JOHN SURRATT:
The Lincoln Assassin Who Got Away

JOHN SURRATT:
The Lincoln Assassin Who Got Away

by Michael Schein

History Publishing Company
Palisades, New York

Copyright©2015 by Schein, Michael (Michael T.)

LCCN: 2015935701
ISBN: 978-1-940773-11-7 (softcover)
ISBN: 978-1-940773-12-4 (ebook)
SAN: 850-5942

Schein, Michael (Michael T.)

John Surratt : the Lincoln assassin who got away / by Michael Schein. -
- First edition. -- Palisades, New York : History Publishing Company,
[2015]

pages ; cm.

ISBN: 978-1-940773-11-7
Includes bibliographical references and index.
Summary: This is the story of John Wilkes Booth's closest
associate prior to the assassination of Abraham Lincoln. It traces
Surratt's worldwide flight from Ford's Theatre to Italy and shows
that he was a conspirator who may be the missing link between
Jefferson Davis and Lincoln's death. The book culminates in the trial
of Surratt after he was brought back to America from Italy and was
set free due to the trial ending in a hung jury.--Publisher.

1. Surratt, John H. (John Harrison), 1844-1916. 2. Lincoln,
Abraham, 1809-1865--Assassination. 3. Assassins--United States--
Biography. 4. Fugitives from justice--United States--Biography. 5.
Conspiracies--United States--History--19th century. 6. Booth, John
Wilkes, 1838-1865--Friends and associates. 7. Davis, Jefferson,
1808-1889--Friends and associates. 8. Confederate States of
America--History. 9. Surratt, John H. (John Harrison), 1844-1916--
Trials, litigation, etc. 10. Trials (Assassination)--Washington (D.C.)
I. Title.

E457.5.S972 S34   2015 2015935701

973.7/092--dc23   1504

Published in the United States of America by
History Publishing Company, LLC
Palisades, New York

Printed in the United States on acid-free paper

First Edition

TABLE OF CONTENTS

Year that trembled and reel'd beneath me!
Your summer wind was warm enough, yet the air I breathed froze me,
A thick gloom fell through the sunshine and darken'd me,
Must I change my triumphant songs? said I to myself,
Must I indeed learn to chant the cold dirges of the baffled?
And sullen hymns of defeat?

—Walt Whitman, 1865

"[T]he reverse of truth has a hundred thousand shapes, and a field indefinite, without bound or limit."

—Michel de Montaigne

CHAPTER ONE

A NEATLY DRESSED GENTLEMAN

GOOD FRIDAY, APRIL 14, 1865. FORD'S THEATRE. SOMETIME BETWEEN 9¹/2 and 10 o'clock. Though after dark, a large lamp lights the front of the theatre. Union Sergeant Joseph M. Dye sits on the platform out front while his comrade in arms, Sergeant Robert H. Cooper, paces up and down the pavement. Together they had viewed the torchlight parade down Pennsylvania Avenue to celebrate a victorious end to the cursed War of Rebellion, then stopped at Ford's on the walk back, hoping to catch a glimpse of their commander-in-chief. As a man will do while idling, Sergeant Dye begins to notice people.[1]

First he sees the famous actor, John Wilkes Booth, out front of the theatre. Booth is conversing with a low, short, "villainous-looking" person. A neatly dressed gentleman joins Booth's conversation. Intermission sends the theatre-goers rushing out. Dye hears Booth say, "he will come now," apparently referring to the President. Sergeant Dye eagerly searches for Mr. Lincoln's unmistakable visage towering above the crowd, but in vain.

Booth and his companions disperse – Booth to Taltavul's Saloon for a quick shot, the villainous-looking man to examine the President's carriage. Not long afterwards Booth returns, fortified by whiskey, and stands by the alley leading to the stage door. The neatly dressed gentleman steps to the front of the theatre, looks at the clock in the vestibule, calls the time, then spins on his heel and briskly marches up 10th Avenue towards H Street. A few minutes later the gentleman returns. He calls the time again; again he marches up towards H Street.

1

Feeling that something is awry, Sergeant Dye reaches into the breast pocket of his artillery jacket to unwrap the handkerchief from around his revolver. Dye watches closely as the gentleman returns to the front of Ford's Theatre. As the mysterious man looks at the clock, the light shines clearly on his excited pale face. He calls the time once more – ten minutes past ten o'clock – then hurries away towards H Street. John Wilkes Booth walks directly into the theatre.

Sergeant Dye points out the gent's strange behavior to Sergeant Cooper. Cooper shrugs his shoulders. "I'm hungry," he says, and together they step into an oyster saloon. Their oysters are not yet delivered when a man bursts in to proclaim: "The President has been shot!"

At the trial of John H. Surratt for conspiracy in the murder of Abraham Lincoln, Sergeant Dye testifies about the neatly dressed gentleman who called the time:

> Mr. Pierrepont (for the Government): Did you see that man distinctly?
> Sergeant Dye: I did.
> Q: Very distinctly?
> A: I did very distinctly.
> Q: Do you see him now?
> A: I do. . . .
> Q: Tell us where he is.
> A: He sits there (pointing to the prisoner [John H. Surratt].)
> Q: Is that the man?
> A: It is. I have seen his face often since, while I have been sleeping – it was so exceedingly pale.[2]

In all, eleven witnesses testify to seeing John H. Surratt in Washington on that terrible Good Friday, April 14, 1865, the day of the assassination.[3]

Yet there is another version of the same events . . .[4]

Thursday or Friday, April 13 or 14. Stewart & Ufford, Men's Furnishings, a tidy shop located at Nos. 20 and 22 Lake Street, Elmira, New York, roughly two-hundred eighty miles from Washington. Some time around two o'clock – definitely after lunch – the shop's very sober bookkeeper, town alderman Frank H. Atkinson, watches as a distinctive young gentleman engages in ten or twenty minutes of conversation with their cutter, Mr. Carroll. The gentleman is memorable for his unusual coat, buttoned up with a full row of buttons on the front, and a belt fastened about the waist. Mr. Carroll confirms this, and adds that the man came in twice – once on the 13th, *and again on the 14th.*

At his trial, John H. Surratt is instructed to rise.

Mr. Bradley (for the Defense): Is that the same man?
Mr. Atkinson: I have no doubt but that is the same man.[5]

Mr. Bradley: Is that the man?
Mr. Carroll: That is the man.[6]

Five witnesses testify to seeing John H. Surratt in Elmira at various times on April 13, 14 and 15.[7] *But what of the man calling time in front of Ford's Theatre?*

Mr. C.B. Hess, an actor, is pleased to be included in the evening's entertainment on April 14. Though not in the cast of *An American Cousin*, he's been engaged to sing a patriotic song at the conclusion of the show in honor of the President and the great Union victory.[8] Filled with the nervous energy that always precedes a performance, Mr. Hess steps from the stage door and sees Lewis Carland, a costumer and actor, and James J. Gifford, a stage carpenter, standing out front. Carland and Gifford had just come from the adjoining saloon, where they'd ducked in the side door just in time to catch a glimpse of Mr. Booth leaving by the front door. Mr. Hess asks the time. Mr. Carland walks to the front entrance, peers at the clock, then returns with the news that it is ten minutes past ten. Mr. Hess repeats, "Ten minutes past ten – I'll be wanted in a few minutes," and he ducks back in at the stage entrance.[9] Not more than two minutes later he hears the report of a pistol, and suddenly all is chaos.

* * *

History is slippery like that. We want to know what really happened, but the evidence cannot always be reconciled. Eyewitness testimony is notoriously unreliable. The passage of time erodes memory. Documents are lost. False documents are created.[10] We want to know so badly that sometimes we fill in the gaps, consciously or unconsciously. Conspiracy theorists jump in to fill the voids created by honest uncertainty. Versions feed off of other versions. The more shocking the event, the more versions there are.

There was no more shocking event in the Nineteenth Century than the assassination of Abraham Lincoln. At the very height of Lincoln's power, the moment of triumph after four years of bloody struggle, a blow was struck to decapitate the government of the United States. The grief that followed was deepened by the heights of the victory just won. On the night before the assassination, "Washington was all ablaze with glory. The very heavens seemed to have come down, and the stars twinkled in a sort of faded way, as if the solar system was out of order and the earth had become the great luminary."[11]

> O, what an elevation! but alas, alas, what a fall! Our joy is suddenly turned into deepest sorrow. The emblem of freedom which recently floated so proudly over land and sea is draped with the emblems of mourning, and a nation in tears follow their beloved and honored chief to a patriot's and martyr's grave.[12]

Literally overnight, the United States plunged from ecstasy into unfathomable and terrifying despair.

What can be known about this epoch-changing event? Who was responsible? Was there a conspiracy? If so, did it reach from the Confederate high command in Richmond to Washington? We want to know, we must know – and it is inconceivable that, perhaps, we cannot know everything about it.

This much can be known: the Lincoln assassination was part of a conspiracy to kill the key leaders of the American government – the President, the Vice-President, the Secretary of State, and possibly also Union General Grant. Regardless of whether John H. Surratt was in Washington or Elmira on the night of the assassination, he was deeply involved in the plot against Lincoln and the government of the United States. What's more, of all the conspirators, John Surratt was the one who was a bona fide Confederate secret agent, with ties to the highest levels of Confederate government. And of all the known conspirators involved in the crime of the century, Surratt was the only one who got away with it!

Who was John H. Surratt? To some he was a patriot, fighting to defend the Southern way of life and the freedom bequeathed by the Declaration of Independence to secede from tyrannical government. To others, he was a spy and assassin, dedicated to preserving the unholy rule of the slaveholders at any cost, who would just as soon shoot a Yankee in the back as give him the time of day. To many of his supporters, Surratt was a courageous young man unjustly accused by vengeful victors of complicity in a crime of which he knew nothing; a Southern soldier who was hounded to the ends of the earth, then dragged back to stand trial based on the same perjured evidence that had unjustly condemned his mother to hang. To many of his detractors, he was as guilty as Booth of the assassination of the sainted Lincoln, a coward who had allowed his mother to swing on the gallows for his own crimes, who nonetheless escaped all punishment due to the protection of powerful allies such as the Catholic Church.

Can it be possible that a boy barely twenty-one on the day Lincoln was shot could have shared Booth's guilt, yet have gotten away with murder? Can it be believed that a Confederate spy is perhaps the missing link between the assassination of Abraham Lincoln, and the top command of the Confederacy right up to President Jefferson Davis? Can it be that a young man whose face was next to Booth's atop the assassination "WANTED" posters and who once held the undivided attention of a deeply divided nation, could have been mostly forgotten by history? The Lincoln assassination, in Churchill's felicitous phrase, "is a riddle, wrapped in a mystery, inside an enigma; but perhaps there is a key."[13] That key might be a forgotten young man, John Harrison Surratt, whose last name is pronounced "Sir Rat"!

---

[1] This version of events is drawn from the sworn testimony of Sergeant Joseph M. Dye, *Trial of John H. Surratt in the Criminal Court for the District*

of Columbia, Vol. I, pp. 131-35 (Washington: French & Richardson; Philadelphia: J.B. Lippincott & Co. 1867) (hereafter "[vol.#] JHS Trial [p.#]").

2 1 JHS Trial 135.

3 2 JHS Trial 1117. The prosecution in argument counts "thirteen," but that includes alleged admissions made by Surratt to others.

4 2 JHS Trial 729-34.

5 2 JHS Trial 730.

6 2 JHS Trial 734.

7 1 JHS Trial 724, 725-26; 2 JHS Trial 730, 734, 863-64,

8 1 JHS Trial 565. The following account is taken from 1 JHS Trial 557-71, testimony of James Gifford, C.B. Hess, and Lewis J. Carland.

9 1 JHS Trial 566.

10 A likely example is "The Hanson-Hiss Article," published in the *Washington Post* on April 3, 1898, purportedly a lengthy interview with John H. Surratt, Jr. *The Hanson-Hiss Article* (hereafter "*Hanson-Hiss*, Weichmann"), *reprinted in* Louis J. Weichmann, *A True History of the Assassination of Abraham Lincoln and the Conspiracy of 1865*, pp.441-52 (Floyd Risvold, ed. Alfred A. Knopf, NY 1975) (hereafter "Weichmann"). It is probably a fraud. This was the conclusion of diligent Surratt researcher James O. Hall, based on the fact that John H. Surratt was notoriously tight-lipped after his trial and his first attempts at lecturing brought him renewed obloquy. *James O. Hall Research Center, Mr. Hall's Papers on Lincoln Assassination*, Surratt House Museum ("JOH Papers") - JHS, *Letter to Joan Chaconas* (Aug. 7, 1981). It is also the view of James E.T. Lange and Katherine DeWitt, Jr., persuasively argued based on numerous easily checkable inaccuracies in the Hanson-Hiss article. Surratt Society, *The Lincoln Assassination: From the Pages of the Surratt Courier*, vol. 2 (Surratt Society, Clinton, MD 2000) (hereafter "*LA from Surratt Courier*"), James E.T. Lange and Katherine DeWitt, Jr., *Hanson Hiss Article a Fraud*, p. X-37 (Nov. 1994). I agree, and therefore I will not rely upon it in this book. However, it will be referred to occasionally just for fun (but always with the largest of caveats), and the reader is of course welcome to seek it out and peruse it.

11 *Washington Evening Star*, April 14, 1865, *quoted in*, James L. Swanson and Daniel R. Weinberg, *Lincoln's Assassins: Their Trial and Execution*, p. 11 (William Morrow 2006) ("Swanson & Weinberg").

12 2 JHS Trial 1078 (closing argument of D.A. Carrington).

13 "The Russian Enigma," Speech by Winston Churchill, Oct. 1, 1939, http://www.churchill-society-london.org.uk/RusnEnig.html (accessed Jan. 1, 2014).

CHAPTER TWO

YOUNG MASTER JOHN

JOHN HARRISON SURRATT, JR. WAS BORN AT FOXHALL ESTATE IN Maryland, on April 13, 1844, twenty-one years and one day before Lincoln was shot.[14] At least, that is the birth date he always claimed and that history generally accepts, although the ten dollar charge made by the Surratt family doctor on April 10 suggests that he might actually have been born three days earlier.[15] It is typical of this mysterious man that we can't even pinpoint his date of birth with absolute certainty.

The doctor who attended young John's birth, Dr. Bayne, was scarred by personal tragedy. About ten years earlier he had lost two sons and a seven month old daughter to arsenic poisoning. "Judith" – one of Dr. Bayne's house slaves – admitted poisoning the children's rice and milk, for which she was hanged.[16] The slave society into which John was born was fraught with peril hidden beneath the veneer of grace and comfort.

Young master John was the third and final child born to John H. Surratt, Sr. and Mary Eugenia Jenkins Surratt.[17] John's brother Isaac was born in 1841, and his sister Elizabeth Susanna – called "Anna" or "Annie" – was born in 1843.[18] When John was just over one year old, John Sr.'s foster mother, Sarah Neale, gave to each child their first slave – Nace, a 20-year old, to serve brother Isaac; Jane, a 15-year old, to serve sister Anna; and for young master John, a fellow named George, whose age is not stated.[19] Interestingly, the grants to Isaac and John were for twenty-six and thirty-four years respectively, with the named servants to be freed upon the expiration of those terms. Jane's service

7

to Anna was to be for life, along with "all her increase" – meaning of course her children.[20] Emancipation came to all these servants much sooner than this grant contemplated when, under pressure from Lincoln's Emancipation Proclamation and the promise of freedom to any slave who enlisted in the Union army, Maryland abolished slavery effective November 1, 1864.[21] John personally felt the financial sting of abolition and emancipation.

* * *

John's great-great grandfather came to the New World from England, and originally settled in Fairfax County, Virginia. He was of French extraction as the family name "Surratt" would indicate.[22] John's father, John Sr., was raised by Richard and Sarah Neale, a childless couple who owned a large estate known as Foxhall, located on Oxon Hill, straddling the border between Maryland and the District of Columbia.[23] John's mother, Mary, was born in 1823 in Prince George's County, Maryland, to an old Protestant family of high respectability, numerous connections, and great wealth. She was educated first by private tutors, then in Washington, and finally at Sisters of Charity Catholic convent in Alexandria, where she converted to Catholicism.[24] Till the day of her death by hanging, Mary had a convert's zeal towards her adopted religion.

John Surratt, Sr. and Mary Eugenia Jenkins met when Mary was just a schoolgirl. They were married in 1840, shortly after her graduation.[25] Through a combination of purchases and inheritance in the early 1840s, the young couple obtained Foxhall, along with $60,000 in gold and a number of slaves, from John Sr.'s stepparents, the Neales.[26] Mary and John Sr. lived at Foxhall until 1851, when the mansion was destroyed by fire. Although arson by a slave was suspected, it was never proven.[27]

* * *

The fire was the beginning of troubles for Mary Surratt. Now with three children to care for, she was thrown onto the kindness of her cousin, Thomas Jenkins, while awaiting new living arrangements. Instead of rebuilding at Foxhall, however, John Sr. developed land he purchased at a crossroads in Prince George's County into a tavern and inn.[28] Soon the surrounding settlement would come to bear his name – Surrattsville. It is known to history as the place where Booth made his first stop after shooting Abraham Lincoln. Once a proud name, after the assassination Surrattsville was renamed Robeystown, and then in 1879 changed again to Clinton, and so it stands today.[29]

Though a knocked-down version of the family's prior wealth, Surratt's Tavern was a nine-room house on 287 acres – spacious enough for the family of five and their servants.[30] We don't have any records of what young master John did to occupy himself as a boy, but we can make good guesses. We know that later, when he was a fugitive in Canada, John liked to pass the time hunting, so it is likely that as a young boy he hunted for birds and game in rural Prince George's County.[31] John's father – before he became too dissipated from drink – was a noted hunter who kept a fine pack of fox and deer hounds.[32] When he was old enough, John likely learned from his father how to ride and shoot and dress game with his knife, all prized skills for a young gentleman in antebellum Maryland. He would not have learned to ride and shoot willy-nilly, like some bumpkin. He would have learned the Southern gentleman's way, straight and tall in the saddle, immaculately coifed and outfitted, blowing his foxhunting horn and commanding his pack of dogs with studied ferocity. In short, young master John probably learned military-type command and discipline from an early age.

* * *

John was sent away to school at a fairly young age. Mary was concerned about the effects of raising her children in a tavern, and therefore prevailed upon Catholic priests to find suitable schooling for each of them. Anna was sent to St. Mary's Female Institute in Bryantown, Maryland, which is known to history as the town where Dr. Samuel Mudd treated John Wilkes Booth's injured leg. In 1855, Isaac and John were enrolled in St. Thomas Manor, located near Port Tobacco, Maryland.[33] It was an important part of the Southern Maryland countryside for young John to get to know. Ten years later he would be back to purchase a boat for his friend Booth.

St. Thomas closed in 1857, throwing the boys back into a home situation in which their father was drunk nearly every day. We do not know for certain, but it is likely that during those two years from 1857 until he went away to school again in 1859, [34] thirteen to fifteen year old John tried – and likely failed – to protect his mother from his father's drunkenness.

* * *

. As namesake of the new community, John H. Surratt, Sr. was prominent in its affairs. He was elected magistrate and, in 1854, he was appointed postmaster. [35] Surratt's Tavern was the local watering hole and meeting place for horse-trading, gossip and politics, a crossroads and lodging for travelers from South to North and vice-versa. From the Fugitive Slave Act of 1850 to bleeding Kansas to the Dred Scott decision to fanatical abolitionism and John Brown's attack on the Federal arsenal at Harper's Ferry, all the news of the day was chewed over and spat out with the tobacco juice at Surratt's Tavern. [36] Prince George's County was conservative, it was pro-slavery, and it was proud of the Southern way of life.

Politics at Surrattsville meant protecting that way of life against the abolitionists and their Northern appeasers, the Republicans – the party of Lincoln. When the time came, Prince George's County, like most of Southern and Eastern Maryland, was "seccesh." [37] It may be that Maryland was only prevented from joining the Confederacy and cutting off Washington City from the rest of the Union by imposition of martial law in April, 1861 by the strong – some said "despotic" – hand of Abraham Lincoln. [38] While those events were still in the future when young master John was growing up at Surrattsville, the passion for defending the Southern way of life was as visceral as the land he hunted. A bright young boy helping his father move the whiskey kegs and sort the mail could not have avoided breathing the nascent Confederacy so deeply that it would become a part of him, no different from his own white skin.

* * *

In the fall of 1859, when he was fifteen years old, John Jr. was sent off again to boarding school, this time at St. Charles College in Ellicott City, Maryland.[39] St. Charles was a six-year minor seminary that fed into St. Mary's major seminary in Baltimore.[40] As such, it was roughly the equivalent of modern high school plus the first two years of college, run with the intention that some portion of the students would go to major seminary to become Catholic priests.[41] The course of study was classical, including Latin and Greek, Cicero, Virgil, Homer, St. Luke's Gospel and the Catholic Fathers; plus algebra, geometry, English, and French.[42] It is not insignificant, in light of later developments, that most of the faculty at St. Charles were French and Canadian priests.[43]

In addition to academic studies, students at St. Charles were expected to work in the fields. The college had a large farm where grain, meat and vegetables for the community were raised. To build character and *esprit de corps*, the students worked side-by-side with their professors on the spring planting and autumn harvest.[44]

The living conditions at St. Charles were Spartan. The third-floor dormitory was heated only by a single woodstove.[45] The politics were decidedly seccesh. According to one student account:

> When the war broke out, the whole school was, with few exceptions, favorable to the success of the Rebellion. The teachers seemed to have little enthusiasm for the liberty of opinion, the secular education, and the republican civilization of the North, and most of the students either came from slave states, or meditated ministering in them. . . . Surratt, with the rest, sang Secession songs very frequently . . . .[46]

* * *

It was at St. Charles that Surratt met a young man who would become his lifelong nemesis. The man known to history as Louis J. Weichmann[47] first registered at St. Charles as "Aloy H. Wiechman, of Philadelphia Pennsylvania," on March 1, 1859.[48] "Aloy" was short for the then-common name, Aloysius. It is not far from "Aloysius" to Louis.

Throughout this history we will rely on Louis J. Weichmann's testimony, interviews, and memoir. In doing so, I do not discount the strong likelihood that he was a secessionist fellow traveler, turned Government witness for the primary motive of saving his own hide – what Surratt would call moral cowardice. During his lifetime, he was (perhaps unjustly) reviled for testimony that allegedly sent Mary Surratt to her grave. Others – her tenant John M. Lloyd, President Andrew Johnson, the whole system of military trial – probably had more to do with that than Weichmann, though he undoubtedly played a part. Take what Weichmann has to say with a grain of salt – but also remember that, while there is evidence of Weichmann's self-justification and probable deception to avoid self-incrimination, there is no reliable evidence that he committed perjury on the principal points of his testimony against either mother or son, despite the strongest efforts among the friends of the Surratts to unmask him.[49]

If opposites attract, there could be no doubt that John H. Surratt Jr. and Louis J. Weichmann would immediately become fast friends, and they did.[50] John was slender, popular, handsome, of good family, courageous, clever, a crack shot and an accomplished horseman.[51] Louis was doughy – "fatty" they called him in the casual cruelty of the schoolyard – clumsy, homely, "poor white," cowardly (at least in popular reputation), frivolous with regard to study, and to make matters worse, he spoke with a lisp and was useless in the manly arts.[52]

Whether, in addition, Louis was a liar and moral coward, or a courageous witness willing to endure popular censure in the interest of truth, remains one of history's great mysteries. It is tempting to look at clues from childhood, on the theory that the man is in the boy. But in this twisted case, even the clues are suspect. One Surratt family tale has Anna spying young Louis out the window on a moonlit night, taking fright at his own shadow.[53] Apocryphal? Probably. And so, from the very start, this unlikely friendship challenges our understanding.

* * *

Unlikely or not, the fates of John H. Surratt, Jr. and Louis J. Weichmann were entangled from the first. They both left St. Charles on the same day in July 1862.[54] Neither of them had completed their course of study. Lincoln researcher Alfred Isacsson believes that John

Surratt was dismissed from St. Charles.[55] This is supported by Weichmann's statement that John was in tears, and had to be reassured by the President of the College that he had been a good boy and would be remembered.[56]

The reason commonly given for John's departure is the need for him to help out at home because his father was ailing.[57] That does not seem accurate, both because his father died suddenly and unexpectedly of "apoplexy" (i.e., stroke) in late August, 1862, more than a month after John left St. Charles,[58] and because it appears that shortly after leaving school John enlisted in the Confederate service and was sent for training.[59] Nonetheless, Isacsson may be over-reading the evidence. There was an annual vacation from July to August,[60] and young John may have simply quit school at this time to enlist. John's eagerness to fight for the South seems the simplest explanation for his premature departure from St. Charles.

The common reason stated for Louis Weichmann's departure from St. Charles also seems suspect. Supposedly, he was removed because the social standing of his family would prevent him from being accepted as a priest by the people of the Richmond Diocese. But Richmond was hardly the only Diocese available to a young priest, and Louis had been on financial assistance from the start, so why would this suddenly warrant dismissal at this time?[61]

It may be coincidence that these two young friends left school on the same day without completing their studies. The possibility exists, however, that Isacsson is correct that they were dismissed for some infraction, and then John simply seized on his sudden freedom to enlist. The commonly stated causes for their departure may be cover stories to hide something nobody wanted to discuss.

Perhaps a clue lies in Weichmann's narrative of May 16, 1867, given to correspondent George Alfred Townsend. We must preface this by noting that it was common for men to sleep together in a single bed in the Nineteenth Century – even Abraham Lincoln was known to partake of co-sleeping.[62] Nonetheless, among the first words spoken by Weichmann about Surratt on the very eve of Surratt's trial are these:

He was then a fresh-faced fellow of sixteen, straight and

thin, with a good, broad forehead, and deeply sunken eyes. *We were not allowed to sleep with one another, the monastic system being enforced . . . .*[63]

In his memoir, Weichmann describes Surratt at St. Charles as "one of the best young men I ever knew, [who] . . . could not have been excelled by anyone." He adds that Surratt "was neatly dressed, and . . . provoked the risibilities of the older students by wearing a white necktie."[64] At nearly two years John's senior, Weichmann was one of the older boys.[65] Was it mere friendship between them, or something more? Perhaps a suspected violation of the "monastic system" played a role in their joint departure from St. Charles. Later, when living together in Washington, they again shared the same bed.[66] Though we cannot know, we can tuck away the possibility of a romantic relationship as perhaps a useful speculation for understanding the intensity of their subsequent enmity.

[14] Surratt Society, *In Pursuit Of . . . Continuing Research in the Field of the Lincoln Assassination* (Surratt Society, Clinton, MD 1990) (hereafter *"In Pursuit Of"*), *The Children of Mary Surratt*, p.221; The Surratt Family Tree, http://www.surrattmuseum.org/genealogy/su_gen1.html (accessed March 17, 2014); Elizabeth Steger Trindal, *Mary Surratt: An American Tragedy*, pp.22-24 (Pelican Publishing Co. Louisiana 1996) (hereafter *American Tragedy*).

[15] *American Tragedy*, pp.22-24; JOH Papers - HBSM, *Dr. Bayne*, Note by James O. Hall.

[16] JOH Papers - HBSM, *Alexandria Gazette* (Nov. 12, 1834), and undated article; *American Tragedy*, p.21.

[17] JOH Papers, *A Biography of John Surratt by Alfred Isacsson, O.Carm. - A Dissertation to Faculty of Grad School of Arts & Sciences of Saint Bonaventure University for MA degree*, p. 1 (July 1957, Saint Bonaventure, NY) (hereafter *"Isacsson Dissertation"*).

[18] *In Pursuit Of, The Children of Mary Surratt*, p.221; *LA from Surratt Courier*, vol. 2, Alfred Isacsson, *Mary Surratt and Her Offspring, Anna and Isaac*, p. VII-31 (May 1986) (hereafter *"Mary's Offspring"*); JOH Papers - JHS, 1880 Baltimore Census - John H. Surratt Household (June 8, 1880).

[19] Email from Sandra Walia, Research Librarian, James O. Hall Research Facility, Surratt House Museum, to author (Nov. 7, 2013) (quoting from Indenture).

20 *Ibid.*

21 The Emancipation Proclamation (Jan. 1, 1863), http://www.archives.gov/exhibits/featured_documents/emancipation_procl amation/ (accessed Nov. 7, 2013), did not have the effect of abolishing slavery in loyal border states, such as Maryland. However, Maryland adopted a new Constitution effective November 1, 1864, which did have this effect. Univ. of Maryland Library, *Slavery in Maryland,* http://lib.guides.umd.edu/marylandslavery (accessed Nov. 11, 2013). Since slavery was abolished in the District of Columbia by an Act signed by President Lincoln, effective April 16, 1862, the Surratts' later move to Washington did not undo the emancipation of their servants. *Abolition in the District of Columbia,* http://memory.loc.gov/ammem/today/apr16.html (accessed Nov. 11, 2013).

22 *LA from Surratt Courier,* vol.2, *His Mother's Memories,* (Interview of Dr. Reginald I. Tonry of Baltimore, grandson of Mary E. Surratt, son of Anna Surratt, by David Rankin Barbee, Nov. 13, 1931) p. XI-24 (April 1987) (hereafter "His Mother's Memories").

23 *American Tragedy,* pp.19, 22; *His Mother's Memories,* p. XI-24.

24 *His Mother's Memories* p. XI-24; *Surratt Family Tree,* http://www.surrattmuseum.org/genealogy/su_gen1.html (accessed Jan. 1, 2013); Public docent display at Surratt House Museum.

25 *Ibid.; Isacsson Dissertation,* p.1; *Surratt Family Tree,* http://www.surrattmuseum.org/genealogy/su_gen1.html (accessed Jan. 1, 2013).

26 *His Mother's Memories,* p. XI-24; *American Tragedy,* pp.19, 22, 24.

27 *American Tragedy,* p.35.

28 *Ibid.*

29 Email from Joan Chaconas, History Specialist, Surratt House Museum, to author (March 28, 2014); *Clinton Maryland Tourism,* http://www.marylandtravelrecreation.com/maryland-cities/clinton-travel.html (accessed Nov. 26, 2013). Although, oddly enough, the town high school is still called "Surrattsville High". http://www1.pgcps.org/surrattsville/ (accessed Nov. 26, 2013). Mary and her son John would be spinning in their graves to see the proud, free, largely African-American faculty and student body at Surrattsville High! "Time wounds all heels."

30 *American Tragedy,* p.36. The acreage comes from public docent display at Surratt House Museum.

31 Andrea Lee Levin, *This Awful Drama: General Edwin Gray Lee and his Family,* p.165 (Vantage Press NY 1987) (hereafter "E.G. Lee"); 2 JHS Trial 905.

32 *His Mother's Memories,* p. XI-24.

33 *Mary's Offspring,* p.VII-31; *American Tragedy,* pp.41-42; *Manor House History,*

http://www.chapelpoint.org/historyManor.asp (accessed March 17, 2014).

34 *American Tragedy*, pp.45-46.

35 *His Mother's Memories*, p. XI-24; *Isacsson Dissertation*, pp.1-2.

36 Helen Jones Campbell, *The Case for Mrs. Surratt*, p.38 (G.P. Putnam & Sons, New York 1943).

37 The common term for favoring the Confederate policy of state secession from the Union.

38 Pratt Library, *Maryland in the Civil War*, http://www.prattlibrary.org/uploadedFiles/www/locations/central/maryland/md_cw_complete.pdf (accessed Nov. 7, 2013); *Ex Parte Merryman*, http://www.princeton.edu/~achaney/tmve/wiki100k/docs/Ex_parte_Merryman.html (accessed Nov. 7, 2013).

39 *Isacsson Dissertation*, p.2.

40 *Ibid.*

41 *LA from Surratt Courier*, vol. 2, Alfred Isacsson, *Some Points Concerning John Harrison Surratt, Jr.*, p. X-9 (August 1995) (hereafter *"Points Concerning"*).

42 *Isacsson Dissertation*, pp.2-3.

43 JOH Papers - HBSM, *Sulpician Educational Institutions*.

44 *Isacsson Dissertation*, p.4.

45 *Ibid.*, p.3.

46 *LA from Surratt Courier*, vol.2, *Townsend Interviews Weichmann, May 16, 1867*, p. IX-18 (August 1991) (hereafter *"Townsend Interviews Weichmann"*).

47 Weichmann spelled his name differently at different times in his life. 1 JHS Trial 369. I use the spelling preferred by Floyd E. Risvold, editor of Weichmann's memoir. Weichmann, p.14.

48 JOH Papers, *List of Students - Saint Charles' College - Ellicott City, Maryland* (Press of the Mission of the Immaculate Virgin, Staton Island, NY 1898).

49 JOH Papers - HBSM, *Letter from James O. Hall* (August 8, 2000). Mr. Hall states in this letter that he does not believe Weichmann committed perjury. I disagree, and think Weichmann committed perjury to avoid incriminating himself, but told the truth with respect to Mrs. Surratt and John Surratt. When asked how I can rely on a witness whom I believe is less than truthful, I can only say that in my experience I have seen many witnesses who are partly truthful and partly deceptive. Most of them follow Weichmann's pattern: truthful about things that don't touch their own legal vulnerability, and deceptive about things that might harm them before the law.

50 *Isacsson Dissertation*, p.5.

51 Weichmann, p.14.

52 *Isacsson Dissertation*, p.5; *His Mother's Memories*, p. XI-25; *Townsend Interviews Weichmann*, p. IX-17; "The Rockville Lecture" p.435 (Dec. 6, 1870), *reprinted in* Weichmann, pp.428-40 (hereafter *"Rockville Lecture,* Weichmann"); *American Tragedy*, p.154.

53 *His Mother's Memories*, p. XI-25.
54 Pitman, Ben, *The Trial: The Assassination of President Lincoln and the Trial of the Conspirators*, p.113 (Weichmann testimony) (Edward Steers, Jr., ed., Univ. Press of Kentucky 2003) (hereafter "*Trial of the Conspirators*").
55 *Points Concerning*, p. X-9.
56 *Townsend Interviews Weichmann*, p. IX-18.
57 *Isacsson Dissertation*, p.5.
58 *Surratt Courier*, Vol. XXXVIII No. 6, *President's Message*, p.1, *reprinting, Letter from Anna Surratt, September 16, 1862* (August 2013) (hereafter "Anna Letter Sept. 16") (commenting on "the suddenness of his death").
Isacsson Dissertation, p.6; JOH Papers, *Letter to Members of Madame Tussaud's Headhunters Society, from "Tyrone" (a/k/a "Dexter")* (April 3, 1990) (hereafter "Tyrone Letter").
Weichmann, p.14.
59 *Isacsson Dissertation*, p.5.
60 *The Atlantic, But Were They Gay? The Mystery of Same-Sex Love in the 19th*
61 *Century*, (Sept. 7, 2012),
62 http://www.theatlantic.com/national/archive/2012/09/but-were-they-gay-the-mystery-of-same-sex-love-in-the-19th-century/262117/ (accessed Nov. 11, 2013).
63 *Townsend Interviews Weichmann*, p. IX-18 (emphasis added).
64 Weichmann, p.14.
65 *Ibid.*, p.12.
66 1 JHS Trial 374.

CHAPTER THREE

REBEL SPY

W<small>E</small> TEND TO FORGET THAT FOR FULLY FOUR BLOODY YEARS, FROM 1861-1865, we were two independent nations. That the Confederate States of America had its own Constitution, its own Senate and House of Representatives, its own Executive Branch, courts and laws.[67] That it flew the Stars and Bars, not the Stars and Stripes. That the state of Mississippi still flies the Stars and Bars as an integral part of its official State flag, and when Georgia abandoned it in 2001, within two years popular demand forced a return to a design based on the original Confederate flag.[68] That the CSA had its own diplomatic relations with foreign nations. That to this day, downtown Richmond is dominated by reverent monuments to this foreign Christian Confederacy of Slaveholders. That of all the Presidential tombstones in Richmond's Hollywood Hills Cemetery, the tallest and best maintained is that of President Jefferson Davis. That the distance between the capitals of these two great warring nations was barely more than one hundred miles. That the distance as the crow flies from the Executive Mansion[69] where Lincoln slept to enemy territory was less than two miles.[70]

On April 12, 1861, the day before young Surratt's seventeenth birthday, Fort Sumter came under Union bombardment, and the war was on. As a hot-blooded young patriot of the Confederacy, John was probably itching to join the action.[71] On March 7, 1861, at the news of the inauguration of Mr. Lincoln, John's elder brother Isaac struck out for Texas. Isaac enlisted in the 1st Texas Cavalry (Confederate) on May 4, 1862. John joined up shortly after leaving St. Charles in July, 1862, and with his intimate knowledge of the Potomac region of Southern Maryland, he was sent for training as a Confederate courier.[72]

Surratt dived into his new life as Rebel spy with all the reckless abandon and arrogance of youth. As he later stated in a lecture delivered December 6, 1870 at Rockville, Maryland:

> I was not more than eighteen years of age, and was mostly engaged in sending information regarding the movements of the United States army stationed in Washington and elsewhere, and carrying dispatches to the Confederate boats on the Potomac. We had a regular established line from Washington to the Potomac . . . . I devised various ways to carry the dispatches – sometimes in the heel of my boots, sometimes between the planks of the buggy. I confess that never in my life did I come across a more stupid set of detectives than those generally employed by the U.S. Government. They seemed to have no idea whatever how to search men. . . . It seemed as if I could not do too much or run too great a risk.[73]

Aside from his own lecture, another possible source of information about Surratt's adventures is the so-called "Pilgrim Interview," first published in the *Philadelphia Times* of October 4, 1885.[74] Through diligent historical sleuthing, this interview resurfaced in 1981. Although probably not genuine,[75] the Pilgrim Interview draws on historically accurate information common to all Civil War couriers, so it is of some value. Here is its re-creation of Surratt's days as a Rebel spy:

> Surratt: There is much I cannot tell. Under the circumstances you come to me, I will tell, I believe, most of what you want to know. . . . What is the starting point?
> Pilgrim: Suppose I say the first experience you had as secret agent of the Confederacy and some of the trips you made, their difficulties, and how you overcame them.
> Surratt: Well, there were not many difficulties. The fact is, sir, that the North was so honey-combed by latent rebel-

lion and resident sympathizers that the difficulty was how to avoid hospitality and accept the best aid in traversing it. There was no trouble. Once on the Maryland side, coming north, and the rest was as easy as traveling now. The same was true on the return journey, but the Potomac was closely guarded, and it was a serious matter to get across. Our disguises were manifold, however, and whatever dispatches we had were towed and weighted astern of the boats so that, in case of capture, we could dispose of them effectually. We were – at least I was and so were all the people engaged as agents – fired at a score of times both by cannon and rifle, but I was not hit. Other people were, occassionaly [*sic*.], less fortunate. We used to choose dark, rainy nights for our expeditions and usually managed to avoid the patrol boats. . . . [76]

Another tale of Surratt's exploits as a secret agent comes to us second hand, through the testimony of Dr. Lewis J.A. McMillan. Dr. McMillan was befriended by Surratt during a voyage to Europe.[77] He testified at Surratt's trial to the following story:

I remember [Surratt] stating one day that there were several of them crossing the Potomac in a boat – it was in the evening, I believe – when they were perceived by a gunboat and hailed. They were ordered to surrender, or else they would be fired upon. They immediately said they would surrender. The gunboat sent a small boat to them; . . . they waited until the gunboat came immediately alongside of them, then fired right into them, and escaped to the shore.[78]

It is important to pause for a moment to consider the import of Surratt's Rockville lecture and Dr. McMillan's testimony. *There is no speculation that John H. Surratt was a Rebel* spy, committed wholeheartedly to the success of the Confederate cause, and willing to risk his life for that cause. This is established fact, based not merely on circumstantial historical evidence – of which there is plenty – but also based on his own admissions.

There is another point of great interest concerning Surratt's secret service to the Confederacy that has been overlooked by other researchers. From April to July 1866, a committee of the House of Representatives known as the Boutwell Committee (after its chairman, George Boutwell of Massachusetts), investigated the possibility of a connection between Jefferson Davis and the Lincoln assassination.[79] One of the witnesses was former CSA Secret Service Agent James H. Fowle, son of an Episcopal minister from Virginia.[80] When asked when he first heard of John H. Surratt as a Confederate agent, he replied:

> Ever since the 16th of May 1863. . . . On the 16th of May 1863 I . . . was put into the 17th Infantry and detailed to Signal duties and then put in the secret service. I was intimately acquainted with Mr. Davis. As a [2 unreadable words] went to him every night with dispatches. I need to read his cipher dispatches. . . . Only a man from our Dep't. could decipher them. He will not read them himself.[81]

The significance is startling: Fowle learned of Surratt's activities as a Rebel spy *by reading Jefferson Davis's cipher dispatches.* If Fowle is telling the truth, then as far back as 1863 either Surratt was in direct communication with Confederate President Davis, or his activities were sufficiently important that others were reporting on him to President Davis.

* * *

Neither John nor Isaac was home when their father died during the night of August 25-26, 1862.[82] Despite his formerly respectable status, John Sr. was an alcoholic who, by the time of his death, had dissipated the once-substantial family resources.[83] Anna was probably the only mourner at his funeral. Mary Surratt's letters show a deep and abiding animosity for "Pa . . . drunk almost every day." [84] John did not get back to Surrattsville until about September 1, 1862.[85] Now eighteen years old, six feet tall, rail-thin but wiry strong, with sandy brown hair combed straight back, a prominent forehead, grey-blue inquisitive eyes fringed with dark, pretty lashes, a wisp of a moustache over the suggestion of a smile – the gallant young Rebel spy would have been a welcome sight to mother and sister upon his return to Surrattsville.[86]

At the same time that Surratt was serving the government of the CSA as a spy and courier, he was employed by the government of the USA as postmaster for Surrattsville. His appointment as postmaster began immediately upon his return home, on September 1. "It was, of course, necessary for the postmaster to take the oath of allegiance to the United States Government."[87] Surratt learned at an early age the necessity of lying under oath to serve the Confederate cause.

Lying about his allegiance enabled Surratt to render another valuable service to the Confederacy: facilitating communication to and from Confederate agents and sympathizers living in the North. Here's how the system worked.[88] Letters from south to north were properly addressed but the envelopes bore no return address, or a false return address, and no stamp. They were assembled in batches in Richmond, and carried across the lower Potomac by a Confederate mail runner. Then the mail would be turned over to a trusted agent who took the letters to a cooperating post office – such as John Surratt's office at Surrattsville. There, the letters were stamped and sent on their way, leaving the Yankees to do the work of delivering Confederate mail.

For north to south communication, a properly addressed envelope aimed at a person living in the South would be placed inside a covering envelope, which was sent to a fictional addressee at a cooperating post office in southern Maryland.[89] All correspondence to that fictional addressee was segregated from the rest of the mail, the hidden letters extracted, and the bundle turned over to a Confederate mail runner.

John H. Surratt's fictional name for mail bound to the Confederacy was "C.H. Baker."[90] Based on a postal investigation into this practice carried out in 1863, Surratt was removed as postmaster effective November 17, 1863, but no further action was taken against him.[91]

* * *

On "a damp, dark, and murky day" in March, 1863, Louis J. Weichmann came back into Surratt's life with a weekend-long visit to Surrattsville.[92] Weichmann was employed at the time as the principal of St. Matthew's Institute for Boys in Washington. Though he took his meals at a nearby boardinghouse, Weichmann slept at night at the Institute. Surratt had stopped by – they "chatted gaily about old times" – and Surratt invited Weichmann down for a visit.[93]

Mrs. Mary Surratt and Anna Surratt welcomed Weichmann. "A cheery fire of wood was blazing on the hearth in the parlor, and the warmth of the room was, indeed, a pleasant contrast to the chilling atmosphere outside."[94] Weichmann describes John's sister Anna as "tall, well-proportioned," "fair-complexioned," well educated and cultured.[95] Anna was, according to Weichmann, an accomplished pianist and a "furious secessionist" possessed of a violent temper.[96] He describes John's mother, Mary E. Surratt, as:

> [A]bout forty-five years of age, of erect bearing, and rather
> above medium height with a ruddy and fair complexion.
> Her eye of steel gray was quick and penetrating. Her hair
> was a dark brown with not a white streak visible in it. Her
> manner was genial and social and she had the rare faculty
> of making a stranger feel at home at once in her company.[97]

But to this domestic description Weichmann adds "that here was a woman devoted, body and soul, to the cause of the South," and that he never met another "who so earnestly . . . defended and justified the Southern cause as she."[98]

Weichmann was not alone in this observation. John T. Tibbett, an admitted Confederate mail runner, testified at John Surratt's trial that in 1863 he heard Mrs. Surratt, in the presence of John, "say she would give any one $1,000 if they would kill Lincoln."[99] Mother's teachings were well received by the son. Tibbett reported John Surratt saying, "the damned Northern army and the leader thereof ought to be sent to hell."[100]

On the first night of Weichmann's March 1863 visit to Surratt's Tavern, the boys (and possibly Anna) sat around playing cards with "two Jewish persons who had carpet-bags with them."[101] Mrs. Surratt took the men's bags and held them for safekeeping overnight. The two men left the next morning before daylight, and by the next day news trickled back that one of them had been arrested crossing the Potomac with $50,000 on him.[102] By March 1863 Surratt's Tavern was already a safe-house for Confederate spies and blockade runners. This fact is further confirmed by a Confederate Signal Bureau document located in the National Archives by Erick F. Davis.[103] It seems likely that Mrs. Surratt was a knowing and active participant in these activities.

* * *

On the Saturday morning of this March visit, Weichmann was awakened by the sounds of a military band. Surratt called him downstairs. Dressing quickly, he came down to find the Marine Band of Washington, which had come down the previous evening to serenade some newly elected county officials.[104] This was not unusual; Surrattsville lay only ten miles southeast of the Navy Yard Bridge out of Washington.[105] But what proved to be significant was Surratt's introduction of Weichmann to one of the company, "a seedy, frowsy, monkey-faced boy" "who seemed to be a kind of hail-fellow-well-met among the whole party."[106] The young man's name was David E. Herold.[107] Two years and one month later Mr. Herold would return on horseback to Surratt's Tavern just after midnight on the night of the assassination, the first stop in a futile attempt to elude pursuit by a small army of detectives and enraged Union troops. His riding companion that night would be John Wilkes Booth.[108] Less than three months after that, Herold would be hanged for that ride.

After the weekend visit, on Monday morning, Surratt accompanied Weichmann back to Washington. Upon arriving in Washington, Surratt stopped the buggy in front of a drugstore near the Navy Yard. They went inside to chat with David E. Herold, who was employed there as a prescription clerk.[109] Later, druggist William S. Thompson would testify at Surratt's trial that Herold was employed by him, and that President Lincoln got his medicines from him.[110] Were Surratt and Herold discussing the possibility of poisoning Lincoln?

One of the strangest pieces of evidence introduced at Surratt's trial was the so-called "Charles Selby" letter. The story goes as follows.[111] Mary Hudspeth, a widow,[112] was riding with her young daughter on the Third Avenue streetcar in New York City on November 14, 1864.[113]

Her attention was drawn to two men, deep in conversation. One was a well-educated gentleman with a fair hand and fair skin, but what particularly drew her attention was the fact that he appeared to be in disguise – whenever his hat bumped forward, it moved a wig and false whiskers!

The other man was coarser and shorter, and he was called "Johnson." The more gentlemanly of the two reached for some letters in his vest pocket, and in doing so revealed a pistol in his belt. The two men got off just before Mary and her daughter. On their way out, the daughter picked up some unsealed letters, which Mary put with her own letters, not noticing that they were not hers. Later, when she looked more closely, she realized her mistake, and saw that they were suspicious. She took them to General Winfield Scott, who said they were of great importance.[114]

One was a plea from an abandoned wife to her husband to return home – a plaintive, but common, wartime story. The other, however, is quite dramatic:

> Dear Louis: The time has at last come that we have all so wished for, and upon you everything depends. As it was decided before you left, we were to cast lots. Accordingly we did so, and you are to be the Charlotte Corday[115] of the nineteenth century. When you remember the fearful, solemn vow that was taken by us, you will feel there is no drawback. Abe must die, and now. You can choose your weapons – the cup, the knife, the bullet. The cup failed us once, and might again. Johnson, who will give you this, has been like an enraged demon since the meeting, because it has not fallen upon him to rid the world of the monster. . . . Strike for your home, strike for your country; bide your time, but strike sure. Get introduced, congratulate him, listen to his stories – not many more will the brute tell to earthly friends. . . . I wish I could go to you, but duty calls me to the West. You will, probably, hear from me in Washington. Sanders is doing us no good in Canada.
>
> Believe me, your brother in love,
> /s/ Charles Selby [116]

Who is "Louis"? Who is "Charles Selby"? Is this a fraud, and if so, why would Mary Hudspeth manufacture such evidence? It certainly seems like a fraud, because it is unlikely that serious conspirators would lay out their designs so frankly in writing. Yet the Selby letter was not manufactured after the assassination, and it has a sound "chain of custody." It was forwarded from Generals Scott and Dix to President Lincoln in November 1864, and Lincoln showed it to Secretary of War Stanton in a private meeting. Stanton remembered the letter as he stood by Lincoln's deathbed listening to the mortally-wounded President's labored breathing, and he sent his assistant Charles A. Dana to the Executive Mansion to retrieve it. Dana found it in a drawer of Lincoln's private desk, with an inscription in Lincoln's own handwriting across the back – "Assassination"! [117]

Is the prior failure of "the cup" mentioned in the letter a reference to an earlier attempt by David E. Herold to poison the President with adulterated medicine? This was argued at Surratt's trial. [118] The letter is tantalizing, but we cannot know to any level of certainty.

Could Weichmann be "Dear Louis"? While the conclusion is tempting, it seems unlikely that the conspirators would have disguised everyone's name except the name of the intended assassin himself. [119] What's more, Weichmann was totally unfit for the job of striking the fatal blow. As Surratt said in his Rockville Lecture, Weichmann "was constantly importuning me to let him become an active member [of the conspiracy, but] . . . I refused, for the simple reason that I told him he could neither ride a horse nor shoot a pistol, which was a fact." [120]

It does seem possible that "Charles Selby" was John Wilkes Booth. Booth lived in New York City at the time, although, to be fair, so did 726,000 other souls and the usual stream of visitors and billeted troops. [121] But Booth has a much closer tie to this particular alias: the real Charles Selby was a deceased playwright who wrote, among other works, *The Marble Heart* – a play that ran at Ford's Theatre on November 9, 1863. The star of that show was John Wilkes Booth, and in the audience that night was none other than President Abraham Lincoln. [122]

One witness at Surratt's trial testified that the Selby letter was written by Booth in a "disguised hand." [123] Booth was fair-skinned enough to fit the bill as the disguised gentleman. He had been to Canada in mid-October, so he would have known of the failures of Confederate operative George Sanders.[124] He would have recently been "west" – as western Pennsylvania was then called – on business, and might use it as a cover or have been planning to go again.[125]

Surratt might do for the disguised gentleman as well. He could have been passing along Booth's note to Powell or Herold or Atzerodt – one of the lesser luminaries among the conspirators. But all this is rank speculation. So far as we know, Surratt and Booth never met before December 1864. And just as one witness attributed the Selby letter to Booth's hand, another witness who knew Booth's hand quite well – John T. Ford of Ford's Theatre – testified that the Selby letter was *not* written by Booth.[126] Why should two random suspicious characters on a streetcar in November 1864 prove to be Booth or Surratt or some other combination of the ultimate conspirators? The most likely reason we think they might be is that we know these are among the persons who were ultimately involved in the one successful plot of the many plots against Lincoln. It is said that hindsight is 20-20, but in the reconstruction of historical events hindsight is often plagued by hallucinations. The human mind is wired to fill gaps, and in doing so it grabs the information it already has in store.

Ultimately, all we can say about the Selby letter is that it may be evidence that Booth plotted to kill Lincoln as early as November 1864, that Surratt may have been involved through his friend Herold, and Herold may have previously tried to poison Lincoln. Or not. When things appear too good to be true in historical research, they usually are.

* * *

Weichmann and Surratt got back together during Easter weekend, 1863, to visit their alma mater, St. Charles College. Easter came early that year, so the two arrived on Thursday, April 2, and left on Good Friday, April 3.[127] Weichmann also wanted to visit with Father William Mahoney, a "clerical friend" with whom he'd lived from November to December of 1862, so from St. Charles Surratt and Weichmann rode to the small Maryland town of Ellangowan, also known as "Little Texas."[128]

It was at Little Texas that the two friends met the Canadian adventurer Henri Beaumont de Sainte Marie. Ste. Marie fascinated Weichmann:

> He could speak French and Italian fluently, touch the guitar lightly, and was a fine tenor singer. He was charming in conversation and had a considerable fund of anecdote.[129]

Ste. Marie's recollections of this first meeting were not so lyrical. He recalls that "a great deal was said about the war and slavery," that both Surratt and Weichmann revealed themselves as "more than strongly secessionists," and that Surratt "said that President Lincoln would certainly pay for all the men that were slain during the war."[130]

Ste. Marie mentioned that he was contemplating going south. "Surratt . . . told me that his house was the rendezvous of all land blockade runners to Richmond, that he often went to Richmond and was in communication with preeminent men there."[131] Surratt then offered to help Ste. Marie go south.[132] A handwritten letter dated April 24, 1863, in Surrattsville, from "J. Harrison Surratt" to "Mons. H De Ste. Marie," still exists:

> If you have made up your mind to go S– I can send you all safely. Do not have the least doubt of it. Times are better than they were. All you have to do is to let me know what day you will be in Washington, and I will meet you. You can carry a hand trunk with you.
>
> There will not be the least difficulty, only perhaps you will [need] to remain among us some two or three weeks. Still we can easily make the time pass agreeably.[133]

Not to be outdone, Weichmann writes that "I became interested in [Ste. Marie] to such an extent that I promised to help him secure a different position in life from that which he was holding."[134] Weichmann's efforts on Ste. Marie's behalf led to a brief appointment at St. Matthew's Institute, Weichmann's own school. Whether there was something more to this arrangement is not known. Whatever it entailed, Ste. Marie's appointment ended quickly, with Weichmann "waking up one morning about three weeks or a month after acceptance of the position under me to find my friend had left. He had gone, completely gone, with baggage and all."[135]   Later, in a statement given to the United States Government in court proceedings, Ste. Marie specified that he left this position and Washington due to "difficulties with Weichmann."[136]

In the Townsend interviews of 1867, Weichmann says that Ste. Marie was thoroughly "unprincipled."[137] Was this pure pique, or based on frank evaluation of his character? There were witnesses at Surratt's trial on both sides of the question of whether Ste. Marie is a person worthy of belief.[138]   Add another grain of salt to the pile, but we will not discount Ste. Marie too quickly because much of what he says is corroborated.

Surratt visited every week while Ste. Marie was staying with Weichmann.[139] Clearly, Surratt and Weichmann were becoming very close. It is significant that Ste. Marie attributes strong secessionist views not merely to Surratt, but also to Weichmann. Shortly after the assassination Ste. Marie wrote to the U.S. Consul-General in Montreal to express his shock that Weichmann had not been arrested. "By their conversation," he said, "I understood that they were strong secessionists, *and more particularly Weichman* [*sic*]."[140] A close friendship in time of war such as that between Surratt and Weichmann demanded shared political sentiments, especially with at least one of the friends so actively risking his life for the Confederacy.

* * *

Surratt continued to spy for the Confederacy throughout 1863 into 1864. At the same time he needed to support his mother, and he hit upon the perfect plan to serve both masters. On October 17, 1863, he wrote a most respectful letter to Union Secretary of War Edwin M. Stanton, seeking employment as a clerk in his department. According to Surratt, "I am firmly convinced that you will . . . not cast aside my petition, especially, when you reflect that I am the only son of a widow dependent, in a great measure, on me for support."[141] Perhaps aware of the postal inspection into Surratt's duplicity, or perhaps simply due to the crush of other business, there is no record that Secretary Stanton ever responded to this inquiry, and thus he spared his department from taking on a mole. If Stanton did not notice Surratt then, he would learn the name soon enough.

When the school year ended in July 1863, Weichmann returned home to Philadelphia for summer vacation. He renewed his attempts to enter a seminary, but for reasons that are not disclosed he was unable to obtain the requisite letter of recommendation from his Bishop. Weichmann returned to teaching that fall, but his fortunes changed for the better when, in early January 1864, he secured a clerkship in the War Department.[142] This meant not only more than double his previous salary, but also something more precious than gold – the very access to U.S. Government secrets that Surratt had failed to gain.

In the same paragraph of his history in which he recounts this new appointment, Weichmann adds:

> John H. Surratt now came to see me frequently, sometimes spending a few days with me at my boardinghouse. He was always welcome; whatever I possessed was his own, as much as mine.[143]

How much was Surratt genuinely fond of Weichmann, and how much was he simply using him? Years later Ste. Marie met Surratt in a distant land, and swears to the following conversation:

> Surratt then said he was in the secret service of the South. And Weichmann, who was in some Department there, used to steal copies of the despatches [*sic.*] and forward them to him, and thence to Richmond.[144]

Although Weichmann steadfastly denies this charge, it is reported as true by several other researchers.[145] It is highly credible, and was corroborated and expanded upon by Surratt himself in the Rockville lecture, after he was beyond the reach of any prosecution:

> Booth sometimes was rather suspicious of [Weichmann], and asked me if I thought he could be trusted. Said I, "Certainly he can. Weichman [*sic*.] is a Southern man," and I always believed it until I had good reason to believe otherwise, because he had furnished information for the Confederate government, besides allowing me access to the government records after office hours.[146]

If this is true, Weichmann not only stole sensitive documents and passed information to his dear friend, the Rebel spy, but he actually opened the doors of the War Department in Washington to Surratt for late-night plunder! Just in case there is any doubt, Weichmann's actions would constitute espionage in time of war – a hanging offense.

* * *

Mary E. Surratt moved from Surrattsville to 541 H Street in Washington in October 1864.[147] She began to take in permanent lodgers to help shore up the shaky family finances. The H Street house was conveniently located not far from Ford's Theatre, the National Hotel, and Herndon House, all of which were important landmarks for events yet to come.[148]

John Surratt was left to manage Surratt's Tavern until the new tenant, John M. Lloyd, took over on December 1, 1864.[149] Lloyd was a pro-slavery man, a former blockade runner who had been arrested, but then pardoned.[150] There was no question that he was qualified by political inclination to carry on the pro-Confederate clandestine activities of Surratt's Tavern.[151]

It was, perhaps, a lonely time for Surratt. On November 12, 1864, he wrote a cryptic letter addressed to "Dear Al." "Al" is short for "Aloysius," Louis J. Weichmann's proper name that was known to Surratt from St. Charles College days. The letter may never have been mailed: it was found at Surrattsville, and Weichmann testified that he never received it.[152] Regardless, it is a tantalizing if inconclusive glimpse into Surratt's mind on the cusp of his move to Washington:

> "Surratt's Villa," Nov. 12th 1864
> Dear Al:
> Sorry I could not get up. Will be up on Sunday [November 13]. Hope you are getting along well. How are times, and all the pretty girls? My most pious regards to the latter; as for the former, I care not a continental d—n. Have you been to the fair – if so, what have we won! I'm interested in the 'Bedstead.' . . . Am very happy I do not belong to the 'firm.' Been busy all week taking care of and securing the crops. Next Tuesday, and the jig's up. Good by, Surrattsville. Good by, God forsaken country. Old Abe, the good old soul! May the devil take pity on him!
> Surrattsville, Md.   /s/ John H. Surratt
> To: Louis J. Weichmann, Esq., Washington city, D.C.[153]

The "Dear Al" letter is another one of those partial glimpses into the past that seems to mean more than we can know. It may be significant code, or it may just be innocent juvenile banter. Could "the firm" be the plot against Lincoln? The War Department? Nobody still alive can answer that question. The best we can really get from it is that Surratt liked to tease Weichmann about girls and flirt with him about "the bedstead"; he was dissatisfied in a general way with the times (Lincoln had just won re-election); and he was perhaps committing to paper a mild back-handed threat towards Lincoln. If the "Dear Al" letter can even be read to mean that Surratt didn't like Lincoln, that's hardly new or significant information. What's more, dislike and even hatred towards Lincoln in November 1864 was virtually a cottage industry – an attitude shared with millions of men and women from both sides of the Mason-Dixon line who would nonetheless not turn to assassination. Compare the mild jibe of the "Dear Al" letter with the much more pointed threat published by Wisconsin newspaper editor Marcus M. Pomeroy during the campaign of 1864:

The man who votes for Lincoln now is a traitor and murderer. . . . And if he is elected to misgovern for another four years, we trust some bold hand will pierce his heart with dagger point for the public good.[154]

More interesting than what "Dear Al" says or doesn't say is that it marks the end of a period of unfocused dissatisfaction. The next day, John H. Surratt would move to the nerve center of enemy territory, where his actions could have much larger consequences. Surratt was about to meet the most infamous actor in all American history. From that moment until one bullet changed the world, Surratt's life would be a frenzy of action focused on one objective: *getting Lincoln.*

[67] Yale Univ., *Constitution of the Confederate States*, March 11, 1861, http://avalon.law.yale.edu/19th_century/csa_csa.asp (accessed Nov. 8, 2013).

[68] *The Mississippi State Flag*, http://www.netstate.com/states/symb/flags/ms_flag.htm (accessed Nov. 8, 2013); *The Georgia State Flag*, http://www.netstate.com/states/symb/flags/ga_flag.htm (accessed Nov. 8, 2013).

[69] Now known as "the White House".

[70] Calculated by use of the wonderful interactive maps on the site *Civil War Maps*, http://civilwardc.org/maps/ (accessed Nov. 8, 2013).

[71] There is a story attributed to school-boy Surratt in the fraudulent Hanson-Hiss article, which might have accidentally struck upon something close to the truth:

> [W]e were all on the campus, which directly faced Charles Carroll of Carrollton's beautiful estate, Dourehegan Manor, when there issued from the main driveway opposite a troop of Confederate cavalry on their way to join the Army of Northern Virginia. . . . They were a magnificent set of young men, full of fire, dash, and vim, and presented a splendid appearance. I was fired with martial ardor at the sight, and tossing my cap into the air, I cheered and cheered again. In fact I cheered myself hoarse.
>
> *Hanson-Hiss*, Weichmann, p.443.

[72] *Townsend Interviews Weichmann*, p. IX-19; *Mary's Offspring*, p. VII-31; Tyrone Letter; *In Pursuit Of, The Children of Mary Surratt*, pp.221, 223; *American Tragedy*, p.54; *Isacsson Dissertation* p.6.

[73] *Rockville Lecture*, Weichmann, p.430.

[74] JOH Papers - JHS, *Philadelphia Times* (Oct. 4, 1885), *reprinted in Pilgrim Magazine, reprinted in* Surratt Courier, *Pilgrim Interview*, p.3 (July 1981)

(hereafter "*Pilgrim*").

75 The correspondent's summary of the Surratt trial proceedings is riddled with obvious inaccuracies, demonstrating sloppy work. Some parts of the so-called "interview" are consistent with other known facts, but it leaves out Surratt's offer to help his mother, which one might think Surratt would never have left out. *Ibid.*, p.6. It also bumps up against the assertion by Clara Laughlin, who was introduced to Surratt in his home by one of his daughters, that Surratt "never gave interviews." Clara Laughlin, *Travelling Through Life*, pp.109-110 (Houghton Mifflin, NY 1934). The correspondent claims to have a letter of introduction from no less a luminary than Judah P. Benjamin, former Secretary of State of the Confederate States of America, then living in England. *Pilgrim*, p.3. It seems unlikely that Benjamin would give his letter of introduction to a newspaperman. There was nothing to be gained and too much sensitive information that needed to be protected. I conclude that the Pilgrim Interview is probably not genuine.

76 *Pilgrim*, p.5.

77 1 JHS Trial 463.

78 1 JHS Trial 468.

79 JOH Papers - JHS, *Notes of James O. Hall and Testimony of James H. Fowle, May 1866*, p.1 (hereafter "JOH Fowle Testimony"); JOH Papers, *Boutwell Committee Final Report*, 39th Congress, 1st Session, Report No. 104.

80 JOH Fowle Testimony, p.1.

81 *Ibid.*, pp.1-2, question #873.

82 *Surratt Family Tree*, http://www.surrattmuseum.org/genealogy/su_gen1.html (accessed Jan. 1, 2014).

83 *American Tragedy*, p.65.

84 *Ibid.*

85 *American Tragedy*, p.65; *Tyrone Letter*; *Anna Letter Sept. 16*, p.2.

86 *Weichmann*, p.14; *LA from Surratt Courier*, Vol. 2, at X-13, George Alfred Townsend article, *Cleveland Leader*, Oct. 4, 1868, *reprinted in* President's Message, *The Trials of John Surratt* (Sept. 1988) ("*Townsend re: Trial of Surratt*").

87 JOH Papers, *Typed Notes*, citing letter from JL Bristow, 4th Assistant Postmaster General, dated May 8, 1898.

88 I am indebted to James O. Hall's JHS notes for this information, compiled on a sheet following the letter of April 20, 1863, from C.A. Welborn to Col. Lafayette, investigating the Surrattsville post office.

89 *Ibid.*

90 JOH Papers - JHS, *Letter from C.A. Welborn, official of the Philadelphia post office, to Col. Lafayette* (April 20, 1863).

91 *Ibid.*; JOH Papers - JHS, *Letter from J.L. Bristow, 4th Assistant Postmaster*

General (May 8, 1898).

92 Weichmann, p.19; 1 JHS Trial 369; *Townsend Interviews Weichmann*, p. IX-19.

93 Weichmann, pp.17-18.

94 *Ibid.*, p.19.

95 *Ibid.*, p.20.

96 *LA in Surratt Courier*, vol.2, John C. Brennan, *Regarding George Alfred Townsend's 1867 Interview with Louis J. Weichmann*, p.IX-15 (July 1991) (hereafter *"Re: Townsend Interviews Weichmann"*).

97 Weichmann, p.20.

98 *Ibid.*

99 1 JHS Trial 179.

100 1 JHS Trial 180.

101 *Townsend Interviews Weichmann*, p. IX-19.

102 *Ibid.*

103 Edward Steers, Jr., *His Name is Still Mudd* (Thomas Publications, 2013), Kindle edition at loc.438-42 & n.30 (hereafter "Still Mudd").

104 Weichmann, p.22.

105 1 JHS Trial, pp.369-70.

106 *Townsend Interviews Weichmann*, p. IX-19; Weichmann, p.22.

107 *Ibid.*

108 1 JHS Trial 282-86; James L. Swanson, *Manhunt: the 12-Day Chase for Lincoln's Killer*, pp.103-06 (HarperCollins 2007) (hereafter *"Manhunt"*).

109 Weichmann, p.22.

110 1 JHS Trial 510.

111 1 JHS Trial 352-55.

112 She had remarried by the time of John H. Surratt's trial, so her name was Mary Benson. 1 JHS Trial 352.

113 1 JHS Trial 352.

114 1 JHS Trial 353.

115 The Royalist who stabbed the French Revolutionary Jean-Paul Marat to death in his bathtub. *Charlotte Corday*, http://www.britannica.com/EBchecked/topic/137301/Charlotte-Corday (accessed Nov. 9, 2013).

116 1 JHS Trial 354-55.

117 Weichmann, pp.65-66; *Trial of the Conspirators*, pp.40-41.

118 1 JHS Trial 1306.

119 I note the use of the name "Johnson," and that some later said that Andrew Johnson was a conspirator in Lincoln's death - just as some believe Lyndon Johnson was a conspirator in the death of John F. Kennedy. Neither charge passes my sniff test.

120 *Rockville Lecture*, Weichmann, p.435.

121 *New York Times,* "Census of 1865," http://query.nytimes.com/mem/archivefree/pdf?res=F10915FC3E59137A 93CBA9178AD85F4 (accessed Nov. 9, 2013).

122 Gene Smith, *American Gothic: the Story of America's Legendary Theatrical Family, Junius, Edwin, and John Wilkes Booth,* p.101 (New York; Simon & Schuster 1992); Michael W. Kaufman, *American Brutus,* p.125 (Random House 2004) (hereafter *"American Brutus"*); William Tidwell, James O. Hall and David Winfred Gaddy, *Come Retribution: The Confederate Secret Service and the Assassination of Lincoln,* p.259 (Univ. Press of Mississippi 1988) (hereafter *"Come Retribution"*). That night the President and Mrs. Lincoln occupied combined boxes 7 and 8, upper tier, audience right - the same boxes in which Booth would shoot the President seventeen months later. *Come Retribution,* p.259.

123 1 JHS Trial 509 (testimony of David H. Bates).

124 *Come Retribution,* p.265.

125 *Ibid.*

126 1 JHS Trial 548. Yet a third witness agreed with this conclusion, but his admitted lack of handwriting analysis expertise led to his testimony being stricken. 1 JHS Trial 861, 863.

127 Weichmann, pp.22-23.

128 *Ibid.,* pp.17 & 23; *Townsend Interviews Weichmann,* p. IX-19.

129 Weichmann, p.24.

130 *Henri B. Ste. Marie v. United States,* United States Court of Claims, Docket No. 6415 (1872), *Additional Statement of Henri B. Ste. Marie,* p.22 (July 10, 1866) (Google digital book scanned from Harvard College Library, Bequest of Evert Jansen Wendell, 1918) (*"Ste. Marie v. United States"*).

131 JHS, *Enclosure with May 23, 1865 letter from Consul-General Potter to Acting Secretary of State Hunter - Letter from Henri B. Ste. Marie, Laprairie Canada East,* p.2 (May 20, 1865) (hereafter *"Ste. Marie Letter of May 20, 1865"*).

132 *Ibid.*

133 JOH Papers - JHS, *Letter from J. Harrison Surratt to H. De Ste. Marie* (April 24, 1863).

134 Weichmann, p.24.

135 *Ibid.*

136 *Ste. Marie v. United States, Statement of Henri B. Ste. Marie* ¶1, pp.20-21 (June 21, 1866).

137 *Townsend Interviews Weichmann,* p. IX-19.

138 *Compare,* 2 JHS Trial 851, 854, 856, with, 2 JHS Trial 990, 991.

139 *Ste. Marie v. United States, Additional Statement of Henri B. Ste. Marie,* p.22 (July 10, 1866).

140 *Ste. Marie Letter of May 20, 1865,* p.1. Another witness who attributes strong Secessionist views to Weichmann was John P. Brophy, who signed an

affidavit on the date of the execution of the conspirators in an attempt to prevent Mrs. Surratt's hanging and to get Weichmann indicted for perjury. JOH Papers - JHS, *Affidavit of John P. Brophy* ¶12 (July 7, 1865) (*"Brophy Affidavit"*).

141 Swanson & Weinberg, p.127.
142 Weichmann, pp.25-26.
143 *Ibid.*, p.26.
144 *Ste. Marie v. United States, Additional Statement of Henri B. Ste. Marie*, p.23 (July 10, 1866).
145 *Isacsson Dissertation*, p.7 ("Louis Weichmann was associated with Surratt in this work of carrying dispatches. . . . Weichmann pilfered copies of dispatches from the War Department, where he worked and would turn them over to Surratt."); Guy W. Moore, *The Case of Mrs. Surratt*, pp.92-93 (Norman: University of OK Press, 1954).
146 *Rockville Lecture*, Weichmann, p.435.
147 *Isacsson Dissertation*, p.9; *American Tragedy*, p.80.
148 *American Tragedy*, pp.78-80.
149 *Ibid.; Isacsson Dissertation*, p.9.
150 *American Tragedy*, p.79 (*quoting, Boston Globe* (May 15, 1865)).
151 JOH Fowle Testimony, pp.3-4, questions ##1016-1021.
152 JOH Papers - JHS, *"Dear Al" Letter from John H. Surratt to Louis J. Weichmann* (Nov. 12, 1864); 1 JHS Trial 403, 406.
153 This is an amalgam of the photostat from the National Archives microfilm, Frame 0069, Roll #3, *Investigation and Trial Papers Relating to the Assassination of President Lincoln*, Microcopy No. 599, and the version read into the trial record, 1 JHS Trial 405.
154 Don E Fehrenbacher, *Journal of the Abraham Lincoln Ass'n*, "The Anti-Lincoln Tradition," TAN 13, vol. 4, issue 1 (1982), Permalink: http://hdl.handle.net/2027/spo.2629860.0004.103 (accessed Nov. 9, 2013).

CHAPTER FOUR

JOHN WILKES BOOTH AND THE "OIL" BUSINESS

THE HOUSE AT 541 H STREET INTO WHICH JOHN SURRATT MOVED IN mid-November was a tall, narrow brick affair on the south side of the street with a wooden staircase stuck on its front like a crooked snout.[155] Every inch of its three stories was put to use.[156] The first floor was an English basement entered directly from the street by a service and family entrance. This door led into a long hallway extending the length of the house on the west side of the house (the right side facing it from the street). The hallway opened to the left onto a public sitting room in front, dining room in the middle, and kitchen to the rear. The second floor was accessed off a formal entrance at the top of the front staircase. This entrance led to a hallway the length of the house just over the one below, which opened to the left into a large family sitting room, a parlor, and a back double bedroom shared by Mrs. Surratt and a 19-year-old boarder named Honora Fitzpatrick. Mrs. Surratt's daughter, Anna Surratt, and her cousin, Olivia Jenkins, shared two rooms way up in the attic behind dormer windows facing H Street. An 11-year-old orphan boarder, Appolonia Dean, may have shared a bed in one of the dormer rooms, or with Miss Fitzpatrick; she was part of the household, but the chamber she occupied is not clear. There was a small servant's room occupied by the "negress" Susan Ann Jackson for about three weeks prior to the date of the assassination.[157] The front two rooms on the third floor were occupied by Mr. Hollohan, his wife and daughter.

The back room on the third floor was shared by John Surratt and Louis J. Weichmann. The frequent shuttling between Surrattsville and

Washington was no longer necessary for the two young friends. Weichmann moved in to Mrs. Surratt's on November 1, 1864, and John took up residence there shortly after writing the "Dear Al" letter.[158] For a time, they were as close as two friends could be. As testified to by Weichmann at Surratt's trial:

> Mr. Pierrepont: At Mrs. Surratt's house, at this time, where was your room in the house in relation to Surratt's room?
> Mr. Weichmann: Well, Surratt and I were so friendly and so intimate with one another that we occupied the same room.
> Q: How about the bed?
> A: We occupied the same bed.[159]

To be clear, Surratt's later relationships strongly suggest that he was predominantly heterosexual, so if there was anything more than close friendship in their relationship, it was probably either Surratt toying with Weichmann's affections to achieve other purposes, or perhaps a bit of youthful experimentation. But whatever the exact nature of their intimacy, it would be short-lived. Between the two friends there soon fell the shadow of one of the most dashing and charismatic men of the day – John Wilkes Booth.

* * *

It was probably December 23, 1864 that John Wilkes Booth and John Harrison Surratt first met.[160] I say "probably" because at the military trial of the conspirators Weichmann testified that it was January 15, 1865, and then at Surratt's trial, when the January date had proved to be impossible, changed his testimony to just before Christmas, 1864.[161] One would think that testimony given in May 1865, concerning events in the recent past, would be more accurate than testimony given in June 1867. But there is enough corroborating evidence to accept that Weichmann made a mistake estimating time in his earlier testimony, including Surratt's own statement in his 1870 Rockville Lecture that the meeting first took place in "the fall of 1864 . . .,"[162] and a sworn statement by the man who introduced Booth to Surratt that the correct date was December 23, 1864.[163] Recognizing that reconstructing history involves weighing evidence and making a choice, we will join other researchers who accept December 23rd as the jumping off point for one of history's most consequential collaborations.[164]

If the date is uncertain, the particulars of what occurred are not. Weichmann provides a picturesque reconstruction in his memoirs:

> In the evening after dinner on that day, about six o'clock, while standing on the pavement in front of the Surratt house and having a very pleasant time with John, we agreed to take a stroll along Pennsylvania Avenue. I was anxious to purchase a few Christmas presents for my sisters. We went down Seventh Street together. It was a delightful evening. The store windows looked very gay. Surratt, I am sure, had no expectation of meeting any acquaintance, nor had I. When directly opposite Odd Fellows' Hall someone suddenly called out, "Surratt, Surratt." "John, someone is calling you," said I. My companion, turning around, recognized an old friend from Charles County, Maryland, named Samuel A. Mudd.[165]

Dr. Mudd was calling to Surratt for the purpose of introducing him to the handsome man at his side, John Wilkes Booth. Booth had stayed over at Mudd's house in Maryland in November, and again on December 18. It is likely that Booth specifically asked Mudd to provide him with an introduction to Surratt, the daring young blockade runner who knew all the ways out of Maryland into Virginia.[166] This is the same Dr. Samuel A. Mudd who would later treat Booth's broken leg in the early morning hours of April 15, 1865, shelter him for that first day following the assassination, and then pretend to pursuing Union troops not to know the "stranger" with the broken leg that he treated.[167]

Weichmann's memoirs claim that Mudd introduced Booth as "Mr. Boone," and that it was not until they returned home that night that Surratt told him that "Boone" was Booth, the famous actor.[168] Curiously, his trial testimony overlooks this point, naming Mudd's companion "Booth," which surely he was.[169] Weichmann describes Booth at this first meeting:

I noticed that he was a young man of medium figure, apparently about twenty-eight years of age.[170] A heavy black mustache rendered the pallor of his countenance very noticeable. He possessed an abundance of black curly hair and a voice that was musical and rich in its tones. His bearing was that of a man of the world and a gentleman. In dress, he was faultless.[171]

At Booth's invitation, the foursome went to his room at the National Hotel.[172] Booth pulled a call bell and ordered up "milk punches and cigars for four."[173] Weichmann, ever fastidious, remarked upon the neatness of the room. Booth replied that it had previously been occupied by Senator Wilkeson, who'd left behind a sheaf of documents that would make "a nice read."[174] After sipping their drinks and making polite conversation for a while, Dr. Mudd called Booth out into the hallway, where they conversed for about five minutes. Then they called for Surratt, and the three of them conferred in the hall for another several minutes before returning. Mudd apologized to Weichmann, saying that Booth wanted to purchase his farm but would not offer enough for it.[175] Booth and Surratt later offered the identical excuse, with Surratt explaining that the men wanted him as their agent for the transaction[176] – an odd choice considering that Surratt now lived in Washington and had just met Booth. Surratt, Booth and Mudd then conferred at a table conveniently located (per Weichmann's testimony) at a distance that made their speech audible but not intelligible, where they held an animated discussion of some twenty minutes duration. During the conversation, Booth made marks as if diagramming something on an envelope, while the other two men watched intently.[177]

The foursome then adjourned to Dr. Mudd's lodgings at the Pennsylvania House on C Street. Mudd and Weichmann talked together, while Booth and Surratt sat by the hearth.[178] A distinct note of jealousy creeps into Weichmann's account, as he strives to portray his friend Surratt as an innocent entrapped:

> Boone [Booth] and Surratt, were meanwhile having a jolly
> time together, Boone taking letters and photographs from

his pocket and exhibiting them to his companion, who, tossing his head in the air, replied with animated laughter. Probably by this time Surratt was duly impressed with the greatness of his new-found friend. . . . What pictures Boone drew before this country boy's vision, what glittering baubles he held out to him, no one knows. Boone, at any rate, found him an easy victim, for from that hour Surratt was his, as completely as Doctor Faust belonged to Mephistopheles.[179]

Whether Booth was Surratt's puppeteer or equal partner remains to be seen. What we do know, from Surratt's own confession in the Rockville lecture, are the main outlines of what Booth proposed, either at that first meeting or over the course of several subsequent meetings. Surratt says that Booth "seemed to be very reticent with regard to his purposes," but upon receiving Surratt's assurance that "I am a Southern man," Booth agreed to confide in him.[180] First, Booth explained that his motives were to force the North to resume prisoner exchanges, because the South "cannot spare one man, whereas the United States Government is willing to let their own soldiers remain in our prisons because she has no need of the men."[181] According to Surratt:

> There was a long and ominous silence, which I at last was compelled to break by asking, "Well, Sir, what is your proposition?"
> He [Booth] sat quiet for an instant, and then, before answering me, arose and looked under the bed, into the wardrobe, in the doorway and the passage, and then said, "We will have to be careful; walls have ears." He then drew his chair close to me and in a whisper said, "It is to kidnap President Lincoln, and carry him off to Richmond!"
> "Kidnap President Lincoln!" I said. I confess that I stood aghast at the proposition, and looked upon it as a foolhardy undertaking. To think of successfully seizing Mr. Lincoln in the capital of the United States surrounded by

thousands of his soldiers, and carrying him off to Richmond, looked to me like a foolish idea. I told him as much.[182]

At this point in the tale, it seems that Surratt is going to balk at involvement in anything so risky. Booth explained "in minute detail" his plans, including the various parts each conspirator would play, and the possibility that Lincoln could be seized in one of his various rides to and from the Soldiers' Home.[183] Then the most amazing thing happens: see how quickly Surratt flips from resistance against to embrace of the plot:

> I was amazed – thunderstruck – and in fact, I might also say, frightened at the unparalleled audacity of this scheme. *After two days' reflection I told him I was willing to try it.*[184]

Thus, in a public lecture in 1870, John Harrison Surratt confessed his complicity in a conspiracy with John Wilkes Booth to commit the felony of kidnapping the President of the United States.

* * *

Let us pause at Surratt's phrase, "unparalleled audacity." Forgetting for a moment the obvious irony that Surratt, in light of his admission that he "was willing to try it," would have the *audacity* to claim fright at the plot's *unparalleled audacity*, this may be a carefully chosen turn of phrase. Perhaps Surratt, ever the Confederate secret agent, is engaging in a bit of what has come to be known in espionage circles as disinformation. Surratt probably joined the conspiracy in December 1864. Just that August, a bullet had put a hole through Lincoln's trademark stovepipe hat on his ride from the Old Soldiers' Home to the Executive Mansion.[185] Outwardly, Lincoln laughed it off as the accidental act of some "foolish gunner," and swore the private who found the hat to secrecy. The incident, however, was taken seriously by U.S. Marshal for the District of Columbia, Ward Hill Lamon, who assigned a guard to ride with the President.[186] Another fresh plot in 1864-65, detailed later, was laid by Captain Thomas Nelson Conrad, and involved kidnapping Lincoln on his route towards the Old Soldiers' Home.[187] Confederate Colonel Bradley T. Johnson undertook maneuvers towards carrying out the same plot in the summer of 1864.[188]

All these plots may have their genesis in an 1862 plan of Confederate Colonel Joseph Walker Taylor, nephew of former President Zachary Taylor. According to Jefferson Davis's aide-de-camp, William Preston Johnson, Colonel Taylor met with Confederate President Davis and Johnson in the summer of 1862 to propose kidnapping Abraham Lincoln as he rode from his summer quarters at the Old Soldiers' Home to the Executive Mansion.[189] Davis rejected the plan, allegedly stating:

> I suppose Lincoln is a man of courage. . . . He would undoubtedly resist being captured. . . . I could not stand the imputation of having consented to let Mr. Lincoln be assassinated.[190]

If Jefferson Davis is quoted (or even paraphrased) correctly, he immediately recognized the obvious: *that a plot to kidnap the President is tantamount to a plot to murder him.*[191]

There was nothing "unparalleled" about Booth's plot, and Surratt likely knew that – if not at the moment he agreed to join in, then certainly by the time of his Rockville Lecture. Booth certainly knew there was competition to "get" Lincoln. According to fellow conspirator George A. Atzerodt, Booth told him that he had met parties in New York City who planned to blow up the Executive Mansion with Lincoln in it, and "Booth said if he did not get him quick, the NY crowd would."[192] If Booth knew it, then it is likely that Surratt knew it. But after the deed was done and the full enormity of the crime struck everyone, the Confederacy had to wash its hands of all involvement in the Lincoln assassination in order to "win the peace," and Surratt knew that too. Thus, Booth's plot had to be isolated from everything the Confederate Government had ever done or thought of doing. It had to be portrayed as the "unparalleled audacity" of a madman.[193]

* * *

Mad or sane, Surratt joined a conspiracy that was already in progress. According to Sam Arnold's statement of April 18, 1865, he was summoned to see his old schoolmate John Wilkes Booth in late August or early September 1864, at the Barnum Hotel in Baltimore. He hadn't seen Booth for twelve years. As they jawed about school days over wine and cigars a knock came at the door, and in walked Michael O'Loughlen, another childhood chum of Booth's.[194] At this meeting, Booth introduced the idea of capturing Lincoln en route from the Soldiers' Home, carrying him to Richmond, and exchanging him for all the Rebel POWs.[195] If this sounds suspiciously like Colonel Taylor's plan, that's because it is. But by the date of this meeting at the Barnum Hotel, the plan had a new urgency to it. After Gettysburg, the balance of POWs tilted distinctly against the South, which lacked resources to feed and care for Union POWs. To avoid "a war of extermination," the North halted all prisoner exchanges by order of General Grant on April 17, 1864, and this policy was confirmed again on August 18, shortly before Booth met with Arnold and O'Loughlen.[196]

As an afterthought, Booth mentioned a possible back-up scenario to the Soldiers' Home: Booth suggested that Lincoln could be taken at Ford's Theatre. No one thought much of this at the time; Arnold even forgot about it until later events pricked his memory.[197]

After the Barnum meeting, Booth headed to New York, then to Pennsylvania, where he hastily sold off his oil investment properties at a loss of $6,000.[198] Though divested of the real thing, Booth and his associates usually referred to their plot against Lincoln by the code name, *the "oil business."*[199]

Booth then headed to Montreal, Canada, where he registered at St. Lawrence Hall on Tuesday, October 18, at 9:30 p.m.[200] Canada was a staging area for guerilla raids and so-called "black flag" clandestine warfare directed against the North by Confederate agents stationed there.[201] Of the five million dollars appropriated for the Confederate Secret Service, one million dollars was set aside for Canadian operations, under the control of Confederate Secretary of State Judah P. Benjamin.[202] On the day after Booth arrived, Lieutenant Bennett H. Young, acting under orders of Confederate Agent Clement C. Clay,[203] led a raid out of Canada upon the town of St. Albans, Vermont. The so-called "St. Albans raiders" stole $200,000 from three banks, terrorized the citizens (mortally wounding one), and unsuccessfully attempted to burn the town to the ground.[204] The St. Albans raid was merely one in a stew of plots against the Union cooked up by the Confederates in Canada, which included primitive biological warfare in the form of yellow-fever infected clothing shipped into northern cities,[205] an ill-fated attempt by John Yates Beall to intercept a POW train (which led to his capture and execution), and a failed attempt to use "Greek fire" to set New York City ablaze.[206]

To the very nerve center of this operation went Booth in October 1864. "Beginning in early 1864, the St. Lawrence Hall was increasingly used as a headquarters for Confederate agents in Canada."[207] The St. Lawrence Hall was elegant and welcoming to Southerners, "the only hotel in the Canadas whose bar served mint juleps."[208] What did Booth do there? We know from Sam Arnold's admissions that he was already plotting to kidnap Lincoln. We know that Booth spent at least ten days in Montreal.[209] He certainly did not go there for the scenery. Montreal is a dreary, cold place in late October, with the autumn colors already several weeks gone by.[210]

In the spring of 1864, President Davis had appointed Jacob Thompson and Clement C. Clay to lead Confederate operations in Canada.[211] There is no definitive historical evidence that Booth obtained their support, or even managed to get an audience with them. While in Canada, however, Booth did meet with at least two well-known Confederate agents, George Sanders and blockade-runner Patrick Charles Martin.[212] Sanders was a zealot who believed so deeply in Giuseppe Mazzini's so-called "Theory of the Dagger" under which tyrannicide is deemed justified, that as U.S. Consul in London in the mid-1850s he became involved in a plot to assassinate Louis Napoleon.[213] As for Patrick Charles Martin, in October 1865, while a Union prisoner, he told two fellow prisoners that he had met Booth for drinks and they discussed the possibility of assassinating Lincoln.[214] They might even have done more than just talk. Booth returned with a draft for $1,500 (worth about $22,000 in 2014), which may have come from Martin or other Confederate sources.[215]

* * *

After he left Canada, Booth was energized and focused on sacrificing himself to the cause of the South. The "Charles Selby" incident, already detailed above, occurred November 14, 1864. Also in November, Booth left a mysterious sealed envelope for safekeeping with his beloved sister Asia.[216] Opened after the assassination, the letter is deeply revealing of Booth's state of mind at the time:

TO WHOM IT MAY CONCERN:
Right or wrong. God judge me, not man. For be my motive good or bad, of one thing I am sure, the lasting condemnation of the North.

* * *

People of the North, to hate tyranny, to love liberty and justice, to strike at wrong and oppression, was the teaching of our fathers. . . .
This country was formed for the <u>white</u>, not for the black man. . . .

* * *

The South can make no choice. It is either extermination or slavery for <u>themselves</u> (worse than death) to draw from. I would know <u>my</u> choice.

* * *

. . . I know how foolish I shall be deemed for undertaking such a step as this, where, on the one side, I have many friends, and everything to make me happy, where my profession <u>alone</u> has gained me an income of <u>more than</u> twenty thousand dollars a year . . .. On the other hand, the South have never bestowed upon me one kind word . . .. To give up all of the <u>former</u> for the <u>latter</u>, besides my mother and sisters whom I love so dearly, . . . seems insane; but God is my judge. I love <u>justice</u> more than I do a country that disowns it; more than fame and wealth; . . . more than a happy home. . . .

* * *

. . . How I have loved the old flag, can never, now, be

known. . . . But I have of late been seeing and hearing of the
<u>bloody deeds</u> of which she has <u>been made the emblem</u> . . ..
O, how I have longed to see her break from the mist of
blood and death that circles round her folds, spoiling her
beauty and tarnishing her honor. But no, day by day has she
been draged [*sic.*] deeper and deeper into cruelty and
oppression, till now (in my eyes) her once bright red stripes
look like bloody gashes on the face of Heaven. I look now
upon my early admiration of her glories as a dream. My love
(as things stand to-day) is for the South alone. *Nor do I deem
it a dishonor in attempting to make for her a prisoner of this man,
to whom she owes so much of misery.* . . .

A Confederate, doing duty upon his own responsibility.

—J. Wilkes Booth [217]

Booth came away from Montreal not only with fresh determination, but also with a valuable letter of introduction from Martin to Dr.
William Queen and Dr. Samuel Mudd. Both men lived near the Zekiah
Swamp in the Bryantown area of Charles County, and both were active
in the Confederate secret transport line through southern Maryland.[218]
In November 1864, under pretext of seeking to purchase land in
Charles County, Maryland, Booth was able to use this letter of introduction to recruit Dr. Mudd and a high-ranking Confederate agent of
the Signal Corps, Thomas Harbin, into the conspiracy.[219] These contacts were an essential part of enlisting the Confederate Signal Corps
"secret line" down through Maryland, into Virginia, into the plot to
kidnap Lincoln.[220] At Dr. Mudd's recommendation, Booth also purchased a high-spirited one-eyed saddle horse from Mudd's neighbor.[221]
Far from the "madman" he was later portrayed to be, Booth was
methodically assembling the pieces needed to move a captive Lincoln
from Washington to Richmond. *The next key piece was John H. Surratt.*
    Shortly after meeting Booth on December 23, Surratt explained his
travels and the sudden influx of $3,000 in cash to Weichmann by say-

ing that now he was in cotton speculation.[222] Then he changed his story. No, it was oil stock; he was in the oil business.[223]

[155] Photo, *American Tragedy*, p.81. The building still stands at 604 H Street (renumbered), with a historical plaque on the front as the only token of its significance. At the time of my visit in March 2014, it was a sushi and pan-Asian restaurant called "Wok & Roll." Nothing original could be seen in the restaurant.

[156] House lay-out and rooming arrangements come from the following sources: *In Pursuit Of, reprinting*, Harold O. Wang, "A Visit to the Surratt Boardinghouse," p.121-22 (*Surratt Society News*, August 1982); *American Tragedy*, pp. 82-83; *Isacsson Dissertation* p.11; LA in Surratt Courier, vol. 2, Alfred Isacsson, *John Surratt: the Assassination, Flight, Capture and Trial*, p. X-3 (July 1993) (hereafter "Isacsson, *AFCT*"); 1 JHS Trial 373-74, 376, 669-70, 713.

[157] *Isacsson Dissertation* p.11; 1 JHS Trial 363.

[158] 1 JHS Trial 370; Weichmann, p.28. Weichmann says in his memoirs that "John was there from the start," *ibid.*, but he is probably confusing John's frequent visits with actual living arrangements, since it is clear from the "Dear Al" letter and other sources that he didn't move in for several weeks. He also says that Mrs. Surratt did not move in until December 1st, but he testified at John's trial that she moved in on November 1st, which better accords with other sources. 1 JHS Trial 370.

[159] 1 JHS Trial 374.

[160] Weichmann, pp.32, 69.

[161] *Compare, Trial of the Conspirators*, p.114, with, 1 JHS Trial 371, 415; *see also, Townsend Interviews Weichmann*, p. IX-20 ("a few days before Christmas").

[162] *Rockville Lecture*, Weichmann, p.430.

[163] *Still Mudd*, Appendix 9 ¶3, at Loc. 2489-2493.

[164] December 23, 1864, is the date accepted by Mr. Hall. JOH Papers - HBSM, *Hall's Handwritten JHS Timeline* (hereafter "*Hall JHS Timeline*"). *See also*, Isacsson, *AFCT*, p. X-3; *American Brutus*, p.154; *Still Mudd* at Loc. 912, 932-42.

[165] Weichmann, p.32.

[166] *Still Mudd* at Loc. 912-46.

[167] Surratt Society, *From War Department Files: Statements Made by the Alleged Lincoln Conspirators Under Examination, 1865* (Nov. 1980) (hereafter "*Statements*"), *Voluntary Statement of Dr. S.A. Mudd*, pp.29-30 (undated, believed to precede Mudd Statement signed April 22, 1865, per *Still Mudd* at Loc. 657-62). For a thorough and - in this author's estimate - deserved debunking of the popular myth that Dr. Mudd was innocent of complicity

in the plot against Lincoln, the reader is directed to Mr. Steers' fine book, *His Name is Still Mudd*.

168 Weichmann, pp.32-34.

169 1 JHS Trial p.371; *accord, Trial of the Conspirators*, p.114.

170 Actually, twenty-six and a half, at this time, born May 10, 1838. *American Brutus*, p.82.

171 Weichmann, p.32.

172 *Ibid.* Even Mrs. Surratt corroborates this part of the story, letting slip in her statement of April 28, 1865, that "Mr. Wieckman [*sic.*] was with my son when they met [Booth] at some hotel, the National I presume, and there made his [Booth's] acquaintance." *Statements, Statement of Mrs. Mary E. Surratt, Carroll Prison, April 28, 1865, p.49 (hereafter "Mary Surratt 4/28").*

173 Weichmann, pp.32-33; 1 JHS Trial 371. One might presume that the "punch" was added by rum.

174 Weichmann, p.33.

175 *Ibid.*; 1 JHS Trial 371.

176 Weichmann, pp.33, 34.

177 *Ibid.*p.33; 1 JHS Trial 371-72; *Trial of the Conspirators*, p.114. This meeting at the National was later confirmed in general outline by Dr. Mudd, *Still Mudd* Appendix 9; *see also*, Affidavit of George W. Dutton, who held Dr. Mudd in confinement, and says that he "confessed he was with Booth at the National Hotel" per Weichmann's testimony. *Trial of the Conspirators, Affidavit of George W. Dutton*, p.421 (August 22, 1865).

178 Weichmann, pp.33-34; 1 JHS Trial 372.

179 Weichmann, p.34.

180 *Rockville Lecture*, Weichmann, p.430.

181 *Ibid.*, p.431.

182 *Ibid.* (paragraph formatting added).

183 *Ibid.*

184 *Ibid.* (emphasis added).

185 *Come Retribution*, p.237, *citing, Cincinnati Enquirer*, "Account of Private John Nichols, Company K, 150th Pennsylvania Volunteers," (August 15, 1885).

186 *Come Retribution*, pp.237-38.

187 *Ibid.*, pp.281-95.

188 *Ibid.*, pp.235-36; JOH Papers - *JHS, Unfiled Papers & Slips Belonging in Compiled Confederate Service Records*, M-347, Reel 194, *Philadelphia Weekly Press*, "The Attempt To Capture President Lincoln," p.4, col.5 (March 13, 1880) (*"Attempt to Capture"*).

189 *Still Mudd*, at Locs. 254, 276-81.

190 *Still Mudd*, at Loc. 281-87; *see Come Retribution*, p.237. This comes from the first published account of the episode, in the *Confederate Veteran* of

April, 1903, and is itself to be taken with the proverbial grain of salt.

191 Weichmann says about the same thing: "Yet abduction was only a road to assassination, and the man or men who had guilty knowledge of it were morally just as guilty of murder as he who fired the fatal shot which ended Mr. Lincoln's life." Weichmann, p.62.

192 *LA from Surratt Courier*, vol. 1, at III-19, *Unpublished Atzerodt Confession Revealed Here for the First Time, p. III-21* (Oct. 1988), *reprinting, Statement of George A. Atzerodt to Prov. Mar. McPhail in Presence of John L. Smith* (May 1, 1865) (hereafter *"Lost Atzerodt Statement"*); *Come Retribution*, p.418.

193 *Come Retribution*, p.329.

194 *American Brutus*, p.86, 132; *Statements, Statement of Samuel Bland Arnold Made at Baltimore Maryland, April 18, 1865*, p.20 (hereafter "Arnold Statement").

195 *Statements, Arnold Statement*, p.20.

196 *Exchange of Prisoners in the Civil War*, http://www.civilwarhome.com/prisonerexchange.htm (accessed Nov. 27, 2013).

197 *Statements, Arnold Statement*, p.20.

198 *Come Retribution*, p.265.

199 *Statements, Arnold Statement*, p.21; *Statements, Statement of David E. Herold, Made before Hon. John A. Bingham, Special Judge Advocate, on April 27, 1865, on Board the Monitor "Montauk,"* p.3 (hereafter *"Herold Statement"*).

200 *Come Retribution*, p.265.

201 *Ibid.*, ch. 8.

202 *Ibid.*, pp.165-66.

203 Clay was from the CSA War Department, and jointly ran the Canadian operation with Jacob Thompson, of the CSA State Department. *American Brutus*, p.138.

204 *Come Retribution*, p.201; *E.G. Lee*, p. 145; *American Brutus*, p.140. Booth had nothing to do with the St. Albans raid.

205 *Come Retribution*, pp.185-86.

206 *Ibid.*, pp.202-03.

207 *Ibid.*, p.263; accord, *American Brutus*, p.140.

208 *E.G. Lee*, p.144.

209 *American Brutus*, p.141.

210 The author's personal experience, having grown up in Northern Vermont.

211 *Come Retribution*, p.189.

212 *Still Mudd*, Loc.782.

213 *Come Retribution*, p.331-32.

214 *Ibid.*, pp.335-36.

215 Edward Steers, Jr., *Blood on the Moon: The Assassination of Abraham Lincoln*, p.73 (Univ. Press of Kentucky 2001) (hereafter *"Blood on the Moon"*) - value

updated from 2000 to 2014. The authors of *Come Retribution* say that this money may have been furnished by the Confederacy, or it may have been Booth's own money. *Come Retribution*, p.335. Therefore, it cannot be relied upon as a definitive link between Booth and the Confederacy.

216 *Blood on the Moon*, p.111.

217 National Parks Service, Ford's Theatre Collection, *J. Wilkes Booth "To Whom it May Concern" Letter of 1864* (underlining in original; italics added by author).

218 *Still Mudd*, Locs. 775-78 & 791; *Come Retribution*, p.331.

219 *Ibid.*, Locs. 775-801; Weichmann, p.48.

220 *Still Mudd*, Locs. 775-801; *Come Retribution*, pp.89-90, 301, 320.

221 *American Brutus*, p.152.

222 1 JHS Trial 406-07; Weichmann, p.69.

223 1 JHS Trial 407.

CHAPTER FIVE

A JANUARY ATTEMPT

O<small>N</small> F<small>RIDAY</small>, D<small>ECEMBER</small> 30, 1864, J<small>OHN</small> S<small>URRATT</small> <small>BEGAN A NEW JOB AS</small> a clerk in the freight department of Adams Express Company. The job was in Washington City, and paid $50 per month.[224] Although in his application for employment Surratt stated that he had been out of work for some time and "was exceedingly anxious to have a position,"[225] about two weeks later he asked Mr. Dunn, the agent in charge, for a leave of absence. Surratt's stated reason was that his mother was going down to Prince George's County, and he needed to accompany her as protector. Mr. Dunn expressed astonishment that Surratt would request leave so soon after starting his new job, and he denied the request.[226]

The next morning, Mrs. Surratt appeared at the offices of Adams Express to personally request that a leave be granted to her son so he could accompany her to Prince George's County. Mr. Dunn replied that he had no reason to change his mind; the son's application for leave was refused. Mrs. Surratt stood her ground and pleaded for the requested leave. Mr. Dunn again refused, adding that Surratt could take leave without his consent, but if he did so he should not return to work.[227]

Surratt left the office that day, January 13, and never came back. He left his pay for the first two weeks of January unclaimed.[228] Almost two years later, a card marked "J. Harrison Surratt" dropped out of one of Booth's black velvet vests that had been locked away in the luggage room of the National Hotel since the night of the assassination.[229] In

Surratt's own handwriting, the card says:

> I tried to secure leave but failed.
>   J. Harrison Surratt.[230]

The implications are clear: *both Surratts* – mother and son – were now doing Booth's bidding.

* * *

From January until the very afternoon of the assassination, John Wilkes Booth was a constant visitor at Mrs. Surratt's house in Washington. Daughter Anna and Mrs. Surratt, the 41-year-old widow, [231] each vied for the attention of the dashing young thespian who shared their fanatical devotion to the cause of Southern liberty.[232] In private, Mrs. Surratt called Booth "my pet."[233] After her arrest, a search of her room uncovered a card with *sic semper tyrannis* written on it – "thus always to tyrants" – the very words spoken by Booth at the moment of the President's assassination.[234] Also, on Mrs. Surratt's mantle, there was a picture frame with an image of "Morning, Noon, and Night" in it. Hidden on the back of this innocent image was John Wilkes Booth's *carte-de-visite* with his photograph on it.[235]

Mrs. Surratt was undoubtedly concealing her true understanding of Booth's purposes in her government examination on April 28, 1865:

> Colonel Olcutt: When did you get acquainted with Mr. Booth?
> Mrs. Surratt: Some three months ago. . . .
> Q: Were his visits always visits of courtesy?
> A: Yes, Sir.
> Q: Any business discussed?
> A: No, sir; not political affairs. I do not think that his longest stay
>   was over one hour.
> Q: What part of the day did he used to come?
> A: Sometimes in the day and sometimes in the evening.
> Q: Did not an attachment spring up between him and your
>   daughter?
> A: Not particularly I should suppose, not that I knew of.

Q: He was a handsome man?

A: He was a handsome man and gentlemanly; that is all we knew
of him. I did not suppose he had the devil he certainly
possessed in his heart.[236]

* * *

By January, the plan was moving into high gear, with an attempt to
be made as soon as practicable. On Tuesday, January 3, 1865, John
Surratt executed a deed of all his interest in the estate of his father to
Mrs. Surratt. This deed was recorded on January 23 in the land records
of Upper Marlboro.[237] Was Surratt eschewing worldly possessions?
Unlikely. Although we cannot be certain, we can speculate that
Surratt's motive was to protect against forfeiture and fines if he was captured and charged with treason. Little did he suspect that he might get
away while his mother might be the one arrested and charged.

Just about the time that Surratt was pleading for a leave of absence,
Booth showed up in Baltimore to check in with Sam Arnold and
Michael O'Laughlen. Booth's trunk was too heavy – he'd need help
with it. When they opened it, they could see why. Inside were two
Spencer carbines, six Colt revolvers, three Bowie knives, plus caps, car-
tridges, belts, two pairs of handcuffs and a fully outfitted canteen that
Booth had purchased in New York.[238] Spencer carbines were military-
grade rifles introduced in 1863, and they were difficult to obtain.[239]
Arnold and O'Laughlen shipped the weapons to Washington, perhaps
unwilling to be caught red-handed with them, then took the wagon,
harness and draft horse they'd bought with Booth's money, and headed
to Washington to claim the weapons shipment.[240]

Sometime in January – likely before leaving his employ at Adams
Express – Surratt paid a call on his pharmacist friend David E. Herold.
If Herold wasn't previously involved in a plot against Lincoln, Surratt
probably recruited him at this time. Herold, twenty-two years of age,
lived with his widowed mother near the Navy Yard in Washington,
close by a key bridge crossing to Union Town, and from there into
Maryland. In addition to his pharmacological talents, Herold was an
avid bird-hunter, familiar with the wilds of lower Maryland along the
Potomac.[241] As such, he would prove valuable to the conspiracy when

he guided an injured Booth through Maryland and across the Potomac in the days immediately following the assassination.[242]

* * *

On January 13, when Surratt took what he called "French leave" from Adams Express, what did he do? He rode with CSA Signal Corpsman Tom Harbin to Port Tobacco, Maryland, the village near his old school on the banks of the Potomac.[243] Port Tobacco was a nest of blockade runners, spies and counterspies. While there, Surratt contacted and recruited into the conspiracy George A. Atzerodt, a 29-year-old Prussian immigrant who made his living by ferrying people across the Potomac, no questions asked.[244] Atzerodt, a wagon maker and smith by trade, "was a valuable man because of his knowledge of the river and of the adjacent country in Maryland and Virginia."[245] He is described by Kauffman as "an insignificant man" who:

> . . . seemed to come right out of a Dickens novel. Grimy and consumptive, he looked like a man who might go for years without a change of clothing, then boast of the fact. A spinal curvature gave him a stooped appearance, and he walked with his head tilted a little to one side.[246]

With Atzerodt's help, Surratt shopped for boats, and purchased at least one from Dick Smoot and James Brawner for $300, paying another $100 to have it hidden until needed at Goose or Nanjemoy Creek.[247] Not bad for a fellow who had been desperately in need of a job barely two weeks earlier, who'd just quit a job that only paid $50 per month, and who had not even bothered to pick up his pay.

Atzerodt soon became a regular fixture at Mrs. Surratt's Washington boarding house, where he was known to the ladies as "Port Tobacco." Weichmann first met him there in the latter part of January, and estimates that he visited approximately twenty times up until the date of the assassination.[248]

* * *

Eddy Martin was one of the men loitering around Port Tobacco at that time, waiting to get across the Potomac. Martin claimed to be a respectable cotton merchant who, with the knowledge and at least tacit consent of Lincoln himself, was exploring whether he could broker the sale of the South's entire cotton crop for the year.[249] Martin testified that he met Surratt at Port Tobacco, and that Surratt told Martin he was on three days' leave of absence from his job at Adams Express.[250]

But that's not the most interesting part of Martin's testimony. On the night Surratt left Port Tobacco – probably Sunday, January 15 – Martin had a fascinating conversation with George Atzerodt, who tended to talk too much. "I accused [Atzerodt] of intending to cross over that night with other parties," said Martin; "told him I had been paying him all that he asked, and that I must cross by the first boat." Atzerodt's reply was that "no one was going to cross that night, but on Wednesday night [January 18] a large party would cross of ten or twelve persons; that he had been engaged that day in buying boats; that they were going to have relays of horses on the road between Port Tobacco and Washington."[251]

It appears that something big was planned for January 18, but what? When Martin asked point blank, Atzerodt suddenly clammed up: "He said he could not tell." Martin suggested that some Confederate officers were going to be sprung from prison, and that Atzerodt had been engaged to convey them to Virginia. Atzerodt quickly agreed: "Yes, and I am going to get well paid for it."[252] But in light of the fact that Surratt had recently joined Booth's kidnap plot, that Surratt was clearly doing Booth's bidding in Port Tobacco, and that Atzerodt had been working for Surratt that day, it seems far more likely that the conspirators had marked Wednesday, January 18, as the date they would attempt to abduct the President.[253]

Booth's doings in Washington align well with the January 18 attempt theory. Upon the arrival of Arnold and O'Laughlen with the buggy and team, and receipt of the trunk loaded with weapons and supplies, Booth took his two old friends to dinner. At this dinner, Booth revived the theatre plan. Arnold and O'Laughlen were skeptical, but Booth was at his charming, persuasive best. Because Lincoln was no longer making regular trips to the country, Booth thought they should focus on the venue he knew best: Ford's Theatre, with its passageways, exits and alleys. Booth took the two men to the theatre that night and showed them every nook and cranny. He had even rented a stable behind Fords' that was perfect to hold the buggy in which the President would be carried to Virginia.[254] Booth reminded them that Lincoln loved the theatre, and that his favorite actor, Edwin Forrest, happened to be playing at Ford's that very Wednesday, January 18.[255]

Surratt was back in town by then, frequently meeting with Booth. According to Arnold's statement:

> Met him [Booth] next day went to Breakfast together, he was always pressed with business with a man unknown and then only by name John Surratt, most of his Booth's [*sic.*] time was spent with him.[256]

According to Isacsson, Surratt's role in the January 18th plot was to turn off the main gas valve in order to plunge the theatre into darkness.[257]

In the days leading up to January 18, Booth redoubled previous attempts to recruit actor Samuel Knapp Chester to the plot, and in doing so Booth had to divulge the plan to kidnap Lincoln from Ford's Theatre.[258] Chester refused to be drawn in, but he testified to the existence of this plot at the military trial of the conspirators on May 12, 1865.[259] All of Booth's theatrical bravado must have been stirred by the thought of it, for the play on January 18 was *Jack Cade, Bondman of Kent*, about an English dissident and revolutionary who started an uprising in Kent in 1450 to protest the bad rule of feeble-minded King Henry VI.[260] Cade, like Booth in four months time, was wounded for his trouble and died from his wounds. But Booth's "uprising" of January 18th – if such it was – failed for the simple reason that the President apparently never had any intention of attending the theatre on the night in question.[261] Without the guest of honor, a kidnapping was out of the question.

* * *

With the first attempt come to naught, on January 20 Arnold and O'Laughlen took a room in the home of widow Mary Van Tyne, 420 D Street, Washington. According to Arnold they lived there "nearly two months seeing him [Booth] perhaps three or four times per week," though when Booth was seen it was "but a short time" due to his "pressing business always on hand vis. John Surratt."[262]

Meanwhile, Weichmann was in communication with his "patron," the Right Reverend John McGill, Catholic Bishop of Richmond, Virginia – the Confederate capital. Weichmann claimed that he was trying to resume his studies for the priesthood, for which he was still seeking the oft-delayed permission from his Bishop.[263] The upshot was that Father Dubreuil of Baltimore received a letter from Weichmann's Bishop, and perhaps wanted to sugar-coat bad news in person:

> You may depend, my dear friend, on my interest in you. All that I could do to make your bishop favorable to you, I have done. Now, I wish to have a talk with you on this matter. Come to Baltimore, at least for a few hours. . . .
> Yours affectionately devoted in Christ,
> F. Paul Dubreuil [264]

Surratt, home but a few days from Port Tobacco, was eager to accompany Weichmann to Baltimore. The two young friends left together on Saturday, January 21, and shared room #127 that night at the Maltby House in Baltimore.[265] Life may have seemed to Weichmann to be returning to normal, but on Sunday morning, January 22, Surratt turned mysterious once again. He called for a carriage, stating that he had $300 in his possession, and needed to see a gentleman on private business. Weichmann's account continues:

> [Surratt] informed me in a sort of a nonchalant way that he did not want me to go along. His language nettled me and I politely answered him that I was not anxious to go with him or know his affairs as I had business of my own to look after.[266]

Surratt was back at the hotel for Sunday dinner by three o'clock that afternoon.[267] On whom did he pay his mysterious call? We cannot know for certain. Since Arnold and O'Laughlen had just taken lodging with Mrs. Van Tyne in Washington, it is unlikely that they were in Baltimore that day. But there is another more sinister character who figures large in the history of the assassination, who had recently taken boarding with Mrs. Margaret Branson, on Eutaw Street, in Baltimore: Lewis Thornton Powell, alias Payne or Paine, alias Mosby, alias Wood.[268]

Tall, with jet-black hair, blue eyes, well-developed muscles and rugged good looks, Powell was a one-man military asset. He had served as a private in Company B, Forty-third Battalion of the Virginia Cavalry – probably the most famous unit in the Confederate army, known and feared by the Bluecoats as "Mosby's Rangers."[269] They were a hardened, well-disciplined band of fierce, partisan-style guerilla warriors.[270] Whether through actual surrender or, more likely, as a subterfuge to pass through enemy lines for the purpose of waging "black-flag" warfare, Powell appeared at a Union encampment at Fairfax Court House in Virginia on January 13, 1865, and applied to the provost marshal for protection as a civilian refugee, using the alias "Lewis Paine." Powell/Paine's false tale of woe was swallowed whole; he was sent to Alexandria where he took the oath of allegiance to the Union, and was then discharged from custody.[271]

Powell sold his horse and made his way to Miller's Hotel in Baltimore, arriving a few days before Weichmann and Surratt. The news of Powell's availability probably reached Preston Parr, a china dealer who was a Confederate man and friend of Surratt's, and Parr may have set up an interview.[272] Less than three months later, at the same time that Booth was shooting Lincoln, Powell would viciously attack Secretary of State William H. Seward. He inflicted multiple stab wounds from a Bowie knife and left Seward for dead, leaving a trail of blood the length of the grand staircase that included near-mortal wounds to one son, Assistant Secretary of State Frederick Seward, serious wounds to the nurse, Private George T. Robinson, and lesser wounds to another son, Colonel Augustus Seward.[273] Secretary Seward's life was surely saved by the intrepid nurse (a private with the Eighth Maine Volunteers), by the jaw support he was wearing as a consequence of a recent carriage accident that made it more difficult to slit his throat, by his deceptively thin frame under the covers, and by his own quick thinking in rolling off the bed.[274]

Having personally recruited Atzerodt, Herold and Powell/Paine into the plot, and of course being the reason his mother became involved with Booth, John H. Surratt is directly responsible for the involvement of *all four of the conspirators who were sentenced to hang for the murder of Abraham Lincoln.*[275]

* * *

By January 25, Surratt was back in Washington and ready to ride again. At about three o'clock on that cold and rainy afternoon, he appeared at the livery stable of "Doc" William E. Cleaver, a doctor of veterinary medicine, located on Sixth between B Street and Maryland Avenue.[276] Doc Cleaver stabled two horses brought in on New Year's Day by John Wilkes Booth – the first, the one-eyed bay horse he had purchased with Dr. Mudd in Maryland, and the second, a light bay horse that Atzerodt described as the smaller of the two.[277] Doc had known John Surratt for about twelve years.[278] Around this time Surratt usually came in with Booth, although Doc had also recently hired horses out to Surratt to ride with Sam Arnold. On January 25, Surratt ordered Doc to have the horses ready by seven o'clock that night.[279]

When Surratt showed up at the appointed hour it was still raining hard. Doc asked him if he was planning to go to the country on such a night, and Surratt replied yes, "he was going down to T.B.[280] to a dance party."[281] Later, while waiting in Doc's office, Surratt supposedly admitted that they were going down to T.B. not for a dance, but "to meet a party and help them across the river . . .."[282] According to Doc, Booth showed up about eight o'clock, Surratt chastised him for coming so late, and the two men headed out together.[283]

Aside from what is shown directly in his account books, all of Doc Cleaver's testimony is suspect, but the balance of what he said concerning that night is not at all credible (other than perhaps Doc's explanation that Surratt was drunk).[284] Doc had just been convicted of rape at the time of his testimony in 1867, and he was a known associate of Charles Dunham alias "Sanford Conover," the notorious perjurer, who had been buying up false testimony in a desperate attempt to connect Jefferson Davis with the assassination during the military trial of the conspirators.[285] Nonetheless, here's what Doc had to say about what transpired while he and Surratt were waiting for Booth in Doc's office:

> [Surratt] told me . . . that he and Booth had some bloody work to do; that they were going to kill Abe Lincoln, the d – d old scoundrel; that he had ruined Maryland and the country. He said that if nobody did it, he would do it himself, and pulled out a pistol and laid it on the desk.[286]

If Surratt was so reckless as to reveal secret murderous designs on the President while in the thick of the plot, it was the only time. There was absolutely no reason to say such things to a fellow like Doc Cleaver, unless by virtue of knowing him since childhood and too much to drink, Surratt uncharacteristically let his guard down. I don't believe it, but I report it here so that you may draw your own conclusions.

224 1 JHS Trial 356, 436.
225 1 JHS Trial 436.
226 1 JHS Trial 437.
227 *Ibid.*
228 1 JHS Trial 356, 437.
229 1 JHS Trial 337-38.
230 Weichmann, p.71; 1 JHS Trial 402.
231 *Surratt Family Tree,*
   http://www.surrattmuseum.org/genealogy/su_gen1.html (accessed Nov. 28, 2013).
232 *Re: Townsend Interview of Weichmann*, p. IX-15.
233 *Townsend Interview of Weichmann*, p. IX-20; 1 JHS Trial 400.
234 1 JHS Trial 125, 310, 343; *American Brutus*, p.226; *Blood on the Moon*, p.118.
235 1 JHS Trial 344-46.
236 *Statements, Mary Surratt* (April 28, 1865), p.49.
237 JOH Papers - JHS, James ET Lange and Katherine DeWitt, Jr., *The Gift Of John Harrison Surratt, Jr.,* citing, Upper Marlboro, Maryland Land Records, Liber F.S.2, folio 368.
238 *Statements, Arnold Statement*, p.20; *American Brutus*, p.160; Weichmann, p.73.
239 *Come Retribution*, pp.336-37; *The Spencer Carbine,*
   http://amhistory.si.edu/militaryhistory/collection/object.asp?ID=117 (accessed Dec. 1, 2013).

[240] *Statements, Arnold Statement*, p.20; *American Brutus*, pp. 153, 160-61.

[241] *Come Retribution*, p.341.

[242] Swanson & Weinberg, p.51.

[243] *American Brutus*, p.161; 1 JHS Trial 215, 372.

[244] *American Brutus*, p.161.

[245] Weichmann, p.76.

[246] *American Brutus*, p.161.

[247] *Ibid.; Lost Atzerodt Statement*, p. III-20; *LA from Surratt Courier*, vol.1, at III-27, *George A. Atzerodt Confession in the Jan. 18, 1869 Baltimore American*, p.III-28 (hereafter *"Atzerodt Baltimore American Statement"*). There's another version of these events attributed to Smoot that gives the price at $250, but I use the price stated by Atzerodt, $300. *Compare, Lost Atzerodt Statement*, p. III-20, *with, Come Retribution* p.339, and 344 n.34. It doesn't really matter.

[248] 1 JHS Trial 374-75.

[249] 1 JHS Trial 213-14. And if you believe that one, I've got a bridge for sale in Arizona that you'll just love.

[250] 1 JHS Trial 215.

[251] *Ibid.*

[252] 1 JHS Trial 215.

[253] I am not the only researcher who has concluded that this is likely. Alfred Isacsson states positively that there was to be an attempt on January 18th. *Isacsson Dissertation*, p.14. He cites for this, Jim Bishop's book, *The Day Lincoln was Shot*, p.76 (NY: Harper & Brothers, 1955). A note found in Mr. Hall's HB Ste. Marie files calls this theory "highly unlikely." JOH Papers - HBSM, *Notes on 2 Plays*. This is one of the rare instances in which I must respectfully disagree with Mr. Hall.

[254] *Statements, Arnold Statement*, p.20; Weichmann, p.73. The draft horse was stabled at Naylor's. *Come Retribution*, p.339.

[255] *American Brutus*, pp.162-63; *Statements, Arnold Statement*, p.20.

[256] *Ibid.*, p.20.

[257] *Isacsson Dissertation*, p.14.

[258] *Trial of the Conspirators*, p.44.

[259] *Ibid.*

[260] JOH Papers - HBSM, *Notes on 2 Plays*.

[261] *Ibid.*

[262] *Statements, Arnold Statement*, pp.20-21; *American Brutus*, p.169.

[263] Weichmann, p.74.

[264] *Ibid.*

[265] *Ibid.*; 1 JHS Trial 373.

[266] Weichmann, p.75; 1 JHS Trial 373.

[267] 1 JHS Trial 374.

268 Weichmann, p.75; *Come Retribution*, p.339.
269 *Come Retribution*, p.339; Swanson and Weinberg, pp.64-67.
270 *Come Retribution*, pp.135-36.
271 *Ibid.*, p.339.
272 *Ibid.*; *American Brutus*, p.166. An alternate version of Powell's recruitment to the plot, given in an 1882 newspaper account and reprinted in Weichmann, pp.82-84, is so riddled with inaccuracies of timing and location as to forfeit all claim of credibility.
273 1 JHS Trial 247-55, 261-65. For a chilling but fairly accurate recreation of this attack, see the film *Killing Lincoln* (2013).
274 1 JHS Trial 261-65; discussion with Jim Garrett at Surratt Society Conference, March 15, 2014.
275 Swanson & Weinberg, p.23.
276 1 JHS Trial 204-05, 206-07. Although much of Cleaver's testimony is unreliable, he used stable books to establish the names and dates of persons taking horses, so these basic facts are reliable. *Ibid.*, pp. 204, 205, 206.
277 *Come Retribution*, p.338-39; 1 JHS Trial 205-06; *Statements, Atzerodt Statement of April 25, 1865, Taken by Col. H.H. Wells Aboard the Monitor "Montauk,"* p.60 (hereafter *"Atzerodt Wells Statement"*).
278 1 JHS Trial 205.
279 1 JHS Trial 206.
280 "T.B." was a small settlement five miles from Surrattsville, in the direction of Port Tobacco. 1 JHS Trial 300, 512.
281 1 JHS Trial 206.
282 *Ibid.*
283 1 JHS Trial 207.
284 1 JHS Trial 206.
285 1 JHS Trial 210-13; see, Seymour J. Frank, *The Conspiracy to Implicate the Confederate Leaders in Lincoln's Assassination*, Mississippi Valley Historical Rev. 629, http://www.journalofamericanhistory.org/projects/lincoln/bibliography/articles/pdf/LIJ-Article-1950s.pdf (accessed Nov. 29, 2013) (hereafter *"Conspiracy re: Confederate Leaders"*). We are indebted to Mr. Frank for his careful and accurate perusal of this sorry incident. It strikes me, however, that one of the most serious casualties of Judge Holt's and Conover's championing of perjured testimony is lost accurate evidence of the possibility that their big lie - that Jefferson Davis knew of and authorized the Lincoln assassination - might actually have been true. Having discredited this entire line of inquiry for nearly 150 years, they effectively played into the hands of their enemies.
286 1 JHS Trial 206.

CHAPTER SIX

SURRATT AND THE VEILED LADY

As Booth and Surratt ride south into the rain and mist that January 25th, Surratt's tracks become murkier. For nearly a month, it is not possible to follow him day by day.[287] But there are some crucial events in Surratt's life in February, not least of which is meeting Mrs. Sarah Antoinette "Nettie" Slater, alias Kate Brown, alias Kate Thompson, alias A. Reynaud, the mysterious veiled "widow" whose husband was not dead.[288] For one thing, Surratt and Slater may have fallen in love. For another, if anyone carried from Richmond to Washington an order to kill Lincoln, it was Surratt and Slater.

Mrs. Slater, called "Nettie" by her family, was born Sarah Antoinette Gilbert on January 12, 1843 at Middletown, Connecticut.[289] The exotic spice in her family tree came through her paternal grandfather, Ebenezer Gilbert, who married Dèsiré Boutin, a beauty from the French island of Martinique. Nettie's father was born in Martinique, and in 1832 he married Antoinette Reynaud, an 18-year-old French girl, who was born at Port of Spain, Trinidad.[290] Their daughter Nettie became fluent in French at an early age (a skill she had in common with Mrs. Surratt), and could easily pass herself as French or Canadian. Sometime around 1859 her father moved to North Carolina, although her mother stayed in Connecticut. Shortly thereafter, Nettie and her younger brother Frederick followed their father south.[291]

Nettie settled in New Bern, North Carolina, where she met the charming Rowan Slater, a musician and town dancing-master. On June 12, 1861 the couple married despite the uncertainties of war swirling around them.[292] In light of the new realities, Mr. Slater was fortunate to obtain a job as purchasing agent for the Confederacy in Goldsboro, which kept him at home for a good part of the war. In 1863 Mr. and Mrs. Slater moved to a farm just outside of Salisbury, Rowan County, North Carolina, which enabled them to stay together as late as July 14, 1864.[293]

Few lives were untouched by the great conflict. Mrs. Slater's beloved younger brother Frederick enlisted in March 1863, and was killed on June 6, 1863 at the tender age of seenteen.[294] After Frederick's death, Mrs. Slater's older brothers Eugene and Robert were in and out of trouble with their commanders. Eugene was court-martialed in Goldsboro and convicted of advising soldiers to desert. He was cashiered on November 9, 1863. While Eugene's review was pending, he and brother Robert deserted and headed back to New Bern, which was under Union control.[295]

On July 23, 1864, Rowan Slater enlisted in Company A, 20th North Carolina Infantry. With her brothers dead or AWOL, and her husband off to war, Mrs. Slater was freed of all domestic responsibilities. James O. Hall has her enlisting in the Confederate Secret Service in mid-January 1865. His version of events is that she decided to apply for passage to the North to go live with her mother and sister in New York City. A letter dated January 16, 1865, signed by two Confederate Congressmen, supported Mrs. Slater's application. It was kicked upstairs to Confederate Secretary of War James Seddon, the man in charge of the Signal Corps, where it was approved. Supplied with money and the necessary transit papers – as well as secret papers to document that the St. Albans Raiders were acting under Confederate orders and therefore not subject to trial as common criminals – Mrs. Slater left Richmond on her first mission for the Confederacy on approximately January 31, 1865.[296]

The problem with this version of events is that it fails to account for contrary evidence in the register of the St. Lawrence Hall in Montreal. On January 10, 1865 at twelve o'clock noon, a Mr. "T.F. Hendrickson" registered. Squeezed in next to his name in a curlicue script is written "+ Miss Slater."[297] "Hendrickson" is undoubtedly an alias, but it is one that appears again at a crucial date in relation to Mrs. Slater and John H. Surratt, so this entry is probably genuine. If so, then the entire mid-

January application for passage to the North was simply a charade to bolster Mrs. Slater's cover for future missions. This might help explain why two Congressmen could be found to support her petition, and why it received the personal attention of the Confederate Secretary of War.

Regardless of how Mrs. Slater became a Confederate agent, there is no mistaking why she would be considered a highly valuable asset. Slim, with dark eyes and hair, the twenty-two-year-old beauty feigning widowhood[298] from behind a coquettish veil could easily melt the hearts of the most jaded sentries, obtain favors from "gallant" officers, and gain access wherever men guarded the gates.[299] The paternalistic assumptions of the time were such that women could pass unsuspected where men could not. Indeed, the prosecution in Surratt's trial argued that Mrs. Surratt had to "unsex herself" to participate in the assassination plot.[300]

Although perhaps not her first mission, Hall is undoubtedly correct that Mrs. Slater left Richmond approximately January 31, carrying documents in support of the St. Albans Raiders.[301] She probably took one of the common Confederate courier routes, "along the Richmond, Fredericksburg, and Potomac Rail Road to Milford station in Caroline County, then to Bowling Green, to the Rappahannock River ferry at Port Royal, and on to a signal corps camp near the mouth of Mattox Creek on the Virginia side of the Potomac River in Westmoreland County."[302] On February 1, she was spotted by Confederate agent James H. Fowle in Westmoreland County, heading north en route from Richmond.[303] At Mattox Creek Mrs. Slater was likely put in the care of August "Gus" Howell, a twenty-seven-year-old experienced Confederate agent and blockade runner. According to Mr. Hall, Howell accompanied Mrs. Slater across the Potomac and along the usual route through Southern Maryland, "through Captico, Charlotte Hall, Bryantown, T.B., Surrattsville, and on to Washington," via a network of safe houses provided by Confederate sympathizers.[304]

When in Washington, Mrs. Slater, like John Wilkes Booth, would often stay at the National Hotel.[305] It is interesting to note that John H. Surratt also checked in to the National Hotel for the night of February 1-2, 1865.[306] Why would Surratt stay in a hotel in his own home town? Did he reserve the room under his name for Howell and

Mrs. Slater? Did he stay with Mrs. Slater that night? We cannot know, but we do know that the two would become very close.

From Washington, Howell continued with Mrs. Slater as far as the European Hotel in New York City.[307] She checked into Montreal's St. Lawrence Hall as "Miss N. Slater" of New York at three o'clock the morning of February 16, perhaps accompanied by a "Wm. Polley" of New York, who checked in at the same time.[308] And there, for the moment, we will leave the veiled lady.

* * *

We know that Surratt was home on Monday, February 6, 1865, because he wrote to his cousin, Belle Seaman on that day. His letter is a domestic idyll. He told Miss Seaman that he and his sister Anna were planning to go to a "regular country hoedown."[309] He painted the blissful scene for his cousin:

> I have just taken a peek in the parlor. Would you like to know what I saw there? Well, Ma was sitting on the sofa, nodding first to one chair, then to another next to [the] piano. Anna sitting in [a] corner, dreaming, I expect, of J.W. Booth. Well, who is J.W. Booth? She can answer the question. Miss Fitzpatrick playing with her favorite cat – a good sign of an old maid – the detested creatures. Miss Dean fixing her hair, which is filled with rats and mice.
>
> But hark! the doorbell rings, and Mr. J.W. Booth is announced and listen [to the] scamperings . . .. Such brushing and fixing.[310]

Surratt is charming, witty, and rather patronizing. Not unexpectedly for a military man, he reveals his distaste for cats, creatures not known to take orders from anyone. He is attuned to his sister's feelings for the charming actor he has introduced to the household. Whether he is aware of the risk that his involvement with Booth will soon destroy their domestic peace, he does not say.

* * *

Gus Howell returned to Washington alone on February 20, and stayed for two nights at Mrs. Surratt's on H Street. Under the alias "Mr. Spencer," Howell successfully pumped Weichmann for sensitive troop strength information, and taught Weichmann the Confederate cipher system based on the alphabetical "Vigenère Square." Weichmann, who thought it came from a magician's book, made himself one of the 27x27 squares. It was identical to the one found among the effects of John Wilkes Booth.[311] Weichmann claims that he "never made any use of it except to translate a few poems into [code]."[312]

It was about this time that a tall, black-haired visitor clad in a seedy black overcoat called for John Surratt at Mrs. Surratt's house.[313] Finding that the son was not at home, the visitor asked to speak with the mother. He gave his name as "Mr. Wood," though of course it was Lewis Powell, the Mosby Ranger recruited by Surratt in January.[314] Mrs. Surratt requested that he be brought to the parlor and introduced.[315] At Mrs. Surratt's direction, Weichmann brought dinner up to his room for "Mr. Wood."[316] Weichmann questioned him while he was eating, but got little response. "I am from Baltimore, and a clerk in the china store of Mr. Parr," was the most the stranger would reveal.[317] "Wood" slept in the attic, and was gone by the next morning.[318]

'

* * *

With Gus Howell already in Washington, who would escort Mrs. Slater from New York? This pleasant task fell to John H. Surratt.[319] While in New York on this errand, Surratt accepted John Wilkes Booth's invitation to visit him at his brother Edwin's mansion at 28 East 19th Street. There, Surratt met members of the famous acting family, and was impressed by their elegance and charm.[320]

The day after his soiree at the Booths, Surratt may have made his way to Broadway and stood on the pavement beneath a particular hotel, keeping an eye out for a small switch with a waxed end and a piece of red ribbon on the butt, held horizontally between the fingers. That was the signal by which he located Mrs. Slater – or so he told Atzerodt.[321] Perhaps he was just being "cloak-and-dagger." However they managed their rendezvous, Surratt successfully escorted the lady spy from New

York to Washington. According to Weichmann:

> About the 22nd of [February] . . ., a buggy was driven one evening to the house by John H. Surratt with a lady in it. . . . The woman was rather diminutive in height, but very active and sprightly in all her movements. She wore what was called in those days a "mask," a kind of short veil, covering the face only as far as the chin. . . . She was not introduced to me, but afterwards I ascertained her name to be Mrs. Slater, at least that was the name under which she was traveling. She remained in the house only one night, and I gave up my room to her use.[322]

But did Surratt also give up his room for the whole night? Weichmann's account continues:

> After her departure I discovered in the closet of my room a delicate pair of ladies' shoes, evidently belonging to someone who was the owner of a small foot. I laughingly made some remark about this to Mrs. Surratt, but she grew angry, and gave me to understand that it was none of my business.[323]

The plan was that George Atzerodt would ride down to Port Tobacco, and row Gus Howell and Mrs. Slater across the Potomac to Virginia.[324] Surratt wrote a note for the proprietor of Howard's stables on G street:

> Mr. Howard,
> Will please let the bearer, Mr. Azworth [*sic*.] have my horse whenever he wishes to ride, and also my leggings and gloves, and oblige,
>
> Yours etc.,
J.H. Surratt
>
> Feb. 22, 1865
> 541H St. Bet 6 and 7th Sts.

On February 23rd, Surratt and Mrs. Slater, now joined by Gus Howell, continued the trip southward from their H Street house in Washington. While at the Surrattsville Tavern, they came upon James H. Fowle, who mistakenly called Howell "Gus Howard" in his testimony to the Boutwell Committee. Howell introduced Fowle to Surratt at that meeting.[326] A few days later, probably February 26 or 27, Atzerodt rowed Howell, Fowle and Mrs. Slater across the Potomac from Great Goose Creek to Mathias Point.[327] Fowle also testified that he saw Mrs. Slater in Richmond, so there is no question that she arrived safely.[328] Most likely, Surratt did not accompany Mrs. Slater all the way to Richmond at this time.

* * *

But perhaps he did! Fowle's testimony before the Boutwell Committee establishes that Surratt went to Richmond some time between late January and the end of February 1865.[329] As we've just seen, Fowle was rowed south across the Potomac by Atzerodt, along with Howell and Mrs. Slater, at the very end of February. They separated at Mathias Point, and Howell and Slater – and perhaps Surratt? – went on to Richmond ahead of Fowle.[330] When Fowle arrived, he was told that Surratt had already been there.[331] What's more, he was told this by Judah P. Benjamin, the Confederate Secretary of State in charge of the Secret Service and Canadian operations, and by Benjamin's assistant, Quinton Washington.[332] It may be that Surratt went all the way to Richmond with Howell and Mrs. Slater in late February. Or it may be that Surratt began his trip to Richmond the night that he and John Wilkes Booth rode off from Doc Cleaver's stables into the rainy mist on January 25.[333] Most likely Surratt went sometime in mid-February. A secret mission to Richmond would account for why researchers have had difficulty placing him during the period from February 6, when he wrote to Miss Seaman,[334] until February 20, when he headed to New York to see the Booths and pick up Mrs. Slater.

A clue that Surratt's mission to Richmond ended just before he went to New York is provided by Weichmann, who says that "[n]o sooner had Surratt returned from Port Tobacco . . . than he found it necessary to go to New York."[335] Port Tobacco is on the way back from

Richmond, and we know that Surratt went to New York to retrieve Mrs. Slater on about February 20, since Weichmann himself dates their return in the carriage as February 22.[336]

The important point is not exactly when Surratt went to Richmond, but that he probably did go. As stated by Weichmann:

> Surratt, in fact, at this time [late January to February 22], was continually on the go and away from his home much of the time. He was not now busying himself about getting an appointment or securing work. He always appeared to have plenty of money and had the air and actions of a man thoroughly preoccupied with important business affairs.[337]

Weichmann hit the nail on the head with his remark about the importance of Surratt's business affairs. Regardless of when in late January to February he went to Richmond, Surratt apparently met personally with the highest official in the Confederate Secret Service, Judah P. Benjamin.[338] He did this as he was in the very midst of collaborating with John Wilkes Booth on the plot against President Lincoln. Whatever he was up to, by his own admission it was deadly serious business. He stayed one night at the home of Mr. E.L. Smoot of Surrattsville, who needled him about going to Richmond. While Surratt never told him exactly what he was up to, he did say this: "If the Yankees knew what I'm up to, they would stretch this old neck of mine." Then Surratt smiled, threw his head back and yanked on an imaginary rope.[339]

It is no wonder that Surratt was no longer hurting for cash. According to testimony by Dr. Lewis J.A. McMillan, ship's doctor on the Steamship *Peruvian* whom Surratt befriended on a voyage bound for Liverpool:

> McMillan: He [Surratt] told me he had received money in
>   Richmond from the Secretary of State, Benjamin, several times.
> Pierrepont: Did he tell you how much?
> McMillan: I remember two amounts, $30,000 and $70,000. I do
>   not remember at what times he received them; he stated
>   particular times. I remember these amounts.[340]

It is likely that Surratt or McMillan exaggerated the amounts given to Surratt. But support is support; the rest is simply haggling over the price.

Judah Benjamin's office was located on the floor just below Jefferson Davis's, in the old Customs Building in Richmond.[341] They conferred frequently. Calling Judah Benjamin President Jefferson Davis's "hatchet man," researcher Sandy Prindle states:

> That didn't mean that Jefferson Davis made every decision and took every action involving the Confederate Secret Service. He certainly made the big decisions.[342]

There could be no bigger decision than providing financial support to Confederate Agents planning to kidnap or kill the enemy Commander in Chief.

[287] *Hall JOH Timeline*, p.5 (Hall loses Surratt from February 1 to February 22).

[288] James O. Hall, *The Veiled Lady, from North & South: The Official Magazine of the Civil War Society*, vol. 3, number 6, pp.35, 38 (2000) (hereafter "The Veiled Lady").

[289] *The Veiled Lady*, p.36.

[290] *Ibid.*

[291] *The Veiled Lady*, pp.35, 37; *E.G. Lee*, p.145.

[292] *The Veiled Lady*, p.37; JOH Papers - *SS*, *State of North Carolina Marriage License, Wayne County, June 12, 1861*.

[293] *The Veiled Lady*, pp.37-38.

[294] *Ibid.*, p.38; JOH Papers - *SS*, *Muster roll, dated Aug. 3, 1863, M-270, Roll 221, Compiled Service Records of Confederate Soldiers from North Carolina*.

[295] *The Veiled Lady*, p.38; JOH Papers - *SS*, *Robert J. Gilbert Service Record, Confederate Company I - 2 NC*; JOH Papers - *SS*, *Military record* (Jan. 25, 1864).

[296] *The Veiled Lady*, pp.38-39.

[297] JOH Papers - *Microfilm of St. Lawrence Hall Register* (January 10, 1865).

[298] Rowan Slater was captured April 6, 1865, at Farmville, Virginia, during Robert E. Lee's retreat. He took oath of allegiance at Newport News on June 26 and was released. *The Veiled Lady*, p.38.

[299] *Ibid.*

[300] 2 JHS Trial 1111, 1115.

[301] JOH Papers - *SS*, *Surratt Courier*, vol. XXXII No.2, John F. Stanton, *Some Thoughts on Sarah Slater*, p.4 (Feb. 2007), *citing*, John W. Headley,

Confederate Operations in Canada and New York.

302 *The Veiled Lady*, p.39.

303 JOH Papers - SS, *Additional Fowle Testimony to Boutwell Committee 1866*, questions ##223, 224, 225 (hereafter "*Additional Fowle Testimony*").

304 *The Veiled Lady*, p.39.

305 *Atzerodt Baltimore American Statement*, p. III-27; *Lost Atzerodt Statement*, p. III-21.

306 *Hall JHS Timeline*, p.4, citing, *The Daily Morning Chronicle* (Feb. 2, 1865).

307 *The Veiled Lady*, p.39.

308 JOH Papers, *Microfilm of St. Lawrence Hall Register* (Feb. 15, 1865).

309 *American Tragedy, p.95*, quoting, *Letter from John H. Surratt to Belle Seaman* (Feb. 6, 1865).

310 *Ibid.*

311 *Trial of the Conspirators*, p.133; Weichmann, p.86; *The Veiled Lady*, p.39; *LA from Surratt Courier*, vol. 1, at VI-11, David Winfred Gaddy, *The Enigma of the Rebel Ciphers*, p. VI-11 (Sept. 1997).

312 Weichmann, p.86.

313 Weichmann dates this visit to the latter part of February, at the time Surratt went to see Booth in New York, in his Surratt trial testimony, 1 JHS Trial 375, and to just before the arrival of Mrs. Slater (February 22nd), in his memoir, Weichmann, pp.84-85. He dates it to early March in his testimony in the military trial of the conspirators. *Trial of the Conspirators*, p.114. I think February makes more sense for this first visit, based on how often Surratt was away.

314 *Trial of the Conspirators*, p.114.

315 1 JHS Trial 376; Weichmann, p.84.

316 1 JHS Trial 376.

317 Weichmann, p.85; 1 JHS Trial 377.

318 *Ibid.*

319 *The Veiled Lady*, p.40; 1 JHS Trial 418.

320 *American Brutus*, p.171; Maria A. Dering, *The Twilight of Edwin Booth*, in *The New York Researcher*, p.80 (Fall 2005), http://mariadering.com/pdf/TheTwilightOfEdwinBooth.pdf (accessed Nov. 30, 2013).

321 *Atzerodt Baltimore American Statement*, p. III-27.

322 Weichmann, p.85.

323 Weichmann, pp.85-86.

324 *The Veiled Lady*, p.40.

325 *Ibid.*, p.40; Weichmann, pp.107-08. Weichmann gives the name as "Atzerodt" in his memoirs, but Mr. Hall says it is scribbled and, though perhaps intended to be Atzerodt, in fact looks like "Azworth." It may also be that Surratt was reflexively disguising Atzerodt's name.

326 *JOH Fowle Testimony*, p.1, question #871; *ibid.*, p.4, questions ##1149-53; *The Veiled Lady*, pp.40-41.

327 *Ibid.; Trial of the Conspirators*, p.134.

328 *Additional Fowle Testimony*, question #228.

329 *JOH Fowle Testimony*, p.1, question #871; *ibid.*, p.2, questions ##875-876; *ibid.*, pp.3, questions 904, 908; pp.5-7, notes & questions ##834, 835, 836.

330 *Veiled Lady*, p.41.

331 *JOH Fowle Testimony*, pp.5-6, notes and question #834.

332 *Ibid.*, p.2, question ##876-877; *ibid.*, p.3, question #909.

333 This is the view of the authors of *Come Retribution*, p.340.

334 *Hall JHS Timeline*, p.4, *citing, The Daily Morning Chronicle* (Feb. 2, 1865); *American Tragedy*, p.95.

335 Weichmann, p.78.

336 *Ibid.*, p.85. Although Weichmann dates this particular visit to New York to "early February," he's been wrong about dates before. Or it may be that Surratt visited New York twice in February.

337 Weichmann, p.78.

338 *JOH Fowle Testimony*, p.2, question ##876-877; *ibid.*, p.3, question #909; *Come Retribution*, p.340.

339 1 JHS Trial 190.

340 1 JHS Trial 467-68.

341 *Come Retribution*, p.166.

342 Hon. Sandy Prindle, *Judah Benjamin: A Person of Interest*, p.7 (*Surratt Courier*, April 2013) (hereafter *"Person of Interest"*).

Chapter Seven

BEWARE THE IDES OF MARCH

Mᴀʀᴄʜ 4, 1865 ᴡᴀs ᴛʜᴇ ᴅᴀʏ ᴀᴘᴘᴏɪɴᴛᴇᴅ ғᴏʀ ᴛʜᴇ sᴇᴄᴏɴᴅ ɪɴᴀᴜɢᴜ-ʀᴀᴛɪᴏɴ of Abraham Lincoln. On the eve of that ceremony Weichmann came upon Surratt and Booth at a restaurant located at the corner of Pennsylvania Avenue and Sixth Street. The three men walked together to the Capitol, where Congress was still in session. They ascended to the gallery of the House of Representatives.[343]

> As we reached the landing, Booth saw a bust standing on a pedestal in a corner. Turning to me, he asked whose it was. Why, said I, that is Lincoln. What is *he* doing in here before his time, said Booth . . .?[344]

The next day, Lincoln took the oath of office in the old Senate chamber, then walked to the freshly-domed Capitol's east facade to deliver his second-most famous speech.[345] As the President emerged hatless and unscathed yet again despite the venom and death threats swirling around him,[346] the sun broke through the clouds to illuminate his careworn face.[347] Thousands of people swarmed the streets to catch a glimpse of the momentous event, though only a few hundred were near enough to hear the unamplified words. They are remembered as words of compassion for his enemies:

> With malice toward none, with charity for all, with firm-ness in the right as God gives us to see the right, let us

strive on to finish the work we are in, to bind up the nation's wounds, to care for him who shall have borne the battle and for his widow and his orphan, to do all which may achieve and cherish a just and lasting peace among ourselves and with all nations.[348]

Yet few remember the Biblical words of vengeance immediately preceding these:

The Almighty has His own purposes. "Woe unto the world because of offenses; for it must needs be that offenses come, but woe to that man by whom the offense cometh." . . . Fondly do we hope, fervently do we pray, that this mighty scourge of war may speedily pass away. Yet, if God wills that it continue until all the wealth piled by the bondsman's two hundred and fifty years of unrequited toil shall be sunk, and until every drop of blood drawn with the lash shall be paid by another drawn with the sword, as was said three thousand years ago, so still it must be said "the judgments of the Lord are true and righteous altogether."[349]

Many in the South already believed that the atrocities they had suffered at the hands of overzealous Union troops "were the result of a deliberate Union policy of savagery," the objective of which was the total annihilation of the South.[350] This passage from the Second Inaugural Address inflamed those fears.

As Lincoln delivered his address, Alexander Gardner removed the lens cap from his pre-focused camera for several long seconds, exposing the collodion-coated glass plate to create the most famous image of Lincoln's second inaugural.[351] On a fenced balcony about a hundred feet behind Lincoln's left shoulder, we can see the mustachioed face of a top-hatted gent who is probably John Wilkes Booth.[352]

"What an excellent chance I had to kill the President, if I had wished, on inauguration day!" Booth later bragged to his actor friend, Samuel K. Chester. Booth told Chester he got as near to the President on inauguration day as he was to Chester at that moment.[353] Was

Booth exaggerating, or did he get even closer than the mustachioed man in the photograph?

* * *

One of the many strange stories surrounding Lincoln's last weeks can be found in little-known affidavits from 1876, which tell the tale of a possible assassination attempt at the second inaugural. John W. Westfall says that he was a private in the Washington police force, detailed to Capitol security on March 4th. A crowd had been admitted to the rotunda by ticket, where they could see the Presidential procession pass through on the way to the speaker's platform on the east portico. The procession had begun to move and the President and Justices had just passed through the door when a man from the crowd broke through the south line in an attempt to follow them. Officer Westfall states that he grabbed the man, who struggled violently and insisted on his right to pass. At one point the man broke from his grasp, but other officers had joined the struggle and caught hold of him again, and together they forced him back into the crowd. During this brief altercation, the door was shut and the procession behind the President was halted for a few moments.[354]

According to Westfall, after the assassination he went around looking for a photograph of Booth, finally finding one in the office of Colonel L.C. Baker, Chief of the National Detective Police. Westfall claims that he immediately recognized Booth as the man from the second inaugural who tried to break through the lines at the rotunda. According to Westfall, he took a photo of Booth to show to several other officers, including Major French, his commander, and they all recognized Booth as the man who tried to break through the lines at the second inauguration.[355]

The basic facts of this story, supported by six affidavits, are probably true.[356] If this happened today the disruptive man would have been arrested or shot, but March 1865 lay near the end of a more innocent era. Although there had been one unsuccessful attempt on Andrew Jackson back in 1835, no American President had ever been assassinated.[357] So it is also credible that the police simply pushed the unruly man back into the crowd and forgot about it until later.

There is one thing in this account, however, that stands out as suspect: the post-hoc identification of the disruptive man as Booth. It seems unlikely that none of the officers or the many bystanders would have recognized one of the most famous actors in America at the time that the disturbance happened. After the assassination, of course, things were different. Suddenly, everyone had seen Booth everywhere.

It is often claimed that most of the conspirators can be seen in Gardner's photograph of the second inaugural, directly beneath the stone buttress in front of Lincoln: tall Lewis Powell (Paine) in a slouch hat, as well as Atzerodt in a conductor's cap, Spangler below him in a derby, and Herold peeking from behind the large bearded man to their right.[358] Perhaps; though hindsight is prone to conjure up synchronicity. Powell was more likely in Baltimore at the time, Atzerodt had just rowed across the Potomac the night before, and Herold was probably laid up with a sprained ankle in Maryland.[359] Still, there is one more curious figure standing just below the President, wearing what appears for all the world to be Confederate Greys with a jaunty Rebel cap pushed forward on his head. That man bears an uncanny resemblance to John H. Surratt.[360]

* * *

On March 14, Surratt summoned Powell back from Baltimore by telegram.[361] Powell's violent streak almost kept him from his date with history. On March 12, he was arrested for the brutal beating of a "negro" maid at Branson's boardinghouse. But the slippery Powell retook the oath of allegiance and talked his way out of jail.[362]

Upon answering the door for Powell/Wood at Mrs. Surratt's house, Weichmann had forgotten his name. Unable to keep his aliases straight, Powell gave the name "Mr. Paine."[363] Weichmann remembered the man's previous alias when "Paine" came into the parlor and several of the young ladies of the house referred to him as "Mr. Wood." Rather than clerking at Mr. Parr's china shop, "Paine/Wood" was now a Baptist preacher.[364] When apprised of these inconsistencies, Mrs. Holohan reportedly remarked, "Queer preacher. I don't think he will convert many souls."[365]

The next day Surratt arrived home. Powell/Paine asked, "Is this Mr.

Surratt?" When told that it was, he requested a private audience with him.[366] Weichmann surmises that the inquiry was a ruse because there seemed to be "a recognition" between the two men, and in light of the telegram summoning him and the fact that Surratt probably recruited Powell on their earlier trip to Baltimore, this hunch is probably correct.[367]

Upon his return from work on March 15, Weichmann found a false mustache on the table in his room, which he threw into a toilet box. Climbing the steps to the attic, he walked in on Powell and Surratt seated on the bed, surrounded by two revolvers, eight brand-new spurs, and two bowie knives. The two conspirators startled and began to hide the weapons, then saw who it was and regained their composure.[368] Weichmann went to Mrs. Surratt to express his unease. She told him that, "John was in the habit of riding into the country and needs these things for protection. You shouldn't think anything of it," she added.[369]

Weichmann could not help but think of it. His suspicions aroused, he made a confidant of Captain Gleason in the War Department. Together, they speculated about Surratt's purposes. According to Weichmann, an article in the March 19th issue of the *New York Tribune* discussing the risk that Lincoln might be captured prodded him to ask Captain Gleason whether such a thing was possible. "He laughed and hooted at the idea."[370] Weichmann put it out of his mind.

* * *

The same evening of the false mustache and revolvers, Surratt showed Weichmann a ten dollar ticket for a private box at Ford's Theatre. Weichmann wanted to go. According to his account:

> I wrested the ticket from [Surratt], and told him I was going to the theatre. "No," said he, "you are not. I don't want you to go to the theatre this evening for private reasons." He then struck me in the pit of the stomach, and took the ticket away from me again. He was very anxious that evening to take the smallest ladies in the house.[371]

Surratt's ticket was a gift from John Wilkes Booth to see *Jane Shore* from a box seat at Ford's Theatre on March 15, 1865, the only night it played at Ford's. Surratt invited thirteen-year-old Miss Holohan, who declined the invitation, likely at the direction of her parents. Surratt and Powell ended up escorting nineteen-year-old Miss Fitzpatrick and the eleven-year-old orphan, Miss Dean, to the theatre that night.[372] It is difficult to tell what Miss Dean would have made of the sophisticated plot centered on the life of English courtesan Jane Shore, who became the mistress of Edward IV, then navigated complex court politics through Richard III's reputed reign of terror.[373] According to Miss Fitzpatrick's testimony, the drama of fifteenth-century murder and passion could not even compete for the gentlemen's attention once John Wilkes Booth came to the box to pay a call. Surratt and Powell stepped out into the hall behind the box to engage in a private conversation with Booth, leaving the two young ladies on their own for a few minutes.[374] James O. Hall's view, stated in the vernacular of the twentieth century, is that they were "casing the joint."[375]

* * *

After escorting the young ladies home to 541 H Street, Surratt and Powell grabbed a deck of playing cards and went out again. According to Weichmann, "[t]hey remained out all night – something I had never known Surratt to do before when in the city."[376] Where did they go?

The answer lies in Surratt's offhand remark made a few days later, and the statements given by Atzerodt and Arnold: *they attended the first known general meeting of the conspirators, to plan the imminent kidnapping of Abraham Lincoln.* Surratt, in conversation with another gentleman in Weichmann's presence, let slip that he had spent the night of the 15th – the ides of March – "with a party of sociables at Gautier's saloon, and that he would like to introduce us, but that he could not as it was a private club."[377] But according to Atzerodt's third-person statement published by the *National Intelligencer* on July 9, 1865, two days after Atzerodt's execution:

> The first meeting of all the conspirators actively engaged was at a saloon on Pennsylvania Avenue called Gautier's. At this meeting O'Laughlen, Arnold, Booth, Surratt, Herold, and Atzerodt were present.[378]

Arnold's better-documented sworn statement of April 18, 1865 corroborates this, and discusses the meeting in some detail. A man who must have been David E. Herold, but whose name Arnold never caught, approached him between eleven and twelve o'clock the night of March 15, to say that Booth wanted him and O'Laughlen right away at Gautier's. Arnold grabbed O'Laughlen, who had just returned from Baltimore in response to the following telegram:

Washington, March 13th, 1865

To M. O'Laughlen, Esq.,
No. 57 N. Exeter St., Baltimore, Md.
Don't fear to neglect your business. You had better come at once.

J. Booth[379]

Herold, Arnold and O'Laughlen hurried to Gautier's, where they were ushered into a private dining room containing all the conspirators named by Atzerodt, plus "Mosby [a/k/a Powell/Paine/Wood] making in all seven persons."[380]

At this meeting, Booth presented his audacious plan to kidnap Lincoln from the Presidential box at Ford's Theatre. Each had their part in Booth's dramatic production. Arnold was to rush the box and seize the President while Booth and Atzerodt would handcuff him and lower him to the stage. "Mosby was to catch him and hold him until we all got down."[381] Surratt and Herold were to be on the other side of the bridge to facilitate their escape into Maryland. O'Laughlen was to put out the gas in order to plunge the theatre into darkness while they struck.[382] The various roles shifted around a bit, but the absurdity of the plan did not. Soon Arnold and O'Laughlen were in a heated argument with Booth, culminating (if Arnold is to be believed) with Arnold saying to Booth, "You can be my leader but not my executioner." Booth replied angrily that Arnold was "liable to be shot," to which Arnold retorted, "I shall defend myself."[383] The meeting didn't break up until six or seven o'clock in the morning of March 16th, but it appears that the resistance was sufficiently stiff to cause Booth to consider other plans, as they were soon focused on a different kidnap scheme.[384]

At least, that's the story handed down by the historical evidence. One might reasonably doubt whether a smart fellow like Booth ever (even back at the time of the January attempt) intended to kidnap Lincoln in front of an entire theatre audience of Union partisans, as opposed to simply shooting him. The plan as detailed at Gautier's is particularly incredible. The idea that they could lower a handcuffed President of the United States twelve feet down from his box to the stage in pitch darkness, then hold him there while the other conspirators climbed down without injuring themselves or getting mobbed by his defenders, is farfetched enough to dissuade any thinking person from the attempt. Then – if by some miracle they were not yet captured or killed – the plan to spirit him away from near the center of a capital swarming with Union troops to Maryland in a *buggy* without getting caught by swift pursuers on *horseback*, is so laughable that it seems strange that some historians have been taking it seriously for 150 years.[385] What's more, it cannot be ignored that the principal motive for the earlier kidnap schemes – forcing the North to recommence prisoner exchanges – had been mooted by General Grant's agreement on January 18 to exchange prisoners, which went into effect in February.[386]

Therefore, it is far more likely that any discussion at Gautier's involving Ford's Theatre would have concerned a somewhat different plan than the one confessed to by the captured participants – a plan of assassination. *Sic semper tyrannis.* Or, as Shakespeare's soothsayer says to the Emperor Caesar, "beware the ides of March!"[387]

A kernel of truth for this speculation lies in the highly guarded, self-serving admissions buried in Surratt's Rockville lecture. Though none of the statements given by the other conspirators mention Surratt as one who stood up to Booth in any way, Surratt discusses "a meeting in Washington for the purpose of discussing matters in general," at which he supposedly proposed the abandonment of the plot.

> At this meeting I . . . stated that I was confident the government had wind of our movements, and that the best thing we could do would be to throw up the whole project. Everyone seemed to coincide in my opinion, except Booth,

who sat silent and abstracted. Arising at last and bringing his fist upon the table he said: "Well, gentlemen, if the worst comes to the worst, *I shall know what to do.*"[388]

Surratt claims that hard words then passed between Booth and four of the party, one saying, "If I understand you to intimate anything more than the capture of Mr. Lincoln, I for one will bid you goodbye."[389] When, supposedly, "everyone expressed the same opinion," Booth was compelled to apologize that his rash words were uttered under the influence of "too much champagne," and then they parted amicably at five o'clock in the morning.[390]   But the salient point remains: Surratt admits that Booth spoke of killing Lincoln at this meeting at Gautier's on March 15th, in words that were understood as such by his fellow conspirators at the time.

The Rockville lecture was given in December 1870, by which time Lincoln was well on his way to sainthood in the American political pantheon, and the assassination was seen – even through the lens of *realpolitik* – as detrimental to the reconstruction of the South. Any breath of complicity in Lincoln's actual murder at that time was a sure path to at least ostracism, if not vigilante retribution. Sentiments like those previously expressed by Surratt and his mother (and thousands of others) about sending Lincoln to hell were no longer politically or socially acceptable. Surratt, in his lecture, was playing to the *zeitgeist* of the time. But Surratt's claim that he or any other of the Lincoln conspirators would object to the idea of killing Lincoln – as opposed to the chance of getting caught – is pure pretense. More likely, Surratt built his version of the meeting at Gautier's around a kernel of truth that, on the Ides of March, Booth and all the conspirators discussed the possibility of assassinating Lincoln. Ford's Theatre was never much good for a kidnapping. But it proved to be perfect for an assassination.

* * *

What happened next is dated by Weichmann as March 16, by Hall as March 17, and by Arnold as "Sunday," which would be March 19.[391] I would think March 17 is correct, but the important thing is what took place, not exactly when it took place. According to Surratt's Rockville lecture, he and Booth received word that Lincoln was planning to attend a production of the play *Still Waters Run Deep* at Campbell Hospital near the Old Soldier's Home on the Seventh Street Road at the outskirts of Washington. Unlike Ford's Theatre, this was a pretty good scene for a kidnapping because the road was relatively isolated and close to Maryland. Although the conspirators only received word about three-quarters of an hour prior to the appointed time, "so perfect was our communication that we were instantly in our saddles on the way to the hospital."[392]   Surratt, Booth, Paine, Atzerodt and Herold met up in front of Mrs. Surratt's boardinghouse in Washington, and all but Herold galloped off towards Campbell Hospital at about two o'clock.[393]   Herold was dispatched to pick up Booth's buggy and head for Surrattsville, carrying with him the arsenal of weapons and the canteen that Booth had collected.[394]

According to Atzerodt, "[t]he plan was to seize the coach of the President, Surratt to jump on the box, as he was considered the best driver, and make for 'T.B.' by way of Long Old Fields, to the Potomac River in the vicinity of Nanjemoy Creek, where they had a boat waiting with men to carry over the party."[395]   Somewhere en route they would meet up with Herold and switch to Booth's buggy, which was well equipped with food and firepower.

Thus, it was John Surratt who was chosen as the man to actually commandeer the President's carriage, and to drive the President to the same boat he had purchased with Atzerodt's help and Booth's money back in January, while on "French leave" doing Booth's bidding. Surratt was as thick in this plot as a man could be. Meanwhile, Mrs. Surratt sat home weeping, and skipped dinner.[396]   One might reasonably conclude that she knew something of what her son was up to.

The efforts of the conspirators were once again in vain. Either their intelligence was faulty or at the last minute Lincoln changed his plans. Either way, he did not attend the play at Campbell Hospital.[397] The conspirators feared that a last minute change in plans meant that the Federals were on to them.[398]   According to Weichmann:

> [A]t about half past six Surratt burst into the apartment. I looked at him and saw that he was very much excited. His pantaloons were in his boot tops, and he wore spurs. He held a small four-barreled Sharp's revolver in his hand; one

that could easily be carried in one's vest pocket. I asked him what was the matter. He leveled his pistol at me and exclaimed, "Weichmann, my prospects are gone; my hopes are blasted . . .."[399]

Ten minutes later Powell rushed into the room, his face flushed with excitement. When he pulled up his waistcoat, Weichmann noticed a large revolver on his hip. Booth came in next, and marched about the room two or three times flicking the riding crop in his hand. At a signal from Booth, the three men went up to the attic to confer. Then they left the house.[400]

* * *

Meanwhile, "Herold hung around the [Surrattsville] tavern for a while but nobody showed up with Lincoln a prisoner."[401] So Herold headed towards T.B., where he arrived at the hotel of John C. Thompson about eight o'clock that night. William Norton helped Herold move a trunk into the barroom. This was Booth's trunk, heavy with two carbines, a couple of double-barrel shotguns, a pistol, a knife, a sword, rope and a wrench.[402] Herold claimed he was going duck hunting. He asked whether John Surratt had come by, and let it be known that Surratt was expected. The next morning, most likely March 18, Herold had breakfast, shot off his pistols into the air (perhaps as a signal), then started back towards Surrattsville.[403]

Surratt and Atzerodt had fled Washington and were headed towards T.B. to find Herold. The three met up on the road between T.B. and Surrattsville.[404] According to the testimony of John M. Lloyd, Mrs. Surratt's tenant at Surratt's Tavern, the three men came in, took a drink, and started playing cards. Then Surratt called Lloyd into the front parlor, where he had Booth's carbines laid out on the sofa, along with a cartridge box, coiled rope and a monkey wrench.[405] The monkey wrench was to be used to remove the wheels from Lincoln's carriage, so that it could be more easily ferried across the Potomac, and the rope was to be stretched across the road to break the pursuit of any cavalry that might follow.[406]

Surratt insisted that Lloyd hide the carbines in the house; Lloyd claims he objected and had to be persuaded by Surratt, but more likely he was a willing participant.[407] Surratt, who had grown up in that house, knew just the place. He led Lloyd upstairs with the carbines to a sealed attic off the storeroom where the butt ends of the ceiling joists above the dining room were exposed above the attached kitchen. Surratt slipped the carbines between the joists.[408]

There the carbines stayed, until about midnight on the night of the assassination, when Booth and Herold came to call for them.[409] *One of these same carbines was in Booth's hands when he was shot by Boston Corbett at Garrett's barn in Maryland.*[410]

* * *

His work done, Surratt headed back to Washington, arriving in time to use two guest passes to Ford's Theatre, signed by John Wilkes Booth. This time Surratt invited Weichmann to accompany him. They met up with Atzerodt, Herold, and Mr. Holohan at the theatre. On that historic night they witnessed Booth's last performance. Booth played Pescara, Duke of Alva, in *The Apostate*, the story of an "apostate" Moor who is hunted down by the Spanish Inquisition. In the words of the *New York Times*, Pescara "fills the centre of the picture, dealing out destruction to all who cross his path, gloating over the contrivance of new cruelties, and reveling in the accumulation of horrors which form the substance of the play."[411] According to Weichmann:

> In one of the scenes, a female was dragged on the stage by Pescara and subjected to torture on the wheel. Never in my life did I witness a man play with so much intensity and passion as did Booth on that occasion. The hideous, malevolent expression of his distorted countenance, the fierce glare and ugly roll of his eyes, which seemed ready to burst from their sockets as he seized his victim by the hair and, placing her on the wheel, exclaimed, "Now behold Pescara's masterpiece!" are yet present with me. I cannot use language forcible enough to describe Booth's actions on that night.[412]

Powerful though it was, Booth's next time on that stage would be even more dramatic.

343 JOH Papers - *Letter from Louis J. Weichmann to Thomas Donaldson* (April 20, 1886).

344 *Ibid.* (emphasis in original).

345 *American Brutus*, p.174. The most famous is the Gettysburg Address.

346 National Parks Service, Ford's Theatre Collection, *Affidavit of John W. Westfall* (May 13, 1876) (hereafter *"Westfall Affidavit"*).

347 *American Brutus*, p.174; Jay Winik, *April 1865*, p.31 (Perennial, Harper Collins 2002) (hereafter *"April 1865"*); Weichmann, p.89.

348 Yale Univ., Second Inaugural Address of Abraham Lincoln, http://avalon.law.yale.edu/19th_century/lincoln2.asp (accessed Dec. 4, 2013).

349 *Ibid.*

350 *Come Retribution*, p.245.

351 Weichmann, plate IX; *American Memory, Lincoln's Second Inaugural Photograph*, http://memory.loc.gov/cgi-bin/query/r?ammem/pin:@field(NUMBER+ @band(ppmsc+02928)) (accessed Dec. 4, 2013); Alexander Gardner, http://www.civilwar.org/education/history/biographies/alexander-gardner.html (accessed Dec. 4, 2013); *Photography and the Civil War*, http://www.civilwar.org/photos/3d-photography-special/photography-and-the-civil-war.html (accessed Dec. 4, 2013).

352 Weichmann, plate IX; *April, 1865*, p.38.

353 *Trial of the Conspirators*, p.45.

354 *Westfall Affidavit*; Weichmann, pp.90-93.

355 *Westfall Affidavit*; *American Brutus*, p.257; Weichmann, p.90-93.

356 *Ibid.*

357 "Jan. 30, 1865: *Andrew Jackson Narrowly Escapes Assassination*, http://www.history.com/this-day-in-history/andrew-jackson-narrowly-escapes-assassination (accessed March 29, 2014).

358 Weichmann, plate IX.

359 *American Brutus*, p.437 n.41.

360 Weichmann, plate IX. Mr. Hall believed it was Surratt. *Hall JHS Timeline*, p.6.

361 *Come Retribution*, p.413; *Hall JHS Timeline*, p.6 (citing National Archives, M-599, reel 3, frames 1047-1048). Weichmann places the date of Powell's return to Mrs. Surratt's house on March 13. Weichmann, pp.96-97. A day or two doesn't really make any difference.

362 *Come Retribution*, p.413.

363 Weichmann, p.97; 1 JHS Trial 377. Weichmann spells it "Payne," but again, no difference.

364 Weichmann, p.97; 1 JHS Trial 377.

365 Weichmann, p.97.

366 *Ibid.*; 1 JHS Trial 377.

367 Weichmann, p.97; 1 JHS Trial 428-29.

368 1 JHS Trial 377; Weichmann, pp.97-98.

369 Weichmann, p.98; 1 JHS Trial 378.
370 *Trial of the Conspirators*, pp.119-20.
371 1 JHS Trial 378.
372 Weichmann, p.98; JOH Papers - HBSM, *Notes on 2 Plays*.
373 JOH Papers - HBSM, *Notes on 2 Plays*.
374 1 JHS Trial 234.
375 *Hall JHS Timeline*, p.7.
376 Weichmann, p.98.
377 *Ibid.*
378 *LA from Surratt Courier, Atzerodt's Confession in the 7/9/1865 National Intelligencer*, p. III-23 (hereafter *"Atzerodt National Intelligencer Statement"*).
379 Weichmann, p.96; 1 JHS Trial 401.
380 *Statements, Arnold Statement*, p.21.
381 *Ibid.*
382 *Ibid.*
383 *Ibid.*
384 *Ibid.*, pp.21-22.
385 Not every historian. Michael W. Kauffman shares my view that this "ridiculous scenario" was a mere cover for assassination. *American Brutus*, p.181.
386 *American Brutus*, pp.181, 438 n.11.
387 William Shakespeare, *Julius Caesar*, Act I, scene 2.
388 *Rockville Lecture*, Weichmann, p.431 (emphasis added).
389 *Ibid.*, p.432.
390 *Ibid.*
391 Weichmann, p.101; *Hall JHS Timeline*, p.6; *Statements, Arnold Statement*, p.22.
392 *Rockville Lecture*, Weichmann, p.432.
393 Weichmann, p.101.
394 *LA from Surratt Courier*, vol.1, at I-19, James O. Hall, *Hiding the Shooting Irons*, p. I-19 (March 1986) (hereafter *"Hiding the Shooting Irons"*); *Atzerodt National Intelligencer Statement*, p. III-23.
395 *Atzerodt National Intelligencer Statement*, pp. III-23-24.
396 Weichmann, p.101.
397 *Isacsson Dissertation*, pp.16-17; *Rockville Lecture*, Weichmann, p.432; *Atzeroldt National Intelligencer Statement*, p. III-24.
398 *Isacsson Dissertation*, p.17.
399 Weichmann, pp.101-02.
400 Weichmann, p.102.
401 *Hiding the Shooting Irons*, p. I-19.
402 Weichmann, p.117; 1 JHS Trial 511, 515.
403 1 JHS Trial 511-12, 515; Weichmann, p.118.
404 *Hiding the Shooting Irons*, p. I-19.
405 1 JHS Trial 277-78, 300.

406 *Atzerodt Baltimore American Statement*, p. III-28; Weichmann, p.119.

407 1 JHS Trial 277.

408 1 JHS Trial 278.

409 1JHS Trial 282; *Hiding the Shooting Irons*, p. I-19. Booth was too badly injured to carry a carbine, so they only took one and Lloyd put the other one back. One carbine was recovered at Garrett's farm, and the other was found hanging by twine from the joists at Surrattsville Tavern. Both carbines are on display at the museum in the basement of Ford's Theatre. *Ibid.* If you visit the Surratt House Museum in Clinton, Maryland, you can take a tour of the house and see the place where the carbines were hidden by Surratt and Lloyd.

410 *Manhunt*, pp.334-35; *Trial of the Conspirators*, p.94.

411 *New York Times, Mr. [Edwin] Booth as Pescara*, http://query.nytimes.com/mem/archive -free/pdf?res=F60C15FC3A5C15738DDDA80B94D9405B8584F0D3 (accessed Dec. 6, 2013). Although the Times' description is for a performance of the same play by John's elder brother, Edwin, it was John Wilkes Booth on stage for the performance viewed by Weichmann and Surratt on March 18, 1865.

412 Weichmann, p.119.

CHAPTER EIGHT

SHOOT THE DAMNED YANKEES

Having failed again to kidnap Lincoln the conspirators dispersed, Booth to New York, Arnold and O'Laughlen to Baltimore, the elusive Powell to New York or Baltimore, Herold to a new job in an army hospital.[413] This is the point at which Surratt later claimed he abandoned the whole idea of kidnapping Lincoln,[414] yet the evidence reveals that he was back at work on the plot within a few days of seeing *The Apostate*. On March 20, he picked up a letter addressed to "James Sturdy" from "Mr. Wood," which he conceded under questioning by Weichmann was actually from Powell/Paine. On March 23, a telegram was delivered to Weichmann at his place of employment in Mr. Stanton's War Department, addressed to "Wickmann" from "J. Booth" in New York. The telegram instructed Weichmann: "Tell John to telegraph number and street at once." Weichmann brought the telegram home and asked Surratt what it meant. "Don't be so damned inquisitive," Surratt snapped back.[415]

Yet if Surratt really wanted Weichmann in the dark, his next move is inexplicable.[416] According to Weichmann, Surratt invited him for a walk that evening. They first called on Miss Annie Ward, who seems to have been in league with Surratt.[417] Afterwards, they went to Herndon House, a boardinghouse at the corner of Ninth and F Streets. Surratt addressed the proprietor, Miss Murray, who was sufficiently hard of hearing that Weichmann was able to overhear the conversation:

"Perhaps Miss Annie Ward had spoken to you about a

91

room. Did she not speak to you about engaging a room for a delicate gentleman who was to have his meals sent up to him?"[418]

Surratt wanted the room on Monday, March 27. Weichmann soon learned why from Atzerodt, who was less than discreet. The room was for Lewis Powell, hardly a "delicate gentleman," but surely one who did not want his face seen by the other guests.[419] The telegram to "Wickman" was Booth's way of finding out from Surratt where Powell would be housed, while avoiding direct communication between the two principal conspirators.

Is it accurate to call Surratt one of the *two principal conspirators* with Booth? I believe that it is. Atzerodt's *National Intelligencer* statement contains the following clue to Surratt's rank among the conspirators:

> Surratt introduced Atzerodt to Booth, who feasted him and furnished him with money and horses, the horses being held in the name of Surratt, *who appeared to be the principal in the absence of Booth*.[420]

Add this clue to what we already know of Surratt's experience in the Confederate Secret Service, and the fact that Surratt and Booth were often together and regularly in communication for the several months just prior to the assassination, and "principal conspirators" does not seem too much of a leap. But whether it was Booth or Surratt or someone even higher up who called the shots in the Lincoln conspiracy may depend on what happened next, when Surratt and Mrs. Slater visited Richmond again.

* * *

As Washington was celebrating Lincoln's swearing in, Mrs. Slater was busily shuttling back and forth between Richmond and Montreal. On March 9 at 11:30 p.m., she checked into the St. Lawrence Hall using her mother's maiden name as an alias – "A. Reynaud" of New York.[421] She arrived in the company of "William H. Power" of New York, probably the same agent who previously checked in with her under the name "Wm. Polley."[422] Two days later, "E.G. Lee and Lady" checked in at the St. Lawrence.[423] This was Robert E. Lee's cousin, General Edwin G. Lee, who had been sent by Secretary of State Judah P. Benjamin to replace Jacob Thompson as the man in charge of all Confederate operations in Canada.[424]

We don't know exactly what Mrs. Slater did over the next few weeks, but most likely she was sent on a local mission, because she checked back in to St. Lawrence Hall on March 17, at 8:00 a.m. under the "Reynaud" alias.[425] It is probable that Mrs. Slater's local mission involved the St. Albans raiders, who had been discharged based on the papers that she first carried to Canada.[426] Some of those Confederate guerilla fighters had been re-arrested near Quebec City.[427] A contemporary account states that "a widow only 24 years old employed by the Confederate Government for Secret Service . . . had come to Montreal and called on the prisoners in the jail."[428] This is close enough that it seems to describe Mrs. Slater. If she called on them at the jail in Montreal, she may well have called on them again at the jail in Quebec City. When she checked back in at the St. Lawrence Hall on March 17, it was in the company of "J. Fryffe King from Quebec & c.,"[429] an obvious alias but also a clue to where they had just been.

Another possibility is that Mrs. Slater was sent back as far as New York or even Washington, met another courier from Richmond there, and then returned to Montreal with fresh dispatches. Because Mr. Hall did not appreciate the "A. Reynaud" alias first ferreted out by John F. Stanton,[430] and therefore was not aware that she checked in on March 9, he was of the view that Mrs. Slater brought fresh dispatches from Richmond on March 17.[431] This is supported by the cryptic diary entry of General Edwin G. Lee, commander of the Confederate Secret Service operations in Canada:

> St. Patrick's day. Great procession. At 8p.m. Col. [Jacob] Thompson read me his dispatch from Richmond. *Extremely interesting – no news.*[432]

On March 22, General Lee wrote again in his diary, "Fixed up and sent off my letter to Mr. B, and helped . . . to get the messenger off. I pray she may go safely."[433] The "B" in question is Judah P. Benjamin; the "she" in question was undoubtedly Sarah Nettie Slater, alias Reynaud, alias Kate Thompson or Kate Brown.[434]

Sometime between March 20 and 21 Surratt received a cryptic letter from "R.D. Watson" of 178 Water Street in New York, urging him to come to New York "on important business if you can spare the time," and to telegraph his intentions immediately upon receipt.[435] Roderick D. Watson, who had been arrested once for blockade running and once for subversion, was a Marylander relocated to New York who was active in the Confederate underground.[436] While there is no evidence that Surratt actually went to New York in response to this call, Mr. Hall speculates that it was a signal to retrieve or expect the veiled lady spy on her return trip from New York.[437]

Sure enough, on the morning of March 25th Mrs. Slater appeared in front of Mrs. Surratt's house. She probably took the overnight train from New York to Washington that arrived at 7:30 a.m., with the debonair John Wilkes Booth as her escort, and was then whisked from the station to Mrs. Surratt's in a carriage rented by John Surratt.[438] As stated in Weichmann's trial testimony:

> Mr. Pierrepont: [T]he 25th of March, 1865. Did you see John Surratt on that day?
> Weichmann: Yes, sir. As I went to breakfast, and looked out of the dining-room window, I saw John Surratt, his mother, and Mrs. Slater, who had been at the house previously, in a carriage containing four seats, to which were attached a pair of white horses.[439]

The plan was to escort Mrs. Slater as far as Surrattsville, where they would be met once again by Confederate Agent Gus Howell, who would accompany Mrs. Slater the rest of the way to Richmond.[440] John Lloyd confirms that on March 25th Surratt "came with his mother and another lady in the carriage."[441] The lady was introduced by Surratt as "Mrs. Brown."[442] Lloyd had some disturbing news for travelers engaged in Confederate business: Federal cavalry from Piscataway had raided the tavern the night before, and arrested Gus

Howell.[443] Clearly, the Yankees were on to Surratt's Tavern, watching it closely. With urgent and incriminating dispatches in her possession, Mrs. Slater could not stay, could not go back, and could not go forward without an experienced escort. Fate forced Surratt's hand: he would accompany Mrs. Slater to Richmond.[444]

* * *

It is likely that Surratt was more than willing to accompany the beautiful faux-widow into danger. He quickly arranged for David Barry, a former Confederate soldier and one of the more trustworthy tipplers at Surratt's Tavern, to go with them as far as Port Tobacco. From there, Barry would drive the buggy and team back to Washington.[445] They put Mrs. Surratt on the stagecoach back to Washington, where she arrived on the evening of the same day they had departed, March 25.[446] According to Weichmann:

> I asked Mrs. Surratt what had become of her son. She said he had gone to Richmond with Mrs. Slater to get a clerk-ship. This seemed to me a rather queer proceeding; he had never said anything to me about it, and had not even thought enough of me to say goodbye.[447]

Alas, poor Weichmann! Thrown over for a pretty face and a physique with which he could never compete.

Probably Surratt was seriously smitten, although it is also possible that romance made a good cover story. The two young spies arrived at Port Tobacco and stayed overnight at Brawner's Hotel.[448] The next morning Surratt dashed off a note to "Mr. Brooks," who was actually Brooks Stabler, proprietor of the livery stable from which he had rented the team and carriage:

> March 26th, 1865
>
> Mr. Brooks:
>   As business will detain me for a few days in the country, I thought I would send your team back. Mr. Barry will deliver it and pay the hire of it.

If Mr. Booth my friend should want my horses let him have them, but no one else. If you should want any money on them he will let you have it. I should like to have kept the team for several days but it is too expensive – especially since I have "woman on the brain" and may be away for a week or so.

Yours respectfully,

J. Harrison Surratt [449]

Dizzy with "woman on the brain," Surratt and Slater headed across the Potomac on an exciting and possibly harrowing mission. Although Union troops were generally concentrated south of Richmond around Petersburg, Virginia,[450] leaving a fairly clear path to Richmond, it is possible that the "gunship" incident in which Surratt pretended to surrender and then fired into the skiff took place on this very crossing of the Potomac.[451] But there is a more disturbing incident attributed to Surratt and Slater on this eleventh-hour mission to Richmond. The story was testified to by Dr. McMillan,[452] the ship's doctor on the *Peruvian* who was befriended by Surratt on a voyage to Liverpool:

> Dr. McMillan: . . . [F]rom Washington [Surratt] started on the way to Richmond with [Slater] and four or five others; . . . after a great deal of trouble they managed to cross the Potomac; . . . after they got south of Fredericksburg they were driven on a platform-car drawn, or pushed, by negroes. As they were drawn along they saw some men coming towards them – five or six if I recollect right. They ascertained that these men were . . . Union soldiers escaped from southern prisons; they were, he said, nearly starved to death . . ..
>
> Mr. Pierrepont: What further did [Surratt] say about the condition of these men?
>
> Dr. McMillan: I understood him to say they were in a very miserable way; that they had been obliged to hide

themselves in swamps and other places, and I understood him to say they were almost dead.[453]

These Union soldiers who had been to hell and nearly back again, never made it home. According to Dr. McMillan, Mrs. Slater said:

> "Let's shoot the damned Yankee soldiers." She had hardly said the word when they all drew their revolvers and shot them, and went right along, paying no more attention to them.[454]

If this story is true – and Dr. McMillan bears the mark of a truthful witness [455] – it reveals that Surratt and Slater hated all things "Yankee" with such passion that this hatred had molded them into cold-blooded killers.

* * *

Surratt and Slater reached Richmond on March 29. Surratt (presumably with Mrs. Slater) registered at the Spotswood Hotel under the alias "Harry Sherman,"[456] the name possibly chosen to mock the famous Union General who practiced total warfare against civilian populations.[457] Surratt and Slater were in Richmond together for three days, leaving early in the morning of April 1, carrying important dispatches.[458] What they did there, and what those dispatches said, is one of the greatest mysteries of the Lincoln assassination.

Surratt and Slater met with an old friend of Surratt's, Sergeant Harry Brogden, who was on detail to Secretary of State Benjamin, and with Lucius Quintus Washington, Benjamin's personal secretary.[459] More importantly, Surratt and Slater also met with Secretary of State Benjamin himself.[460] Surratt admits as much – and more – in his Rockville lecture:

> On my arrival [in Richmond] I went to Spotswood Hotel, where I was told that Mr. Benjamin, the then Secretary of War of the Confederate States, wanted to see me. I accord-

ingly sought his presence. He asked me if I would carry some dispatches to Canada for him. I replied "yes." That evening he gave me the dispatches and $200 in gold with which to pay my way to Canada.[461]

In this passage Surratt admits: first, that he was well enough known to the Confederate Secretary of State and important enough that, on the very eve of the fall of Richmond, Mr. Benjamin asked to see him; and second, that Mr. Benjamin gave him dispatches to carry and gold in payment.

Surratt elides any mention of Mrs. Slater who, by the time of his Rockville lecture, had eluded capture and vanished. He assures his listeners, two sentences later, "that this scheme of abduction was concocted without the knowledge or the assistance of the Confederate government in any shape or form."[462] Thus, Surratt asks us to believe that the principal project that had consumed the preceding three months of his life, and which vitally concerned the interests of the Confederacy, was not even mentioned to the head of the Confederate Secret Service. We have no documents or direct testimony to the contrary, so we cannot positively say that Surratt is a liar. We do know, however, that he was willing to lie on behalf of the Confederacy, and this very unlikely denial of high-level Confederate knowledge of the Booth-Surratt plot is exactly what he would want us to believe.

* * *

Surratt briefly stopped in at home upon his return from Richmond, on April 3, arriving at about half past six. Weichmann, whose eye for sartorial detail misses nothing, observed that Surratt was neatly dressed, wearing a new pair of pants.[463] Weichmann greeted Surratt from his spot on the parlor sofa, and testified to the following exchange:

I asked [Surratt] where he had been. His answer was to Richmond. I then said, "Richmond is evacuated. Did you not hear the news?" "No, it is not," he said; "I saw Benjamin and Davis in Richmond, and they told me it would not be evacuated."[464]

"Benjamin *and Davis.*" *Surratt may have met with Confederate President Jefferson Davis about two weeks prior to the assassination of President Lincoln.* What would they have discussed at such a meeting?

One theory – the one put forward by Benjamin's assistant L.Q. Washington – is that Surratt was "unusually mutton-headed," and though he was sent back with a letter for Jacob Thompson in Canada directing him to transfer Confederate funds to England and France, Surratt "never knew what was in that letter."[465] Nothing that is known about Surratt supports the assessment that he was in any way "mutton-headed." What's more, the Confederate agents haven't even got their story straight. Surratt admits to knowing the contents of the dispatches he carried, although he agrees that they "were only accounts of some money transactions – nothing more or less."[466] With an acerbic rather than "mutton-headed" wit, Surratt got a laugh out of carrying these dispatches folded inside a book entitled *The Life of John Brown.*[467]

Of course there is another, more sinister, interpretation of these events. If the only purpose of the meeting was to notify agents in Canada to transfer Confederate funds to England and France, President Davis's personal participation would not have been necessary. Surratt is single-minded in his devotion to the Confederate cause and devious in his reporting at Rockville – he completely leaves President Davis and Mrs. Slater out of the picture – and therefore his assurance, given in 1870 while Jefferson Davis was still alive, that the Confederate government had nothing to do with the plot against Lincoln, has no more credibility than his oath of loyalty to the Union taken in 1862 for the purpose of appointment as postmaster. The most likely conclusion is that Surratt was in Richmond from March 29 to April 1, 1865 for the purpose of discussing with the highest leaders of the Confederacy the conspiracy against Lincoln that he and John Wilkes Booth were leading. The possibility exists, although it is beyond direct proof, that the dispatches or even oral instructions carried by Surratt and Slater out of Richmond as it was on the brink of falling to the hated Yankees was an order of vengeance: *shoot the damned Yankee President.*

---

[413] *Statements, Arnold Statement,* p.22; Weichmann, p.120; *Atzerodt Baltimore American Statement,* p. III-28; *American Brutus,* p.188.

[414] *Rockville Lecture*, Weichmann, p.432.

[415] Weichmann, p.120; 1 JHS Trial 380, 381, 431.

[416] Kauffman offers an explanation: Booth and Surratt wanted to sufficiently implicate Weichmann in the plot that he would be forced to keep silent, or at least be discredited. *American Brutus*, pp.190-91. If that was their aim, they mostly succeeded.

[417] Weichmann, p.121. On about April 10, Miss Ward brought a letter from Surratt to Mrs. Surratt's, and it was passed among a gathering that included Booth. *Ibid.*, pp.130-31.

[418] *Ibid.*, p.121; 1 JHS 382.

[419] Weichmann, p.121.

[420] *Atzerodt National Intelligencer Statement*, p. III-23.

[421] JOH Papers, *Microfilm of St. Lawrence Hall Register* (March 9, 1865). It is puzzling that Judah Benjamin's ledger book for March 8 states, "Payment in gold to defray expense of dispatch messenger to Canada: $100." *E.G. Lee*, p.147. Obviously, Mrs. Slater could not travel from Richmond to Montreal in a single day. This may have been a different messenger.

[422] JOH Papers, *Microfilm of St. Lawrence Hall Register* (March 9 and February 15, 1865).

[423] *Ibid.* (March 11 at noon).

[424] *E.G. Lee*, pp.121-24, 142-43.

[425] JOH Papers, *Microfilm of St. Lawrence Hall Register* (March 17, 1865).

[426] Or possibly a duplicate set carried by the Reverend Stephen Cameron at about the same time. *The Veiled Lady*, pp.39-40.

[427] *E.G. Lee*, at 146-47.

[428] JOH Papers - SS, John F. Stanton, *Some Thoughts on Sarah Slater*, p.3 (*Surratt Courier*, vol. XXXII No.2 Feb. 2007) (hereafter *"Thoughts on Slater"*), *quoting*, John W. Headley, *Confederate Operations in Canada and New York*. Although described as a "Kentucky" lady, it may well have been the slippery Sarah Slater.

[429] JOH Papers - *St. Lawrence Hall Register* (March 17, 1865).

[430] JOH Papers - SS, John F. Stanton, *Attention Sarah Slater Seekers*, p.4 (Surratt Courier, Vol. XXX, No.9, Sept. 2010) (hereafter *"Attention Slater Seekers"*).

[431] *The Veiled Lady*, p.41.

[432] *Ibid.* (emphasis added).

[433] *E.G. Lee*, p.144.

[434] These latter two aliases are mentioned by Atzerodt. *Lost Atzerodt Statement*, p. III-21; *Atzerodt Baltimore American Statement*, p. III-27. The "Thompson" alias is given by the authors of *Come Retribution*, p.415.

[435] *The Veiled Lady*, p.41; *Come Retribution*, p.415.

[436] *Come Retribution*, pp. 65, 415.

[437] *The Veiled Lady*, p.41.

[438] *American Brutus*, p.192.

[439] 1 JHS Trial 393; Weichmann, pp.122-23.

[440] *The Veiled Lady*, p.42.

[441] 1 JHS Trial 301.

[442] 1 JHS Trial 752.

[443] *The Veiled Lady*, p.42; 1 JHS Trial 390; *Atzerodt National Intelligencer Statement*, p. III-24.

[444] *The Veiled Lady*, p.42; *Rockville Lecture*, Weichmann, p.432. An offer of proof submitted in Surratt's trial by Surratt admits this trip to Richmond, departing March 25, but omits any mention of Mrs. Slater. National Archives, RG 21, *United States v. John H. Surratt*, Criminal Case #4731, *E.G. Lee* Offer of Proof ¶3 (July 15, 1867) (hereafter "*E.G. Lee Offer of Proof*").

[445] *The Veiled Lady*, p.42; 2 JHS Trial 751-52.

[446] Weichmann, p.123.

[447] *Ibid.*

[448] *The Veiled Lady*, p.42.

[449] *Ibid.*; Weichmann, p.123; 1 JHS Trial 217; 2 JHS Trial 752.

[450] *The Siege of Petersburg*, http://www.nps.gov/history/history/online_books/civil_war_series/20/sec8.htm (accessed Dec. 14, 2013).

[451] 1 JHS Trial 468.

[452] McMillan suggests that Surratt had gone to get Mrs. Slater in New York on this occasion. 1 JHS Trial 467. That seems to mix together the previous mission in February, when Surratt did not accompany Mrs. Surratt to Richmond, with the current trip, when Surratt met her at the train station. But it could be that Surratt did fetch Mrs. Slater from New York this time as well.

[453] 1 JHS Trial 467.

[454] *Ibid.*

[455] For example, asked whether these half-dead soldiers were armed, McMillan responded, "I do not recollect whether he said anything as to whether they were armed or not." 1 JHS Trial 467. A perjurer out to get Surratt would likely "remember" this fact unfavorably to Surratt.

[456] 2 JHS Trial 789-91.

[457] *William T. Sherman*, http://www.civilwar.org/education/history/biographies/william-t-sherman.html (accessed Dec. 14, 2013).

[458] *The Veiled Lady*, p.43.

[459] *Ibid.*

[460] *E.G. Lee Offer of Proof*, ¶3.

[461] *Rockville Lecture*, Weichmann, pp.432-33.

462 *Ibid.*, p.433.
463 1 JHS Trial 387.
464 *Ibid.*
465 *The Veiled Lady*, p.43; *E.G. Lee Offer of Proof*, ¶¶1, 3.
466 *Rockville Lecture*, Weichmann, p.434.
467 *Ibid.*, p.433.

CHAPTER NINE

THE PLOTS THICKEN

THE WORDS ATTRIBUTED TO JEFFERSON DAVIS IN THE SUMMER OF 1862 are, "I could not stand the imputation of having consented to let Mr. Lincoln be assassinated."[468] Did something change between that remark and April of 1865? Approximately 250,000 of the total 289,000 Confederate dead. Antietam, Stone's River, Gettysburg.[469] The imminent end of everything for which the Confederate leaders had gambled their lives, their sacred honor, and the lives of hundreds of thousands of their best young men. Desperate times call for desperate measures. But there was even more to it than that. The origins of Davis's probable approval of plots against Lincoln may lie in Lincoln's probable approval of a plot against Davis.

In early February 1864, Union prisoners who had managed to escape from Richmond's notorious Libby Prison reached Union lines with tales of harsh treatment and near starvation.[470] This triggered intense political pressure for bold action in support of Union POWs. In response, it appears that Lincoln indulged his penchant to meddle in operational military planning.[471]

The operation in question was under the command of Brigadier General Judson Kilpatrick, but it will forever be remembered as "Dahlgren's raid" due to the involvement of Colonel Ulric Dahlgren. Colonel Dahlgren was the son of Admiral John A. Dahlgren, a good friend of Lincoln's who was also commander of the South Atlantic Blocking Squadron engaged in the endless siege on Charleston.[472] The son was a resilient soldier who was determined to be effective on horseback despite the encumbrance of a wooden leg in place of the leg he'd lost at Gettysburg.[473]

On February 11, 1864, Lincoln met with General Kilpatrick about the idea of staging a cavalry raid on Richmond's Libby and Belle Isle prisons in order to free the Union prisoners held there. In approving the plan, Lincoln overrode Kilpatrick's superior, General George G. Meade. Possibly at the request of his friend Admiral Dahlgren, he ordered Kilpatrick to take Colonel Dahlgren with him.[474]

On February 28, 1864, about four thousand Union cavalry launched the raid on Richmond's military prisons by crossing the Rappahannock above Fredericksburg, past Lee's right flank. Colonel Dahlgren, leading five hundred men, headed west and south to cross the James upriver of Richmond, then attack the mostly unguarded southern side of the capital. The plan was that Kilpatrick, leading the main force, would attack from the north and draw off the few defenders, leaving Richmond wide open to Dahlgren's force.[475]

As is common in war, what looks good on paper is churned to chaos in the field. Bad weather set in, delaying both groups. The raiders' couriers were intercepted, triggering an alarm that drew a large defense force to the Confederate capital before they could reach it. The James was too swollen by fresh rain to be crossed, so Dahlgren changed his plan and followed the northern bank towards Richmond, aiming at an attack from the west. Kilpatrick arrived before Dahlgren and commenced an uncoordinated attack that was repulsed by the stronger-than-expected defense force. He gave up and fled southeast before Dahlgren even arrived.[476]

Dahlgren's attack from the west was repulsed, so he headed around Richmond's northern flank in an effort to catch up to the fleeing Kilpatrick. At some point in the confusion his force was broken into two contingents. Disoriented and increasingly desperate, Dahlgren's men ran into a Confederate ambush in the wee hours of March 2-3, 1864, and Colonel Dahlgren was killed.[477]

Lying there in the Virginia mud like so many other gallant young men on both sides, Dahlgren would have been forgotten if not for some papers found in his pocket. One was a draft of a speech he had apparently intended to give to his men, encouraging them "to destroy and

burn the hateful city," and to "not allow rebel leader Davis and his traitorous crew to escape."[478] More damning than a Colonel's possibly
overzealous remarks was the unsigned "special order" stating:

> The men must keep together and well in hand, and, once in
> the city, it must be destroyed and *Jeff Davis and his Cabinet
> killed.*[479]

The Dahlgren papers were transmitted directly to their intended
victim, Jefferson Davis. At the Confederate President's direction,
General Lee wrote to General Meade to demand whether this order
represented official Union policy. General Meade denied that it did.
There were claims of forgery in the North, but the South had photo-
graphic reproductions of the papers circulated to Union newspapers
and to foreign governments, and the consensus was that they were
genuine.[480]

Regardless of the bona fides of Dahlgren's "special orders," the
important fact is that the leaders of the Confederacy apparently
believed they were genuine and that they were now under personal
attack. Putting the pieces together, Dahlgren's effort to kill or capture
Confederate leaders began to appear as one part of a concerted policy.
Just three weeks before the Dahlgren raid, a District of Columbia cavalry company under the command of Brigadier General Isaac J. Wistar
attempted a raid on Richmond, but had to abort when he ran into a key
bridge over the Chickahominy River that was strongly defended
because the Confederates had gained access to key intelligence about
the raid. Did the Confederates also know that a note from General
Butler to Wistar instructed him to destroy public buildings and capture
leaders of the Confederacy?[481] If so, then it is no wonder that General
Meade's disclaimer of Dahlgren's orders did little to dissuade Jefferson
Davis from the growing belief that suddenly the great Civil War was
personal – mano a mano, Lincoln or Davis.

* * *

The Dahlgren raid brought about a shift in public opinion in the
South. Referring to the first documented Lincoln assassination

attempt, when Lincoln had to sneak through Baltimore allegedly wearing "a Scotch plaid cap and a very long military cloak" to avoid a pre-inauguration plot in February 1861,[482] the *Richmond Sentinel's* March 5, 1864 editorial on the Dahlgren papers stated:

> Let Lincoln and Kilpatrick remember that they have bidden their subordinates give no quarter to the Confederate chiefs. Perhaps even a Scotch cap and a military cloak will not prevent a just and stern vengeance from overtaking them.[483]

There was a corresponding shift in the intensity of "black flag" warfare by the Confederates. The first well-documented attempt to kidnap Lincoln from the Old Soldiers' Home was planned for June 1864, under General Bradley T. Johnson, Commander of the 1st Regiment of the Maryland Cavalry (CSA).[484] The plan was to cross the Potomac River above Washington with 200 cavalrymen to make a quick strike on Lincoln's summer residence on the outskirts of town.[485] "The assassination of the President was not contemplated, and it was merely intended to make him a prisoner of war and carry him to Richmond."[486] Although they did march towards Washington they were diverted when General Jubal Early ordered General Johnson to cover his rear flank.[487] General Early expressed an interest in joining with General Johnson on his mission as soon as they could rid themselves of Union General David Hunter's forces, but the promotion and transfer of General Johnson ended the mission.[488] Though the Johnson mission was aborted, it is significant that it had the approval of General Wade Hampton, leader of the cavalry corps. It is an educated guess that "General Wade Hampton would never have given his approval to Johnson without clearing the idea with Secretary of War Seddon and probably with General Robert E. Lee and President Davis."[489]

Soon after the Johnson kidnap plan was abandoned, a far more sinister plot against the North generally – but also against Lincoln personally – reached fruition. This was nothing less than primitive biological warfare: spreading yellow fever epidemics in Union territory by shipping infected clothing to key Northern cities for distribution to the residents. The plot was laid in Canada and led by Dr. Luke P. Blackburn of Kentucky, an authority on the treatment of yellow fever.[490] In July 1864, Dr. Blackburn's recruits, including Godfrey J. Hyams, unloaded trunks of infected clothing that Blackburn had shipped from Havana and Bermuda to Halifax. Hyams shipped his share of the infected trunks to Boston, and then to Philadelphia, where he was able to place them in the hands of an auctioneer for sale to the general public.[491] Significantly, according to Hyams's later statement to Union authorities, Dr. Blackburn wanted Hyams to bring a special valise loaded with elegant shirts infected with yellow fever bacilli to President Lincoln, but Hyams refused to do so.[492] The entire plot foundered on the fact that yellow fever is transmitted through the bite of a mosquito, not through contact with infected clothing, but it was a serious attempt based on the existing state of medical knowledge.

The next attempt by the Confederacy to get Lincoln was more conventional, under the operational command of Captain Thomas Nelson Conrad, Chaplain of the Third Virginia Cavalry Regiment. According to Conrad's own postwar account, he reported to President Davis in Richmond in late August 1864, was placed on the rolls of the Confederate Secret Service, and sent in September to Washington on a secret mission run directly by Secretary of War Seddon.[493] Prior to embarking, Conrad conferred with the "big three" in the CSA Executive Branch: Confederate President Davis, Secretary of War Seddon, and Secretary of State Benjamin.[494] His book *A Confederate Spy* adheres to the Confederate post-assassination dogma that the CSA leadership had nothing to do with any plot against Lincoln,[495] but nonetheless details the level of intelligence he was gathering towards a possible kidnapping. Conrad conducted extensive reconnaissance on the White House, "[p]artially concealed by the large trees of" Lafayette Park, "only a stone's throw" from the entrance, from where he found no difficulty in observing Lincoln's "ingress and egress, noting about what hours of the day he might venture forth, size of the accompanying escort, if any; and all other details. . . ."[496] Conrad identifies the exact route traveled by Lincoln's carriage to the Old Soldier's Home, stating that "[w]e had to determine at what point it would be most expedient to capture the carriage and take possession of Mr. Lincoln" to deliver him to Colonel Mosby "for transportation to Richmond."[497]

There is clear documentation that Conrad requested funding from Secretary of War Seddon, who passed the requests on to President Davis, and that these requests were approved. It is not credible that President Davis would not understand the substance of the mission for which he was providing funding. Secretary of State Benjamin was also involved in funding Conrad.[498] Thus, from September 1864 to January 1865, *all three of the top Confederate leaders were providing active support to reconnoiter the kidnapping of Lincoln.*

* * *

Captain Conrad was an old friend of the Surratt family. He had known them from before the war, when he had often stopped at Surratt's Tavern for hunting trips, and in the company of his sister. He came to know the Surratt family even better during the war, as he was one of the agents using the tavern as a safe house during wartime missions. Conrad received several invitations to visit the H Street house in Washington, although it does not appear he did so.[499] Nonetheless, Conrad was probably in touch with the Surratts during the time that John Surratt was involved in the Booth plot, and with such strongly overlapping interests, it seems likely that information was shared between the two groups of plotters. Conrad's commanders, Davis and Seddon, would likely have learned of Booth's plot through Conrad, if they were not already aware of it.

Indeed, the evidence suggests that Booth had been fed intelligence about the means and methods of a Soldiers' Home kidnapping as early as the summer of 1864. Recall that when Booth met with Arnold and O'Laughlen at the Barnum Hotel in Baltimore in late August or early September of that year, he already knew enough to outline operational details of a plan to kidnap Lincoln from the Old Soldiers' Home.[500] There is no record that Booth had been in Washington since November 1863, so where did he get that knowledge? This important point was first highlighted by the authors of *Come Retribution*:

> Booth came [to Barnum's] with precise information about Lincoln's habits and movements. He knew that Lincoln

disliked the trappings of a military guard and that he often went to the Soldiers' home without them. Yet, so far as can be learned, Booth had not been in Washington since November 1863 when he last performed at Ford's Theatre. This suggests that intelligence was being fed to him. Also, Booth's Soldiers' Home scenario was in principle the same as that proposed earlier . . .. And it corresponds exactly with the plan approved by Seddon, who sent a group under command of Captain Thomas N. Conrad to Washington in mid-September 1864 to explore possibilities.[501]

Viewed in the cold light of historical context, Surratt's assurance "that this scheme of abduction was concocted without the knowledge or the assistance of the Confederate government in any shape or form"[502] appears no better than a bald-faced lie.

* * *

This brings us face to face with the question whether Confederate President Davis, Secretary of State Benjamin, or the new CSA Secretary of War, John C. Breckinridge, were actually involved in plots to assassinate Lincoln, and not merely to kidnap him. Let us leave aside the fancy chemises tainted with yellow fever as the work of Dr. Blackburn's fevered mind. Let us leave aside for the moment even the truth recognized by every thinking person, including Jefferson Davis himself, that any plot to kidnap a sitting President of the United States must necessarily entail a high risk of killing him. Let us look simply at whether there is any historical evidence linking Davis, Benjamin and the CSA Secretary of War to a plot to kill Lincoln.

A chilling clue to the change in the Confederate attitude about extending the war to *ad hominum* attacks against the enemy Commander in Chief was the Confederate code phrase used as a key for messages encrypted by the Vigenère square. In January 1865, the phrase was "Complete Victory." On February 1, 1865, it was changed. The new phrase was, "Come Retribution."[503] The implication is that the assassination of Lincoln was a form of retribution for the wartime suffering inflicted on the South. But that phrase only grows in meaning when viewed in hindsight in light of the events of April 14, 1865. A punishing Confederate offensive against purely military targets could be as much "retribution" for the suffering of the South as any particular attack on the President or even the United States Government. What's more, the military situation of the South was not yet hopeless in February 1865.[504] "Come Retribution" is a riddle, not a proof.

By April 1865, however, the only operation against Lincoln that could conceivably benefit the Confederacy was assassination, not kidnapping. It was too late to reap meaningful military advantage from the release of POWs.[505] Nor could more favorable terms in surrender be expected on ransom of Lincoln without being willing to kill him – and even short of that, any deal made under duress of such a threat would hardly be deemed enforceable after his release. Yet on or about April 1st, the Confederate Torpedo Bureau in Richmond dispatched a small company, including one of its top experts in explosive devices, Sergeant Thomas F. Harney, to join up with Colonel Mosby's unit in Fauquier County, Virginia. Based on their actions, it appears that their orders were to infiltrate Washington. What were they to do when they got there? Their plan was nothing less than to blow up the Executive Mansion, with Lincoln and his cabinet inside it.[506]

When Richmond fell from April 2-3, 1865, the Confederate government fled towards Danville, South Carolina, with the full intention to keep on fighting.[507] According to an account by Colonel Edward H. Ripley of the Ninth Vermont Infantry, one of the first Union officers to occupy the fallen capital, a Confederate enlisted man named Snyder from the Torpedo Bureau sought an urgent audience with him on April 4. Snyder's message was chilling: he was tired of all the killing, and wanted to warn the Yankees that a party had been dispatched on a secret mission against Lincoln just before the city fell. Although secrecy within the bureau precluded Snyder from giving names or dates for the planned attack, he warned, "that the President of the United States was in great danger."[508] The warning was brought to the attention of the President, who is said to have responded, "I cannot bring myself to believe that any human being lives who would do me harm."[509] Lincoln's comment can only be ascribed to a mix of fatalism and public relations.

On April 8, a mixed force very much intent on doing Lincoln harm, including explosives expert Harney and one hundred fifty men, departed Fauquier County on the fifty-mile ride due east towards the Executive Mansion in Washington City. But on April 10, just fifteen miles from their target, they ran into a detachment from the Eighth Illinois Cavalry, and Harney was captured. An action report on the capture states that Harney had "brought ordnance to Colonel Mosby," indicating that either someone talked, or explosives were captured among his equipage.[510] The Harney plot was dead.

Is it possible to link Harney to Davis, Benjamin or Breckinridge? Only indirectly. The Confederate Torpedo Bureau was under the command of Brigadier General Gabriel Rains.[511] General Rains and President Davis were old friends who attended West Point together in the mid-1820s.[512] We might assume that an operation of this importance had to be known and approved at the highest levels, but I have seen no direct evidence of this.

Of course, it is likely that the orders for such a sensitive mission were never put in writing in the first place. In speaking of General Edwin G. Lee, his commander in Canada, Benjamin wrote in the dispatch authorizing a transition in power to Lee from Jacob Thompson:

> I have stated to Genl. Lee many things which could not well be committed to paper . . ..[513]

General Lee was tight-lipped; recall his diary entry of March 17: "Extremely interesting – no news."[514] What's more, even if something had been put in writing, it is well known that Judah Benjamin personally destroyed many of the Secret Service files just before evacuating Richmond.[515] Any file containing evidence of CSA complicity in a plot against Lincoln's life would be first into the incinerator.

Researcher Sandy Prindle states that Benjamin gave Harney gold to blow up the White House with Lincoln inside, but there is no citation to evidence, and therefore this speculation cannot be accepted as fact.[516] We know that Judah Benjamin drew $24,250 in gold for "foreign intercourse" on March 23, $1,000 in gold on March 28, and $1,500 in gold on April 1, 1865, but aside from the $200 given to John Surratt, we do not know where this money went.[517]

* * *

What of evidence linking the top CSA executive officials to the Surratt-Booth plot against Lincoln? Neither Surratt nor Slater nor anyone else was clumsy enough to allow Dahlgren-type orders (if they even existed) to fall into enemy hands. But to have actually struck down the enemy Commander in Chief, whom you viewed as a great tyrant – and, what's more, to have gotten away with it – and yet to be unable to whisper a word of it, is a burden heavy enough to bend even the most iron will. Was Surratt up to the task? Later, while in flight, Surratt let fall a few clues to the possible involvement of the Confederate government. Jefferson Davis did so almost immediately.

If the heart of a crime is the *mens rea* – the "guilty intent" – then Jefferson Davis appeared to have it. On May 30, 1865, Lewis F. Bates, Superintendent of the Southern Express Company for the State of North Carolina, testified at the military commission trial of the conspirators. According to Mr. Bates, Jefferson Davis had stopped at his house in Charlotte on April 19 to make a speech from the front steps, when he was handed a telegram from Confederate Secretary of War John C. Breckinridge.[518] In concluding his remarks, President Davis read the telegram to the assembled crowd:

> President Lincoln was assassinated in the theatre in Washington on the night of the 11th instant [*sic*]. Seward's house was entered on the same night, and he is probably mortally wounded.[519]

Looking up from the telegram, Davis was moved to paraphrase the assassin of good King Duncan, Macbeth himself: "If it were to be done, it were better it were well done."[520] The exact quotation from Shakespeare's *Macbeth* is, "If it were done when 'tis done, then 'twere well it were done quickly. If the assassination could trammel up the consequence, and catch with his surcease success; that but this blow might be the be-all and the end-all . . . ."[521]

Two days later Davis and Breckinridge got together at Bates' house. Breckinridge said he regretted the assassination, "that it was very unfortunate for the people of the South . . .."[522] Davis disagreed:

> Well, General, I don't know, if it were to be done at all, it
> were better that it were well done; and if the same had been
> done to Andy Johnson, the beast, and to Secretary Stanton,
> the job would then be complete.[523]

The man who once "could not stand the imputation of having consented to let Mr. Lincoln be assassinated,"[524] now objected only to the
fact that the assassins had not made complete work of the entire executive branch of the United States.

[468] *Still Mudd*, at Loc. 281-87; see, *Come Retribution*, p.237. Even as late as
August 1863, Confederate Secretary of War James Seddon rejected a pro-
posal to eliminate high Union government officials, saying, "The laws of
war and morality, as well as Christian principles and sound policy forbid the
use of such means." Ibid., p.235.

[469] *The Ten Costliest Battles of the Civil War*,
http://www.civilwarhome.com/Battles.htm (accessed Dec. 22, 2013); *Civil
War Statistics*,
http://www.phil.muni.cz/~vndrzl/amstudies/civilwar_stats.htm
(accessed Dec. 22, 2013).

[470] *Come Retribution*, p.242; *Encyclopedia Virginia - Libby Prison*,
http://www.encyclopediavirginia.org/Libby_Prison (accessed Dec. 21, 2013).

[471] *Come Retribution*, p.242.

[472] *Ibid.*; *Biographies in Naval History - Rear Admiral John A. Dahlgren*,
http://www.history.navy.mil/bios/dahlgren.htm (accessed Dec. 21, 2013).

[473] *Come Retribution*, p.242.

[474] *Person of Interest*, p.7; *Come Retribution*, p.242.

[475] *Come Retribution*, pp.241, 242.

[476] *Ibid.*, p.243.

[477] *Ibid.*

[478] *Ibid.*

[479] *Ibid.*, pp.243-45 (emphasis added).

[480] *Ibid.*, p.246.

[481] *Ibid.*, p.247.

[482] *Ibid.*, p.246.

[483] *Ibid.*, p.245.

[484] *Attempt to Capture*, p.4, col.5. The authors of *Come Retribution* give
Johnson's rank as Colonel, but the more contemporaneous account states

"General".
485 *Come Retribution*, pp.235-26.
486 *Attempt to Capture*, p.4, col.5.
487 *Ibid.*
488 *Come Retribution*, p.236.
489 *Ibid.*; Wade Hampton, http://www.history.com/topics/wade-hampton (accessed Dec. 23, 2013).
490 *Come Retribution*, p.185.
491 *Ibid.*, p.186.
492 *Ibid.*; *Person of Interest*, p.7.
493 *Come Retribution*, pp.283-85, *citing*, Thomas Nelson Conrad, *The Rebel Scout*, pp.94-97 (National Publishing Co., Washington DC 1904).
494 *Come Retribution*, p.288.
495 *Ibid.*, p.291.
496 Thomas Nelson Conrad, *A Confederate Spy*, p.72 (J.S. Ogilvie, New York 1892).
497 *Ibid.*
498 *Come Retribution*, pp.324, 409.
499 *Ibid.*
500 *American Brutus*, p.86, 132; *Statements, Arnold Statement*, p.20.
501 *Come Retribution*, p.264.
502 *Rockville Lecture*, Weichmann, p.433.
503 *Come Retribution*, pp.24, 346.
504 *Come Retribution*, p.370; JOH Papers, Clark Larsen, *Who Started It?* p.4 (*Surratt Courier* Vol. XXXVIII, No. 6, June 2013) (hereafter *"Who Started It?"*).
505 *Come Retribution*, p.27.
506 *Ibid.*, pp.27, 418-19; *Lost Atzerodt Statement*, p. III-21; *Blood on the Moon*, pp.89-90; *Person of Interest*, p.9.
507 *Who Started It?* p.4.
508 Edward H. Ripley, *The Capture and Occupation of Richmond, April 3, 1865*, pp.23-24 (G.P. Putnam & Sons, New York 1907).
509 *Ibid.*, p.25.
510 *Come Retribution*, pp.27, 419-20.
511 *Blood on the Moon*, p.89.
512 *Brigadier General Garbriel J. Rains, "Father of Modern Mine Warfare,"* http://gabrielrains.com/ (accessed Dec. 26, 2013).
513 Library of Congress, *Letterbooks of Confederate State Papers, Canada, Feb. 15 1864-Jan. 8, 1865*, at Dec. 6, 1864.
514 *The Veiled Lady*, p.41.
515 *Come Retribution*, p.101.
516 *Person of Interest*, pp.8-9.
517 JOH Papers - JHS, Judah Benjamin files, M-13744, LC, reel 19, frame 011488, Requisition 96; Library of Congress, *Confederate State Papers,*

Control #mm 78016550, Reel #19, *Warrant in Response to Req. 93.*

[518] *Trial of the Conspirators*, pp.46-47.

[519] *Ibid.*, p.47.

[520] *Ibid.*

[521] *Macbeth*, Act. 1, Scene 7. The author is grateful to his extraordinary high school drama teacher, Peggy O'Brien, for making him memorize this soliloquy.

[522] *Trial of the Conspirators*, p.47.

[523] *Ibid.*

[524] *Still Mudd*, at Loc. 281-87; see, *Come Retribution*, p.237.

CHAPTER TEN

THE MAN IN TWO PLACES AT ONCE

SURRATT AND SLATER LEFT RICHMOND THE MORNING OF SATURDAY, April 1, 1865, the same day that Harney left carrying explosives, the day before the Confederate government fled towards Danville, and three days before President Lincoln walked the streets of the conquered capital.[525] The two couriers made a quick trip north, crossing the Potomac into Maryland the morning of Monday, April 3. Although Surratt never mentioned that Slater was with him, we know she was thanks to one of the many statements given by the garrulous Atzerodt:

> Kate Thompson, alias Kate Brown, came from Richmond with John Surratt about the time that Richmond fell. . . . This woman was about 21 years of age, spruce and neat, medium size, black eyes and fair complexion.[526]

"As soon as I reached the Maryland shore," says Surratt, "I understood that the detectives knew of my trip South and were on the lookout for me."[527] But the twenty-one-year-old Surratt and the equally nimble Slater were unlikely to be captured along the back roads of Southern Maryland that John had memorized since childhood. They made it safely to Washington by four o'clock that afternoon.[528] It was not until about half past six that Surratt appeared alone in the parlor of his mother's house on H Street.[529] What did he do with himself in the intervening time?

First, he likely deposited "Miss Brown" at the Metropolitan Hotel, to which he would return later.[530] Surratt says that he stopped over that night at a hotel rather than at his mother's house, because "a detective had been to my house inquiring of the servant my whereabouts."[531] Of course, Slater's charms cannot be overlooked as another inducement to prefer the hotel.

The Metropolitan may have been chosen as safer than the National, though the National was the likely spot to find Booth. Surratt may have checked there, only to find that Booth had left for New York and Boston. Booth would not be back in Washington until April 8.[532] Surratt reports that he met "one of our party" – i.e., a co-conspirator – on Seventh Street, who asked after Booth. Perhaps it was Atzerodt, who said that Surratt borrowed some money off him because he was going to New York with a lady.[533] Although Surratt had gold, he needed greenbacks to make his way without attracting suspicion. He probably also met David Herold, who said in a statement given April 27th that he had last seen Surratt "about one month ago."[534] Herold says they shared a glass of ale at Kloman's, then went to Wilson's on Pennsylvania Avenue where Surratt ordered some groceries, then went together to a barber shop where Surratt got shaved and had his hair dressed.[535] Certainly he wanted to clean up after the arduous trek from Richmond. And with the "woman on the brain" waiting back at the hotel, naturally Surratt wanted to look and smell his best.

What did Surratt and Herold discuss? First, Booth's whereabouts. Other than that, Surratt says that he told Herold he'd been to Richmond, that he was on his way to Canada, that Richmond had fallen and the jig was up, that all hopes of abducting Lincoln were blasted and he should "go home and go to work."[536] Yet a few hours later, when Surratt was told by Weichmann that Richmond was evacuated, Surratt didn't believe it because President Davis and Secretary Benjamin had told him it would not be evacuated.[537] Once again, Surratt is providing us with a whitewashed version of events. What he actually told Herold can never be known. What he might have told Herold is that Davis and Benjamin had decided that it was too late to kidnap Lincoln, and instead had personally authorized the assassination of Lincoln and other key Union Government executive officers. On the other hand, it is not clear that Surratt would have trusted Herold with such sensitive information. So, piling inference upon the inference that there even was such an order, it is most probable that Surratt would have kept it to himself at this point.

Surratt was only at his mother's house about one-half hour. At first he sat at the dinner table. Mrs. Surratt claims that she brought up the question of a draft of money that was owed to her by a gentleman in Maryland, which Surratt was supposed to have collected on her behalf. "He . . . told me to never mind the draft."[538] She scolded her son, who left the table vexed and ran upstairs.[539] If this is a true account and the witnesses were correct who saw Surratt in Elmira around the time of the assassination, then this pathetic little quarrel was the last time Surratt and his mother ever saw one another alive.

There is another possibility, which I do not believe has previously appeared in print. If Surratt would not trust Atzerodt or Herold with the order to kill Lincoln, he would certainly have trusted his own mother. Possession of that information would explain many things, including the meeting between Booth and Mrs. Surratt on the afternoon of the assassination, and John Lloyd's and Weichmann's testimony demonstrating Mrs. Surratt's foreknowledge of the ghastly events. *Did Mrs. Surratt pass the order to kill Lincoln from her son to John Wilkes Booth?* We have no evidence of it, and if so, then this secret was taken by all three to their graves. Still, it is a tantalizing possibility.

* * *

Weichmann says that Surratt "was very neatly dressed, unusually so," wearing "a new suit of clothes," and that he went up to "my room" to put on clean underclothes.[540] Surratt called him upstairs, but Weichmann may have been disappointed to find that Surratt "had very little to say to me," and that all he wanted was to exchange forty dollars in gold for greenbacks.[541] Surratt showed Weichmann about ten $20 gold pieces that he was carrying, before exchanging $40 worth for $60 in cash with Mr. Holohan, the boarder across the hall.[542]

By seven o'clock, Surratt and Weichmann were out the door and off to dine at an oyster saloon located at 4½ Street and Pennsylvania Avenue. The two then walked together to the Metropolitan, where they parted for the last time as friends. The next time they would lay eyes on one another, Surratt would be on trial for the murder of Abraham Lincoln, and Weichmann would be a key prosecution witness whose testimony had also helped send Mrs. Surratt to the gallows.

* * *

Surratt arrived back at the Metropolitan immaculately coifed and dressed to the nines for his night with Nettie Slater. Propelled by the vigor of youth, they caught the early train the next morning, April 4, bound for New York.[544] Upon their arrival the first place they went was to Booth's house, but they missed him – he had left suddenly that morning on pretext of a theatre engagement in Boston.[545] He never played there that April, and though the sudden trip under false cover "has the feel of an appointment with some member of the Confederate apparatus in Canada," we do not know what he did there.[546]

If Surratt and Slater were carrying the authorization to assassinate Lincoln, and Surratt had not told his mother about it, then they had a dilemma. Surratt had a dispatch to carry to Canada, and was therefore bound for Montreal. But any message – whatever it might have been – from Davis and Benjamin to John Wilkes Booth, had not yet been delivered. One possibility, therefore, is that Surratt and Slater split up at this point. That would have been perfectly natural, since Slater lived with her sister in New York and could easily blend in there. Slater could stay behind to deliver the message to Booth when he returned from Boston, and Surratt could continue on to Canada.[547]

Surratt arrived in Montreal on the morning of Thursday, April 6, and registered at the St. Lawrence Hall at 10:30 a.m. under the name "John Harrison."[548] But something curious occurred – he was assigned two rooms, numbers 13 and 50.[549] Why was he assigned two rooms, especially two rooms so widely separated, if he was traveling alone? Room 13 was rented out again later that same day.[550] This suggests that Surratt and Slater arrived together, went through the charade of taking two rooms, then settled into one and gave back the other. If that's true then nobody was left to deliver the order to Booth – or the order was safely entrusted to Mrs. Surratt, or there was no such order. We just don't know.

My guess – and I stress, this is merely speculation – is that there was a verbal order from Davis and Benjamin to strike Lincoln and other high U.S. government officers, and that it was delivered by Surratt to his mother and by Mrs. Surratt to John Wilkes Booth. This might go a long way to explaining how the son could sit in hiding for weeks in Canada while his mother was put on trial for her life, and ultimately hung, without rushing to her aid. If Mrs. Surratt was not the innocent portrayed by her many supporters, but instead had been deeply and crucially involved in the plot, then some of the moral imperative on the son of coming to his mother's rescue vanishes.

* * *

General Edwin G. Lee, commander of Confederate Secret Service operations in Canada, was also staying at the St. Lawrence Hall in that first week of April 1865.[551] General Lee's codename for Surratt was "Charley Armstrong."[552] General Lee's diary for April 6 contains the bland entry: "Letter by Charley from Mr. Benjamin; my last rec'd all safe."[553] If Surratt carried any orders or had anything whatsoever to say on the subject of President Lincoln, General Lee was not about to commit it to paper. One might infer that General Lee expected his diary to become public from the fact that he never says anything revealing, he uses aliases for the key players, and he edits himself. Thus, the entry for Saturday, April 15 reads:

> News of Lincoln's death came this morning, exciting universal shock of horror and amazement.[554]

On April 7 Surratt visited a Montreal tailor on Notre Dame Street by the name of John J. Reeves. It appears likely that Reeves was not an average tradesman from off the street, but was a Confederate sympathizer, because he sheltered Surratt for several days shortly after the assassination.[555] Reeves measured Surratt for a Garibaldi jacket and a pair of pantaloons on April 7, which he delivered on April 9 or 10.[556] A Garibaldi is a front-pleated belted jacket with four front buttons, and a skirt gathered under the waist. It was not the style in the United States, but was useful for passing as a Canadian. Anybody wearing such a garment in the United States would be conspicuous.[557]

* * *

While in Montreal, Surratt had the leisure to write letters. One such letter reached Miss Annie Ward on April 10. Miss Ward was the woman who had helped Surratt secure lodging for Powell/Paine at Herndon House.[558] Miss Ward brought the letter to Mrs. Surratt's house at about seven or eight o'clock in the evening, and none other than John Wilkes Booth was present. Weichmann walked in after they were all assembled in the parlor. After some general discussion, Booth arose and approached Miss Ward, saying, "Please allow me to see the address of that lady again."[559] Miss Ward handed him the letter to peruse. After Booth and Ward had left, Anna Surratt gave Weichmann the letter from "brother John," which he read. Weichmann noticed that no lady's name was mentioned.[560] Miss Surratt told Weichmann that they meant to deceive him.[561] It is possible that there was more to the letter that was withheld from Weichmann. It is possible that some sort of coded message conveying or confirming an order to assassinate Lincoln and other government officials was contained in this letter. It is also possible that Booth simply wanted to see Surratt's address in Montreal. This letter, which may have contained the most important message in Nineteenth Century American history, was never recovered in the very thorough search of Mrs. Surratt's house. Most likely, Mrs. Surratt burned it.

That same evening, Booth protested vigorously when Weichmann suggested that the Confederacy was finished. Booth used maps to show Weichmann how Confederate General Joseph E. Johnston could hold out. When Weichmann asked Booth why he was no longer acting, Booth snapped that he was done with play acting; that the only play he cared to present was *Venice Preserved.*[562] Though Weichmann says this play is about a plot to assassinate the officials of Venice,[563] this is a half-truth; it is about a *foiled* plot to assassinate the Senators of Venice, the perfidy of the Senators, and the honor of the would-be assassin.[564] This demonstrates that Booth had assassination on his mind by April 10, after reading Surratt's letter. Nor was this the first time. We have already seen that Booth discussed killing Lincoln at the meeting at Gautier's, in mid-March. Booth also had assassination on his mind on

April 7 when in New York with his fellow actor, Samuel K. Chester, he bemoaned the missed opportunity to shoot Lincoln at the second inaugural.[565] And if you believe that the ludicrous theatre-kidnap plot was a cover for assassination, or that Booth wrote the Selby letter, it would seem that he had long had assassination on his mind.

* * *

Surratt also wrote to his cousin, Miss Belle Seaman, on April 10. Although full of fluff and misdirection, this letter suggests a young man in love:

> Montreal is really a beautiful city and what pleases me more there are a great many pretty girls here. It is more than probable that I shall lose my heart with some of them and then I ask myself have I one to give away. The answer comes back fully satisfactory. . . .
>
> I am enjoying myself to my heart's content. Nothing in the wide world to do but visit with the ladies and go to church. How are your Grant and Lee? I always knew the old Confederacy would go up the spout and the flag that Washington left us would wave again o'er North and South. . . .
>
> Your cousin,
> John Harrison
> St. Lawrence Hall
> Montreal C.E.[566]

This letter feels like a document written to be read to a jury some day.

Surratt wrote to his mother from Montreal on April 12, and Mrs. Surratt showed the letter to Weichmann on April 14.[567] Detective Clarvoe, who first searched Mrs. Surratt's house in the wee hours of the morning after the assassination, confirms that Mrs. Surratt claimed to have received a letter from her son on April 14, showing that he was in Canada at the time that it was mailed. Like the letter received April 10, the letter received April 14 was never found.[568] With the exception of the fluff sent to Belle Seaman, Surratt's correspondence just before the assassination had a habit of quickly disappearing.

* * *

Surratt paid his bill at the St. Lawrence on April 10 as if to leave, but then changed his mind; instead, he stayed until April 12.[569] His stated intention on April 10 was to go to New York, but he only went as far as the train depot before returning to the hotel.[570] This false start is unexplained. Much later, Surratt told the ship's doctor on the *Peruvian*, Dr. McMillan, that he started off from Montreal immediately upon receipt of a letter from Booth.[571] This letter may have been the reason that Surratt boarded the three o'clock afternoon New York train from Montreal on April 12, 1865.[572] Did Surratt receive Booth's letter on April 10 or April 12? Probably the latter, based on the likelihood that Booth did not get Surratt's address off the letter brought to Mrs. Surratt's house by Miss Ward until the evening of April 10.

Surratt also told Dr. McMillan that he and Booth had first plotted to abduct the President, but then decided they could not succeed "and they thought it was necessary to change their plan." [573] Surratt told Dr. McMillan that he was in Montreal when he received Booth's letter.[574] Testimony about this letter is key evidence that, even if Surratt did not carry an order from Richmond, *Surratt knew that the plan was changed from kidnapping to assassination.*

From his experience traveling from Washington to New York in fifty hours on the way up, it would have been possible for him to arrive in Washington in time to participate in the assassination, which took place at approximately 10:15 p.m., April 14. Surratt says no, he was in Elmira at the time of the Lincoln assassination.[575] As described in Chapter One, so much credible evidence has been heaped on both sides of that question that it is impossible to know with absolute certainty where he was. Judge Fisher, who presided at Surratt's trial, privately believed that Surratt was in Washington.[576] On the other hand, Weichmann, who had every reason to believe the worst of Surratt but could rarely bring himself to do it, expressed the opinion that he was probably not in Washington.[577] Like an electron, Surratt's whereabouts from April 12 to April 18 flit about with a vexing uncertainty, often depending on the point of view of the observer. Let's look at the key evidence on both sides of this question to see whether we can puzzle out a satisfactory answer to this central mystery.

* * *

Surratt presented an Offer of Proof at his trial, outlining the proposed testimony of General Edwin G. Lee, after General Lee's testimony about Surratt's whereabouts was ruled inadmissible.[578] General Lee offered to testify that on April 12, 1865 he dispatched Surratt on a secret surveillance mission:

> . . . to visit Elmira [N.Y.] with the intent to ascertain the position and condition of the Confederate prisoners confined at or near said town of Elmira & to make sketches of the stationing of the guards, and of the approaches to said prison, [unreadable] the numbers of the forces stationed there . . ..[579]

To confirm that Surratt had indeed carried out these orders, General Lee adds that Surratt was absent from Montreal from April 12 to April 17 or 18, when "he returned to Montreal and made his report, and brought back with him [unreadable] sketches of the said prison [unreadable] approaches, the numbering of the forces, etc. & that he [General Lee] paid . . . [Surratt] his expenses & for his services."[580] General Lee's diary entry for April 19 states, "Expenses + $100. services. (Charley)"[581] – although it bears telltale signs of having been filled in after-the-fact. Not only does it reference "See May 4," which is another entry pertaining to "Charley"/Surratt, but the line immediately preceding the note about paying "Charley" says, "This day *or the 20th* – Gave messenger $40."[582] Once a diary is no longer a contemporaneous account, it becomes suspect for possible *ex post facto* creation of false evidence. For all we know, the entry about paying "Charley" could have been written closer to 1867, when the Offer of Proof was presented.

Despite these fine points, the basic outline of Surratt's alibi is clear: he was in Elmira, New York, at the time of the assassination, gathering intelligence for the Canadian branch of the Confederate Secret Service on the prisoners of war held there. This is also the story told by Surratt himself in the Rockville lecture. Surratt says that he arrived in Elmira on Wednesday, April 12, and registered at Brainard House as "John Harrison."[583] This is why Surratt was spotted at Stewart & Ufford Men's Furnishings on Lake Street in Elmira by bookkeeper Frank H. Atkinson and cutter Joseph Carroll, on April 13, 14 and 15.[584] This is why no fewer than five witnesses testified to seeing Surratt in Elmira roughly the day before and the day after the assassination.[585] Although in plain clothes dressed in a Garibaldi jacket and round-top hat to disguise himself as a Canadian while spying in enemy territory,[586] at least Surratt was not at the scene of the most dastardly crime of the Nineteenth Century.[587]

* * *

At Surratt's trial in 1867, the Government made a serious tactical blunder by initially staking their case on proving that Surratt was in Washington at the time of the assassination.[588] As a consequence, once Surratt's alibi was presented, the Government had to spend a lot of time backpedaling with arguments to the effect that a co-conspirator who has provided material assistance to the plot is equally guilty with the man who actually pulled the trigger.[589] While perhaps legally accurate, the Government's shift in position made it appear duplicitous.

At the same time, the Government never entirely gave up on its theory that Surratt was present at Ford's Theatre, based on the testimony of eleven witnesses who claimed to have seen him about town on April 14th, and one who claimed that Surratt admitted he had been in Washington.[590] Charles Wood, a barber, claimed to have shaved Surratt at about nine o'clock that morning, when he came in to Booker & Stewart's barbershop on E Street with John Wilkes Booth, Michael O'Laughlen, and one other gentleman.[591] Theodore Benjamin Rhodes, a clock and watch repairman, walked into Ford's Theatre to have a look around at about half past eleven o'clock, and saw a man he identified beyond any doubt as Surratt boring a small hole in the door to the President's box in order to fit a board into it so the President "won't be disturbed."[592] David C. Reed, who had known Surratt since he was a boy, thinks that he passed him in the street on Pennsylvania Avenue just below the National Hotel, about two or half-past two on that Good Friday afternoon, and they nodded to one another.[593] Sometime that afternoon, a New York City lawyer named Benjamin W. Vanderpoel, who claimed to be very good with faces, purportedly saw Surratt (whom he had never met) seated at a round table with John Wilkes Booth (whom he did know) in a music hall on Pennsylvania Avenue.[594] Another fellow who thinks he saw Surratt on the Avenue between three and five o'clock that afternoon, though he "might be mistaken," was John Lee, a Union soldier from Vicksburg Mississippi, who knew Surratt by sight and had seen him around town about a dozen times previously.[595] "Doc" Cleaver, the stableman who rather incredibly testified that Surratt announced that he and Booth were going to kill Lincoln back in January, and who was an associate of the perjurer Conover, testified that he saw Surratt on April 14 at four o'clock on H Street, riding a chestnut sorrel horse, that he said, "How are you, John," and that Surratt nodded back to him.[596] Sometime after five o'clock that afternoon, a restaurateur named Sciapiano Grillo walked with David Herold over to Willard's on Pennsylvania Avenue, where they met up with a young man Grillo identified as Surratt, who assured Herold that he was "going tonight."[597] Walter Coleman, head of a division of the Office of the Treasury, testified that he and an associate, George W. Cushing, were walking up Pennsylvania Avenue between 10th and 11th Streets towards Willards at about six o'clock that evening, when they saw John Wilkes Booth engaged in intense conversation with a man he identified as looking "very much like" Surratt.[598] Mr. Cushing, on the other hand, testified that the young man with whom Booth was conferring did not look very much like Surratt.[599] Frank Heaton, who lived near Ford's Theatre, came out to see the President's carriage arrive, and claims to have seen Surratt in front of the theatre between a quarter to and a quarter past eight.[600] Sometime between eight and nine o'clock, the Surratt's new servant Susan Ann Jackson, claims to have served tea to Mrs. Surratt and a man whom she introduced to Susan as "my son," Mrs. Surratt asking "did he not look like his sister Annie?"[601] Sergeant Dye, as explained in great detail in Chapter One, very positively identified Surratt as the man calling time in front of the theatre in the final half hour leading up to the assassination.[602] Many of these statements were subjected to rebuttal and impeachment, but the sheer number counsels against dismissing the possibility that Surratt was in Washington on that worst of Good Fridays.

There were also two second-hand accounts placing Surratt in Washington on the night of the assassination. Remember Henri Beaumont de Sainte Marie, the Canadian that Surratt and Weichmann helped out of Little Texas? Ste. Marie testified that Surratt later told him that he was in Washington on the night of the assassination, and that he had a very difficult time getting out.[603] But perhaps the most intriguing statement was one attributed to Surratt's co-conspirator, George Atzerodt. Atzerodt's Baltimore American statement contains damning evidence against Surratt:

> Booth told me Surratt was in the Herndon House; on the night of the murder, the 14th of April, we were not altogether at the Herndon House. Booth told me Surratt was to help in the box. . . . The words of Booth were "I saw Surratt a few moments ago." All the parties appeared to be engaged at something that night, and were not together.[604]

Thus, according to Atzerodt, no less of an authority than Booth himself supports the view that Surratt was in Washington at the time of the assassination.

* * *

But could he have physically gotten there? In the face of Surratt's unimpeachable alibi witnesses, the Government was forced to concede that Surratt was in Elmira on April 13, the day before the assassination.[605] Therefore, the Government had to provide a credible scenario by which Surratt could have traveled to Washington from Elmira in time to call time in front of Ford's Theatre the night of April 14 – and preferably, in time to be seen by its many witnesses placing him around town from nine o'clock in the morning onward. This was complicated by the fact that the testimony of Atkinson placed Surratt in his men's clothing shop *after lunch*,[606] which, if accurate, meant that Surratt could not have left Elmira until the afternoon of April 13 at the earliest.[607]

The initial testimony on this point, given by John Dubarry, General Superintendent of the Northern Central Railroad, must have been discouraging to the Government. Mr. Dubarry testified that there was no train leaving Elmira after noon on April 13; rather, the train left at eight o'clock in the morning.[608] But then it emerged that a special train left Elmira on that date at ten or half past ten in the morning, which arrived at Williamsport about half-past noon.[609] This still was not after lunch, but it was more in the ballpark, and the Government seemed content to run with it. The Williamsport trainmaster, Ezra B. Westfall, claimed to have been accosted by a suspicious character who asked about getting through, since the rail beyond Williamsport was washed out, but Mr. Westfall cut him short because he suspected him of being either a Rebel spy or a Government detective – equally bad in his view![610] A ferryman at Williamsport named Morris Drohan testified that he ferried a man wearing a peculiar jacket across the west branch of the Susquehanna on April 13th.[611] Both Westfall and Drohan identified Surratt as the man they encountered that day.[612]

The town on the other side of the Susquehanna was Sunbury. The quickest route from Sunbury to Washington is via Baltimore.[613] A freight train that also carried passengers departed Sunbury on April 13 at half-past four in the afternoon, and arrived in Baltimore on the morning of April 14 at 3:50 a.m.[614] The regular passenger train departed Sunbury at 12:13 a.m., and arrived in Baltimore at 7:25 a.m., on April 14. Surratt could have been in Baltimore as early as 3:50 a.m., and easily by 7:25 a.m., on the day of the assassination. On that morning, trains from Baltimore to Washington had the following departure and arrival times:

April 14, 1865

Depart Baltimore	Arrive Washington
4:20 a.m.	5:45 a.m.
5:30 a.m.	7:20 a.m.
7:00 a.m.	8:43 a.m.

8:50 a.m.	10:25 a.m.
9:40 a.m.	11:30 a.m.[615]

This evidence still fails to account for Mr. Atkinson seeing Surratt in Elmira after lunch on the 13th. It is also not credible that Surratt would have undertaken this journey wearing his Garibaldi jacket, since he would not have wanted to attract notice. That in turn calls into question the testimony of the ferryman.

Nonetheless, it is physically possible that John H. Surratt paraded around Elmira attracting attention in his Garibaldi jacket precisely to manufacture an alibi, and then made it to Washington in time for all the witnesses who claimed to have seen him there on the day of the assassination to be both accurate and truthful.[616] Another credible scenario is that Surratt had already played his part in the assassination plot, and was deliberately showing himself all around Elmira in his Garibaldi jacket the full time from April 13-15 in order to establish an alibi.

In the final analysis, I am inclined to agree with researcher Sandy Prindle, whose argument is simply this: "If Surratt had been in Washington on the night of the assassination, would he be calling time in front of Ford's Theatre, or would he be the one assigned to kill Andrew Johnson?"[617] The plain implication of this rhetorical question is that Surratt was in Elmira at the time of the assassination. If Surratt had been in Washington, it is unlikely that an unreliable asset like Atzerodt would have been assigned to kill an important target such as the Vice-President. If the conspirators felt it was necessary to call time – which is itself unlikely in light of the testimony of Gifford, Hess and Carland,[618] not to mention the invention of the pocket watch long before 1865 – that's the sort of job Booth might have selected for Atzerodt, preferring to save Surratt for the tough work. If Surratt had been in Washington, in all likelihood Johnson would have been dead by morning.

There are many possible answers to the question, "where's Johnny" – and to the further question, "why was he there?" Most likely, those answers are not the ones Surratt himself gave. Surratt was the man who was everywhere at once, and nowhere at all. He was probably at his most candid when he said to Mr. Smoot, "if the Yankees knew what I'm up to, they'd stretch my neck."[619]

* * *

Surratt would have us believe that he had no idea the plan had been changed from kidnapping to assassination, and he was simply on a bona fide mission to surveil the prison. Most historians to date have accepted this version of the story, but it has at least three significant flaws that call it into question. First, as previously discussed, by this late in the war there could be no point in kidnapping Lincoln. Second, as previously discussed, Surratt told Dr. McMillan that he had received a letter from Booth stating that the plan had changed. While Surratt did not tell McMillan from what to what, we already know what the plan was, and we also know what the plan became. The key point here is that Surratt's own admission when he felt he was safely escaping on a ship bound for Europe ties him to knowledge of the change from kidnapping to murder.

Third, the very fact that Surratt claims he went on a surveillance mission aimed at releasing Confederate prisoners strongly suggests foreknowledge of the planned decapitation of the Union Government. Absent a desperate and decisive blow, the Confederacy was finished. Therefore, without the planned assassination of Lincoln and his cabinet, the surveillance mission was simply a fool's errand. Indeed, because the Confederacy had previously given up on Elmira, the mission looks on its face like a mere pretext for parading John Surratt around Elmira in his Garibaldi jacket to build an alibi while the assassination went forward, or (if you believe he was in Washington) perhaps a cover story for sneaking him down to the scene of the crime.

How do we know that the Confederacy had given up on Elmira? In the words of Jacob Thompson's December 3, 1864 report to Judah Benjamin, the Elmira plan was abandoned back when it might have made a more timely difference in the war effort to rescue and repatriate these Confederate prisoners:

> [A]ll the different places where our prisoners are confined, [including] . . . Elmira, ha[ve] been thoroughly examined, and the conclusion was forced upon us that *all efforts to*

release them without an outside co-operation would bring disaster, upon the prisoners and result in no good.[620]

Colonel Thompson adds that "[a]ll prospects of that sort were abandoned."[621] General Lee, who had regular communication with both Benjamin and Thompson, must have learned about this if he was planning another attempt at Elmira. The prisoners at Elmira were half-starved, diseased, and in terrible condition.[622] It would be some time before they could recover their health and the will to fight, and be transported from upstate New York to the battlefield. More likely, they would be recaptured or shot for escaping – the "disaster upon the prisoners" mentioned in Thompson's report. With the state of affairs as known to General Lee in mid-April – including the fall of Richmond – these troops could make no difference in the war effort absent some kind of game-changing blow such as the assassination plot.

Thus, either the surveillance mission was merely a ruse to build Surratt's alibi, or it had once again become the real thing solely because the plot to decapitate the Union Government gave new reason to hope that the Confederacy could be rescued from the ashes.[623] *Either way, Surratt's so-called "alibi" in fact suggests foreknowledge of the plot against Lincoln and his cabinet.*

525 *Rockville Lecture*, Weichmann, p.433; *April 1865*, pp.105-08, 118-19; *E.G. Lee*, p.151.
526 *Atzerodt Baltimore American Statement*, p. III-27.
527 *Rockville Lecture*, Weichmann, p.433.
528 *Ibid.*
529 1 JHS Trial 387; Weichmann, p.128.
530 1 JHS Trial 388; Weichmann, p.128.
531 *Rockville Lecture*, Weichmann, p.433.
532 *Come Retribution*, p.416; Weichmann, p.127.
533 *Statements, Atzerodt Wells Statement*, p.60.
534 *Statements, Herold Statement*, p.14.
535 *Ibid.*
536 *Rockville Lecture*, Weichmann, p.433.
537 Weichmann, p.128; 1 JHS Testimony 387.
538 *Statements, Statement of Mrs. Mary E. Surratt to General Augur, April 17,*

1865, p.33 (*"Mary Surratt 4/17"*) p.33; *Statements, Mary Surratt 4/28*, p.44.

539 *Ibid.*; Weichman p.128.

540 Weichmann, p.128.

541 *Ibid.*; 1 JHS Trial 387-88.

542 Weichmann, p.128; 1 JHS Trial 387-88; Isacsson, *AFCT*, p.4. Weichmann says Surratt got $40 in cash but Holohan testified that he gave Surratt $60 in cash for $40 in gold.

543 Weichmann, p.128; 1 JHS Trial 388, 670.

544 *Statements, Atzerodt Wells Statement, p.60; Atzerodt National Intelligencer Statement*, p. III-24; Isacsson, *AFCT*, p.4.

545 *Rockville Lecture*, Weichmann p.433.

546 *Come Retribution*, p.416.

547 *See*, Isacsson, *AFCT*, p.4, in which he assumes that Slater stopped in New York, and Surratt continued on.

548 JOH Papers, *Microfilm of St. Lawrence Hall Register* (April 6, 1865); *E.G. Lee Offer of Proof* ¶¶1, 3.

549 *E.G. Lee*, p.151 n.2.

550 JOH Papers, *Microfilm of St. Lawrence Hall Register* (April 6, 1865).

551 *E.G. Lee*, p.151; JOH Papers, *Microfilm of St. Lawrence Hall Register* (April 4, 1865) (room 19).

552 *E.G. Lee*, p.151.

553 JOH Papers, *Diary of E.G. Lee* (April 6, 1865) (hereafter *"Lee Diary"*); *E.G. Lee*, p.151.

554 *Lee Diary* (April 15, 1865); *E.G. Lee*, p.153.

555 2 JHS Trial 840, 842, 845, 894.

556 2 JHS Trial 841, 844, 894 (witness says "Monday, April 9" but April 9 was a Sunday).

557 1 JHS Trial 725; 2 JHS Trial 729-31, 733, 841.

558 Weichmann, p.130.

559 *Ibid.*, pp.130-31; 1 JHS Trial 388.

560 *Ibid.*, p.131; 1 JHS Trial 388.

561 Weichmann, p.131.

562 *Ibid.*

563 *Ibid.*

564 *Venice Preserved* by Thomas Otway, http://www.gutenberg.org/files/21515/21515-h/21515-h.htm (accessed Dec. 28, 2013).

565 *Trial of the Conspirators*, p.45.

566 JOH Papers - JHS, *Letter from John H. Surratt to Belle Seaman* (April 10, 1865) (copied from War Department Archives, May 16, 1933, by D.R. Barbee).

567 1 JHS Trial 393, 449; 2 JHS Trial 836.

568 2 JHS Trial 698, 708.

569 1 JHS Trial 166-67.

570 JOH Papers, C.W. Taylor, *Report of Proceedings in Canada*, p.1 (hereafter *"Taylor Report"*).

571 JOH Papers - *Report of the Committee of the Judiciary, Testimony of L.J. McMillan*, p.13 (March 2, 1867) (hereafter *"McMillan Judiciary Testimony"*).

572 *Ibid.*; 1 JHS Trial 471, 477.

573 1 JHS Trial 471.

574 1 JHS Trial 167.

575 *Rockville Lecture*, Weichmann, p.434.

576 *LA from Surratt Courier*, vol.2, Alfred Isacsson, *Judge Fisher's Account of the John H. Surratt Trial*, pp. X-17 to 18 (May 1987) (hereafter *"Judge Fisher's Account"*).

577 Weichmann, pp.371-72.

578 *E.G. Lee Offer of Proof.*

579 *Ibid.*, ¶2.

580 *Ibid.*

581 *Lee Diary* (April 19, 1865).

582 *Ibid.* (emphasis added).

583 *Rockville Lecture*, Weichmann, p.434.

584 2 JHS Trial 729-34.

585 1 JHS Trial 724, 725-26, 2 JHS Trial 730, 734, 863-64.

586 1 JHS Trial 473, 725; 2 JHS Trial 729-31, 733, 1200; *Rockville Lecture*, Weichmann, p.438.

587 That does not mean that Surratt had nothing to do with it. Not only were his previous actions (even absent the speculation about delivery of an order) sufficient to convict him as a co conspirator or accessory before the fact, but he may have continued his involvement from afar. Dr. McMillan testified that Surratt told him that he went from Montreal to Elmira, and then telegraphed to John Wilkes Booth in New York, but he had already left. 1 JHS Trial 471-72. This suggests that, although Surratt was not trying to get to Washington in time for the assassination, he was nonetheless still attempting to provide aid and support to the conspiracy.

588 1 JHS Trial 118-19.

589 *E.g.*, 1 JHS Trial 860-61, 1061, 1064, 1066, 1080, 1083, 1085, 1089, 1110, 1115, 1150-52, 1154.

590 2 JHS Trial 1117.

591 1 JHS Trial 494-97.

592 1 JHS Trial 501-02.

593 1 JHS Trial 158-59.

594 1 JHS Trial 240-42.

595 1 JHS Trial 195-203.

[596] 1 JHS Trial 207.

[597] 1 JHS Trial 166-67.

[598] 1 JHS Trial 520-22.

[599] 1 JHS Trial 523.

[600] 1 JHS Trial 500.

[601] 1 JHS Trial 163.

[602] 1 JHS Trial 135.

[603] 1 JHS Trial 492.

[604] *Atzerodt Baltimore American Statement*, p. III-28; *see also, Atzerodt National Intelligencer Statement*, p. III-24 ("Booth told Atzerodt that Surratt was in the city. He had just left.").

[605] 2 JHS Trial 1117, 1358.

[606] 2 JHS Trial 732.

[607] What's more, the jury would have to conclude that Carroll was mistaken when he said that Surratt came back in on April 14. 2 JHS Trial 733, 739, 743, 745. Cross-examination suggested that he had previously told an investigator that he saw Surratt on April 12 and 13, but Carroll's testimony never wavered. *Ibid.*

[608] 2 JHS Trial 772.

[609] 2 JHS Trial 916-17, 936.

[610] 2 JHS Trial 936.

[611] 2 JHS Trial 917, 924-25.

[612] 2 JHS Trial 925, 936.

[613] 2 JHS Trial 1025.

[614] 2 JHS Trial 928, 1024.

[615] 2 JHS Trial 1027-28.

[616] There might even have been a Surratt look-alike parading about in a Garibaldi jacket into the afternoon of the 13th, while Surratt was already on the train.

[617] Conversation between the author and Judge Sandy Prindle, Surratt Society Annual Meeting, March 14, 2014.

[618] 1 JHS Trial 559, 566, 571.

[619] 1 JHS Trial 190.

[620] Library of Congress, *Confederate State Papers*, control #mm78016560, Reel #6, Document #14, *Toronto, Letter from Jacob Thompson to Judah Benjamin*, pp.12-13 (Dec. 3, 1864) (not received until Feb. 13, 1865) (emphasis added).

[621] *Ibid.*, p.13.

[622] *E.G. Lee*, pp.153-54, contains a description of the harsh conditions at the prison in Elmira.

[623] With respect to the possibility that it was a ruse, one might say that it made more sense to keep Surratt in Canada, since he ended up scrambling back

to Montreal after the assassination. But Elmira always worked best for Surratt's main narrative that he was going about his usual business without any consciousness of the unfolding events in Washington. Montreal was already the supposed nest of plotters, and Confederates there risked prosecution for violation of the Neutrality Act. Better to push the messenger from the nest for his own and everyone's protection.

CHAPTER ELEVEN

GLADNESS TO SORROW

O<small>N</small> T<small>UESDAY</small>, A<small>PRIL</small> 11, W<small>EICHMANN</small> <small>DROVE</small> M<small>RS</small>. S<small>URRATT</small> <small>TO</small> Surrattsville in a carriage rented with Booth's money, on business supposedly concerning debts owed to her.[624] Mrs. Surratt's tenant, John Lloyd, who stated at John Surratt's trial that, "I do not wish to state one solitary word more than I am compelled to,"[625] nonetheless testified to a whispered conversation he had with Mrs. Surratt when they met on the road between Washington and Surrattsville:

> Mr. Lloyd: She tried to draw my attention to something.
> Mr. Merrick: . . . State what she did say and did do.
> A: She finally came out and asked me about some shooting irons that were there.
> Q: Where?
> A: At Surrattsville, as I supposed. . . ..
> Q: . . . [S]tate what you recollect she said, not your impressions. . . .
> A: As well as I recollect, in speaking of the shooting irons, she told me to have them ready; that they would be called for, or wanted, soon . . . ..[626]

The "shooting irons" referred to are the Spencer carbines purchased by John Wilkes Booth and hidden between the ceiling joists at Surratt's Tavern by John H. Surratt.

On Good Friday, April 14, at about 2:20 p.m., Mrs. Surratt knocked at the door to Weichmann's room, and asked him to rent a horse and buggy in order to take her to the country again, supposedly to see John Nothey about a debt that was owed her. As Weichmann sped out the door with Mrs. Surratt's ten dollars in his pocket, he came face to face with John Wilkes Booth. They shook hands, and Booth proceeded into the parlor as Weichmann went to the stable. Weichmann was back by about 2:40 p.m., and saw Booth and Mrs. Surratt in close conversation near the hearth. Booth left and waved goodbye to Weichmann; it was the last time Weichmann saw the actor alive. Mrs. Surratt came down to the buggy but had to go back because she had forgotten "those things of Mr. Booth." She fetched two packages tied up in coarse brown paper, one of which she said was glass. It proved to be the very field glass that was used by Booth and Herold during their attempted escape through Maryland and Virginia.[627]

Weichmann and Mrs. Surratt had an uneventful trip to Surrattsville, except that when they spied some Union soldiers along the road Mrs. Surratt stopped the carriage to ask a local farmer about them. He told her they were pickets, but they generally withdrew about eight o'clock at night. "I am glad to know it," said Mrs. Surratt.[628]

They arrived at Surrattsville about half past four. Mr. Nothey was not there; he lived another five miles south of Surrattsville, but they never continued on. Instead, Mrs. Surratt had Weichmann write a letter to Mr. Nothey that she later tried to use in her defense, in order to show that she was on a legitimate business trip rather than an errand for the conspiracy.[629] Of course, she could have written the letter from Washington as easily as from Surrattsville. The real reason for this trip made on the day Lincoln was shot is revealed by Mr. Lloyd:

> Mrs. Surratt . . . handed me a package, and told me, as well as I remember, to get the guns, or those things – I really forget now which, though my impression is that "guns" was the expression she made use of – and a couple of bottles of whiskey, and give them to whoever should call for them that night.[630]

It is necessary to pause a moment here. The worst against Mrs. Surratt has now been stated by the two witnesses whose testimony most contributed to her hanging: John Lloyd and Louis J. Weichmann. It is important to recognize that Lloyd was probably involved in the conspiracy against Lincoln to some extent, and Weichmann had his own misdeeds at the War Department to cover up, and therefore each had a strong motive to turn Government witness in order to save his own hide.

John P. Brophy, a friend of the Surratt family who also sidled up to Weichmann after the trial, gave a sworn affidavit dated July 7, 1865 that was used in the eleventh-hour attempt to obtain commutation of Mrs. Surratt's execution. This most fascinating document includes the following testimony:

¶2 Weichmann "told me that he was arrested as a conspirator and threatened with death by Mr. Stanton . . . unless he would at once reveal all about the assassination . . .."

¶3 Weichmann "told me he would rather be hooted at as a spy and informer and do anything rather than be tried as a conspirator . . .."

¶¶ 5 & 6 Weichmann "admitted to me that he was a liar" and "[t]hat he swore to a deliberate falsehood on the witness stand."

¶¶ 9-10 Weichmann said Mrs. Surratt "wept bitterly" at John Surratt going to Richmond, and implored him not to go and to stop whatever was going on, but John would not stop and would not tell her what was going on.

¶11 Weichmann "told me he thought Mrs. Surratt to be innocent, saying her son John was the guilty one . . .."

¶12 Weichmann "was an avowed Secessionist . . .."[631]

To the extent that Weichmann or Lloyd were peripherally involved co-conspirators who were "turned" by the Government to obtain testimony under a promise of immunity, that is standard operating procedure in criminal prosecutions. With respect to Weichmann, his testimony against Mrs. Surratt was not all that damning anyway – recall that he claimed not to hear the most incriminating statements about getting the shooting irons ready. To the extent that he may have lied under oath, it seems likely that it was to minimize his own involvement, rather than to directly condemn Mrs. Surratt. For example, when Weichmann denies secessionist sentiments, or that he leaked information from the War Department to Surratt, or that he could hear what Lloyd said to Mrs. Surratt on April 11, he may well be lying. But when he talks about where John or Mary Surratt were and who they were with on specific dates, his testimony was never successfully impeached, and it jibes with other known facts.

There is a further embellishment on the story of pressure brought to bear on Weichmann. According to the highly suspect Hanson-Hiss article, Surratt supposedly said this:

> In order to get a confession from [Weichmann] a rope was placed around his neck, the other end of it thrown over a beam, and he was ordered to tell what he knew. He was lifted off his feet. Under such circumstances a man will tell or say anything to get a rope from around his neck.[632]

In direct response to publication of the Hanson-Hiss article, Detective A.C. Richards wrote:

> Now if anyone put a rope around Weichmann's neck and threw it over a beam I did it, and I say that statement is as false in fact and circumstance as it is possible for a statement to be. It was conceived in recklessness, and is a mere figment of imagination.[633]

Detective Richards adds: "In no instance was any statement in relation to the conspiracy made by [Weichmann] found to be false or incorrect, and very many of his statements were subsequently corroborated by undoubted testimony."[634]

* * *

With respect to John Lloyd, it has been alleged that he was hanged by his thumbs till he could no longer stand the pain in order to extract his testimony against Mrs. Surratt.[635] This story directly conflicts with the sworn testimony of George Cottingham, the officer in whose charge he was placed after his arrest. According to Cottingham, Lloyd said nothing about the assassination for the first two days of his captivity. Cottingham told him that it was obvious he was bearing a heavy load, and he would feel better to get rid of it. "O, my God," replied Lloyd, "if I was to make a confession, they would murder me!" Cottingham asked who would murder him, to which Lloyd replied, "These parties that are in the conspiracy." "Well," replied Cottingham, "if you are afraid of being murdered, and let those fellows get out of it, that is your business, not mine."[636]

According to Cottingham, it was through this strategy of persuasion, not by torture, that Lloyd was induced to give his statement. After thinking it over, Lloyd began to talk while being brought to Washington under guard of a squad of cavalry. Lloyd's statement included the story that Mrs. Surratt had come down at five o'clock the day of the assassination, and told him to have the fire-arms ready, and that two men would call for them that night. Then Lloyd broke down in tears and cried out: "O, Mrs. Surratt, that vile woman, she has ruined me! I am to be shot! I am to be shot!"[637]

Cottingham cannot be expected to have admitted torturing Lloyd, so it remains possible that he did so. Yet more likely, the inducement of saving himself from prosecution was sufficient to extract from Lloyd everything he knew of the matter. What's more, we need to ask ourselves this crucial question: *why incriminate Mrs. Surratt if it wasn't true?* Lloyd already had incriminating details against Booth, Herold, and John H. Surratt, giving him plenty of ammunition to trade for his life. There was no reason for Lloyd to go further if he wasn't telling the truth about Mrs. Surratt. To the contrary, in light of the Nineteenth Century taboo against impugning of the sanctity of Woman, there was every reason not to falsely accuse Mrs. Surratt.

It might be argued that Lloyd was induced to implicate Mrs. Surratt because the Government hoped to use its case against Mrs. Surratt to flush out John Surratt. But his statement to Cottingham was given only two days after the assassination. At that point, Mrs. Surratt was not even under arrest, and it was not clear that John Surratt would get away. Mr. Lloyd was a loyal Southern man. He was not interested in saying one word more than he had to on the witness stand. It is not likely that he would have had the motive, or the wit, to make up a story to incriminate Mrs. Surratt.

The other charge against Lloyd, of course, is that he was a drunk who was too inebriated on April 14 to know what Mrs. Surratt told him. Again, there is truth to this – he was unquestionably drinking all that day, as was his habit. Yet, like many alcoholics, he functioned well enough to drive a wagon back to Surrattsville from Marlboro on April 14, and to fix a broken spring on Mrs. Surratt's wagon.[638] While there were likely many details that he did not remember from that day, the message to have the guns ready was by no means a minor or routine matter. Instead, it called upon him to take illegal action in a dreadful conspiracy of the highest order, likely to impress itself on his memory so long as he was even a half shot of whiskey this side of consciousness.

Weichmann and Lloyd are not necessarily shiny paragons of virtue. Rarely are criminals in the company of saints while carrying out their plans. But these are the principal witnesses against Mary Surratt. You have the facts – draw your own conclusions.

* * *

Early in the evening of April 14, Weichmann and Mrs. Surratt drove off in their buggy for the return trip to Washington.[639] On a hill overlooking Washington, they saw the lights of the torchlight parade and celebration illuminating the victorious capital. "I am afraid that all this rejoicing will be turned into mourning and all this gladness to sorrow," said Mrs. Surratt.[640] Weichmann asked her what she meant. She replied that the people were too proud and licentious; that God would punish them.[641] They arrived back home about half past eight.[642] Lincoln had less than two hours to enjoy life.

Ford's Theatre, that vortex of assassination obsession, no longer interests us. Was Surratt there or in Elmira? It doesn't matter. At the very least, Surratt had already helped Booth recruit his action team, arranged for lodging for the man who would nearly kill Secretary Seward, stood ready to drive the kidnap wagon if Lincoln could be seized, and hidden Booth's carbines at Surrattsville. At the most, he had delivered the order to kill. That night, *An American Cousin* was twisted from light comedy to darkest tragedy by a shot fired not by a madman, but by Surratt's comrade-in-arms doing his duty as a Confederate. What happened was the culmination of months of planning and effort. The tragedy plays on the stage but those who write the script and direct the players are invisible.

* * *

According to John Lloyd's testimony at the military trial of the conspirators:

> Just about midnight on Friday [April 14], Herold came into the house and said, "Lloyd, for God's sake, make haste and get those things." I did not make any reply, but went straight and got the carbines, supposing they were the parties Mrs. Surratt had referred to . . .. Mrs. Surratt told me to give the carbines, whisky, and field-glass. . . . Booth didn't come in. I didn't know him; he was a stranger to me. . . . Herold came into the house and got a bottle of whisky, and took it out to him, and he drank while sitting on his horse. . . .[643]

Booth said that he couldn't carry a carbine because his leg was broken, so they only took one with them. [644] This was one of the carbines hidden by Surratt, later found in Booth's hands at the time he was shot by Union soldiers in Garrett's Barn.[645]

Lloyd finished the story as follows:

> Just as they were about leaving, [Booth] . . . said, "I will tell you some news, if you want to hear it," or something to that effect. I said, "I am not particular; use your own pleasure about telling it." "Well," said he, "I am pretty certain

that we have assassinated the President and Secretary Seward."[646]

[624] 1 JHS Trial 389.
[625] 1 JHS Trial 280.
[626] *Ibid.*
[627] Weichmann, pp.164-66; 1 JHS Trial 281-82, 390-91, *Trial of the Conspirators*, p.131.
[638] Weichmann, p.166; 1 JHS Trial 391.
[639] Weichmann, pp.168-69; *Trial of the Conspirators*, p.126.
[630] 1 JHS Trial 281.
[631] JOH Papers - JHS, *Brophy Affidavit.*
[632] *Hanson-Hiss*, Weichmann, p.450.
[633] Weichmann, p.453.
[634] *Ibid.*
[635] *American Tragedy*, p.133 & p.270 n.23.
[636] *Trial of the Conspirators*, p.124.
[637] *Ibid.*
[638] 1 JHS Trial 281.
[639] *Ibid.*
[640] 1 JHS Trial 393.
[641] Ibid.; Weichmann, p.172.
[642] Weichmann, p.172.
[643] *Trial of the Conspirators*, p.86.
[644] *Ibid.*
[645] *Manhunt*, pp.334-35; *Trial of the Conspirators*, p.94.
[646] *Trial of the Conspirators*, p.86.

Chapter Twelve

RUNNING FOR HIS LIFE

All that night of April 14-15, 1865, as the lifeblood drained from Lincoln's insensate body, as Booth and Herold made their bone-jarring escape into the Maryland night, "John Harrison" says he slept like a baby at Brainard House in Elmira. According to Surratt, he laid his head down on his pillow at "[a]bout ten o'clock," not "thinking that on that night a blow would be struck which would forever blast my hopes, and make me a wanderer in a foreign land." Surratt says that he slept the peaceful night through in Elmira, "and came down the next morning little dreaming of the storm then brewing around my head."[647]

What of the other Surratt, the one who was supposedly active in the assassination at Ford's Theatre? The Government presented several scraps of not very convincing testimony tracing Surratt's path out of Washington. First, Mr. Ste. Marie testified that Surratt told him that he had "a very hard time" getting out of Washington the early morning after the assassination; that he left disguised as an Englishman, with a scarf over his shoulders.[648] Charles Ramsdell, an enlisted man with the Third Massachusetts heavy artillery division, testified that between four and five o'clock on the morning after the assassination he met a man on horseback by Fort Bunker Hill, which is located about four miles northeast of Ford's Theatre. Ramsdell makes no mention of the scarf or "Englishman's disguise" testified to by Ste. Marie. According to Ramsdell, the man was "fidgety and nervous," and wanted to know if there would be any trouble getting through the pickets. Ramsdell replied that there would be, and asked the man whether he had heard of the assassination. The man "gave a sneering laugh," looked about, then set off at a brisk gait without reply.[649]

Knowing of Surratt's prowess in the saddle, it is hardly believable that he would only have gotten four miles away from the scene of the crime in a period of six or seven hours. As testified to by Mr. Smoot, when the talk around the bar in Surrattsville turned to Surratt's possible role in the assassination, Joseph T. Nott said, "John knows all about the murder; do you suppose he is going to stay in Washington and let them catch him?"[650] Nonetheless, the Government tried to identify the fidgety man spotted by Ramsdell as Surratt. Surratt was instructed to stand with his back to the witness.

> Mr. Pierrepont: Did you ever see that man (pointing to [Surratt]) before?
> Mr. Ramsdell: I think I have seen that back before.
> Q: Did you see it on that horse?
> A: I think I did.[651]

To this ludicrous identification, there was no cross-examination. Likely, the defense correctly calculated that the Government was capable of making a horse's ass of itself without any help.

* * *

Surratt says that when he came down to breakfast at Brainard House at about nine o'clock on April 15, a gentleman seated to his left asked, "Have you heard the news?" Surratt said he had not, to which the man replied, "President Lincoln and Secretary Seward have been assassinated."[652] Surratt told his Rockville audience that he replied, "it is too early in the morning for jokes," but the gentleman backed up his claim with a fresh newspaper account.[653] Surratt told a slightly different story to Dr. McMillan on the *Peruvian*, saying that he let slip his disbelief that Lincoln and Seward had been assassinated "because the story is too good to be true."[654] Dr. McMillan seems confused about the location – he places this discussion in St. Albans, Vermont, which seems an unlikely place for Surratt to have first heard of the completed assassination, since it is already well on the way back to Canada and he was not there until the following Tuesday. Nor does it seem likely that Surratt would be so unguarded as to make such an incendiary remark in the heart of Yankee territory, whether Elmira or St. Albans. Dr. McMillan may be confusing Surratt's private views with what he actually said.

Surratt asserts that he did not initially believe that Booth or his former conspirators were involved. The first newspaper account viewed by Surratt mentioned no suspects. Surratt supports his supposed credulity with two points: first, he was aware that other plots against Lincoln were afoot, and second, "because I had never heard anything regarding assassination spoken of during my intercourse with . . . Booth or any of the party."[655] This conflicts with his own prior acknowledgement that Booth made a veiled threat of assassination at the Gautier's meeting, which Surratt claimed nearly broke up their conspiracy till Booth passed it off to an excess of champagne.[656] What's more, although the initial accounts did not mention suspects, they did mention that the President was "shot at the theatre," which should have been synonymous in Surratt's mind with "John Wilkes Booth."[657] The interesting thing is not whether Surratt is telling the truth – he almost certainly is not – but why he would lie about this. The answer seems to be to excuse his next action, which is otherwise quite incriminating.

Rising from the breakfast table, Surratt admits that he immediately went to the telegraph office in the hotel lobby, "picked up a blank and wrote 'John Wilkes Booth,' giving the number and street."[658] He then tore the paper up, and for purposes of disguise instead wrote "J.W.B." with directions to Booth's house in New York. The resulting telegram read, in substance:

J.W.B., in New York:
If you are in New York telegraph me.
John Harrison, Elmira, N.Y.[659]

Though the telegraph operator questioned Surratt for a full name, he nonetheless sent the message as is. He had scarcely finished sending it when Surratt heard some men talking about the Booth brothers, and mentioning the name "J. Wilkes Booth." It was then – and only then, in Surratt's version of events – that he suddenly recognized his peril. "The whole truth flashed on me in an instant, and I said to myself, 'My God! What have I done?'"[660]

It is a very good question. If, as Surratt later claimed, he was truly no longer involved in the conspiracy, *why would his very first action upon hearing of the death of Lincoln be to attempt to telegraph the man who pulled the trigger?*

* * *

Surratt tried to snatch back the original of the telegram he had just written, but the operator insisted on keeping it for his files. Surratt headed out onto the street. "The town was in the greatest uproar, flags at half mast, bells tolling," women crying, men huddled around sharing the news, shops closing.[661]

John Cass, who kept a clothing store at the corner of Water and Baldwin Streets in Elmira, got his newspaper at home at about half-past seven o'clock that morning as usual, and saw in it a short bulletin about the assassination. Mr. Cass went to work, arriving at his store about eight o'clock, and soon thereafter went to see his friend, Mr. Palmer, who was the telegraph operator at the shop directly across from his store. No news had arrived since the first bulletin, and so Mr. Cass milled around with some friends, awaiting fresh intelligence. Shortly after nine o'clock, the sad news arrived confirming that Lincoln was dead.[662]

Mr. Cass went across the street to his shop, told his clerks the news, and instructed them to close up for the day. Standing at the front of his store he saw a man crossing whom he at first mistook for a Canadian friend of his. The stranger was clean, not dirty as he would have been after a grueling overnight trip.[663] At about half-past nine, the stranger followed him back into the store and inquired about a particular make of white shirts, which Mr. Cass did not stock. Mr. Cass told the stranger they had received "some very bad news" that morning, "[o]f the death of Abraham Lincoln." The stranger made a remark that Mr. Cass at first took to be disrespectful, but then wrote it off to his belief that the stranger "was a Canadian and had no sympathy with our people."[664] He wore an unusual pleated jacket with a belt around the waist, which Mr. Cass associated with Canadians.[665]

> Mr. Bradley: Have you ever seen that man since?
> Mr. Cass: I have. . ..
> ([Surratt] was requested to stand up.)
> Q: Look at that man (pointing to [Surratt]) and state if he is or not the man.
> A: That is the man I saw there.
> By a Juror: Was that on the 15th?
> A: Yes, sir; while closing the store after seeing the news.[666]

Surratt, appearing clean in Elmira about twelve hours after he was last seen two-hundred eighty miles away in Washington City, was a virtual Nineteenth Century impossibility. The express train between Elmira and New York City – not Baltimore or Washington – took twelve hours.[667] Unless Mr. Cass is lying or mistaken, this is strong evidence that Surratt was in Elmira all along.

* * *

For the next nineteen months Surratt would be running for his life. At first, he ran in the logical direction – north, towards Canada – although he told his Rockville audience that "I left Elmira with the intention of going to Baltimore." His explanation is bizarre, at best: "As there was no train going South that evening I concluded to go to Canandaigua and from there to Baltimore by way of Elmira and New York."[668] The best way to do that, of course, would be to sit tight in Elmira until the southbound train came along. Canandaigua, New York, is about seventy-three miles north and slightly west of Elmira, whereas Baltimore is about two hundred forty-seven miles due south of Elmira. The logic of heading north in order to go south – especially to go back south through the town you are already in – will escape any rational railroad traveler. The logic of avoiding Baltimore and New York at all costs will appeal to any rational fugitive running from the crime of the century just committed in Washington. And to top it off, by naming Baltimore as his intended destination, Surratt seems to be forgetting his cover story and mission – that he had made careful sketches of the prison at Elmira that needed to be delivered to General Lee in Montreal. Surratt's story that he decided to go to Baltimore is therefore further evidence that his secret surveillance mission was a sham.

Surratt probably did go to Canandaigua on Saturday, April 15. Most likely, he registered at Webster House under the name "John Harrison" on Saturday night between eight and ten o'clock.[669] Although the hotel register was offered and excluded from evidence at Surratt's trial on the ground that it was open and available to anybody (including Surratt) to write "John Harrison" in for two years after April 15, the "court of history" has ruled that the hotel register containing Surratt's given and middle names written half-way down the page, sandwiched between other registrants for that day, is reliable evidence that he was there.[670]

Why would Surratt have gone to Canandaigua? Probably because it was on one of the established Confederate routes to Canada, through Niagara Falls.[671] But the next day was Easter Sunday. With no trains going anywhere, Surratt found that he was stuck in Canandaigua, so he went to church.[672] Perhaps he prayed for his mother and sister, whose house had been searched in the wee hours of Saturday morning. But with what we know of Surratt he was probably only thinking of himself and Nettie Slater.

* * *

On Monday morning, April 17, Surratt bought the New York papers. His eye settled on a paragraph that seared itself into memory:

> "The assassin of Secretary Seward is said to be John H. Surratt, a notorious secessionist of Southern Maryland. His name, with that of J. Wilkes Booth, will forever lead the infamous roll of assassins."[673]

Surratt says his mind reeled as "I gazed upon my name, the letters of which seemed . . . sometimes to grow as large as mountains and then to dwindle away to nothing."[674] Claiming that this spurred him to decide "to go direct to Canada" as quickly as possible, he did anything but. From Canandaigua, it was only a little more than one hundred miles northwest to Niagara Falls and the relative safety of Canada. That was the logical route to take since it was the shortest and it headed directly away from the scene of the crime and the expanding manhunt. Yet Surratt defied logic by heading due east over two hundred miles to Albany, then north to Whitehall, New York, then on a Lake Champlain steamer to Burlington, Vermont, and from there a train to Essex Junction, St. Albans, and finally, into Canada – a total journey of approximately four hundred ten miles.[675] *Why?*

We can only speculate. But we do know that he started this journey alone, that by the time he was seen in Burlington he was accompanied by at least one companion, and by the time he arrived in Montreal he probably had two companions. There are only a few things that could cause a young man suspected of the crime of the century to risk his life in this way. Foremost on the list is the gallant rescue of a beautiful young co-conspirator with whom he is in love. It is possible that Surratt telegraphed Nettie Slater in New York, set up a rendezvous somewhere along this route, and that they fled the rest of the way to Canada together.

* * *

About the time Surratt was on the steamer bound for Burlington, his mother and sister heard the scraping steps of men on the front steps at 541 H Street in Washington. It was Major Henry Warren Smith and Captain William M. Wermerskirch, accompanied by two detectives.[676] "Are you Mrs. Surratt?" demanded Major Smith. "I am the widow of John H. Surratt," replied Mary Surratt. "The mother of John H. Surratt, Jr.?" prodded the Major. "I am," the lady replied. "I come to arrest you and all in your house and take you for examination to General Augur's head-quarters."[677]

Together they stepped into the parlor, where John's sister Anna, cousin Olivia Jenkins, and the boarder Honora Fitzpatrick were seated. "Ladies, you will have to get ready as soon as possible and go with me down to General Augur's for examination," announced Major Smith. Anna exclaimed, "Oh, mother, to think of being taken down there for such a crime." As Mrs. Surratt hugged Anna she whispered something in her ear, quieting Anna.[678] The ladies prepared to go out. Mrs. Surratt would never return.

It was nearly eleven o'clock that night when Major Smith heard the sound of heavy footsteps coming up the front stairs. Placing Captain Wermerskirch and Detective Morgan behind the front door, Major Smith stood in the hall when the door-bell rang and the front door opened. Smith found himself face to face with Powell (alias Paine/Wood/Mosby), "standing on the threshold of the door with a pickaxe over his shoulder."[679] Powell's boots were full of mud, his pants were mud-splattered, and he was wearing a headdress fashioned out of the sleeve of an undershirt.[680] According to Major Smith's testimony:

> [Powell] said, "I guess I have mistaken the house." I said, "You have not." He said, "Is this Mrs. Surratt's house?" I said, "Yes." He seemed to hesitate. I drew my revolver and cocked it, and said, "Step in."[681]

Powell did as he was told, and laid down the pickaxe. After some very unsatisfactory lies about coming by so late just to learn where Mrs. Surratt wanted him to dig a ditch, Major Smith called Mrs. Surratt into the hallway. The gas was at half-head, so the hall was dimly lighted. Mrs. Surratt stood only about four to five feet from Powell, who stood just under a gas fixture with the dim light on his face. "Do you know this man?" asked Major Smith. "Did you hire him to dig a ditch for you?" Mrs. Surratt raised both her hands and said, "Before God I do not know this man; I have never seen him; I did not hire him to dig a ditch."[682]

In defense of Mrs. Surratt, Honora Fitzpatrick testified:

> Mrs. Surratt has complained that she could not read or sew at night on account of her sight. I have known of her passing her friend, Mrs. Kirby, on the same side of the street, and not see her at all.[683]

Mrs. Surratt's servant, Rachel Semus, testified that she had to thread Mrs. Surratt's needle for her even in the daylight, and that she had even mistaken a priest for her son, "little Johnny."[684]

The many apologists for Mrs. Surratt have seized upon her "poor eyesight" to excuse this incident.[685] But poor eyesight is reason to say, "I can't tell," not reason for a pious woman to take an oath before God never to have seen the man before. Recall that Powell had been introduced to Mrs. Surratt on about February 20, and again on March 14, when he stayed over at her boarding house for one night. Anna Surratt testified that Powell "called two or three times after that" in the next week or two.[686] It is also likely that Mrs. Surratt conferred with Powell sometime after March 27 at Herndon House, where her son had obtained lodging for him under cover of being a "delicate gentleman."[687] It is apparent that by Monday, April 17, when he appeared on her doorstep, she knew him well enough. An innocent lady with bad eyesight would say she could not tell, or ask for a lantern so she could get a good look to resolve the question. Mrs. Surratt was evidently not that lady.

* * *

Powell, Mary Surratt, Anna Surratt, and the other ladies, were all taken to the office of General Christopher Augur, a man with "a thick, walrus mustache" and "starched and ironed" beard.[688] In the waiting area, presumably under better gaslight, Mrs. Surratt got another chance to see Powell – this time with his makeshift cap removed.[689] There is no record that she corrected her previous denial of recognition, and the statement given to General Augur that night maintains the charade that Powell was a ruffian come to murder her and her daughter.[690]

Mrs. Surratt was interrogated by General Augur that night on several subjects, including the whereabouts of her son, John. She said that she had last seen him Monday, two weeks previous, and that she "supposed he had gone to Canada."[691] Having obtained a spot of truthful information from Mrs. Surratt, General Augur promptly discarded it:

General Augur: No man on the round earth believes he went to
    Canada.
Mrs. Surratt: I believe it.
General Augur: No one can believe it, they would just as soon
    believe that a bird could fly if we cut off his wings. . . .[692]

* * *

But Surratt was flying north up Lake Champlain to Burlington, Vermont. The first boat of the season from Whitehall landed at Burlington about midnight on Monday, April 17. According to Charles H. Blinn, night watchman at the Vermont Central Railway Depot in Burlington, two "men" from off the boat – "one was a tall man, and the other shorter" – requested permission to sleep in the depot until the 4:20 a.m. train departed for Essex Junction and then Montreal. It was the taller of the two who did all the talking. They slept on a bench until Mr. Blinn awakened them at about four o'clock the morning of Tuesday, April 18. Later, when the sun came up, Mr. Blinn noticed a handkerchief on the bench where the taller man's head had lain. The monogram on the handkerchief read, "J.H. Surratt, 2."[693]

Like a cat or Surratt himself, this handkerchief has many lives. One story has the handkerchief passing from Blinn to a Vermont farmer named George F. Chapin, to a detective named Gurnett. According to Chapin, he took a train into Burlington on Wednesday, and while there Mr. Blinn showed him the handkerchief. Chapin, realizing that the handkerchief was important, returned on Tuesday, April 25, with Gurnett, to track down the evidence. They found it at Blinn's home in Winooski Falls, neatly washed and folded by Blinn's mother.[694]

A very different version of the handkerchief story was told by John T. Holohan, the Surratt house boarder who changed gold into greenbacks for Surratt. According to Holohan, he and Weichmann went with detectives McDevitt and Bigley to Canada in pursuit of Surratt. Just before they left on Monday afternoon, April 17, Holohan stopped at Mrs. Surratt's to change his shirt, and he also picked up some handkerchiefs – one of which was marked "John H. Surratt." By Wednesday night, April 19, they had arrived in Burlington, where they registered at a hotel under false names. Holohan is certain that he had the handkerchief in his overcoat pocket with his chewing tobacco at that time. On Thursday morning they were early for the train to Essex Junction, so Holohan lay down on a settee. Between four and five o'clock that morning, while in Essex Junction waiting for the Montreal train, Holohan wandered a few hundred feet from the depot to a shack where liquor was sold. Thus fortified, he returned craving a chew, but discovered that he had lost his tobacco along with the "John H. Surratt" handkerchief.[695]

Holohan's story matters not a whit in the big scheme of things because it is unquestioned that Surratt was in Vermont on Tuesday, April 18, whether his handkerchief was there yet or not. Surratt admits as much, though he engages in a bit of subterfuge when he tells his tale to the Rockville Maryland crowd. Surratt says that he did not leave Elmira until twelve midnight, arriving in Albany "on Tuesday morning in time for breakfast,"[696] when in fact he was all the way to Burlington by Monday night. Perhaps his memory was faulty by 1870, but more likely he was still in the business of throwing pursuers off of Mrs. Slater's scent.

The theory that the "short man" at the depot in Burlington was in fact Nettie Slater in disguise was first floated by researcher John F. Stanton.[697] I think Mr. Stanton is close, but there is one important piece of evidence to the contrary. Mr. Carroll Hobart, conductor on the Vermont Central Railroad run from White River Junction to St. Albans, picked up the two mystery travelers at Essex Junction at five o'clock on the morning of Tuesday, April 18. Hobart described the shorter man as "a short, thick-set man, of sandy complexion, with whiskers around his face," wearing a slouched hat.[698] Hobart would have had several chances to get a good look at this man, in two separate meetings at different parts of the train. While the diminutive Mrs. Slater might conceivably be disguised as a short man, and might even pass on casual observation as a bewhiskered man by application of a false mustache and beard, it seems unlikely that she could pass as a "thick-set" and bewhiskered male upon close observation. It is not impossible, but unlikely.

Close observation is what Surratt received from Mr. Hobart. Surratt sought free passage based on a sob story about being Canadian laborers lured to the United States with the promise of work, who were cheated out of their money, and he promised to pay their fare upon arrival in Canada.[699] The Yankee conductor was not fooled:

This tall man tried to use broken English, as if he were a

Canuck [French-Canadian], but occasionally he would get a little in earnest for fear he was to be put off, and then he would drop the Canuck and speak good square English. . . . His hands were not like those of a laboring man; were not like those of a Canadian who had been used to hard labor. They were white and delicate.[700]

Mr. Hobart told Surratt and his companion that they needed money to travel by rail, and that he would drop them at the next stop. But then he got busy and forgot to put them off until St. Albans. From there, they asked how far to the border crossing at Franklin, and he told them fourteen miles. They said they would walk.[701]

Mr. Hobart's description of the shorter "man" does not necessarily eliminate Mrs. Slater from this trip. Hobart, like Blinn, agrees that the tall man did all the talking.[702] Mrs. Slater might have been wearing cushions to mask her womanly physique, and we already know that Surratt was conversant in the use of false whiskers. Or Surratt might have had another Confederate traveling companion that he met in Albany, and Mrs. Slater might have taken the train directly from New York City to Essex Junction. If so, then she would likely appear as an immaculately coifed veiled lady passenger with no apparent connection to the two vagabonds from the boat. Or, perhaps she was already waiting for Surratt in St. Albans, or even across the border just beyond Franklin. Wherever she was, we have reason to believe that it was not far off.

* * *

General Augur's skepticism notwithstanding, by Tuesday morning the St. Albans into which Surratt and his traveling companion were ejected by Conductor Hobart was a nest of detectives on the lookout for John Harrison Surratt, Jr., or any other suspected conspirator trying to reach Canada. Surratt told the Rockville crowd that his Garibaldi[703] jacket and round-top hat, "peculiar to Canada," "guarded me safely through St. Albans."[704]

I went in [to St. Albans] with the others, and moved

around, with the detectives standing there most of the time looking at us. Of course I was obliged to talk as loud as anybody about the late tragedy.[705]

Surratt's mocking cynicism about Lincoln's murder even five years later is revealing. Any sympathy he may have shown was merely faked for purposes of making a clean getaway. Whether or not Surratt knew of the plan to kill the President before it happened, there can be little doubt that he wanted Lincoln dead and rejoiced when he heard the news. Like Jefferson Davis, Surratt had the *mens rea* – the "guilty mind" – for the crime.

According to what Surratt told ship's doctor McMillan, his breakfast in St. Albans was barely finished when a man rushed in proclaiming that a handkerchief belonging to "John H. Surratt" had just been found in the street.[706] Here is Surratt's version of what happened next:

> After having a hearty meal I lighted a cigar and walked up town. One of the detectives approached me, stared me directly in the face, and I looked him quietly back. In a few moments, I was speeding on my way to Montreal . . ..[707]

Surratt seems to undergo a transformation in St. Albans. He is put off the train as a penniless and "poorly clad" workingman,[708] and suddenly he has a nice breakfast, a good cigar, passes scrutiny as a Canadian gentleman, and then boards the train for Montreal. It seems likely that he met a Confederate contact, washed up, changed his clothes, and obtained some funds. It may even be that his contact was Mrs. Slater.[709]

What are we to make of all these conflicting details? Ultimately, it boils down to this: it was a dangerous and exciting chase, won not just by Surratt, but by Surratt and *those who supported him along the way*. This would become a common theme for Surratt's time as a fugitive from justice. He could not have succeeded without the well-organized and well-financed assistance he received.

At half-past noon on Tuesday, April 18, three names appear in the register of the St. Lawrence Hall in Montreal. One is "John Harrison." The second is "T.F. Hendrickson," the same alias who registered with

"Miss Slater" on January 10. The third, written in a tight hand, is "Miss H.C. Slater."[710] Lincoln was dead and Surratt was safely back in Montreal, apparently with the lady spy of his dreams at his side.

* * *

But could Surratt ever be safe from the consequences of so great a crime, even in Montreal? In those days, Montreal was a city of about one hundred thousand people – good sized for the time, but not big enough to allow a southern boy like Surratt completely to disappear.[711] Two days after he arrived, the United States Government announced a reward, emblazoned on posters and handbills carried everywhere, even into Canada. Surratt's photo was at the top next to John Wilkes Booth himself. In lurid typeface, these posters proclaimed: "$100,000 REWARD! THE MURDERER of our late beloved President, Abraham Lincoln, IS STILL AT LARGE." Fifty thousand dollars was offered for the apprehension of Booth. Twenty-five thousand dollars was offered "for the apprehension of John H. Surratt, one of Booth's accomplices." "Liberal rewards" would be paid for any information leading to Surratt's capture.[712] Surratt's run for his life was just beginning. But how could he run from the prison that held his mother?

[647] *Rockville Lecture*, Weichmann, p.434.
[648] 1 JHS Trial 492-93.
[649] 1 JHS Trial 498-99.
[650] *Trial of the Conspirators*, p.141.
[651] 1 JHS Trial 499-500.
[652] *Rockville Lecture*, Weichmann, p.434.
[653] *Ibid.*
[654] *McMillan Judiciary Testimony*, p.13.
[655] *Rockville Lecture*, Weichmann, p.434.
[656] *Ibid.*, pp.431-32.
[656] Swanson & Weinberg, p.45 (reprinting *New York Herald*, morning edition, April 15, 1865).
[656] *Rockville Lecture*, Weichmann, p.435.
[659] *Ibid.*
[660] *Ibid.*
[661] *Ibid.*
[662] 1 JHS Trial 725, 726.
[663] *Ibid.*, p.726.

664 *Ibid.*, p.725.
665 *Ibid.*; 2 JHS Trial 729.
666 1 JHS Trial 725.
667 *Ibid.*, p.724.
668 *Rockville Lecture*, Weichmann, p.436.
669 *Ibid.*; 2 JHS Trial 748, 761-62, 766.
670 *Rockville Lecture*, Weichmann, pp.436-37.
671 *Come Retribution*, pp.175-76.
672 *Rockville Lecture*, Weichmann, p.436.
673 *Ibid.*, p.437.
674 *Ibid.*
675 *Ibid.*, pp. 437-38; 1 JHS Trial 174-75.
676 *American Tragedy*, p.124.
677 *Trial of the Conspirators*, p.121.
678 1 JHS Trial 332.
679 *Ibid.*, pp.332-33.
680 *Ibid.*, pp.350, 486.
681 *Ibid.*, p.332.
682 *Ibid.*, pp. 332-33, 335.
683 *Trial of the Conspirators*, p.132.
684 *Ibid.*, p.138.
685 *E.g.*, *American Tragedy*, p.126.
686 *Trial of the Conspirators*, p.131.
687 Weichmann, pp.121-22; 1 JHS Trial 715.
688 *American Tragedy*, p.127.
689 *Trial of the Conspirators*, p.132.
690 *Statements, Mary Surratt 4/17*, p.43.
691 *Ibid.*, pp. 33-34.
692 *Ibid.*, p.34.
693 1 JHS Trial 374-75.
694 *Ibid.*, pp.236-39.
695 *Ibid.*, pp.676-83.
696 *Rockville Lecture*, Weichmann, p.437.
697 *Thoughts on Slater*, p.5.
698 1 JHS Trial 169-70.
699 *Ibid.*, p.170.
700 *Ibid.*, pp.170-71.
701 *Ibid.*, p.170.
702 *Ibid.*, pp.170-71.
703 He actually used the term "Oxford" jacket, which is what the Garibaldi was called in Canada. *Rockville Lecture*, Weichmann, p.438; 1 JHS Trial 473.
704 *Rockville Lecture*, Weichmann, p.438.

[705] *Ibid.*

[706] 1 JHS Trial 472. Detective Bigley also thinks that the handkerchief was found in St. Albans, not in Burlington, but he says that Holohan told him he had lost it. 2 JHS Trial 931-32.

[707] *Rockville Lecture*, Weichmann, p.438.

[708] 1 JHS Trial 173.

[709] There is yet another version of Surratt's escape into Canada. Remember the suspect Pilgrim interview published in October 1885? There, Surratt endorses Hobart's testimony as "in the main correct," confirms that he and his companion were temporarily without means, refuses to identify the mysterious traveling companion, and claims that they had to walk the "twelve or fifteen miles" north from St. Albans, after which they "were for the moment safe and in funds at once." *Pilgrim*, pp.5-6. This would suggest that their Confederate savior awaited them just over the border beyond Franklin. However, I don't believe *Pilgrim* is genuine.

[710] *St. Lawrence Hall Register* (April 18, 1865); *ibid.* (Jan. 10, 1865).

[711] Population 90,323 in 1860 and 107,225 in 1870, *Montreal History by Date*, http://www.imtl.org/montreal/histoire.php?periode=1860 & http://www.imtl.org/montreal/histoire.php?periode=1870 (accessed Jan. 22, 2014).

[712] Swanson & Weinberg, *Lincoln's Assassins*, p.50; *Henry B. Ste. Marie v. the United States*, US Court of Claims, *Amended Petition*, pp.1-2 (May 6, 1873).

Young John H. Surratt, Jr., circa 1861-64; *courtesy Surratt House Museum, Clinton, MD / MNCPP.*

SURRATTSVILLE, THE HOME OF JOHN H. SURRATT.—[SKETCHED BY A. M'CALLEN.]

Wood engraving Surrattsville, 1867, from *Harper's Weekly*; *Library of Congress.*

Young Louis J. Weichmann, circa 1861-67; *courtesy Surratt House Museum.*

Anna Surratt, date unknown;
courtesy Surratt House Museum.

Mary Surratt, circa 1851;
courtesy Surratt House Museum.

Surratt's Tavern porch;
photo by the author.

Mary Surratt House, 604 H St. NW, Washington, DC; *Library of Congress.*

Historical Marker; *photo by author.*

Lincoln's Second Inauguration, 1865, by Alexander Gardner; *Library of Congress.*

Howard's Livery Stables, 1865;
Library of Congress.

George A. Atzerodt, alias Port
Tobacco, 1865, by Alexander
Gardner; *Library of Congress.*

Lewis Powell, alias Payne,
Paine, Mosby, or Wood, 1865,
by Alexander Gardner;
Library of Congress.

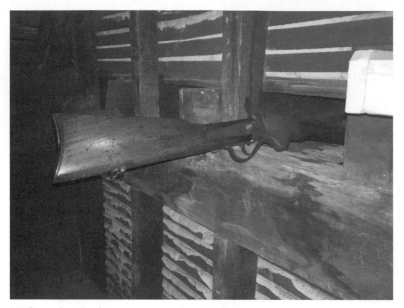

Hiding the Carbines,
Surratt's Tavern;
photo by Lindsey Horn,
*courtesy Surratt House
Museum.*

John H. Surratt, Jr.,
in Garibaldi jacket,
1866, by Mathew Brady;
Library of Congress.

JOHN H. SURRATT.

IN HIS CANADA JACKET,

Entered according to Act of Congress by JOHN H.
SURRATT, in the year 1868, in the Clerk's Office of
the District Court of the District of Columbia.

Clock in
reconstructed Ford's
Theatre lobby;
photo by author.

Microfilm of
St. Lawrence Hall
register, Montreal,
April 18, 1865;
*courtesy James O. Hall
Research Center at
Surratt House
Museum.*

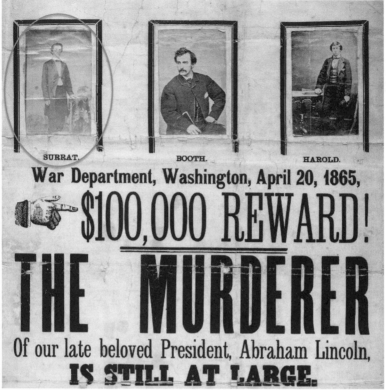

U.S. Government Assassination Wanted Poster, circa April 20, 1865 (cropped); *Library of Congress.*

Hanging of the conspirators (L to R) Mrs. Surratt, Powell, Herold, Atzerodt, July 7, 1865, *by Alexander Gardner; Library of Congress.*

John H. Surratt, Jr., in Zouave uniform, 1867, by Alexander Gardner; *Library of Congress.*

Prison cell door, Veroli, Italy; *photo by the author.*

Veroli, Italy, looking down at the twin wings of the old barracks/prison, connected by a courtyard with Palladian arches; *photo by the author.*

Looking down the steep embankment near where Surratt made his famous leap; *photo by the author.*

A fraudulent "penny-dreadful" account of the famous fugitive's exploits, 1866; Frederick A. Brady publisher, New York.

Hon. George P. Fisher, presiding judge, Surratt trial; *National Archives and Records Administration (NARA).*

The Surratt Jury, 1867, by J. Orville Johnson; *Library of Congress.*

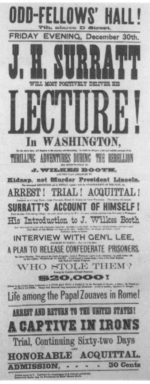

Poster for December 30, 1870, Odd Fellows' Hall Lecture, Washington, DC; *Brown University Digital Repository.*

John H. Surratt in old age, circa 1912-1916; *Courtesy Surratt House Museum.*

CHAPTER THIRTEEN

SURRATT'S CHOICE

SURRATT WAS TOO HOT EVEN FOR ST. LAWRENCE HALL TO HANDLE. Within minutes of his arrival he called on "a friend" – most likely Confederate General Edwin G. Lee – who, in Surratt's words, "advised me to make myself scarce."[713]   General Lee's diary is not helpful because he left this eventful day entirely blank.[714] But it appears that Surratt gathered up his things immediately after his arrival, told the desk clerk that he was bound for Quebec City, but then hid out in General Lee's suite of rooms, waiting for dark.[715] Surratt beguiled his Rockville audience with his story of what happened later when he refused to come down for tea:

> One of the ladies remarked, "I expect you have got Booth
> in there." "Perhaps so," [my friend] answered laughingly.
> That was rather close guessing.[716]

As soon as night fell, Surratt (and perhaps also Nettie Slater) moved under cover of darkness to the house of John Porterfield.[717] Mr. Porterfield was formerly a banker in Nashville who had become a successful Montreal merchant with a large house located at One Prince of Wales Terrace, just behind the Roman Catholic Bishop's palace.[718] Probably because Porterfield was also known as an agent for the Confederacy,[719] even his well-heeled residence could not safely keep Surratt for long. By Wednesday or Thursday, April 19 or 20, Federal detectives had placed Mr. Porterfield's home under surveillance, and it was necessary to devise a plan of escape.[720]

According to the testimony of ship's doctor McMillan:

> [Surratt] said that one evening two carriages were driven in
> front of Mr. Porterfield's house, and that he, and another
> party dressed nearly as he was, came out at the same time,
> and got one into one carriage, and the other in the other,
> and drove off, one carriage driving one way and the other
> in the other.[721]

Researcher John F. Stanton speculates that the identically dressed second "man" was not a man at all, but was instead Nettie Slater.[722] While that is a romantic possibility, we'll never know.

Where did Surratt go next? The key was to place him with someone who was totally reliable yet not obviously associated with the Confederacy. The man who came to mind was John J. Reeves, the Montreal tailor who had made Surratt's Garibaldi jacket. As a native Canadian and working-class tradesman, Reeves was not immediately known to Union agents and his lodgings were inconspicuous. According to Mr. Reeves' testimony, Surratt spent the next two or three days with him, until Saturday.[723]

During this time General Lee was providing for Surratt, alias "Charley Armstrong." According to Lee's diary, either on April 19 or 20 he paid "Charley" $40 expenses, and $100 for "services."[724] His later offer of proof states that this payment was in exchange for "sketches of the . . . prison approaches, the numbering of the forces, etc.," at Elmira.[725] The diary evidences two other payments of $100 made to "Charley," and though that's not very much, events suggest that this was merely the visible tip of an iceberg of support, both financial and operational.[726] Circumstances had made Surratt too important to be abandoned, even by a Confederacy that was itself coming undone.

* * *

From April 20 to approximately April 26, Weichmann was in and out of Montreal with a team of detectives. Their mission was to find and apprehend Surratt, international borders be damned.[727] The actual effect of their presence may have been the opposite. Surratt credits

Weichmann with inadvertently facilitating his escape from Mr. Porterfield's. Perhaps following one of the decoy carriages from Porterfield's, Weichmann sent detectives northward as Surratt went the other way.[728] According to Special Agent C.W. Taylor's report of his doings in Canada, the Chief of Police interrogated a lorry driver named Charles Lorin, who took three men north from Mr. Porterfield's, over Recollet Bridge to the village of St. Vincent de Paul. There he let them out, and they walked away across the fields.[729] There is no indication that Surratt was one of these men.

An intense game of cat-and-mouse was on, in which the mouse outsmarted the cats at every turn. According to Surratt:

> One day I walked out and I saw Weichman [*sic.*] on the lookout for me. He had little idea I was so near.[730]

Apparently Weichmann then swallowed the bait left at St. Lawrence Hall by Surratt about Quebec City. On Friday, April 21 – one week after the assassination – Weichmann and Detective Bigley went to Quebec City in search of Surratt, while Holohan and McDevitt went in the same direction as far as Trois-Rivières.[731]

Surratt was still in Montreal. But that Friday may have been the night that Mr. Reeves returned home at about eleven o'clock to tell Surratt that detectives had offered him $20,000 to disclose Surratt's hiding place.[732] Although Surratt says that Mr. Reeves was directly suspected of hiding him, it seems that if the detectives really knew that much then they would have captured him at the Reeves shop or lodgings. More likely, the detectives were offering a reward all around Montreal. While no reward would have been sufficient to buy off the incorruptible Mr. Reeves, a general offer of $20,000 would have made Surratt's position in populous Montreal untenable.

Surratt was hustled out of Montreal between five and six o'clock in the afternoon of Saturday, April 22.[733] Disguised as a huntsman,[734] Surratt departed in a carriage in the company of Mr. Reeves, the unnamed brother of Father Larcille Lapierre, and a man named Mettevie.[735] Mr. Reeves went with them about thirteen miles to a tavern at Longue-Pointe, towards the southeast along the St. Lawrence in the present-day Mercier-Hochelaga-Maisonneuve borough of Montreal.[736] Mr. Reeves returned, leaving Surratt there in the company of the unnamed brother and Mr. Mettevie.[737]

Surratt says that he was carried by canoe across the St. Lawrence river, and then guided by an unnamed woman to a village lying about forty-five miles southeast of Montreal.[738] He had been brought to the tiny hamlet of St. Liboire, and into the protection of the parish priest, Rev. Father Charles Boucher. According to Father Boucher, Surratt arrived by wagon between nine and ten o'clock on the night of April 22.[739] He was brought to Father Boucher by Joseph F. DuTilly, a local farmer who had at times lived with and rented from the priest.[740] Father Boucher makes no mention of a woman arriving with Surratt. Surratt clearly says he was guided by a woman, yet Boucher says that he arrived in the company of a man, DuTilly. If Slater was along for the journey, it is unlikely that the priest would have revealed that fact. Perhaps Surratt's reference to a woman guide was spun from a kernel of truth about Nettie Slater, but this is merely an educated guess.

Surratt was introduced to Father Boucher by the alias "Charles Armstrong." Father Boucher was told that Mr. Armstrong was in Canada on account of his health, and having been compromised in the war.[741] Mr. Armstrong was hidden in a separate bedroom partitioned off from the parlor, where he convalesced due to ill health.[742]

Surratt's stay with the priest had been prearranged in writing prior to his arrival,[743] which suggests that it was not only the Confederate Government, but also the Catholic Church (at least in Quebec), that had taken an interest in protecting Surratt. Recall that Surratt's connection to Canadian priests goes back to his school days at St. Charles College in Maryland. Father Lapierre not only arranged Surratt's transport to and lodging with Father Boucher, but he was also among the few visitors Surratt received during his time in St. Liboire.[744] Father Lapierre's involvement is strong evidence that the involvement of the Catholic Church was not purely localized, because Lapierre served as Canon to Ignace Bourget, the Catholic Bishop of Montreal.[745]

Within about ten or twelve days, Father Boucher began to suspect that "Armstrong" was really the "John H. Surratt" repeatedly mentioned in the newspapers, who was wanted in connection with the

Lincoln assassination.[746] He asked "Armstrong" if he was Surratt, and Surratt admitted it.[747] Nonetheless, he kept Surratt hidden in his lodgings in St. Liboire for three full months without disclosing his identity or whereabouts.[748] When asked why he answered simply, "[b]ecause I believed him innocent."[749] Surratt had found the perfect hidey-hole, deep in the bosom of the Catholic Church, safe from the powerful storm consuming his mother and the other known conspirators.[750]

* * *

According to Paragraph 148 of General Order 100 of the War Department, April 24, 1863, entitled "Assassination":

> The law of war does not allow proclaiming either an individual belonging to the hostile army, or a citizen . . ., an outlaw, who may be slain with out trial by any captor, any more than the modern law of peace allows such international outlawry; on the contrary, it abhors such outrage. The sternest retaliation should follow the murder committed in consequence of such proclamation, made by whatever authority. Civilized nations look with horror upon offers of rewards for the assassination of enemies, as relapses into barbarism.[751]

On May 1, 1865 President Andrew Johnson issued an executive order requiring the War Department to establish a military tribunal composed of nine military officers to try "persons implicated in the murder of the late President, Abraham Lincoln, and the attempted assassination of the Honorable William H. Seward, Secretary of State, and in an alleged conspiracy to assassinate other officers of the Federal Government at Washington City, and their aiders and abettors . . .."[752] A military tribunal was quickly assembled, and the accused, David E. Herold, George A. Atzerodt, Samuel Arnold, Lewis "Payne" (Powell), Michael O'Laughlen, Edward Spangler, Samuel A. Mudd – *and Mary E. Surratt* – first appeared before it on Tuesday, May 9, 1865.[753] On May 10, the charges were read against them, accusing the defendants of "maliciously" and "traitorously" conspiring with "John H. Surratt, John Wilkes Booth, Jefferson Davis, George N. Sanders [Canada], Beverly Tucker [Canada], Jacob Thompson [Canada]," and others, "within the Military Department of Washington," to murder Abraham Lincoln, President and Commander-in-Chief, Andrew Johnson, Vice-President, William H. Seward, Secretary of State, and General Ulysses S. Grant, commander of the United States Army.[754] Mrs. Surratt was additionally charged that, between March 6 and April 20, 1865, she did "receive, entertain, harbor, and conceal, aid and assist the said John Wilkes Booth, David E. Herold, Lewis "Payne," John H. Surratt, Michael O'Laughlen, George H. Atzerodt, Samuel Arnold, and their confederates, with the knowledge of the murderous and traitorous conspiracy . . . , and with intent to aid, abet, and assist them in the execution thereof, and in escaping from justice after the murder of . . . Abraham Lincoln . . .."[755]

* * *

The military trial was reported diligently in the American press, as well as in the Canadian newspapers in consequence not only of the immensity of the crime, but also the alleged Canadian connection.[756] There is no question that Surratt could have had access to ongoing press reports on the military trial through Father Boucher and the Confederate and Catholic networks that were supporting and hiding him. General Edwin Lee received regular reports on what he called "the farcical court of death" from his friend Henry Kyd Douglas, as well as from an array of newspapers.[757] He also met with Father Lapierre on May 4, after which he sent $100 to "Charley."[758] Certainly, of all matters on earth, the military trial would be the one of greatest interest to Surratt, and it is difficult to imagine that he would not have sought out every scrap of intelligence he could lay his hands on concerning events back in Washington.

If he did, then within days of the May 10th reading of charges Surratt must have known that his mother was accused of conspiring with himself and with Booth in the murder of Lincoln, and that she was on trial for her life. The most damning testimony against Mrs. Surratt was given by John Lloyd on May 13 and May 15, and it was widely reported, so Surratt should have known about that too.[759] On May 23, the *Washington Chronicle* reported that:

> [A] great change has come over Mrs. Surratt. For the first time we read unmistakable letters upon her still features, the record of an ineffable woe. It is not fear, it is not excitement of a mighty doubt, but withering, blasting woe.[760]

Likely, this and similar accounts of his mother's suffering also reached Surratt, either though a couriered copy of the *Washington Chronicle*, or by the common practice of newspapers of the time reprinting stories from other papers. Other reports of his mother's torments at the Old Capitol Prison and then at the Penitentiary at the United States Arsenal – which included confinement to a seven by three and one-half foot cell and filthy rodent-infested conditions – must have reached Surratt after his sister Anna was released from prison on May 11, and although he would have been gratified to learn that his mother had been transferred to a larger cell on May 5, any caring son would still have to have been weighed down by the magnitude of her suffering.[761] Press reports of her soft moans emanating from behind a dark veil during the long trial sessions, clad in a heavy long dress in the hot, fetid air of a Washington summer, were a regular feature of the time. Also reported were the insults and taunts aimed at her – "Isn't she a devil?" and "I hope they'll hang her" – followed by cruel laughter.[762] And although from May 25-26 no fewer than five Catholic priests took the stand to testify as to Mrs. Surratt's piety and good character, this evidence was overwhelmed by the admitted evidence of the many "war crimes" of the South, including mistreatment of Union prisoners, which added fuel to the already vociferous cries for public vengeance.[763] This evidence, too, should have reached Surratt's attention. And so, by the end of May – some five weeks before Mrs. Surratt was hanged – Surratt must have recognized that his mother was in mortal peril.

With one exception not relevant here, the military tribunal's evidence closed June 14.[764] From June 27 to 28, Special Judge Advocate John A. Bingham delivered a searing rebuttal argument on behalf of the

Government. The June 28th portion of Judge Bingham's argument directed at the conduct of Mary E. Surratt summarized all the evidence against her with devastating effect.[765] "By the time . . . [Bingham] had finished, he had expunged any hope that the prisoners may have held."[766] If Surratt was paying attention, and if he obtained a newspaper on June 29 or 30, he would have had no cause for optimism as to her possible acquittal; at most, he might have hoped that she would be spared the death penalty. And although the trial was over, it was still not too late for Surratt to attempt to trade his surrender for leniency towards his mother.

* * *

But Surratt claims that he did not understand any of this. Here is his version of the events:

> It has been asserted over and over again, and for the purpose of damning me in the estimation of every honest man, that I deserted her who gave me birth in the direst hour of her need. Truly would I have merited the execration of every man had such been the case. But such was not the case. . . . [U]pon my arrival . . . [at St. Liboire] I wrote to my friends in Montreal to keep me posted in regard to the approaching trial, and to send me the newspapers regularly. I received letters from them frequently, in all of which they assured me there was no cause of anxiety; that it was only a matter of time, and it would all be well. After a while papers did not come so regularly, and those that did, spoke very encouragingly. A little while afterwards, when they came, sentences were mutilated with ink and pen.[767]

This is the foundation of Surratt's defense against the great charge of matricide by neglect. He relied upon "his friends" – meaning General Lee and the Confederate and Catholic networks – to keep him informed, but instead they only sent him the good news, and hid from him the bad.

Surratt must have known he was being duped when he saw the pen-

and-ink redactions to the newspapers he was given. As a man of action, what did he do? First, "I protested," and the result was that "for some time I received no papers at all."[768] That should have been a clue that something serious was wrong. Becoming uneasy, Surratt says that he wrote and signed an article for publication in the *New York World*, which he sent to his "friends" in Montreal, and that was the last anyone ever saw of it (if it even existed in the first place).[769] It is certainly credible that Surratt might have written an article in an attempt to save his mother, and that the revelations it may have contained could have been vetoed by General Lee. But on the other hand, if Surratt were simply to assert her innocence without implicating others, wouldn't that have served the Confederate cause by throwing a monkey wrench into the machinery of military justice clanking away in Washington? And if he did write an article that was censored, then Surratt must have known that his handlers were controlling the flow of information outward, from which he could easily deduce that they were also controlling the flow of information in to him.

Surratt nonetheless let things go "for some time."[770] It was not until June – after his mother's defense in chief had been presented[771] – that Surratt determined to send an emissary to Washington to get in contact with his mother's lawyers to discover for himself "how the case stood; if there was any danger; and also, to communicate with me if my presence was necessary . . .."[772] "[T]he suspense and anxiety" of Surratt's mind while waiting for a response was excruciating: "I imagined . . . all kinds of things; yet I was powerless to act."[773] But at last, "in the latter part of June," Surratt's emissary returned, "so bright and cheerful . . . that I confess one-half of my fears were dispelled."[774] The message brought back from defense counsel was this:

> "Be under no apprehension as to any serious consequences. Remain perfectly quiet, as any action on your part would only tend to make matters worse. If you can be of any service to us, we will let you know; but keep quiet."[775]

Reverend Father J.A. Walter, who stayed with Mrs. Surratt all the long night before her execution, and took her final confession and statement of innocence made on death's doorstep,[776] read a statement to the United States Catholic Historical Society of New York on May 25, 1891 that includes the following:

> [Surratt] has been accused of deserting his poor mother. This is not true. He sent a person to Washington, furnished him means, and was ready to give himself up in her defence [*sic*.]. This friend saw the counsel of his mother. They advised the friend to return and tell John H. Surratt to remain in Canada, for there was no danger that his mother would be convicted.[777]

Whether Father Walter knew this upon his own personal knowledge, or was merely relying upon Surratt's Rockville lecture, is not clear. But this account seems to make express what is only implied in Surratt's version: that he would be willing to surrender if it would save his mother. The priest then dismisses this offer as foolhardy:

> Everyone knows that had he come to Washington he would have been placed in the docks with the other prisoners and condemned with them. Prudence and common sense demanded the course he followed.[778]

There is – of course! – yet another version of Surratt's overture on behalf of his mother. According to the July 7, 1865 edition of the *Constitutional Union*, during the military trial Mrs. Surratt's defense counsel wrote to Secretary of War Stanton, proposing to bring John H. Surratt down from Canada to testify as a witness for the defense, in exchange for an informal pledge to Surratt of "pardon" (so says the newspaper; possibly they mean "immunity," which is temporary). The article states that counsel for the defense believes that John Surratt would testify that his mother knew nothing of any plot against Lincoln. The offer was rejected "on the ground that Surratt was so deeply implicated in the conspiracy . . . that he could not, under any circumstances, receive a pardon."[779] Thus, under the *Constitutional Union* report, Surratt would not freely surrender himself to save his mother, but would only appear on condition of his own personal immunity from prosecution.

This was the view of pro-Union correspondent George Alfred Townsend, who covered Surratt's trial in 1867. In an article Townsend wrote in 1868, he echoed the by-then familiar refrain that Surratt was a "cowardly deserter of his mother," but added a fascinating detail that I have not seen corroborated by any other source:

> Like Probst, the Philadelphia murderer, who brained the infants because he 'lost courage to spare them' after killing the parents, Surratt had to let his mother swing. He did come as far as Baltimore to get the earliest news of her execution, which was described in very satisfactory detail by the correspondents.[780]

The highly suspect Pilgrim interview completely omits any mention of any overture towards Surratt's surrender.[781] This is almost enough to discount its authenticity. On the other hand, it is possible that the mission to Washington was a creature of Surratt's yearning – what he wished he had done rather than what he actually did – and that he had forgotten the story he told in 1870 by the time he was supposedly interviewed in 1885. Here are the events as allegedly told by Surratt to the correspondent called "Pilgrim":

> Now let me solemnly say that I never knew that my mother was in serious danger. I deemed it only a matter of time – a few months – when she should, by reason of the revulsion of public feeling, be released. In that belief I was confirmed by those about me who insisted that she was to be discharged and kept the newspapers away from me. When I head that she was sentenced to death, I was absolutely crazy. I was restrained by force – physical force which I tried to overcome – from coming to the States, if not to save, to die with her. Alas, I could not do it![782]

Thus, Pilgrim disagrees with Surratt's Rockville account in another important particular. According to Pilgrim, Surratt knew of his mother's fate before she was hanged, but was physically restrained from going to her aid.

* * *

Again, we are left with a welter of conflicting stories. The best we can do is apply deductive reasoning to tease out the most likely truth. First, it is logical that General Lee and the others guarding Surratt would want to shield him from the truth. He was a valuable asset, and they did not want him compromised. On the other hand, it does not seem that a man of John Surratt's intellect and capabilities could be shielded from that which he truly wanted to know. Nor does it seem likely that, once knowing it, he could be kept from acting unless he did not want to act. He was the young soldier of fortune, and who was to hold him back? A middle-aged priest?!

For these reasons, I believe that Surratt made a calculated choice – a kind of reverse *"Sophie's Choice"* – to remain intentionally oblivious and to let his mother stand at risk of possible hanging in order to save himself or to avoid a scenario in which they both might hang. "Surratt's Choice" was to let himself believe it would all work out for the best, because any other choice would almost certainly place his own neck in the noose, even if it might save his mother.

Surratt himself tips his hand about the choice he made, however reluctantly, when he says of the advice brought back by his emissary and by others among his supporters:

> I certainly felt greatly relieved, *though not entirely satisfied.* This news reached me some time in the latter part of June, just before the party of gentlemen . . . arrived. They, too, assured me there was no cause for fear. *What else could I do but accept these unwavering assurances? Even had I thought otherwise, I could not have taken any action resulting in good.*[783]

There's the nub of it: *a choice*, justified by the argument that giving himself up to try to save his mother could do no good.

But can this rationale withstand analysis? Father Walter may have been correct that, had Surratt ventured to Washington in order to testify in defense of his mother, they would have convicted and hanged them both. Like the insatiable beast it had become in the weeks immediately following the unspeakable attack upon it, a wounded government might well have gobbled up the son without spitting back the mother, and licked its lips. *But of course, we cannot know that, and neither could Surratt.* It seems equally likely that the Government would have been willing to take the death penalty off the table for Mrs. Surratt in exchange for John Surratt's surrender with no strings attached. Next to Booth, Surratt had always been the prize, at the top of the wanted poster right next to the triggerman himself. Hanging a woman was anathema to the Nineteenth Century code of paternalism anyway. Imprisonment of Mrs. Surratt for some stiff term would satisfy public justice, especially if Booth's right-hand man, the very fellow who had brought the gold and possibly an order to kill from Richmond, could take her place on the gallows.

If, as Surratt allegedly maintained in private, his mother was perfectly innocent,[784] then of course he could have done some good by giving himself up. He could have served the highest ends of justice by doing everything in his power to try to prevent the execution of an innocent woman falsely accused of his own crime. This is something any guilty man ought to do, but when that man is the son of the supposedly innocent woman, how much higher the duty! Success or failure was not the point. The point was that everything morality, religion and filial love means demands that the effort be made.

A frequently overlooked fly in the ointment is that *there is no record of Surratt maintaining his mother's innocence in public.* A careful reading of the Rockville lecture, and even the suspect Pilgrim interview, discloses that Surratt does not directly assert his mother's innocence.[785] Surratt does not say in Pilgrim that he deemed it only a matter of time that his mother would be released *due to her innocence*, but only due to "the revulsion of public feeling."[786] It fell to Powell, of all people, to repeatedly assert Mrs. Surratt's innocence in the days leading up to the execution.[787] Powell's belief apparently stemmed from an incident in which he mentioned something touching on the plot in the family's presence, and Surratt took him aside to angrily upbraid him, saying that neither his mother nor his sister knew anything of it, and that he didn't want them to know.[788] This generality does not, however, absolve the specific actions later attributed to Mrs. Surratt. Those could only have been carried out with a specific knowledge of the weapons hidden by her son, and the timing of the ongoing plot.

Surratt's failure to proclaim his mother's innocence leads to a startling conclusion: *Surratt's Choice makes the most sense if they were both guilty.* If Mary Surratt were innocent of all involvement in the plot, then the pressure on her son to save her would be virtually irresistible. But if Mary Surratt, like John Surratt, knowingly entered into a plot against Lincoln with all its attendant risks, then she like he – and like Booth himself – was but another Confederate doing her duty, come what may. It was of course psychologically traumatizing to leave her to face the consequences, but the risks were the risks. There was no point in compromising two valuable Confederate assets just because one was already compromised. Better to let her take her chances with the leniency of the tribunal, or the President. Her chances were better than his anyway, by virtue of her age and gender. And so, it appears that Surratt made a calculated choice – one that nearly drove him mad. But the fact that he dealt with Surratt's Choice for the rest of his life by denial and by placing the blame on others – his "friends," Andrew Johnson, Louis Weichmann – does not mean that he did not make the choice.

We may assume that Mrs. Surratt concurred in her son's decision. Few mothers would choose to spare their own lives at the expense of the life of one of their children. Aside from the purported message from her lawyers, which might not even have emanated from her, we do not have direct confirmation of this. What's more, it does not change Surratt's culpability, any more than a person is exonerated from homicide by the victim's request to be killed. Ultimately, as a prisoner, Mrs. Surratt was not in control of the choice anyway. Her son was the one who was free. *It was John Surratt's choice.*

* * *

Surratt told his Rockville audience that he was just leaving St. Liboire for a hunting excursion when a man handed him a newspaper.

Based on Surratt's account, it would have been the afternoon of the hangings:

> That paper informed me that on a day which was then present, and at an hour which had then come and gone, the most hellish of deeds was to be enacted. It had been determined upon and carried out, even before I had intimation that there was any danger. It would be folly for me to attempt to describe my feelings. After gazing at the paper for some time I dropped it on the floor, turning on my heel, and going directly to the house where I had been stopping before. When I entered the room, I found my friend sitting there. As soon as he saw me, he turned deadly pale, but never uttered a word. I said, "You doubtless thought you were acting a friend . . . towards me, but you have deceived me. I may forgive you, but I can never forget it."[789]

Surratt never did forget it. How could he? Surratt's Choice had become as irrevocable as death itself.

[713] *Rockville Lecture*, Weichmann, p.438.

[714] *Lee Diary* (April 18, 1865). Mrs. Levin, author of *This Awful Drama*, asserts that the page was torn out, *E.G.Lee*, p.154, but that is not how I view the photocopy of the microfilm I've looked at. Perhaps she saw the original and has the better view.

[715] *Rockville Lecture*, Weichmann, p.438; JOH Papers - C.W. Taylor, *Report of Proceedings in Canada*, p.2.

[716] *Rockville Lecture*, Weichmann, p.438.

[717] 1 JHS Trial 472; *Rockville Lecture*, Weichmann, p.438.

[718] *E.G. Lee*, pp.154-55; JOH Papers - C.W. Taylor, *Report of Proceedings in Canada*, p.2.

[719] 1 JHS Trial 472.

[720] *Ibid.*

[721] *Ibid.*

[722] John F. Stanton, *Some Thoughts on Sarah Slater*, p.6, *Surratt Courier*, vol. XXXII No.2 (Feb. 2007).

[723] 2 JHS Trial 845, 895.

724 *Lee Diary* (April 19, 1865).

725 *E.G. Lee Offer of Proof* ¶2.

726 *Lee Diary*, May 4 ($100), Sept. 5 ($100).

717 1 JHS Trial 709, 711.

728 *Rockville Lecture*, Weichmann, p.438.

729 JOH Papers - C.W. Taylor, *Report of Proceedings in Canada*, p.2.

730 *Rockville Lecture*, Weichmann, p.438.

731 1 JHS Trial 398, 684.

732 *Ibid.*

733 2 JHS Trial 845, 895. Although one account places the time of departure at half past ten o'clock at night, this account seems to mix the departure from Mr. Porterfield's with the departure from Mr. Reeves', and is therefore unreliable on this point. JOH Papers - C.W. Taylor, *Report of Proceedings in Canada*, p.2.

734 *Rockville Lecture*, Weichmann, p.438.

735 2 JHS Trial 842, 845.

736 2 JHS Trial 842.

737 2 JHS Trial 845-46.

738 *Rockville Lecture*, Weichmann, p.438.

739 *Ibid.*; 1 JHS Trial 473; 2 JHS Trial 903. Surratt positively states that he arrived at three o'clock in the morning on a Wednesday, which would have to be April 26. *Rockville Lecture*, Weichmann, p.438. Surratt is fairly bad with dates and this does not jibe with testimony by Rev. Boucher that Surratt arrived on April 22, and testimony of Mr. Reeves about the duration of Surratt's stay. Oddly, however, Rev. Boucher says that Surratt arrived on April 22, but then later says that he arrived on Wednesday evening around nine or ten o'clock. 2 JHS Trial 895, 903. So, perhaps Surratt left Reeves on Saturday, April 22, and laid over somewhere, not arriving at Boucher's until Wednesday, April 26. Perhaps Surratt did originally go to Trois-Rivières, and stayed a short time at the monastery attached to the church of St. Antoine located there. Special Agent C.W. Taylor reports that he tracked Surratt to this monastery, where they had suspended their usual custom of openness by barring the gates to all visitors for several days. JOH Papers - C.W. Taylor, *Report of Proceedings in Canada*, pp.3-5.

740 2 JHS Trial 857-59, 895, 902.

741 *Ibid.*

742 1 JHS Trial 473; *E.G. Lee*, pp.165-66.

743 2 JHS Trial 903.

744 2 JHS Trial 904.

745 Alexander Lee Levin, *Who Hid John H. Surratt? Maryland Historical Magazine*, vol. 60 no.2, p.178 (June 1965) (hereafter "*Who Hid Surratt?*").

[746] 2 JHS Trial 903-04.

[747] 2 JHS Trial 914.

[748] 2 JHS Trial 906.

[749] 2 JHS Trial 914.

[750] Catholics served honorably on both sides in the Civil War, probably in greater numbers in the Union Army. Acton Institute, Religion & Liberty, *Onward Catholic Soldiers: The Catholic Church During the American Civil War*, http://www.acton.org/pub/religion-liberty/volume-21-number-4/onward-catholic-soldiers-catholic-church-during-am (accessed Jan. 15, 2014). The Church tried to steer a middle course, stating in 1861 that it was above politics, and that the Catholic "unity of spirit" recognized "no North, no South, no East, no West." *Ibid.* But by 1863 the Emancipation Proclamation had alienated even Archbishop of New York John J. Hughes, Carl Sandburg, *Abraham Lincoln: The War Years*, vol. 1, p.568 (Harcourt Brace 1939), and Pope Pius IX wrote a very sympathetic letter to Jefferson Davis, addressing him as "President, Confederate States of America," thus seeming to recognize his separate nation. *Correspondence Between His Holiness Pope Piux IX and President Jefferson Davis*, http://www.danvilleartillery.org/popeletter.htm (accessed Jan. 15, 2014). While I firmly disavow the bigoted nonsense promulgated by characters such as defrocked priest Charles P. Chiniquy about a supposed Jesuit conspiracy behind the Lincoln Assassination, it must be acknowledged that elements of the Church in Maryland, Canada and Europe - including Rome until the Pope finally put a stop to it - played an important role in supporting the Surratts after the fact.

[751] Pittman, p.418.

[752] *Trial of the Conspirators*, p.17.

[753] *Ibid.*, p.18.

[754] *Ibid.*, pp.18-21.

[755] *Ibid.*, p.20.

[756] E.g., *Waterloo Advertiser and Eastern Townships Advocate*, p.2 (Vol. 10, No. 25 Thursday, May 25, 1865) (reprinting charges against, *inter alia*, John H. Surratt and Mary E. Surratt; calling the trial "unquestionably one of the most remarkable and important that the world has seen," this edition reprints evidence of Surratt's trip to Richmond with "Mrs. Slader [*sic.*]" and return April 3 with money, as well as evidence against Mrs. Surratt).

[757] *E.G. Lee*, pp.163-65.

[758] *Who Hid Surratt?* pp.178-79.

[759] *Trial of the Conspirators*, pp.85-87.

[760] *American Tragedy*, p.167.

[761] *Ibid.*, pp.131-32, 139, 143, 145-46, 148.

[762] *Ibid.*, p.169.

[763] *Ibid.*, p.168; *Trial of the Conspirators*, pp.135-36.

[764] *Trial of the Conspirators*, p. ix.

[765] *Trial of the Conspirators*, pp.392-94.

[766] *American Tragedy*, p.199.

[767] *Rockville Lecture*, Weichmann, pp.438-39.

[768] *Ibid.*, p.439.

[769] *Ibid.*

[770] *Ibid.*

[771] *Trial of the Conspirators*, 124-36.

[772] *Rockville Lecture*, Weichmann, p.439.

[773] *Ibid.*

[774] *Ibid.*

[775] *Ibid.*

[776] *American Tragedy*, p.215-20.

[777] Weichmann, p.320.

[778] *Ibid.*

[779] JOH Papers - *Constitutional Union*, p.1 col.4 (July 7, 1865) (handwritten copy).

[780] *Townsend re: Trials of Surratt*, p. X-13.

[781] *Pilgrim*, p.6.

[782] *Ibid.*

[783] *Rockville Lecture*, Weichmann, p.439 (emphasis added).

[784] JOH Papers, *Letter from Henry B. Lee to "My dear Rebecca"* (Nov. 30, 1937), attributes to Surratt the statement that "his mother knew a group of young men were meeting in her basement, but nothing about their plans which were to kidnap Lincoln."

[785] This point is made in a *Washington Evening Star* editorial from December 16, 1870, *reprinted in*, Weichmann, pp.440-41 (hereafter "*Evening Star*, Dec. 16, Weichmann").

[786] *Pilgrim*, p.6.

[787] *American Tragedy*, pp. 209, 210.

[788] *Ibid.*, p.109, citing, *Daily Constitutional Union* (July 7, 1865).

[789] *Rockville Lecture*, Weichmann, p.440.

CHAPTER FOURTEEN

LOOSE LIPS ABOARD SHIP

Surratt told the Rockville audience that, after learning of the deception by his friends, it was his "intention to leave the place immediately."[790] If Surratt's friends had indeed been responsible for keeping news of his mother's impending execution from him, Surratt would justly have acted on this intention. But that does not appear to be what he actually did. Mrs. Surratt was executed on July 7, 1865. According to Father Boucher, Surratt did not leave the safety of his abode until "late July."[791] What's more, it was not anger about trickery by his protectors that forced him out; rather it was discovery.

Recall that Surratt's quarters were partitioned off from the sitting room in the priest's house. There was a hole cut in the partition to accommodate the chimney for the stove, leaving a vacant space about six or eight inches high behind the stove. According to the testimony of ship's doctor McMillan, Surratt told him that he was lying on the sofa in his bedchamber one day, when he was startled by the face of Boucher's servant girl, peering through the gap behind the stove to get a look at the priest's mysterious lodger. Surratt jumped up and ran towards the girl, who fled in terror.[792] But the damage was done.

According to McMillan, "[t]he story was immediately circulated around the village that the priest had a *woman* in his bed-room hiding."[793] Most researchers have dismissed the reference to "a woman" as either the servant girl's mistaken identification in her terror, or McMillan's mistake. That's possible, but with what we know of Nettie Slater's propensity for popping up wherever Surratt went, we cannot dismiss the other possible interpretation of this evidence: that the priest *did* have a woman in the house, and it was Mrs. Slater.[794]

* * *

Secretary of War Stanton had announced that all persons harboring or hiding Surratt would be treated as accessories after the fact in Lincoln's assassination. Soon after the incident with the serving girl, U.S. Government agents were combing through the countryside around St. Liboire.[795] Curiously, the Government still was receiving mixed signals, for on July 28th it arrested a man living in the mountains of Western Pennsylvania named Eugene T. Haines – and accused him of being John H. Surratt.[796] But things were hot enough around St. Liboire that Father Boucher "told [Surratt] that he could keep him no longer; that he must find other quarters."[797]

Surratt probably left in the company of trustworthy local guides, for he was able to elude his pursuers once again. Several accounts have him going directly back to Montreal, but that does not seem to be accurate. Perhaps spooked by his mother's hanging and his own brush with capture, Surratt ran far into the northern wilderness. Traveling with a young Canadian named Bouthillier, he made his way to Murray Bay, located along the St. Lawrence River about four hundred kilometers north-east of Montreal.[798]

It is a fair assumption that Murray Bay forever held a warm spot in Surratt's heart. Not only did he meet General Lee there on August 11, but also a beautiful young lady known in the General's diary as "Miss Young" from New York. Just as Surratt was "Charley Armstrong," "Miss Young" was probably Nettie Slater. Also in the party were Mr. John Lovell and his wife Sarah, and General Lee's witty cousin, Dan Lucas, who suffered from hyperkyphosis (known then as "hunchback"). They all stayed together, first at the Riverton Hotel, and then at the less public boardinghouse of Madame Barger on Grand Lake. That Friday and Saturday in August, "Armstrong" and "Young" boated, swam and fished together, their cares momentarily forgotten. At night General Lee and the Lovells played whist, likely joined by the young couple, who may have watched their elders impatiently for signs of drowsiness. Perhaps their summer idyll lasted a bit longer. From August 12-13,

General Lee, Dan Lucas and Boutillier boated up to Rivière-du-Loup, but there is no indication that either Miss Young or Mr. Armstrong joined them.[799]

* * *

General Lee, the Lovells, Dan Lucas, and their "fair companion" Miss Young, all departed for Quebec City on August 14, and arrived at Montreal on Tuesday, August 15. Surratt must have taken a different route, for he did not arrive in Montreal until Friday, August 18.[800] That night, General Lee took Miss Young to see Charles Kean in a farewell performance as Richard II, and also as Felix, in *The Wonder*.[801] The diary is silent as to whether Mr. "Armstrong" dared to show his face in the theatre that night.

Surratt was hidden on a quiet street behind the Catholic Bishop's Palace, at 116 Old Cemetery Street, in the home of the prosperous shoe merchant, André J. Lapierre. Lapierre's son was Father Larcille Lapierre, the Canon to Bishop Bourget, who had been coordinating Catholic Church protection for Surratt the entire time he had been a fugitive in Quebec. André J. Lapierre's other son was one of the men who had helped spirit Surratt out of Montreal back in April. Surratt occupied a pleasant second-floor room, overlooking the garden of the Bishop's Palace.[802]

On August 21, General Lee observed that Mr. Armstrong was "very devoted" to Miss Young, and so the General gallantly "made an opportunity for him in the Library." But that same night the General "had a very confidential conversation with 'the Young' after returning from theatre at 11 p.m."[803] A few days later, on August 25, Miss Young left Montreal, presumably to return to New York.[804]

Thus ends the last vestige of the suspected affair between Surratt and Slater – there is no documented meeting of the two for the remainder of their natural lives. No historical record explains the parting of Surratt and Mrs. Slater. One might presume that the affair ran the course of young love, burning hot but brief in the crucible of daring espionage. In the six months they had known one another, from February to August, they participated in one of the most successful plots in history – and got away with it. What more could they do? The external pressures on their relationship were intense. Surratt was a known fugitive, and although Slater's name had been bandied about in the military trial of the conspirators, none of Yankee officialdom had any idea where to find her. If she wanted to keep it that way, she would have to put distance between herself and John Surratt. And if Surratt were to continue to elude Federal pursuers, he would have to stay nimble and unencumbered.

Mrs. Slater never reunited with her husband, though he survived the war. Rowan Slater was granted a divorce on November 19, 1866. Poor lonely Rowan was left believing that his dear Nettie was dead.[805] Very much alive, she went on to marry her sister's widower, William Warren Spencer, and then outlived him. Sarah "Nettie" Gilbert / Slater / Reynaud / Kate Thompson / Kate Brown / Miss Young died a wealthy widow, of natural causes, in Poughkeepsie, New York on April 20, 1920, under the alias "Sarah A. Long."[806] The Government never caught up with her. Whatever her crimes, they died with her.

* * *

Holed up behind the Bishop's Palace in Montreal a mere sixty miles over the border, Surratt was feeling insecure. While attending mass at the Notre Dame Basilica of Montreal, Surratt read in the Catholic Newspaper *La Minèvre* of recruiting efforts by the Papal Zouaves – the army of the Pope, then at war with the forces of secular government represented by the Garibaldi movement. Surratt's martial instincts awakened at the thought of a new mission, and he discussed the possibility of enlisting with Father Lapierre. It was not long before Father Lapierre had obtained approval for Surratt's new mission and, together with General Lee, he arranged for Surratt's passage up the St. Lawrence and across the Atlantic.[807] This was a "win-win" scenario: Surratt would repay the Church for its support with his well-honed fighting skills, while effectively vanishing into the anonymous ranks of a distant army.

On the night of Friday, September 15, 1865, three men came out of the Lapierre residence on Old Cemetery Street and got into an open carriage. One, Father Boucher, was wearing his usual clerical garb. The other two were traveling in disguise: Father Lapierre was dressed in civilian clothes in defiance of convention, and John H. Surratt, his hair and mustache dyed dark brown, wore spectacles not to improve his vision, but to deflect the vision of passersby who might otherwise recognize his notorious face.[808] They rode to the river docks, where they boarded the steamer *Montreal* bound for Quebec City.

It was on board the steamer *Montreal* that Surratt was first introduced to Dr. Lewis J.A. McMillan, ship's surgeon on the *Peruvian*.[809] Father Lapierre had come to see Dr. McMillan about a week to ten days before this sailing, to arrange Surratt's passage. By prearrangement, Father Lapierre met with Dr. McMillan on the deck of the *Montreal* that Friday night, and brought him up to a locked stateroom. When Lapierre unlocked the door, McMillan saw a young man with short, dark brown hair, in the company of another man. He appeared thin and careworn. Father Lapierre introduced Dr. McMillan to the young man, calling him "Mr. McCarty."[810]

Talking the night away in Surratt's stateroom – without in any way suspecting who "McCarty" really was – McMillan and the others steamed down the St. Lawrence to Quebec City, arriving between five and six o'clock the morning of September 16. After a nice breakfast on board the *Montreal*, a tug arrived about nine or ten o'clock to transport them to the *Peruvian*, the larger steamer on which they would cross the Atlantic. Father Boucher said his farewells on the deck of the *Montreal*, but Father Lapierre insisted on seeing "McCarty" all the way to the *Peruvian*. At Father Lapierre's request, Dr. McMillan allowed "McCarty" to rest in the doctor's quarters until departure. Satisfied that his charge was safe, Father Lapierre wished the young man *bon voyage*, then left him to Dr. McMillan's care.[811] The *Peruvian* weighed anchor by about half-past ten that morning.[812] As the coastline of North America dropped away, the weary fugitive with dyed hair and an Irish alias huddled in the dark of Dr. McMillan's stateroom must have thought, *good riddance*.

* * *

Dr. McMillan next saw Surratt either just after lunch or dinner on the first day of their voyage. Surratt sidled up to him on deck and, pointing out one of the passengers, asked if McMillan knew him.

McMillan did not; he supposed him to be just another passenger. Surratt did not think so; he thought the man was perhaps an American detective. "I don't believe anything of the kind," replied McMillan. "Besides, what have you done that you should be afraid of an American detective?"

"I have done more things than you are aware of," replied Surratt, "and if you knew of them, it would make you stare."[813] Brushing this curious remark aside, McMillan assured "McCarty" that he was safe – "you are on a British ship, in British waters, and if that American detective had been after you, he would have tried to arrest you before we left port."[814]

"I don't care whether he [i]s after me or not," blustered Surratt, "if he tries to arrest me, *this* will settle him!" And he drew from his waistcoat pocket a small four-barreled revolver.[815] Most likely, this was the four-barreled Sharp's revolver previously described as Surratt's by Weichmann.[816]

While awaiting trial in April 1867, Surratt was interviewed about escaping his many pursuers. He had nothing to say to the interviewer about his escape into Canada, but he did want to talk about his escape from Canada. "[T]here was no secrecy about my leaving Canada," he told the correspondent:

> I went on board a steamer at mid-day, wholly without disguise, and with hundreds of people on and about the wharf. The Steamer had fully 200 passengers, with whom I associated freely during the voyage. Nobody recognized me, though there were those among the passengers that I recognized.[817]

Surratt's statement is hardly accurate. Surratt was disguised and plainly feeling insecure.[818] "He would . . . show signs of nervousness whenever any one came suddenly behind him," McMillan testified. "He would turn round and look about as if he expected some one to come upon him at any moment."[819] In 1867, McMillan told Congress that he was the only person Surratt knew, and that "he seemed not to care for being in the company of any one else."[820] Yet that same year he testified at Surratt's trial that Surratt also spoke with Confederate General Ripley, who was on the *Peruvian* at the same time as Surratt. Still, Surratt's boast that he went on board "wholly without disguise" and that he "associated freely" seems disingenuous, at best. As was characteristic of his few public statements, Surratt had no qualms about lying.

* * *

The most fascinating voyage of Dr. McMillan's life had just begun. However nervous he may have been, Surratt still needed an outlet for all his adventures. Surratt and McMillan spoke every day of the voyage from Quebec City to Londonderry, Ireland, a period of eight days.[822] "He used to come to me when I would be alone," the doctor testified, "and ask me to walk with him on the deck . . . ."[823] On these occasions, Surratt regaled the doctor with tales from his days as a Confederate courier, plying the route between Richmond and Washington, and even as far as Montreal. He told him about the beautiful lady spy, "shooting the damn Yankees," meeting with Secretary of State Judah Benjamin, receiving money from Richmond, his many aliases, and more.[824] Because Dr. McMillan was the man chosen by Father Lapierre to serve as his protector on the voyage, Surratt opened up to him, perhaps not realizing that he was not "one of them" – not a Confederate partisan or Catholic collaborator.

Whether McMillan was a neutral witness or biased towards the Government is an important question. He does not have the best memory and seems to garble facts. For example, as mentioned earlier, he places Surratt's first notice of the completed assassination in St. Albans instead of Elmira. But he lacks a motive to dissemble, and freely admits that there are things he does not remember – such as any directly incriminating admission that Surratt helped plan the killing itself – which separates him from obvious perjurers such as Charles Dunham alias "Sanford Conover." Father Boucher and others testified that McMillan's reputation for truth was bad,[825] but other witnesses testified it was "beyond reproach."[826] Father Boucher was clearly a partisan, with personal quarrels with Dr. McMillan over a supposed unpaid subscription to church renovation, and over the practice which was then called *foeticide*, that we now call abortion. It may be that McMillan was caught in a lie about the church donation quarrel, although even that may be explainable.[828]   But Father Boucher is no angel; under cross-examination he admitted to vacationing in Maine under the alias "Mr. Jary," disguised in civilian clothes and pretending to be a lawyer, so that he could frolic with young women.[829]   On balance, I think McMillan is not deliberately untruthful with respect to his testimony about what Surratt told him.   Admittedly, who to believe once again comes down to a judgment call.

If your judgment concurs with mine, you'll be interested to know McMillan's testimony about what Surratt said he would do if he were arrested by an English officer upon making landfall. Surratt stated that he would shoot the first officer who laid a hand on him. McMillan responded that Surratt would be shown very little leniency in England if he were to do something like that. "I know it, and for that very reason I would do it," was Surratt's calculated answer. "I would rather be hung by an English hangman than by a Yankee one, for I know very well if I go back to the United States I shall swing."[830]

* * *

Dramatic as these revelations are, it is Surratt's confessions to Dr. McMillan about his role in the plot against Lincoln that are of greatest interest.   According to McMillan, Surratt told him that the plot to abduct Lincoln "was concocted solely by John Wilkes Booth and himself."[831]   *Thus, Surratt names himself an equal conspirator with Booth in the original abduction plot.* Surratt told McMillan that he and Booth together had put ten thousand dollars into the affair, in order to hire horses, men, and materials.[832]   As for the change to a plot to assassinate, McMillan says:

> [Surratt] and Booth had planned at first the abduction of President Lincoln; . . . however, they thought they could not succeed in that way, and they thought it was necessary to change their plan.[833]

Surratt also told Dr. McMillan that he got a letter from Booth while in Montreal stating "that it was necessary to act, and to act promptly," and that Surratt started off in response to this letter towards Washington, but only got as far as Elmira. From there, he sent a telegram to Booth, and learned that he had already left New York.[834] This part of McMillan's testimony seems to be partially inaccurate, since Elmira is not the quickest route to Washington. But there is enough that jibes with known evidence to suggest that Surratt obliquely admitted having foreknowledge of the change in plan from kidnapping to assassination.

Upon seeing the coast of Ireland on the evening of September 23, Surratt told McMillan that he hoped he would be able to return to his country in two years. It was not love of country that inspired him. Surratt was holding his revolver in his hand. "I hope to God," he added, "I shall live to see the time when I can serve Andrew Johnson as Abraham Lincoln has been served."[835] McMillan asked why he would say such a thing. Surratt responded, "Because he has been the cause of my mother being hung."[836] Later, in 1867, a dispute would burst into public between President Johnson and General Holt over whether the military commission's recommendation of clemency for Mrs. Surratt had been presented to Johnson along with the verdict and sentences. [837] In September 1865, however, Surratt already had good enough intelligence from Washington to know that President Johnson had suspended a writ of *habeas corpus* and adamantly rebuffed all last-minute clemency appeals, even including those from Surratt's disconsolate sister Anna, and from Mrs. Stephen Douglas, wife of the great Senator.[838] While Surratt's statement about Johnson does not directly implicate him in the Lincoln assassination, it does show that he was not squeamish about the idea of presidential assassination.

* * *

With all the revelations he had heard, McMillan had begun to suspect that "McCarty" was perhaps one of the Lincoln conspirators. Surratt asked him who he thought he was, and McMillan replied, "Surratt or Payne [Powell]." Surratt just laughed. But upon hearing "McCarty" mention that his mother had been hanged, McMillan fixed his identity as Surratt in his own mind.[839] Still, he wanted it from the horse's mouth.

Surratt/McCarty asked McMillan whether he thought he ought to disembark at the very first landfall, in Londonderry, Ireland. McMillan says that he refused to advise him, so Surratt said that he "would go down to Liverpool with you." Nonetheless, between half-past eleven and midnight the very next day, Sunday, September 24, McMillan was called to the after-square where he found Surratt, ready to go ashore. "Are you going ashore?" asked McMillan in surprise. "I thought you were coming down to Liverpool."

"I have thought over the matter," replied Surratt, "and I believe it is better for me to get out here. It is now dark, and there is less chance of being seen." Before he disembarked they drank brandy together, the younger man taking rather too much in an effort to calm his overly excited nerves. As they were parting, McMillan stated frankly his suspicion that "McCarty" was not who he claimed to be. "Will you please give me your own name?"

McMillan says that the young man "looked about to see if there was anybody near, and then whispered in my ear, 'My name is Surratt.'" [840] By then Surratt was so drunk that McMillan had the officer at the gangway lead him down, for fear that the notorious fugitive might meet an ignominious end by falling off the plank and drowning. [841]

Surratt may have been too intoxicated to know it, but he had made it much farther than any other of Booth's immediate co-conspirators – over 3,800 miles from Elmira, all the way to the shores of Europe. But even here he could not feel safe. Within days, his presence would be known to the U.S. Government. Surratt was still running for his life.

790 *Rockville Lecture*, Weichmann, p.440.

791 2 JHS Trial 908.

792 1 JHS Trial 483; *Rockville Lecture*, Weichmann, p.336; *E.G. Lee*, p.166.

793 1 JHS Trial 483 (emphasis added).

794 Intrepid Slater tracker John F. Stanton first suggested this possibility back in 2007. *Thoughts on Slater*, p.6.

795 *E.G. Lee*, pp.166-67.

796 JOH Papers, *Letter from Brig. General Baker to War Department* (July 28, 1865).

797 1 JHS Trial 483.

798 *Lee Diary* (August 11, 1865); *E.G. Lee*, p.167.

799 *Lee Diary* (August 11-13, 1865); *E.G.Lee*, pp. 7, 167.

800 *Lee Diary* (Aug.14-15, Aug. 18, 1865).

801 *Ibid.* (Aug. 18, 1865). Charles Kean is no relation to Laura Keene, who was playing in *Our American Cousin* on the night Lincoln was assassinated.

802 *E.G. Lee*, p.168; 2 JHS Trial 908.

803 *Lee Diary* (August 21, 1865).

804 *Ibid.* (August 25, 1865).

805 *Surratt Courier*, vol. XXXVI No.8, John C. Stanton, *A Mystery No Longer - The Lady in the Veil*, p.5 (August 2011) (hereafter *"Mystery No Longer Pt. 1"*).

806 *Surratt Courier*, vol. XXXVI No.10, John C. Stanton, *A Mystery No Longer - The Lady in the Veil* (Conclusion), p.7, (Oct. 2011) (hereafter *"Mystery No Longer Pt. 2"*).

807 *E.G. Lee*, pp.169-70; 1 JHS Trial 462.

808 1 JHS Trial 465-66; 2 JHS Trial 910-12; *E.G. Lee*, p.169.

809 1 JHS Trial 462; 2 JHS Trial 910; *E.G. Lee*, pp.169-70; *Affidavit* [anonymous, but clearly of L.J. McMillan], p.3 (hereafter *"McMillan Affidavit of Dec. 8, 1866"*), *reprinted in*, 39th Congress, 2nd Session, House Of Representatives, *Message From The President Of The United States, Transmitting A Report Of The Secretary Of State Relating To The Discovery And Arrest Of John H. Surratt* (Dec. 8, 1866) (hereafter *"President's Message re: Surratt"*).

810 1 JHS Trial 462-63, 474.

811 1 JHS Trial 463; 2 JHS Trial 910.

812 1 JHS Trial 463.

813 *Ibid.*

814 1 JHS Trial 464.

815 *Ibid.; McMillan Judiciary Testimony*, p.13.

816 Weichmann, pp.101-02.

817 *New York Times*, "A Visit to Surratt, Tuesday, April 2," (published April 8, 1867) (hereafter *"NY Times*, A Visit to Surratt*"*).

818 *McMillan Judiciary Testimony*, p.14; 1 JHS Trial 465-66.

819 1 JHS Trial 474.

820 *McMillan Judiciary Testimony*, p.13.

821 1 JHS Trial 464.

822 1 JHS Trial 462, 466, 474-75 (they left Quebec City Saturday morning, September 16, and Surratt disembarked in the wee hours of Monday morning, September 25).

823 *McMillan Judiciary Testimony*, p.13.

824 *Ibid.;* 1 JHS Trial 466-68.

825 2 JHS Trial 897.

826 2 JHS Trial 947-49, 989.

827 2 JHS Trial 898, 902.

828 2 JHS Trial 942-43.

829 2 JHS Trial 913-14.

830 1 JHS Trial 469.

831 1 JHS Trial 476; *McMillan Judiciary Testimony*, p.13.

832 *McMillan Judiciary Testimony*, p.13.

833 *Ibid.*

834 *Ibid.*

835 1 JHS Trial 469; Cable #237 from Potter to Seward (Oct. 27, 1865), *reprinted President's Message re: Surratt*, p.6.

836 *McMillan Judiciary Testimony*, p.14.

837 Discussed in detail *infra*, Chapter Twenty-one.

838 *E.G. Lee*, pp.211-13.

839 *McMillan Judiciary Testimony*, p.14.

840 1 JHS Trial 474.

841 1 JHS Trial 475.

CHAPTER FIFTEEN

THE ADVENTURES OF
JOHN WATSON (AND HIS DOG)

DR. MCMILLAN DISEMBARKED FROM THE *PERUVIAN* IN LIVERPOOL later that Monday, September 26, and immediately sought out United States Vice-Consul Henry Wilding. McMillan was eager to reveal all he had learned about the fugitive from the Lincoln assassination.[842] He informed Wilding that Surratt had admitted his complicity in the plot against Lincoln, and that he had disembarked in Londonderry.[843] Vice-Consul Wilding cabled Washington with this fresh intelligence about Surratt's whereabouts and involvement in the plot, attaching a copy of McMillan's sworn statement.[844]

McMillan told Wilding that he expected Surratt in Liverpool within a day or two, and promised to inform him of Surratt's arrival and place of lodging.[845] Sure enough, Surratt took a boat from Londonderry and showed up Wednesday evening on Dr. McMillan's doorstep at his boardinghouse in Birkenhead, just across the Mersey River from Liverpool. Surratt asked McMillan to help him find a particular house to which he had been directed. Still playing the role of friend and confidant, McMillan accompanied Surratt across the river into Liverpool, from where he summoned a cab to take Surratt the rest of the way.[846] Then McMillan updated Wilding on Surratt's whereabouts.

State Department Cable 539, dated September 30, 1865, contains the intelligence that Surratt "has arrived in Liverpool and is now staying at the oratory of the Roman Catholic church of the Holy Cross."[847] Noting that he could do nothing further without the approval of Mr.

Adams, the American Ambassador to England stationed in London, Mr. Wilding added a most undiplomatic plea for action: *"If it be Surratt, such a wretch ought not to escape."*[848]

Surprisingly, this was not the universal view of the United States Government. William Hunter, acting Secretary of State during Seward's long convalescence from Powell's vicious attack, consulted with Secretary of War Stanton and Judge-Advocate General Holt, manager of the conspiracy trial prosecution. Based on this consultation, Hunter cabled Wilding on October 13: "it is thought advisable that no action be taken in regard to the arrest of the supposed John Surratt at present."[849] A few days previously, Mr. Adams had likewise advised Mr. Wilding that nothing should be done immediately to apprehend Surratt due to "our present evidence of identity and complicity."[850] Since the Government's evidence of Surratt's identity and complicity was reasonably strong at this point, one might assume that all this was diplomatic code for political reluctance to seize the son after hanging the mother. Not for the last time, the ghost of Mary Surratt would protect her wayward son. Surratt was still running, but was anyone chasing him?

* * *

After hearing from Vice-Consul Wilding that there would be no immediate prosecution of Surratt, Dr. McMillan agreed to carry Surratt's letter requesting money to his friends in Quebec.[851] But McMillan had not given up on getting Surratt arrested. Whether the motivation was his own conception of justice or the reward still offered by the U.S. Government is not known. Regardless, as soon as McMillan arrived back in Canada he gave full information about Surratt's admissions and whereabouts to John Potter, United States Consul in Montreal. Potter promptly conveyed the information to Washington,[852] but the response was apparently not quick enough to suit him. He followed up in Cable No. 236 to Secretary Seward, dated at Montreal October 25, 1865:

> John H. Surratt left Three Rivers some time in September
> for Liverpool, where he is now awaiting the arrival of the

steamer Nova Scotian, which sails on Saturday next, by which he expects to receive money from parties in this city, by the hand of [blanked out – undoubtedly "Dr. McMillan"] of whom Surratt made a confidant in Liverpool.

I have the information from [McMillan]. It is Surratt's intention to go to Rome. . . .

I requested instructions in my [previous coded] telegram, but hearing nothing yet, I scarcely know what course to take. If an officer could proceed to England in this ship, I have no doubt but that Surratt's arrest might be effected, and thus the last of the conspirators against the lives of the President and Secretary of State be brought to justice.[853]

Mr. Potter also took a lengthy statement from Dr. McMillan, which was forwarded to Washington on October 27 in Cable 237.[854] In this October 27 cable, Potter says that, according to McMillan, "Surratt manifested no signs of penitence, but justified his action, and was bold and defiant when speaking of the assassination."[855]

Surratt's bold defiance was well requited by the Government, which did nothing. Though Potter sent further cables tracking the progress of McMillan's departure, he received no timely response. It was not until November 11 that the flummoxed Mr. Potter received a bland response from Frederick Seward, Assistant Secretary of State. "Your dispatches from No. 235 to No. 241, have been received," it said. "The information communicated in your No. 237 has been properly availed of."[856]

In what manner was it "availed of"? It appears that on November 13, Secretary of State Seward did request that the Attorney General obtain an indictment against Surratt as soon as convenient, with an eye towards demanding that Great Britain surrender him. But some power must have intervened to countermand this request. There is no record that any indictment was actually obtained, and no extradition request was made. Instead, as found by the Boutwell Committee, "the Executive did not send any detective or agent to Liverpool to identify Surratt, or trace his movements." What's more, "the Executive did not cause notice to be given to our minister at Rome that Surratt intended going there, when the government had every reason to believe that such was his intention."[857]

Indeed, not only did the Government do nothing towards capturing Surratt, it actually did worse than nothing. On November 24, 1865 the War Department issued an order revoking the reward for information leading to the arrest of Surratt.[858] In a matter of a few months, Surratt's status had mysteriously changed from the most wanted man in the world, to fugitive *non grata*.

* * *

Why would the Government decide to let Booth's number one henchman, a known Confederate courier who had carried dispatches from Richmond just before the assassination, go free? Because this makes so little sense, into the breach left by Government incompetence and mendacity march the armies of conspiracy.

This is a bit of a tricky topic because unlike the Kennedy assassination, in the Lincoln assassination the question is not whether there was a conspiracy, but how far and in what direction it extended. Still, just as we ask how a cipher like Oswald could bring down a titan like Kennedy, the people of the Nineteenth Century wondered how one supposedly-crazed actor and his motley gang could bring down Lincoln in the heart of the capital on the very eve of Union triumph. Such events are so inconceivable and destabilizing that we sometimes succumb to the need to look beyond the plain facts, though we know full well that any angry weakling or zealot with a gun is a potential assassin. Thus, for example, one of the wilder Lincoln assassination conspiracy theories was that the man killed in Garrett's barn was not John Wilkes Booth, and that Booth went on to live a full life in South America, where he acted under the name Enos until at least 1896.[859] No number of eyewitness accounts of the killing of Booth[860] can dispel such nonsense, because it is a kind of religious fervor, ultimately based not on evidence but faith.

In 1937 Otto Eisenschiml published a book entitled *Why Was Lincoln Murdered*, which set forth the theory that Edwin M. Stanton was behind the Lincoln assassination plot.[861] Eisenschiml argued that

Stanton was the one who stood to benefit most politically from Lincoln's death. He saw the sinister hand of a grand conspiracy at the highest levels of Stanton's War Department in an array of details, including Stanton's refusal of special protection to the President that night, failure to punish the guard who abandoned his post outside the President's box, interruption of some telegraph communications that night, Boston Corbett's shooting of Booth and the disappearance of Booth's body, hooding of the conspirators during their confinement to "silence" them, and – most significantly to our purposes – the unwillingness to arrest Surratt when they knew where he was, and the revocation of the reward for his arrest.[862] Although Eisenschiml's theories have been meticulously debunked,[863] he continues to attract disciples such as Robert Mills, who perpetuates the theory that "allowing John Surratt to remain at large makes sense in the same way that the hooding of his fellow conspirators makes sense . . . to wit, to make certain he didn't talk!"[864]

It seems to me that there are two fatal flaws to this argument. First, the premise that hooding silenced the conspirators is false; during their confinement they gave multiple statements to the Government and – in Atzerodt's case – to the press, they met with their families, Mrs. Surratt was not hooded, and those who were not hanged had ample opportunity to talk later.[865] Second, in the case of John Surratt, it makes no sense to try to silence somebody by letting them run free. As researcher Steven J. Wright points out, "[w]hile Surratt was free and not under control of the government, he would have been able to speak freely about his association with Booth and the other conspirators."[866] Thus, letting Surratt run free was hardly a permanent solution to a "loose cannon" who needed silencing. As organized crime proved time and again in more recent history, the best way to silence someone is simply to kill them. If the Government was really in the hands of a cabal capable of planning and executing the murder of its own head of State, it would have had no qualms about picking Surratt up and then bumping him off on the pretext of attempted escape. Dead men tell no tales.

Still the question lingers unanswered: *why wasn't Surratt arrested in Liverpool or London?* Probably for the same reasons that the

Government never put Jefferson Davis on trial, though it held him prisoner continuously for two years beginning in May 1865.[867] The Government had jumped out of the starting gate prematurely in April 1865, with Secretary Seward and President Johnson both publicly accusing Jefferson Davis and other high Confederates of complicity in the assassination plot.[868] These accusations were based on tales woven by paid witnesses who proved to be base perjurers – Charles Dunham alias "Sanford Conover" and company.[869] Embarrassed, the Government had to pull back from this initial position. Meanwhile, it had hanged four conspirators partly on perjured testimony connecting them with the Confederacy. The entire strategy of proving a Confederate Government connection was thereby thoroughly discredited, even if it may have been accurate.

Furthermore, after the initial retribution of the trial of the conspirators and hangings, the public's desire for vengeance was satisfied – in the case of Mary Surratt, not just satisfied, but glutted to the point where many were having second thoughts about what had been done. It was no longer politically useful to try to link the Lincoln assassination to Richmond. The war was over and the country wanted to move forward, not pick over the many corpses left rotting in the battlefields, both overt and covert. General amnesty was the new watchword; there would be no more Yanks and Rebels, but just one United States again. The last thing that President Johnson's administration needed was John Surratt back in irons, stirring up sectional passions over Confederate involvement in the plot and wrapping himself in the death shroud of his martyred mother.

And so, not for the first nor for the last time, that abstraction "justice" so dear to politicians and the public when it accords with their concrete interests, had to give way to those very interests. The American people had had all the "justice" they could stomach for a while. It was better to forget and just move on. That is not a conspiracy. That is human nature.

This is not to say that there was no conspiracy to kill Lincoln. We know that there was. It says only that failure to pursue Surratt vigorously does not prove that Stanton, or Johnson, or any other of the Union Government officials, were a part of this conspiracy. The more fertile field for inquiry is whether the Lincoln assassination conspiracy reached Judah Benjamin or Jefferson Davis through Surratt. It is likely that it did, but at this late date that is beyond definitive proof.[870]

* * *

The Liverpool into which Surratt landed was still very much Confederate territory. Liverpool had served as the unofficial port of the Confederate Navy during the latter part of the Civil War. There were many Confederate officers located there, and likely Surratt had no difficulty finding sympathetic comrades and support.[871]

One version of Surratt's next steps is given by the very thorough Surratt researcher, Alfred Isacsson. According to Isacsson, Surratt patiently awaited Dr. McMillan's return while hidden by Father Charles Jolivet in a secret chamber at Oratory of the Holy Cross, on Great Crosshall Street in Liverpool.[872] McMillan provides evidence in support of Isacsson's version, saying that he saw Surratt in Liverpool five to six weeks after he first arrived.[873] Surratt must have been disappointed to learn that his "friends" back in Montreal had declined his request for funds, but he was not completely without resources, since Father Jolivet supported him to some extent.[874]

While it does appear that Surratt was hidden by Father Jolivet for a few days and that he may have been back in Liverpool when McMillan returned in late October, it is unlikely that Surratt remained idle and hidden away the whole time. A more complete picture of his activities can be derived from the report of an investigation performed for Congress in 1867 by George H. Sharpe. According to Sharpe, Surratt left Liverpool on Saturday morning, September 30, at nine o'clock in the morning, and arrived at London's Euston Square Station at about two o'clock that same afternoon.[875] Who should be in London at the time but former Confederate Secretary of State Judah P. Benjamin, who had sought refuge in London after the fall of the Confederacy.[876] It seems very likely that Mr. Benjamin met with his valuable and notorious young courier, although there is no particular evidence of it. Mr. Benjamin may even have found additional funds to support Surratt, either immediately or after McMillan returned empty handed.

It is even possible that Surratt was still acting as Benjamin's courier. It is known that Mr. Benjamin instructed Jacob Thompson to deposit a large sum of Confederate funds with Frazer, Trenholm & Co, Liverpool, to be placed at Mr. Benjamin's credit in an account headed "Secret Service."[877] It is hard to imagine Surratt sitting atop a pile of Confederate loot without any idea of its existence, and then visiting Benjamin's newly-adopted city without making a withdrawal for their mutual benefit. I am speculating without direct evidence, but it makes sense that the next phase of Surratt's travels was financed, at least in part, in this manner.

If Surratt went back in Liverpool to meet Dr. McMillan in late October, and then stayed until November 6, 1865, he might have witnessed a poignant moment in the waning history of the Confederacy. There, in the Mersey River, the Confederate steamer *Shenandoah* struck the stars and bars for the last time, and surrendered to the Royal Naval vessel *Donegal*.[878] The *Shenandoah* had circumnavigated the globe, eluding its many pursuers, and would be remembered as the ship that fired the last shot of the Civil War at an American whaler off the shores of the Aleutian Islands.[879]

* * *

On October 12, 1865, a purported Scotsman applied for a passport in London. The passport was issued to "John Watson" of Edinburgh the very next day, October 13. It was unusual for a passport to be granted so quickly, but this one had the support of the Provincial Government of Canada, and was therefore expedited. How the intervention of the Government of Canada was obtained is unexplained.[880] "John Watson" of Edinburgh was in reality the mercurial John H. Surratt of Maryland, alias "Charley Armstrong," alias "John McCarty."

"Watson" next surfaces in Paris, where his passport was stamped by the Papal Nuncio with a visa for entry into the Papal States. The Nuncio's visa was given *gratis* – which is unusual. Mr. Sharpe's inquiry into this was "met with rudeness and discourtesy" by the Nuncio and his secretary. Later, Sharpe was informed that the visa was given upon the assurance that Watson was traveling to Rome for the purpose of enlistment in the Papal Zouaves.[881]

According to Surratt family lore, while in Paris Surratt obtained a bloodhound that stayed by his side until his capture. Surratt also began to transform himself from fugitive to tourist. He visited the palace at Versailles, opulent home of the Sun King Louis XIV and his descendants. Another story has him creating quite a commotion when he dared to eat at a restaurant that the local inhabitants thought was a source of an outbreak of cholera.[882] If the latter is true, and Surratt was willing to draw unnecessary attention to himself, then by the time that he was in Paris he may have been aware that the United States Government was no longer actively seeking his arrest.

Surratt probably travelled overland to Marseilles or Nice, from which he took a ship to Civita Vecchia, a maritime port about seventy kilometers northwest of Rome. Unfortunately for Surratt, he had run through his funds yet again, so he was detained on the cusp of paradise, amongst the umbrella pines and orange groves of central Italy. But once again, the Catholic Church came to his rescue. Apparently he had received a letter of introduction to Dr. Neve, rector of the English College in Rome. The English College was (and still is) a seminary founded in 1579 for English-speaking students preparing for the priesthood who wished to study close by the Vatican. Dr. Neve sent fifty francs to Surratt, and he was released from confinement and brought to Rome, where he stayed for a few weeks at Dr. Neve's college at number 45 Via di Monserrato.[883]

Surratt's great escape over approximately five thousand miles of land and sea was, for the time being, finished.

* * *

The late 1860s were the final years in which the Pope acted as temporal as well as spiritual sovereign.[884] But though the Pope's temporal rule was threatened by the growing forces of the Italian *Risorgimento* – or "unification" – the Rome in which Surratt landed, like Richmond or Washington in 1861, was a relatively peaceful place. The fighting against the Red Shirts of the Garibaldi army in 1866 was confined to outlying areas such as Sezze and Frosinone.[885]

Now that he was more tourist than fugitive, Surratt and his faithful hound dog probably wandered the timeless streets of the city, from the Spanish Steps and Trevi Fountain to the Roman ruins, including the

Coliseum, the Arch of Constantine, and the columns celebrating Rome's many martial triumphs. Without doubt Surratt also visited St. Peter's Cathedral, and perhaps was able to view Michealangelo's masterpiece on the ceiling of the Sistine Chapel or, like other Zouaves, the *Scala Sancta* (Pilatès Stairs) located in Piazza San Giovanni, down which Jesus is said to have walked after receiving his death sentence.[886] But Surratt left no written trace of these times. Just like the French Foreign Legion, it was a precondition of enlistment in the Papal Zouaves that the new recruit must destroy all personal effects, in part to discourage desertion.[887] In all likelihood, Surratt enthusiastically embraced this erasure of his past.

If Surratt met with Cardinal Antonelli, Papal Secretary of State under Pope Pius IX, or even with the Pope himself, there is no record of it. Despite the substantial assistance given by the Church to Surratt at every step of his five thousand mile odyssey, the Vatican claims that there is no record of Surratt or any of his aliases in the Vatican Secret Archives.[888] One-hundred fifty years after the fact, the Catholic Church offers no explanation as to why it played such an instrumental role in helping a key conspirator against Lincoln get away. This does not mean, as charged by the conspiracy theorist and excommunicated priest Charles Chiniquy,[889] or his even more bigoted protégé, Burke McCarty,[890] that (in Chiniquy's words) "[i]t was Rome who directed [Booth's] arm," and "that the President, Abraham Lincoln, was assassinated by the priests and the Jesuits of Rome."[891] Chiniquy's rhetoric is inflamed and his so-called "evidence" is a combination of patently false and exaggerated first-hand encounters with Lincoln, inaccurate assumptions, anti-Catholic prejudice, and speculative guilt by association.[892] The Catholic Church was most likely not an accessory *before the fact* as charged in 1963 by Chiniquy disciple Emmett McLoughlin.[893] But nonetheless, based on an objective view of the evidence, it does appear that significant elements within the Catholic Church made themselves into what the law calls "accessories after the fact," by sheltering the fugitive Surratt and actively facilitating his escape. Most likely, they did so from a combination of the particular political leanings of the bishops and priests involved, partiality towards a faithful Catholic family, eagerness to recruit a proven soldier to the Pope's army, and a true Christian calling to shield a fugitive from likely death if captured. There is no credible evidence of a grand conspiracy directed by the Pope or the Jesuits, though it is possible that such evidence was destroyed or is still being suppressed. There is, however, enough evidence of concerted evasion of civil legal authority to conclude that this was not the Church's finest hour.

842 The statement, dated September 26, is referred to in the trial as having been given on September 27, but that is only the date of the cover letter. *Compare*, Cable #538, U.S. Consulate, Wilding to Stewart (Sept. 27, 1865), *reprinted in President's Message re: Surratt, with*, 1 JHS Trial 476. The statement refers to arriving in Liverpool on September 25, which does not accord with other evidence. *President's Message re: Surratt*, p.3. These small variations are inconsequential.

843 1 JHS Trial 476; Isacsson, *AFCT*, p. X-5.

844 Cable #538, *President's Message re: Surratt*, pp.3-4.

845 *Letter of Sept. 27, 1865, from Wilding to Seward, President's Message re: Surratt*, p.3.

846 1 JHS Trial 475.

847 Cable #539, *President's Message re: Surratt*, p.4.

848 *Ibid.* (emphasis added).

849 Cable #476 (Oct. 13, 1865), *President's Message re: Surratt*, p.5; Isacsson, *AFCT*, p. X-5; Alfred Isacsson, *The Travels, Arrest, and Trial of John H. Surratt*, pp.7 & 11n.5 (Vestigium Press, Middleton, NY (2003) (hereafter, "Isacsson, *TAT*").

850 Cable #544, *President's Message re: Surratt*, p.4; 1 JHS Trial 481.

851 1 JHS Trial 483.

852 Isacsson, *TAT*, pp.7-8.

853 Cable #236, *President's Message re: Surratt*, p.5.

854 Cable #237, *President's Message re: Surratt*, pp.5-6.

855 *Ibid.*, p.6.

856 Cable #164 (Nov. 11, 1865), *President's Message re: Surratt*, p.6.

857 JOH Papers, Boutwell Committee, *Report Of The Committee Of The Judiciary*, pp.1-2 (March 2, 1867) (hereafter "*Boutwell Committee Report*").

858 *Ibid.*, p.2.

859 *LA from Surratt Courier*, vol. 2, Steven G. Miller, *Ripples from the Hanson Hiss Article*, p. X-41 (July 1996); *LA from Surratt Courier*, vol. 2, Erich L. Ewald, *The Butcher's Tale: The Primary Documentation of "Chris Ritter's" Confrontation with Louis J. Weichmann*, p. XI-5 (April 1992).

860 *LA from Surratt Courier*, vol. 2, Rev. Dr. R.B. Garrett, *I Saw John Wilkes Booth Killed, reprinted from Alexandria Gazette* (June 8, 1903), p. XI-11 to 14

(including Booth's dying declarations and the matching of Booth's known India ink tattoo of his initials on his arm with the corpse) (May 1999).

861 Otto Eisenschiml, *Why Was Lincoln Murdered?* (Little Brown and Co., Boston 1937).

862 *Ibid.* pp.199-203, passim.

863 *E.g.*, William Hanchett, *The Lincoln Murder Conspiracies*, chs. 6 & 7 (Urbana, Univ. of Illinois Press 1983); *LA from Surratt Courier*, vol.2, William Hanchett, *We Told You So . . .*, pp. X-29 to 33 (Nov. 1990), *reprinting in part*, William Hanchett, *The Historian as Gamesman, Civil War History*, Vol. XXXVI, No. 1 (March 1990) (hereafter "*Historian as Gamesman*").

864 *LA from Surratt Courier*, vol. 2, Robert Mills, *A Can of Worms*, p. X-27 (Oct. 1990).

865 *Historian as Gamesman*, p. X-31; Statements; *LA from Surratt Courier*, vol.1, pp. III-19 to III-28 (three more Atzerodt confessions).

866 *LA from Surratt Courier*, vol. 2, Steven J. Wright, *More from the "Can of Worms,"* p. X-35 (Dec. 1990).

867 *Blood on the Moon*, p.225.

868 *E.G. Lee*, pp.155-56;

869 *E.G. Lee*, p.157; *Conspiracy re: Confederate Leaders*, pp.633-39.

870 Is this book yet another "conspiracy theory" book because it revives the possible link between the Lincoln assassination and Jefferson Davis? The difference, I hope, is a state of mind - skepticism, not certainty. I am skeptical about the "accepted truth" that Davis was not involved, but at the same time skeptical of ever proving definitively that he was involved. Skepticism may not be as satisfying as certainty, but it seems more intellectually honest than attributing all of history to hyper-efficient dark forces.

871 *When Liverpool Was Dixie*, http://www.whenliverpoolwasdixie.org.uk/index.htm (accessed Jan. 31, 2014).

872 Isacsson, *TAT*, p.8.

873 *McMillan Judiciary Testimony*, p.14.

874 Isacsson, *TAT*, pp.8-9; 1 JHS Trial 483.

875 JOH Papers, *President's Message re: Surratt, A report of George H. Sharpe re: Assassination of President Lincoln*, p.2 (Dec. 17, 1867) (hereafter "*Sharpe Report*").

876 Isacsson, *TAT*, p.9. Mr. Isacsson may read too much into Sharpe's statement that there was no evidence of participation of any former United States citizens in Europe in the escape of Surratt sufficient to warrant further prosecution by the Government. *Sharpe Report*, p.4. Isacsson reads this to mean that Surratt did not visit with Benjamin and therefore did not go to London, even though both Sharpe and Henri Beaumont Ste. Marie

place him in London.
877 *E.G. Lee*, p.143.
878 *Marauders of the Sea: Confederate Naval Vessels of the American Civil War -*
CSS Shenandoah,
http://ahoy.tk-jk.net/MaraudersCivilWar/CSSShenandoah.html (accessed
Jan. 31, 2014).
879 Lynn Schooler, *The Last Shot of the Civil War: the Incredible Story of the CSS*
Shenandoah (Ecco 2005).
880 *Sharpe Report*, p.3.
881 *Ibid.*
882 *His Mother's Memories*, p. XI-26. This story was related in November 1931
by Dr. Reginald I. Tonry, the son of Anna Surratt, nephew of John Surratt,
grandson of Mary Surratt.
883 Isacsson, *TAT*, p.10; *Ste. Marie v. United States*, p.34 (Note attached to Swan
to King, Nov. 25, 1866); *Website of the English College*,
http://www.vecrome.org/ (accessed Feb. 8, 2014). Isacsson believes that
Surratt traveled by ship directly from Liverpool to Civita Vechhia. Isacsson,
TAT, p.10. In my judgment, however, there are too many other accounts
of Surratt in London and Paris for this to be credible.
884 On September 20, 1870, the Italian army entered Rome and deposed the
Pope from temporal power. *Canadian Catholic Historical Ass'n Report*, vol.12
(1944-1945), Howard R. Marraro, Ph.D., *Canadian and American Zouaves in*
the Papal Army, 1868-1870, p.100 (hereafter "Marraro").
885 John Powell, *Two Years in the Pontifical Zouaves: a Narrative of Travel,*
Residence and Experience in the Roman States, p.3 (R. Washbourne, London
1871) (hereafter *"Two Years in the Zouaves"*).
886 *Two Years in the Zouaves*, p.49.
887 *Sharpe Report*, p.3.
888 Emails of January 17 and April 1, 2014, from Dott. Marco Grilli, *Segretario*
della Prefeturra, Archiva Secretum Vaticanum, to author.
889 Charles Ciniquy, *Fifty Years in the Church of Rome* (Fleming H. Revel Co.,
NY, Chicago, Toronto 1886) (hereafter *"Fifty Years"*).
890 Burke McCarty, *The Suppressed Truth About the Assassination of Abraham*
Lincoln (Self-published 1922).
891 *Fifty Years*, p.718.
892 *Journal of the Southern Illinois Historical Society*, vol.69, pp.17-25, Joseph
George, Jr., *The Lincoln Writings of Charles P.T. Chiniquy* (Feb. 1976)
http://www.philvaz.com/apologetics/Charles-Chiniquy-Anti-
Catholic.htm#CONSPIRACY (accessed Feb. 15, 2014).
893 Emmett McLoughlin, *An Inquiry into the Assassination of Abraham Lincoln*
(Lyle Stuart, Inc., New York, 1963).

CHAPTER SIXTEEN

LEAP INTO LEGEND

ACCORDING TO THE ENLISTMENT RECORD FOR "GIOVANNI WATSON," on December 11, 1865 Surratt joined up to fight once again for the forces of reaction against progress.[894] Just one year before, in 1864, Pope Pius IX had issued his notorious "Syllabus of Errors" that condemned some ninety so-called "errors and perverse doctrines" including rationalism, science, Protestantism, any claim that the Catholic Church is not "true and perfect," democracy, separation of Church and state, the liberty of the press and secular education, and ended by renouncing the view that "the Roman Pontiff can and should reconcile himself to and agree with progress, liberalism, and modern civilization."[895] As the *New York Times* would observe on the occasion of the embarkation of a Canadian regiment of Zouaves, "the fall of the last of the old ecclesiastical governments was like the extinction of a decaying race."[896] Back home in the same month as Surratt's enlistment, the United States sprang into a new era with the ratification of the Thirteenth Amendment to the Constitution, which states: "Neither slavery nor involuntary servitude . . . shall exist within the United States, or any place subject to their jurisdiction."[897] The times they were a-changing, but Surratt was as determined as ever to fight to preserve the old ways.

The Papal (or "Pontifical") Zouaves was a mercenary force comprised of Catholic men from around the world, gathered in defense of the Pope's temporal authority. The Zouaves were active in military engagements against the "Red Shirt" brigades of the indigenous

Garibaldi army, which sought to unite the various kingdoms of Italy into a single modern secular state. According to an 1868 report of the *New York Herald*, the Zouaves were then comprised of 4,592 men, of which only 157 were "Romans and Pontifical Subjects," with a scattering from Naples, Tuscany, and other parts of what was to become Italy.[898] The balance of the Zouave force was comprised of 1,910 Dutch, 1,301 French, 686 Belgians, 135 Canadians, 101 Irish, 87 Prussians, 50 English, 14 Americans, and assorted Swiss, Austrians, Germans, Scots (such as "Watson" pretended to be), Spaniards, Portuguese, Poles, Russians, and one each from India, Africa, Peru, Mexico and Circassia.[899] Although undoubtedly fewer in number when Surratt joined up at the end of 1865, the international mix was a predominant feature of the Papal Zouaves at all times.

The uniform of the Papal Zouaves was one of the most fanciful in military history. It combined the uniform of the Zouaves of Africa with that of the French infantry. The color was probably grey with red trimmings, although Zouaves in other theaters of war used light blue, which may account for the colorized image of Surratt in blue.[900] Zouave units had fought on both sides during the Civil War, so this style of uniform may have already been familiar to Surratt.[901] Surratt/Watson wore a red fez with a long fringed pom-pom, an open fronted jacket with red piping and bright red crosses on each breast, buttoned once at the top so it fanned out in a "vee" over a shirt with a single line of red piping up the middle (the three lines of red piping thus forming an arrow aimed towards heaven), a red sash around the waist, dramatic baggy pantaloons cut to mid-calf known as *serouel*, white gaiters, and turned down boots with pointed toes.[902] The overall effect would appear foppish and somewhat silly to modern eyes, if not for the machinery of death toted about by each Zouave. Arms included carbine rifles, belts with sixty rounds of ammunition, revolvers, sabres, and fixed bayonets.[903]

Assuming that Surratt/Watson was treated like any other recruit, he would have been placed in basic training upon first enlisting. His days were then filled with martial routine. Up by five or earlier, he would drill with the other recruits, learning the commands given in French. If he had duty – guard or picket – he would perform it. Special duty befell each recruit only about once a week, and lasted for twenty-four hours, divided between three recruits. Other daily tasks included cleaning arms and tending to ammunition belts, mending uniforms, making up knapsacks with overcoats and tents, pitching and striking camp, conditioning marches with full kit, and inspections. New recruits in Rome also attended religious ceremonies with the Pope, sometimes acting in the role of Papal guards.[904]

After successful completion of basic training the freshly-minted Zouave soldier was assigned out to his company.[905] It is likely that Surratt/Watson progressed quickly through the basics, for by April of 1866 he was already established as a Zouave Third Class in Company C of the Third Regiment, stationed at Sezze, about forty miles southeast of Rome.[906] Most likely based on his prodigious skills, Surratt was placed among the dragoons – the mounted infantry.[907] In a British company by virtue of his purported Scottish identity, he would have sung the song of the British Zouaves as he rode:

Saint George and old England for ever!
Once more her sons arm for the fight,
With the cross on their breasts, to do battle
For God, Holy Church, and the right. . . .

Dishonour our swords shall not tarnish,
We draw them for Rome and the Pope;
Victors still, whether living or dying,
For the Martyr's bright crown is our hope;
If 'tis sweet for our country to perish,
Sweeter far for the cause of to-day; –
Love God, O my soul, love Him only,
And then with light heart go thy way.[908]

For a young man of martial instincts who had lost the only country that ever held his allegiance, what life could be finer than this?

* * *

Probably in March 1866,[909] a Canadian who had once been a school teacher in Little Texas, Maryland, enlisted for a two-year term in the

Papal Zouaves, but he was not motivated by the usual passions for religion and adventure. His sole purpose for enlisting was to find and unmask John H. Surratt.[910] It was Henri Beaumont de Saint Marie, the tenor fluent in Italian whom Surratt and Weichmann first met in Maryland in 1863, and whom Surratt offered to guide to Richmond. Ste. Marie began chasing Surratt about a week after the assassination, diligently tracking him from Quebec to Paris to Italy, and finally into the ranks of the Papal Zouaves.[911]

The Zouaves maintained encampments in the beautiful valley town of Velletri, roughly twenty-four miles southeast of Rome, as well as in the hills leading to Velletri, on the banks of the volcanic caldera, Lake Albano. The encampment by Lake Albano was called Rocca di Papa ("Fortress of the Pope").[912] The turreted guard towers in the center of Velletri can still be seen. Newly-enlisted private Ste. Marie was assigned to the 9th Company of Zouaves in Velletri, where he was learning to drill.[913]

Some time between April 9 and April 15 – almost exactly three years after their first meeting in Little Texas, Maryland, and one year after the assassination of Lincoln – Ste. Marie and "Watson" came face to face.[914] It must have come as quite a shock to Surratt to suddenly be confronted by a familiar face in this distant land. Ste. Marie took "Watson" aside and told him privately, "You are John Surratt, the person I have known in Maryland." Surratt acknowledged his identity, and begged Ste. Marie to keep it secret.[915] Whatever may have been Ste. Marie's response to this plea, he had not come to protect Surratt, but to expose him.

* * *

Before we plunge into Ste. Marie's revelations, let's pause again to explore the question of whether he is worthy of belief, this time going into it more deeply. He was frankly and unabashedly a bounty hunter, but that does not preclude the possibility that the details he provided beyond those strictly necessary to arrest Surratt were not accurate. On the other hand, a Montreal *avocat* called as a witness in defense of Surratt stated that "it is perfectly easy to have a hundred witnesses to swear to [the] fact" that Ste. Marie is not worthy of belief.[916]

Regardless of his rhetoric, however, in the eyes of the law this lawyer was but a single witness, and in fact the defense only called two such witnesses. The prosecution rebutted with three of its own witnesses to testify that Ste. Marie's reputation for truth was good.[917] As is usual with dueling "reputation for truth" testimony, it shed more heat than light on the subject.

More serious is the fact that diligent researcher Alfred Isacsson doubts the veracity of Ste. Marie. The Archdiocese of Montreal and the La Prairie historical society apparently assured Isacsson that there is no record of Ste. Marie's 1833 birth in his claimed hometown of La Prairie. While the Archdiocese might conceivably have motive to impugn Ste. Marie, the historical society presumably would not, so this is a fair point – but a relatively minor one. Records from over 150 years back disappear all the time, and besides, Ste. Marie would have had little to gain by lying about his place of birth. The same is true of Isacsson's inability to locate a record to confirm Ste. Marie's alleged Union service in the last six months of the Civil War. There is a record that the man Ste. Marie said that he substituted for – Edward D. Porter of Delaware – did in fact end his service August 18, 1864, which is about six months (give or take) before the end of the war. Ste. Marie also claimed that earlier in the war he had been imprisoned by the Yankees at Castle Thunder, but was released after informing on his fellow prisoners.[918] This is verified (at least in part) by a clipping from the *Richmond Daily Examiner* of October 21, 1863, that places Ste. Marie in Castle Thunder.[919] As for other minor discrepancies mentioned by Isacsson, it seems to me that differences in minor detail are reassuring, rather than cause for doubting the witness. The only time repeated tellings of the same story are exactly synchronous is when they are fabricated. On balance, I think it is a mistake to write off Ste. Marie's reports. His problem, if he had one, was a tendency to embellish what was probably the truth after he began to feel that he was being ignored, in an effort to spur the Government into action.

* * *

Diplomatic Cable No. 53, dated April 23, 1866 from Rufus King, United States Minister at Rome, to Secretary of State William H.

Seward, stirred up once again all the conflicting passions over Surratt that the Government had tried to suppress back in November 1865. The cable reported that King had been visited by Ste. Marie, a private in the Papal Zouaves, who claimed to have identified John H. Surratt as a fellow Zouave, enlisted under the alias "John Watson."[920] To add to the urgency, the cable promised that the Government might be closing in on two Holy Grails of the assassination case:

> [Ste. Marie] added that Surratt acknowledged his participation in the plot *against Mr. Lincoln's life*, and declared that *Jefferson Davis had incited or was privy to it.*[921]

If true, both points were of deep and fundamental importance. First, Ste. Marie claimed to have Surratt's admission not just that he was part of a plot to *abduct* Lincoln, but also *to kill* Lincoln. Second, Ste. Marie claimed to have an admission of the link to Jefferson Davis from the lips of the courier most likely to have carried the fatal order.

Mr. King followed up on May 11 with a letter from Ste. Marie dated April 23, at Velletri. Ste. Marie said that there was no doubt as to Surratt's identity, since he had mentioned details of their first meeting at Ellangowan (Little Texas), which could only have been known to Surratt. He urged prompt action by the Government, as it appeared likely they would be transferred deeper into the mountains soon, from which communication and capture of the fugitive would be more difficult. Ste. Marie feared for his life at the hands of what Mr. King later called "his wild zouave comrades if it became known that he had betrayed Surratt's secret."[922] Ste. Marie said that any writing sent to him must use only plain paper and envelopes, and "take a form and turn of expression as none but myself will be able to understand." He asked that his enlistment be bought out as soon as possible, at a price of five or six hundred francs, equivalent to about fifty U.S. dollars.[923]

Armed with this vital and time-sensitive information, the Government again commenced to dither. After a flurry of inside correspondence and cables, many of which were aimed at figuring out the correct spelling of Ste. Marie's name, on May 24 Assistant Secretary of State Frederick Seward instructed Mr. King to obtain a sworn statement from Ste. Marie. The statement could not be obtained until June 21, and King sent it to Washington two days later.[924] In it, Ste. Marie swears that Surratt "acknowledged to me that he was the instigator of the murder, and had acted in the instructions and orders of persons he did not name, but some of whom are in New York and others in London." [925] Not satisfied with this, the Government demanded and Ste. Marie provided an additional sworn statement. The statement, dated July 10, 1866, contains the following particulars:

> Speaking of the murder, [Surratt] said they had acted under the orders of men who are not yet known, some of whom are still in New York, and others in London. . . . I have also asked him if he knew Jefferson Davis. He said no, but that he had acted under the instructions of persons under his immediate orders. Being asked if Jefferson Davis had anything to do with the assassination, he said, *"I am not going to tell you."* My impression is that he brought the order from Richmond, as he was in the habit of going there weekly. He must have bribed others to do it [i.e., carry out the assassination], for when the event took place he told me he was in New York, prepared to fly as soon as the deed was done. He says he does not regret what has taken place . . . .. This is the exact truth of what I know about Surratt. More I could not learn, being afraid to awaken his suspicions.[926]

Note the precise nature of Ste. Marie's information. While highly significant, it does not amount to a full confession. Although Mr. King said that Ste. Marie would directly implicate Jefferson Davis, Ste. Marie's actual information does not go quite so far. This is a further indication of truthfulness. Perjurers like "Sanford Conover" simply give their handlers what they want to hear. The truth is generally more nuanced.

What was the identity of the men in London and New York to whom Surratt may have referred? London is easy – that would be Judah P. Benjamin, and possibly also Jacob Thompson. But New York is a puzzle. Booth would be the obvious answer, except that he was both known and, of course, not "still in" New York. Jefferson Davis was a prisoner at Fortress Monroe in Virginia at this time, so he is out. General Edwin G. Lee was back home in Leeland by this timè – although it was now *West* Virginia, much to the General's chagrin.[927] While the extremist Confederate agitator George Sanders was a New Yorker, he was in exile at this time, and did not return to New York until 1872.[928] Surratt apparently told Ste. Marie of a "heavy shipping-firm" in New York "who had much to do with the South, and he is surprised that they have not been suspected."[929] Perhaps the missing link is Confederate agent Roderick D. Watson of 178$^{1/2}$ Water Street, who summoned Surratt to New York in March 1865.[930] Was Surratt displaying bravado to use the alias "Watson" now, flaunting key evidence of a missing link to Confederate involvement? Anything is possible in this enigmatic case.

Although not quite as initially advertised, the information provided to the Government by Ste. Marie as of July 10th was still of tremendous significance. An apparently reputable witness was eager to swear that Surratt was the instigator of the assassination of President Lincoln, and that he acted under the orders of a man in London. It did not take a code-breaker to deduce that the "man in London" was Confederate Secretary of State Judah P. Benjamin, with whom Surratt had met from March 29-April 1, 1865, and for whom Surratt had carried dispatches to Washington immediately afterwards. What's more, evidence that the assassins were acting under the orders of Judah Benjamin strongly suggested that the assassination was carried out with the knowledge and consent of Jefferson Davis.

* * *

On July 16, Secretary of State Seward cabled Mr. King to inform him that Ste. Marie's June 21st statement had been laid before Secretary of War Stanton. It was not until August 15, however, that Secretary Seward acknowledged receipt of the July 10th statement, and said he had presented that to Secretary Stanton.[931] It was already nearly four months after Ste. Marie's first contact with King, and the Government had taken no official steps towards apprehending Surratt.

Privately, however, King had been in communication with Cardinal

Antonelli, Secretary of State for the Papal States. According to King's cable of August 8, "his eminence was greatly interested by [Ste. Marie's information], and intimated that if the American Government desired the surrender of the criminal there would probably be no difficulty in the way."[932] It seemed that the Catholic Church would no longer shelter Surratt. Isacsson speculates that the reason was the uncertainty of the Pope's military position, and the realization that he might need to call upon American warships for protection, or even upon the U.S. Government for asylum, in the not too distant future.[933] Whatever the motivation, everything was in place for Surratt's immediate arrest. All that was needed was for the Americans to give the word and the trap would be sprung.

* * *

Meanwhile, Ste. Marie was getting impatient. On September 12 he wrote a long letter to Mr. Hooker, acting Secretary of the American legation in Rome, to report on a fresh conversation with Surratt, who was "in funds and a little tight . . . ."[934] As with Dr. McMillan on the last night on board the *Peruvian*, it may be that alcohol loosened Surratt's tongue. Alternatively, Ste. Marie may have grown tired of waiting, and embellished the truth in an effort to prod the Government into action. Here is his rather sensational report:

> [Surratt] told me that the plot of the assassination of President Lincoln first originated in Richmond; that Booth and himself were in the habit of visiting Richmond weekly; that, knowing Booth to be a strong-headed man, he proposed to the secretary of state, Benjamin, to have what he called President Lincoln put out of the way, also the other members of his cabinet . . .; that the matter was debated in the rebel cabinet, and they were told to act as they thought the best to accomplish their design, and money was furnished them . . ..[935]

If true, of course this implicated the Confederate government right up to the hilt. But the Government had heard such claims before, and was now wary of them. The claim that Surratt and Booth went to Richmond weekly is hyperbolic. Surratt did not go that often, and no reputable witness saw Booth there despite the fact that, after the assassination, people saw Booth *everywhere*. From a historian's viewpoint, this statement becomes doubly questionable when tied with the rest of the letter, in which Surratt supposedly told Ste. Marie "that the evening on which the assassination took place he waited in Washington till all was prepared for the deed, and left the same night for New York, and from thence to Canada."[936] As already explained, while it is possible that Surratt was in Washington the night of the assassination, it is far more likely that he was in Elmira. Furthermore, even if he was in Washington, he would still want people to believe that he was in Elmira, since he had gone to a lot of trouble to be seen there in order to create an Elmira alibi. Why would he confide in Ste. Marie? Surratt was probably too wary to be taken in by a fellow like Ste. Marie, who was insufficiently macho and single-minded to be viewed even by a drunken Surratt as a close confidant and fellow partisan.

As a final prod to action, Ste. Marie adds that, "[s]trange as it may appear, I know some papers in New York and Philadelphia, who, if they were in possession of this information, would force the Government to act upon it in justice to the memory of President Lincoln."[937] It didn't work. As late as October 23, Ste. Marie was still writing to the American consulate in Rome, begging for a discharge from the Zouaves because he was in fear for his life, and reiterating his charges against Surratt.[938] Like many witnesses to something terrible who refuse to stay quiet, Ste. Marie was becoming an annoyance to the authorities.

Still, odd as his later statements may be, we do not know for certain that the fundamental point about tacit approval by the Confederate cabinet is not accurate. Therefore, it is worth pausing just a moment to consider the significance if this part of Ste. Marie's story was true. *It would mean that there was a high level Confederate plot to kill Abraham Lincoln, which has been mostly lost to history.*

* * *

Instead of springing the trap offered by Cardinal Antonelli, Secretary of State Seward sent a detailed cable instructing King to: (1)

have a confidential third party bring a photograph of Surratt (to be sent by the State Department by subsequent cable) out to wherever Surratt was stationed, in order to "ascertain . . . whether the person indicated by Ste. Marie is really John Surratt"; (2) meet with Cardinal Antonelli to obtain his assurance that, in the absence of an extradition treaty, the Papal States would really surrender Surratt upon request of the American Government; (3) ask Cardinal Antonelli to keep both Surratt and Ste. Marie in the Zouaves until the American Government had time to further communicate concerning them; and (4) pay Ste. Marie $250 in gold "in consideration of the information he has already communicated on the subject."[939]

It was now six months since information had first been received from Ste. Marie. Surratt's company was no longer in Velletri or Sezze – both relatively accessible to Rome – but was now stationed near the monastery of Trisulti, high up Mount Rotonario in the Province of Frosinone, over sixty miles from Rome.[940] The American Government seemed intent on letting Surratt slip through its fingers once again.

* * *

Cardinal Antonelli would not let that happen. Without awaiting a formal request from the United States, he ordered Surratt's arrest. The actual order was issued on Tuesday, November 6, 1866, from the Zouave Commander in Chief, a Bavarian named General Kanzer, to Lieutenant-Colonel M. Allet, a Swiss officer stationed at Velletri, who was in command of Surratt's regiment.[941] The order was terse and to the point:

> Cause the arrest of the zouave Watson, and have him conducted, under secure escort, to the military prison at Rome. It is of much importance that this order be executed with exactness.[942]

Allet passed the command through the lines to Captain De Lambilly, commander of Surratt's company, who dispatched Sergeant Halyerid with six men to Trisulti to seize "Watson."[943]

In human affairs it so often seems as if the best laid plans are no match for chance. Just about the same time that the arrest order was issued, a confidential letter from King to Ste. Marie was misdelivered to a Zouave trumpeter named "Santa Maria." Santa Maria did not speak English, but he knew a comrade who did. He took the letter to his friend "Watson" for translation. Surratt was instantly put on guard and immediately began preparations to desert.[944] He requested and was granted leave, and together with his faithful bloodhound he managed to travel twelve miles across the mountains from Trisulti to the ancient hill town of Veroli, nestled against the *Monti Lepini* range. Surratt's quick exit eluded Sergeant Halyerid's force.[945] From there, it would be a simple matter to slip away down the valley towards Sora, into Garibaldi-held territory. He just needed a bit of time to secure provisions and civilian clothes.

Surratt did not appreciate just how imminent was his peril. Corporal Vanderstroeten of Surratt's own 3rd Company arrested "Zouave Watson" on Wednesday, November 7, in Veroli, and handed him over to Post-Corporal Warrin. Warrin locked Surratt in a sturdy stone prison cell under the barracks in Veroli. Two guards with loaded arms were placed on duty, one at the door of the cell, and the other at the door of the barracks to ensure that Surratt's brothers in arms did not come to his aid.[946]

Surratt's cell was one of three in the ancient guard house built into the steep banks surrounding the ancient hill town. It was commodious for a prison cell – about twelve by fifteen feet[947] – but to a man who had run over five thousand miles and then disappeared into the anonymity of foreign service, it must have felt like a crypt. Through the Roman bars of the single window, the cell afforded a tantalizing view towards the promontory of land on which rested the beautiful Basilica-Cathedral of Santa Maria Salome, and beyond that, the freedom that Surratt had been on the cusp of seizing when he was arrested.

For the first time since the assassination of Abraham Lincoln over one and one-half years before, Surratt was a prisoner. On November 30, Secretary of State Seward wrote to Mr. King: "You cannot express too strongly to Cardinal Antonelli the satisfaction of the President with the friendly and prompt proceedings of the Papal government."[948]

At four o'clock the morning of Thursday, November 8, Corporal Warrin awakened the prisoner "Watson," and ordered him to prepare for immediate transport to Rome. Surratt rose, put on his gaiters and, in the words of Warrin's account, "took his coffee with a calmness and phlegm quite English."[949] In this context, the word "phlegm" is used to describe a sense of "dull or apathetic coldness or indifference."[950] Squeezed between a detail of six armed guards, Surratt was marched out the gate of the prison onto steps leading down onto a courtyard overlooking the countryside.[951]

Surratt was anything but indifferent to his peril. At the far end of the courtyard was a parapet beyond which there was a steep drop of about one hundred feet.[952] Perched on the edge of the cliff were the privies of the barracks. Surratt requested of Corporal Warrin permission to use the privy, which was granted. He walked calmly to one of the privies at the edge of the cliff, seized the parapet and leaped over, disappearing in an instant into the abyss![953]

Captain De Lambilly picks up the astonishing narrative in his report of November 8:

> Corporal Warrin . . . allowed him to stop, very naturally, [never] . . . doubting . . . that their prisoner was going to escape at a place which it seemed quite impossible to us to clear. This perilous leap was, however, . . . to be crowned with success. In fact, Watson, who seemed quiet, seized the balustrade, made a leap, and cast himself into the void, falling on the uneven rocks, where he might have broken his bones a thousand times, and gain[ed] the depths of the valley.[954]

A clue to Surratt's survival can be gleaned from Lieutenant-Colonel Allet's report of November 9 to General Kanzer:

> [Watson] leaped from a height of twenty-three feet on a very narrow rock, beyond which is a precipice. The filth from the barracks accumulated on the rock, and in this manner the fall of Watson was broken.[955]

Thus, Surratt used the excrement piled on a rock ledge beneath the barracks privies to cushion his fall. In a later interview with the *New York Times*, Surratt would correct the twenty-three feet estimate to "about equal to a second-story window, or say twelve feet."[956] Still, the chasm loomed below, and Surratt's aim had to be good to survive. It was a moment of extraordinary courage and bravado, yet simultaneously disgusting and faintly ridiculous.

Whatever you think of Surratt's escape, by making it he had leapt into legend. The covers of the "penny dreadful" novels written about him over the next decade would all feature Surratt in his Zouave uniform, flying over the parapet at Veroli.[957] Though he had thoroughly outfoxed his entire regiment and embarrassed its officers, a note of grudging admiration nonetheless creeps into Lieutenant-Colonel Allet's report to General Kanzer:

> . . . [T]he escape of Watson savors of a prodigy. . . . Had he leaped a little further he would have fallen into an abyss.[958]

Instead, Surratt leapt into the filthy stew of historical legend.

894 State Archives of Rome, *Papal Zouaves Enlistment Records*, vol. 2, record #1857. For this document I am indebted to my colleague Professor Giancarlo Onorati of Sezze, Italia, author of *L'Ultimo dei Cospiratore (The Last Conspirator)* (Latina 2012).

895 Papal Encyclicals Online, *The Syllabus of Errors Condemned by Piux IX*, http://www.papalencyclicals.net/Pius09/p9syll.htm (accessed Feb. 15, 2014).

896 *New York Times* (Feb. 22 & 27, 1868), quoted in Marraro, p.92.

897 U.S. Const., Amend. XIII (ratified Dec. 6, 1865).

898 Marraro, p.83.

899 *Ibid.*, p.83 n.1.

900 *Two Years in the Zouaves*, p.48. Colorized image at http://images.historyinfullcolor.com/assassination3d/h4EF23084#h4ef230 84 (accessed Feb. 8, 2014).

901 *Regiments of the Civil War*, http://www.civilwar.org/education/history/warfare-and-logistics/warfare/regiment.html (accessed Feb. 10, 2014).

902 Colorized image at http://images.historyinfullcolor.com/assassination3d/h4EF23084#h4ef230

84 (accessed Feb. 8, 2014).

903 *Two Years in the Zouaves*, pp.37-38, 62-63, 65, 67.

904 *Ibid.*, pp.48-52, 67.

905 *Ibid.*, pp.53, 60.

906 Isacsson, *TAT*, p.15.

907 *Two Years in the Zouaves*, p.68. Other companies would be artillery, or engineers.

908 *Ibid.*, frontispiece.

909 Ste. Marie's Petition in the Court of Claims gives an enlistment date of April 9, but appended contemporaneous letters suggest that is closer to the date that Ste. Marie first found Surratt, rather than the date Ste. Marie enlisted. *Compare, Ste. Marie v. United States*, p.3, *with, ibid.*, p.16 (letter of April 23, 1866, from Ste. Marie to Rufus King). The March enlistment date is based on when the Petition states Ste. Marie first became aware that Surratt had joined the Papal Zouaves. *Ibid.*, p.3. A possible explanation for the discrepancy in dates is that the Petition was drawn up and sworn to by Ste. Marie's attorney, who probably muddled some of the dates.

910 *Ibid.*, p.16 (letter of April 23, 1866, from Ste. Marie to Rufus King).

911 *Ibid.*, p.3.

912 *Ibid.*, p.22; *Two Years in the Zouaves*, pp.66-68.

913 1 JHS Trial 492. Later correspondence names his company as the 8th. *Ste. Marie v. United States*, p.56. The discrepancy is not explained.

914 1 JHS Trial 492 (trial testimony says April 14 or 15); *Ste. Marie v. United States*, p.16 (letter of April 23, 1866, from Ste. Marie to Rufus King says "about a fortnight ago").

915 *Ste. Marie v. United States*, p.22 (Statement of Ste. Marie, July 10, 1866). I have chosen Ste. Marie's sworn version of their meeting over the probably embellished version given by the *New York Times* on February 16,1867: "While attending a festival St. Marie met Surratt, who approached and asked him if he was not an American. He replied that he was, and whispering said: 'You remind me of an American named Surratt; are you he?' 'Oh no,' replied Surratt. 'All the better for you,' rejoined St. Marie. Subsequently, when excited with wine, Surratt confessed that he was the man of whom St. Marie spoke, and at various times indulged in braggadocio concerning . . . the assassination plot and other cognate matters, greatly to the astonishment of St. Marie and the delight of his associates, many of whom were Canadian refugees and raiders like himself." *New York Times*, "The Surratt Case - Arrival of St. Marie, His Identifier - Surratt Expected Daily" (Feb. 16, 1867).

916 2 JHS Trial 856.

917 *Compare*, 2 JHS Trial 851, 854 (bad), with, 2 JHS Trial 990, 991, 1032 (good).

918 Isacsson, *TAT*, pp.9, 19-20.

919 JOH Papers - HBSM, *Richmond Daily Examiner*, p.1 col.4 (Oct. 21, 1863).
920 *Ste. Marie v. United States*, p.15 (Cable #53).
921 *Ibid.* (emphasis added).
922 *Ibid.*, p.24 (letter King to Seward, July 24, 1866); *see also, ibid.*, p.16 (letter from Ste. Marie to King, April 23, 1866).
923 *Ibid.*, p.16 (letter from Ste. Marie to King, April 23, 1866); *ibid.*, p. 21 (letter King to Seward, June 30, 1866).
924 *Ibid.*, pp.18-19 (Cable #36, May 24, 1866); ibid., pp.20-21 (Cable #57, June 23, 1866).
925 *Ibid.*, p.21 (Ste. Marie Statement, June 21, 1866).
926 *Ibid.*, p.23 (Ste. Marie Statement, July 10, 1866) (emphasis in original).
927 *E.G. Lee*, p.180.
928 Library of Congress, Manuscript Division, *George Nicholas Sanders Family Papers - Finding Aid Biographical Statement*, http://lcweb2.loc.gov/service/mss/eadxmlmss/eadpdfmss/2012/ms012053.pdf (accessed Feb. 9, 2014).
929 *Ste. Marie v. United States*, p.23 (Statement of Ste. Marie, July 10, 1866).
930 *The Veiled Lady*, p.41; *Come Retribution*, p.415. See Chapter Eight.
931 *Ste. Marie v. United States*, p.24 (Cables ##40 and 41, from Seward to King).
932 *Ibid.*, p.24 (Cable #62, from King to Seward, August 8, 1866).
933 Isacsson, *TAT*, p.20.
934 *Ste. Marie v. United States*, p.56 (Ste. Marie to Hooker, Sept. 12, 1866).
935 *Ibid.*
936 *Ibid.*
937 *Ibid.*
938 JOH Papers - HBSM, *Typescript of Letter for Sale by Mr. Charles Appelbaum* (Oct. 23, 1866).
939 *Ste. Marie v. United States*, p.25 (Cable #43, Seward to King, Oct. 16, 1866); *ibid.*, p.47 (Davis to Phillips, Sept. 29, 1873).
940 *Ste. Marie v. US*, p.27 (Letter King to Seward, Nov. 3, 1866); p.28 (Cable #463 from Allet to Kanzer).
941 *Ibid.*, p.28 (Order of Nov. 6, 1866); *Two Years in the Zouaves*, p.54.
942 *Ste. Marie v. United States*, p.28.
943 *Ibid.*, p.30 (De Lambilly to Allet, Nov. 8, 1866).
944 *Ibid.*, pp.5, 30.
945 *Ibid.*, p.30 (De Lambilly to Allet, Nov. 8, 1866).
946 *Ibid.*, p.28 (Cable #463 from Allet to Kanzer, Nov. 7, 1866); *ibid.*, p.30 (De Lambilly to Allet, Nov. 8, 1866).
947 Calculated by the author pacing the cell.
948 *Ibid.*, p.35 (Cable #47, Seward to King, Nov. 30, 1866).
949 *Ibid.*, p.31 (De Lambilly to Allet, Nov. 8, 1866).
950 Merriam-Webster Online Dictionary, Definition 3a, http://www.merriam-

webster.com/dictionary/phlegm (accessed Feb. 10, 2014).

951 *Ste. Marie v. US*, p.31 (De Lambilly to Allet, Nov. 8, 1866).

952 *Ibid.*, p.28 (Allet to Kanzer, *quoting*, DeLambilly to Allet, Nov. 8, 1866).

953 *Ibid.* p.30 (Allet to Kanzer, Nov. 9, 1866); ibid., p.31 (De Lambilly to Allet, Nov. 8, 1866).

954 *Ibid.*, p.31 (De Lambilly to Allet, Nov. 8, 1866).

955 *Ibid.*, p.30 (Allet to Kanzer, Nov. 9, 1866).

956 *NY Times*, "A Visit to Surratt," pp.2-3.

957 Aside from the obvious fictions of the penny dreadfuls and the fraud of Hanson-Hiss, there is another version of Surratt's escape that was published in the *New York Daily Tribune* on February 21, 1881, p.3. In this version a purported comrade of Surratt's named Henry Lipman was part of a guard duty of twelve who conspired to allow Surratt to escape by letting him into the latrine at midnight, and then "forgetting him" until two o'clock in the morning, which gave him time to lower himself through the sewer into the stream below, and escape down the mountain. *Ibid.* But that account is so fraught with obvious inconsistencies when compared with contemporaneous accounts, that in my opinion it is not worthy of belief. For example, Lipman says that he enlisted upon attaining his majority in February 1867, and that he met Surratt several months later. But by 1867 Surratt was in Washington City, standing trial for the murder of Lincoln. This is not a casual mistaken date, because Lipman must know in what year he attained his majority. Another example is the claim that twelve guards were placed on Surratt overnight. Captain De Lambilly - who had every motivation to show Lieutenant-Colonel Allet the stringency of his protective measures - said at the time that only two guards were placed on Surratt overnight. *Ste. Marie v. United States*, p.30 (De Lambilly to Allet, Nov. 8, 1866). Many other details - Surratt's supposedly "black" mustache, his overdramatic nighttime mumblings about his poor mother, calling "St. Mary" (not "Ste. Marie") an "American detective," and more, plainly mark this account as fraudulent.

958 *Ste. Marie v. United States*, p.30 (Allet to Kanzer, Nov. 9, 1866).

CHAPTER SEVENTEEN

"HIS DEATH IS PREFERABLE
TO HIS ESCAPE"

PATROLS WERE IMMEDIATELY ORGANIZED TO PURSUE "WATSON." Initial reports stated that as many as fifty Zouaves were sent in pursuit.[959] One of the search parties came upon a peasant who reported that she had seen an unarmed Zouave heading in the direction of the monastery at Casamari. They followed, but lost his trail.[960] Surratt had once again demonstrated his uncanny ability to elude pursuers.

According to a family tale told by Anna Surratt Tonry to her son Reginald, as Surratt scrambled down the valley towards Casamari and beyond, he heard the baying of bloodhounds in pursuit. Though his back was wrenched and his arm sprained from his daring leap, he was forced to climb a tree. Looking down from his perch he recognized his own loyal hound, wagging her tail. Reunited after being separated the previous day at the time of his arrest, Surratt and his canine accomplice fled together.[961]

This is a nice story, but it doesn't quite ring true. If Surratt really had been treed by hounds there would have been other hounds in the pack who were not so friendly to him, and his pursuers could not have been far behind. It may be, however, that the rank and file Zouaves in pursuit did not have their heart in the chase. "Watson" was a popular comrade in arms, and their sympathies probably were with him regardless of the orders of their superior officers. It is unlikely that they would disobey a direct order to capture "Watson" under the eyes of their officers, but to not quite catch up with him as he fled down the valley was another matter.

At the bottom of the valley the River Liri flows down from the mountains to the east. If Surratt's leap from the parapet really was broken by "the filth" from the barracks privies, he probably took a few moments for a cleansing dip in the river before proceeding further. The well-worn paths along the river formed a natural highway away from Rome into enemy territory, where the Zouaves could not follow. That is the way Surratt went. By choosing to head east into Garibaldi territory in full Zouave uniform, Surratt ran from the proverbial frying pan into the fire.

* * *

At Sora, a town located approximately twenty-five kilometers from Veroli, Surratt found a hospital where his injuries were treated. General Kanzler reported a rumor that Surratt was treated at the "military hospital."[962] It seems odd that a soldier in Zouave uniform would have been treated in a Garibaldi military hospital without then being held as a prisoner of war. The discredited Hanson-Hiss interview says that Surratt ran into a Garibaldi unit while making his escape, and only managed to avoid being shot or held captive by convincing them that he was a Zouave deserter.[963] That interview is not only generally incredible, but it also fails to convince on this specific incident by claiming that Surratt spent a full week with this Garibaldi unit, which we know was not possible since he was already far from Sora by that time. Still, it may be that Hanson-Hiss stumbled upon the explanation for Surratt's ability to thrive in Garibaldi territory while sporting a Zouave uniform. It was demonstrably true that the Pope was now treating Surratt as an enemy and, as the saying goes, *the enemy of my enemy is my friend.*

It is also possible that the General's intelligence – which he described as merely a "rumor" – was faulty, and that Surratt obtained care elsewhere. A likely place for an injured Zouave to seek care in that district would have been on the outskirts of Sora, with the nuns of the convent at the Abbey of San Domenico, which was founded on the River Liri in the year 1011.[964]

Either way, we know that Surratt was able to get care for his injured arm and back in the town of Sora on the very Thursday, November 8, of his daring leap.[965] Meanwhile, the authorities were being unusually ineffective, even by their lugubrious standards. It was not until Friday, November 16 – a full week and one day after the escape – that General Kanzler called upon Mr. King with the intelligence that Surratt may have sought care at the military hospital in Sora.[966] That Surratt might head to Sora should have occurred to his pursuers on the very morning of the escape. They already had the peasant's report that he was headed east towards Casamari, and Sora is the major town located just fifteen kilometers east of Casimari. Probably the best explanation for the delay in placing Surratt in Sora is that, by the bold tactic of crossing enemy lines, Surratt made it much more difficult for the Zouaves to obtain any timely intelligence about him. Another factor may be that "Watson's" former comrades nearest the scene of the getaway failed to cooperate fully with their superiors.

Acting on General Kanzler's November 16 report, Mr. King immediately sent the acting secretary of his legation, Mr. Hooker, by train to Sora to investigate. Mr. Hooker quickly learned that Surratt had been in Sora, but had left on November 8 for Naples, a distance of about eighty-five miles.[967] Hooker telegraphed King, who in turn cabled Frank Swan, American consul in Naples, at eight o'clock on the morning of November 18. Mr. Swan immediately caused the police in Naples and in the surrounding small towns to search for Surratt.[968] As stated by Mr. King in his report, "[o]ur hopes were strong . . . that we should succeed in catching him somewhere in the vicinity of Naples."[969] But where?

* * *

The answer was . . . nowhere. Surratt had already left Naples.

A bedraggled Surratt and his faithful hound dog arrived in the elegant city of Naples on Tuesday or Wednesday, November 13 or 14. He had no passport, was clad in a dirty, tattered uniform, and claimed to be a destitute Canadian named "Walters" who had deserted from the Papal Zouaves. At his own request, "Walters" was held for three days in the town prison, "not exactly as a prisoner," says Mr. Swan in his report, but for surveillance and questioning.[970] This seems to have operated to the mutual advantage of Surratt and the police. The police got to keep a suspicious character under watch, and Surratt was kept out of sight and given bed and board. Meanwhile, Surratt/Walters plied his keepers with a somewhat altered version of the truth, claiming that he had been a tourist in Rome who had enlisted out of necessity when he ran out of money, and that after he had been imprisoned for insubordination, he had escaped by jumping from a high wall, injuring his arm and back in the process.[971]

Surratt rested and healed for three days in the prison at Naples, before asserting his rights as a supposed British subject to be taken to the British consulate. It was probably Friday, November 16, that the British consul obtained his release. Meanwhile the police had searched Surratt's belongings and found that he had twelve scudi, which would have been enough to pay for his own lodgings but for the fact, as he claimed, "that he wished to save his money."[972] Likely the local police were quite content to be rid of him.

"Walters" lounged about the consulate overnight, "giving them some trouble . . . and exciting sympathy by his position, that of a young man of good appearance without money . . .."[973] At the prompting of the British consul, some English gentlemen stood "Walters" his fare for passage to Alexandria, Egypt, and at nine o'clock on the night of Saturday, November 17 – precisely eleven hours *before* the American consul even knew he might be in Naples – Surratt alias Walters set sail on the steamer *Tripoli*.[974] Watching the torch lights of the Royal Palace and Castelnuevo fade into the dark shadows of Mount Vesuvius as he headed out across the Bay of Naples bound for Africa, did Surratt feel the triumph of escape once again? Or had he begun to fear that no matter where he went it could not be far enough; that he would be hunted down to the ends of the earth?

* * *

By two o'clock the next day – Sunday, November 18 – Mr. Swan of the American consulate at Naples learned that Surratt alias "Walters or Watson" was on board the *Tripoli*, bound for Alexandria. The *Tripoli* was scheduled to make one stop at the British island of Malta on Monday, November 19, for the purpose of taking on three hundred tons of coal. As Malta was quarantined (probably due to a cholera outbreak, which was rampant at this time and locale), there was no risk that Surratt could disembark there. Both Swan and King cabled the consul at Malta, Mr. Winthrop, with instructions to have Surratt arrested, but to no avail.[975] The British authorities would not permit his arrest there.[976] Whatever the Americans might claim about the young man in the tattered Zouave uniform, Walters had been launched by the British consul at Naples under the guise of being a British subject. If the attempt to arrest Surratt in Malta had any effect, it was to put him even further on his guard.

Mr. King's backup plan was a cable sent on Tuesday, November 20, to Charles Hale, American consul at Alexandria, with instructions to arrest Surratt there. That plan also began to falter before the vagaries of chance. On Wednesday, November 21, Mr. King received word from the Office of the Pontifical Telegraph that his dispatch had first been sent via Malta, because the Syria-Suez line was interrupted, but upon learning that the Malta to Alexandria line was interrupted and the Syria-Suez line reestablished, they had resent the cable via the latter channel. However, because the Syria-Suez line only took cables as far as Benghazi, the Papal telegraph authorities had directed King's cable to be mailed from Benghazi to Alexandria. Even that attempt failed: "Now they telegraph us from Malta that there being no postal service between Benghazi and Alexandria, the despatch [*sic*] in question was this day sent by steamer from Malta to Alexandria."[977] The net result of these redundant failures meant that the telegraph ordering the arrest of Surratt left Malta by steamer *a day or two after* Surratt himself left Malta by steamer. It had little chance of catching up with him, and Surratt's incredible run of good fortune was apparently holding strong.

The *Tripoli* with Surratt on board docked in Alexandria on Friday, November 23. King's telegram did not even find its way through to Alexandria via Constantinople until November 27.[978] But as any gambler knows, luck doesn't last forever. Surratt must have been furious to learn that, having passed through Malta, he was to be held in quarantine along with all the other third class passengers for six days, until November 29.[979] He must have surmised that even the United States Government could not be that far behind him. All he could do was sit and wait.

* * *

Although there were seventy-eight passengers still in quarantine from the *Tripoli* on the morning of November 27, Mr. Hale had no difficulty picking out John Surratt from his "unmistakable American type countenance" and – even more readily – by the fact that he was still wearing his Zouave uniform. "You are the man I want," said Mr. Hale, "you are an American."

"Yes sir, I am," replied Surratt, his long days in the heat and stench of Egyptian quarantine perhaps addling his brain.

"You doubtless know why I want you," said Hale. "What is your name?"

"Walters," was the prompt reply, as Surratt came to his senses.

"I believe your true name is Surratt," said Hale. "As United States consul-general for Alexandria, I place you under arrest."[980]

Surratt offered no resistance. Under an armed escort provided by the Egyptian authorities, Hale escorted him to a private cell within the quarantine zone. Surratt was quiet, "displaying neither surprise nor irritation." When cautioned that he was not obligated to say anything, but that whatever he said would be taken down in writing, he replied merely, "I have nothing to say. I want nothing but what is right."[981]

Two days later Surratt's quarantine expired, and he was moved to a local prison under the supervision of the United States Consul's office. At that time he was still maintaining "his demeanor of reticence" – *i.e.*, not talking. But he had already said too much. In the absence of a passport or any other documents, by acknowledging his United States citizenship and submitting to arrest by the U.S. Consul Surratt precluded intervention on his behalf by the British or any other government.[982] The Americans had their man at last. But could they keep him?

* * *

This time, the Government did not tarry. On December 4, Mr. Hale learned that the Secretary of the Navy had instructed Admiral Goldsborough to send an armed warship to Alexandria to pick up the "fugitive, charged with the crime of assassination of the late Abraham Lincoln, President of the United States, and of an attempt to assassinate William H. Seward, Secretary of State of the United States . . . ."[983] This must have been a most gratifying telegram to write, as it was signed "WILLIAM H. SEWARD."

It was probably in late November that the United States Naval Screw Sloop Third Rate *Swatara*, armed with ten guns and under the command of William N. Jeffers, had first received instructions to go from Marseilles to Rome to pick up a prisoner. Upon arrival at Civita Vecchia on December 10, Captain Jeffers traveled overland to Rome, where he learned that the prisoner had escaped and been recaptured in Alexandria, Egypt.[984]

On December 14, just before departing Civita Vecchia for Alexandria, the *Swatara* took on board Henri de Beaumont Ste. Marie, whose discharge from the Papal Zouaves had at last been secured by Mr. King. There was immediate friction between Ste. Marie and Captain Jeffers, who considered Ste. Marie to be a braggart.[985] Ste. Marie's view was that he was treated with disrespect by the Captain, officers and crew of the *Swatara*, while Surratt was treated with "marked courtesy and distinction by . . . Captain Jeffers . . .."[986] When they reached Malta, Jeffers refused to allow Ste. Marie to go ashore, allegedly because he did not want Ste. Marie "babbling" about their mission. Initially, Jeffers accused Ste. Marie of refusing to go ashore at Alexandria to identify Surratt, but then in the next breath conceded that he (Jeffers) had refused to permit Ste. Marie to go ashore there.[987] Jeffers admitted that he "entertained the utmost contempt for Ste. Marie," and indeed his testimony strains to assist the "fine looking fellow" he'd taken on board in irons.[988] For example, when asked whether the *Swatara* brought John H. Surratt to Washington as a prisoner, Jeffers' legalistic and uncooperative answer was, "I do not know whether she brought John H. Surratt or not; she brought a prisoner from Alexandria, Egypt."[989]

Jeffers' hair-splitting aside, there is no question that on Friday, December 21, 1866, John H. Surratt was marched up the gangway onto the *Swatara* for the voyage back to the United States.[990] The prisoner taken on board was identified as Surratt by Ste. Marie in his trial testimony, and ultimately even the uncooperative Captain Jeffers admitted as much.[991]

Despite Ste. Marie's charge that Surratt was granted special favor aboard the *Swatara*, the formal orders under which he was held were quite strict. Apparently, Surratt's reputation as an escape artist preceded him. The orders included the following:

> He is not to be allowed to converse with any person whatever. . . .
>
> He will be kept in the room arranged for his reception, in single irons only, so long as he keeps quiet and makes no attempts at escape. The room door to be kept locked. . . .
>
> His meals will be supplied by the ward-room mess. The food to be cut up, and a spoon only to be allowed with which to eat it.
>
> He is to be carefully guarded against attempts at suicide, whether by jumping overboard or otherwise. If he attempts to escape he is to be fired upon by the sentry, the orderly, and the officer of the watch. . . .
>
> . . . [H]is death is preferable to his escape.
>
> If the prisoner becomes violent, he is to be placed in double irons, hands behind him. . . .
>
> The sentry is to be relieved every two hours . . ..
>
> The corporal of the guard and orderly . . . will be present when the prisoner is taken to the water-closet, will see the door locked on his return, and hand the key to the officer of the watch.
>
> When in port the officer of the watch will be present whenever the door is opened.
>
> Meals may be passed in through the window. . . .[992]

Captain Jeffers testified that, "[i]n accordance with these orders, from the day [Surratt] was received on my ship till the moment I delivered him over to the marshal here, he had never spoken a word, and no one has been allowed to speak to him except in reference to his personal wants."[993]

Although he took Surratt on board on December 21, Captain Jeffers was in no particular hurry. He allowed his crew to spend

Christmas in Alexandria before sailing for Port Mahon on the island of Minorca on December 26, and then to Villefranche sur Mer, just by Nice, where Admiral Goldsborough inspected the prisoner and gave Jeffers his final orders.[994] Tensions between Ste. Marie and Jeffers had reached the breaking point by then, and at Ste. Marie's request he was put off at Nice before the *Swatara* headed for the United States.[995]

The *Swatara* left Villefranche sur Mer on January 8, 1867, with arrival expected in late January. But fate once again intervened. Bad storms raked the Atlantic, and a rare freeze extended from Washington City southward for forty miles, closing all the ports. From the *New York Times*, dateline Fortress Monroe, Virginia, February 15, 1867:

> The strong southwest and southerly breezes prevailing lately shifted to the northwest early today. Chesapeake Bay and Hampton Roads are shrouded in a heavy fog, and rain has descended almost incessantly during the day.
>
> There have been no additional arrivals or departures . . . .
>
> An anxious watch is being kept up at the Capes of Virginia for the gunboat Swatara, with Surratt on board, now fully due.[996]

Concern that Surratt might be lost at sea intensified when Ste. Marie, who sailed from France on February 2, arrived on February 16.[997] But the anxiety broke on Sunday, February 17, with the first sightings of the *Swatara* in Chesapeake Bay, anchored near the lightship for Willoughby Spit. The next day she began to make her way in under the guidance of a skilled harbor pilot.[998] On Tuesday, February 19, she lay anchor at the Washington Navy Yard, within view of the bridge crossed by Booth on the night of the assassination. Surratt was led off in irons directly to jail by United States Marshal David Gooding.[999]

It had been one year and ten months since Surratt had set foot on American soil. He had traveled roughly fourteen thousand miles only to end up back at the scene of the crime. But the nation to which he returned was not the one from which he had fled. There would be no military tribunal and quick trip to the gallows for Mary's son.[1000] If John Surratt was to be hanged for complicity in the murder of Abraham

Lincoln, the prosecution would have to convince twelve "good and true" men of the district, including some whose sympathies had been with the Rebels, that he was guilty as charged.

959 *Ibid.*, p.28 (Allet to Kanzer, Nov. 8, 1866).
960 *Ibid.*, p.31 (De Lambilly to Allet, Nov. 8, 1866).
961 *Ibid.*, p.33 (Swan to King, Nov. 21, 1866); *His Mother's Memories*, p. XI-26.
962 *Ste. Marie v. United States*, p.29 (Cable #67, King to Seward, Nov. 19, 1866).
963 *Hanson-Hiss*, Weichmann, p.448.
964 Background on the Abbey taken from signage at the site.
965 *Ste. Marie v. United States*, p.29 (Cable #67, King to Seward, Nov. 19, 1866).
966 *Ibid.*
967 *Ibid.*
968 *Ibid.*, pp.31-32 (Swan to King, Nov. 18, 1866).
969 *Ibid.*, p.29 (Cable #67, King to Seward, Nov. 19, 1866).
970 *Ibid.*, p.33 (Swan to King, Nov. 21, 1866).
971 *Ibid.*; ibid., p.36 (Cable #66 Hale to Seward).
972 *Ibid.*, p.33 (Swan to King, Nov. 21, 1866).
973 *Ibid.*
974 *Ibid.*, pp.31-32 (Swan to King, Nov. 18, 1866), p.33 (Swan to King, Nov. 21, 1866).
975 *Ibid.*, p.29 (Cable #67, King to Seward, Nov. 19, 1866); *ibid.*, p.32 (Swan to King, Nov. 18, 1866); *ibid.*, p.34 (Swan to King, Nov. 21, 1866).
976 *Ibid.*, p.7.
977 *Ibid.*, p.33 (Office of the Pontifical Telegraph to King, Nov. 21, 1866).
978 *Ibid.*, p.36 (Cable #66, Hale to Seward, Nov. 27, 1866).
979 *Ibid.*, p.37.
980 *Ibid.*, p.36 (Cable #66, Hale to Seward, Nov. 27, 1866).
981 *Ibid.*
982 *Ibid.*, p.37 (Cable #66, Hale to Seward, Nov. 27, 1866); *Ibid.*, p.38 (Cable #68, Hale to Seward, Dec. 4, 1866).
983 *Ste. Marie v. United States*, p.38 (Cable #25, Seward to Hale, Dec. 4, 1866).
984 JOH Papers, *Boutwell Committee Report, Testimony of William N. Jeffers*, p.15 (Feb. 20, 1867) (hereafter *"Jeffers Testimony"*); Isacsson, *TAT*, p.26.
985 *Jeffers Testimony*, p.17; *Ste. Marie v. United States*, p.39 (Cable #72, Dec. 17, 1866).
986 *Ste. Marie v. United States*, p.8.
987 *Jeffers Testimony*, p.17.
988 *Ibid.*, p.16.

989   *Ibid.*, p.15.
990   *Ibid.*, p.15.
991   1 JHS Trial 493; *Ste. Marie v. United States*, p.8.
992   *Jeffers Testimony*, pp.15-16.
993   *Ibid.*, p.16.
994   Isacsson, *TAT*, p.27; *Jeffers Testimony*, p.16. The sources call it "Villa Franca," but because that is too easily confused with the Villa Franca on the Amalfi coast of Italy I have used the proper French name for the town.
995   *Ste. Marie v. United States*, p.8; *Jeffers Testimony*, p.17.
996   *New York Times* (Feb. 18, 1867).
997   *New York Times*, "The Surratt Case - Arrival of St. Marie, His Identifier - Surratt Expected Daily" (Feb. 16, 1867); Isacsson, TAT, p.27.
998   *New York Times* (Feb. 18, 1867).
999   Isacsson, *TAT*, pp.27-28.
1000 The Supreme Court held in *Ex Parte Milligan*, 71 U.S. 2 (1866), that so long as the civilian courts were open and functioning, civilians could not be tried in military courts. *Ibid.* pp.136-37. It is questionable whether Surratt could be deemed a "civilian" at the time of his participation in the conspiracy. It was likely the public obloquy that had attached to the military trial of the conspirators that tipped the decision towards a civilian trial for Surratt. It is often argued that the military trial of the conspirators was illegal because of *Ex Parte Milligan*. I disagree. While the writ of habeas corpus in *Milligan* was granted on April 3, the opinion with the Court's reasoning was not issued until December 17, long after the military trial of the conspirators had concluded. *Ibid.* What's more, the coordinated attempt to decapitate the U.S. Government appears to have been an act of war supported and led by Confederate combatants.

Chapter Eighteen

WEICHMANN VERSUS WEICHMANN

At the very moment Surratt stepped from the *Swatara* onto land, Congress was conducting impeachment hearings against President Andrew Johnson.[1001] The actual articles of impeachment would not be passed until one year later,[1002] but the political air was already poisoned by rabid polarization between the enemy camps of Congress and the Executive. Although Surratt had pledged to live long enough to "serve Andrew Johnson as Abraham Lincoln has been served,"[1003] it now appeared that the southern democrat from Tennessee sitting in the White House was at the vanguard of the defunct Confederacy's push to win the peace.

With the conclusion of the Civil War two fundamental political questions rose above all others: first, on what terms would the former southern states be readmitted into the Union; and second, on what terms would the newly freed slaves (the "freedmen") be admitted into the American political community? These questions were inextricably linked. If the southern states were admitted without purging the pre-existing Confederate political structure and with full sovereign control over their people and affairs, then the virtual re-enslavement of the freedmen was a foregone conclusion.

The law of unintended consequences had played a nasty trick on the "victors" who enacted the Thirteenth Amendment to abolish slavery. With that abolishment, the so-called "Three-Fifths Compromise" under which slaves were only counted as three-fifths of a person was consigned (most deservedly) to the dustbin of history. The immediate

231

political effect, however, was to *increase* the potential political clout of the southern states by twenty-eight members of Congress and twenty-eight electoral votes.[1004] Because no southern state had yet agreed to enfranchise the freedmen, there was no imminent influx of new Republican voters to offset the increase in southern political power. If the status quo ante were allowed to survive, the abolition of slavery would paradoxically ensure the seating in Congress of a significant block of implacable racists, states rightists, and rebels.

Nonetheless, during a long period of Congressional recess in the summer and fall of 1865, Andrew Johnson authorized the reinstatement of all the remaining states of the former Confederacy on terms that did not require granting the "negro" vote, and did not in any effective way prevent the participation of former rebels.[1005] "Instead of reconstructed Southern states led by men committed to the Union, Johnson spawned resurrected Confederate governments that bristled with former rebels in high office."[1006] The men selected to sit in Congress from these newly-constituted southern states "included ten former Confederate generals and five more army officers of lower rank, seven former members of the Confederate Congress, and three men who were members of conventions that voted to secede in 1861."[1007]

Into this breach stepped Representative Thaddeus Stevens of Pennsylvania, powerful head of the House Ways and Means Committee. At the age of seventy-two, Stevens was a fiercely egalitarian Radical Republican whose home had served as a way station on the underground railroad in antebellum times.[1008] Stevens was one of three men – along with Senator Charles Sumner and abolitionist lawyer Wendell Phillips – accused by President Johnson of "laboring to destroy" the "fundamental principles of [American] Government . . . ."[1009] Stevens, for his part, had no fondness for the former tailor who had been made President by Booth's bullet. When Stevens was advised that President Johnson was "a self-made man," he replied sharply that he was "glad to hear it, for it relieves God Almighty of a heavy responsibility."[1010]

Under Stevens' guidance, Congress refused to seat the newly-elected southern representatives, and it established a Joint Committee on Reconstruction to investigate the loyalty of the newly-formed state governments, voting rights for freedmen, violations of civil rights, and the virtual re-enslavement of the freedmen in the South under the notorious Black Codes.[1011] Sadly, there was no shortage of abuses to investigate. In May 1866, in the President's home state of Tennessee, the rumor that black troops had killed several white policemen who tried to arrest a black soldier led to white police, firefighters and citizens storming through the black neighborhoods of South Memphis. Forty-six blacks and two whites were killed.[1012] In late July in New Orleans, police attacked a peaceful Louisiana Constitutional Convention attended predominantly by freedmen, killing forty-seven and wounding over one hundred, against one policeman who died, apparently, of sunstroke.[1013]

The fruits of Congress's work in 1866 included the Freedman's Bureau bill, aimed at assisting freedmen with access to the courts and ownership of property, and the first Civil Rights Act, aimed at nullifying the devastating effects of the Black Codes.[1014] When the Freedman's Bureau bill passed, Johnson met with "negro" leaders on February 9, 1866, though he was noncommittal. Still, the very fact of the meeting seemed encouraging. Only later was it learned that he confided to his private secretary after the meeting that Frederick Douglass was "just like any other nigger, & he would sooner cut a white man's throat than not."[1015] Johnson vetoed both acts, although his veto was overridden on the Civil Rights Act.[1016]

On June 13, 1866 Congress passed the Fourteenth Amendment by the required two-thirds majority, and sent it to the states for ratification.[1017] Modern readers are likely familiar with the enduring importance of section one, which abrogates the first holding of *Dred Scott*[1018] and requires that state laws provide "due process" and "equal protection."[1019] But it was on the second section that much of the contemporaneous attention was focused, as an intended remedy for the unintended consequences of the Thirteenth Amendment:

> Representatives shall be apportioned among the several States according to their respective numbers, counting the whole number of persons in each State . . .. But when the right to vote at any election . . . is denied to any of the male inhabitants of such State, being twenty-one years of age,

and citizens of the United States, or in any way abridged, except for participation in rebellion, or other crime, the basis of representation therein shall be reduced . . . [proportionately].[1020]

It was not as strong as what came later – the Fifteenth Amendment's flat-out prohibition on denying the right to vote based on "race, color, or previous condition of servitude," but it was a start.[1021] Unlike the President, Congress was determined not to allow Southern states back into the Union without fair participation of the newly freed slaves who were now citizens and equals before the law.

If all this was the political kindling, 1867 contained the sparks that ignited the firestorm of impeachment: passage by Congress of three Reconstruction Acts aimed at ensuring freedmen participation in the new politics of the South and limiting the power of former Confederates; veto of those acts by President Johnson; overriding of those vetoes by Congress; and then the firing by Johnson of the Secretary of War and military commanders who were enforcing Congressional Reconstruction.[1022] We learn in school that Johnson was impeached for firing Secretary of War Stanton in violation of something called the Tenure of Office Act, which – though accurate – entirely misses the point. The struggle was over Presidential Reconstruction versus Congressional Reconstruction. Who had the power to set the terms under which the South would reenter the Union and be governed? On this question turned two even bigger issues: first, whether the slaves would be set free on the road towards equal citizenship, or re-enslaved by slightly revised forms of law; and second, *who won the Civil War?*

* * *

Into this political tinderbox the *Swatara* dropped John H. Surratt just two weeks before passage and veto of the first Reconstruction Act. With the exception of his sister Anna, nobody was happy to see him. Not Johnson, who didn't want his intransigence over the hanging of John's mother revived in the public press. Not Secretary of War Stanton, ally to the Radical Republicans in Congress, whose department prosecuted Mary Surratt and was tainted by the perjuries of "Sanford Conover," and the resulting inability to make good on its early promises to link Jefferson Davis to the plot. Not the Radical Republicans themselves, who did not want this fresh-faced young rebel to stir up any sympathy for the South. Not Weichmann, who was already wracked by guilt over his testimony against the mother who took him in with great kindness, and now faced the prospect of helping to hang his "very intimate" friend, the son. But Surratt was in Washington, and the Government had no choice but to put him on trial.

Surratt was a cat who always managed to land squarely on his feet. Though confined to jail pending trial,[1023] in the words of a *New York Times* correspondent who gained access to him, "[m]any poor prisoners, whose crimes are scarcely worth mention in comparison with the great crime associated with Surratt's name, would rejoice could their lifetime be spent as comfortably as are the prison hours of this universally accused assassin."[1024] During the daytime hours, Surratt had free run of an entire private jailhouse corridor, thirty feet in length, with its three adjoining cells, as well as the open air of the prison courtyard, and an octagonal wooden structure in the courtyard with seven large windows and a glass door. At night he was more strictly confined to a scantly furnished ten-foot cell, with a stool and a single mattress laid on a stone floor, albeit amply covered. Surratt enjoyed all the comforts of home, provided by his friends and Anna's daily visits. He wore a new dark suit, "cut in the prevailing fashion," and "[u]pon his head he wore a black soft felt hat, also new."

> [H]e is provided with a plentiful assortment of books, embracing the field of literature from Divine truth to the silliest human trash. . . . His cuisine seems to be carefully looked after by outside friends, and no restriction is placed upon the amount or variety that is sent him. Instead of the brown loaf and boiled beef of ordinary prisoners, Surratt has the choicest of domestic cookery, selected with the sole view of pleasing his palate.[1025]

Regardless of the comforts, the four months awaiting trial could not have been easy, even for one with the steel nerves of a spy and soldier. Indeed, for a man of action like Surratt, enforced idleness and waiting might have been the worst torment.

* * *

It was not all idleness. In addition to visiting with Anna, Surratt met with his attorneys to plan his defense, and also with Father Walter, who served him as confessor as he had served his mother.[1026] There may have been more to Father Walter's visits than just religious guidance. He may also have been a conduit for a possible deal: Surratt's life and liberty in exchange for evidence sufficient to hang Confederate President Jefferson Davis.

No more irritating thorn chafed at the Government than Davis, who had been held prisoner at Fortress Monroe since May 19, 1865, but never put on trial.[1027] A hint of the genesis of a possible deal with Surratt for the head of the former Confederacy can be found buried in a *New York Times* article of December 19, 1866, while Surratt was still sitting in jail in Alexandria, Egypt. According to the article:

> The arrest of Surratt may materially alter the complexion of Jeff. Davis' case, and others supposed to have been engaged in the assassination plot.
>
> It is authoritatively stated that the Judicial authorities in Washington are awaiting the arrival of Surratt, and upon his revelations will entirely depend the future action of the Government.[1028]

Nothing more was heard about this publicly until the *New York Herald* broke the story on June 6, 1867, just four days before the start of Surratt's trial. According to this article, the whole object of the prosecution of Surratt was not to exact punishment for his crime, but rather to "obtain from him disclosures and facts implicating Jeff Davis in the assassination, which it is confidently believed the abject coward would readily give to save his own life." The appraisal of cowardice was based on what the correspondent called Surratt's "matricidal conduct in abandoning his mother . . .," and perhaps also an underestimation of Surratt's loyalty to the Confederate cause.[1029] Nonetheless, the article offered interesting particulars about the possible deal:

> It is well known to a few, including your correspondent, that overtures have been made to Surratt to the effect that if he would disclose the names of all who participated in the assassination conspiracy, and the part taken by each, which it is believed would implicate Mr. Davis, a nol. pros. would be entered in his case, and an act passed by Congress relieving him of all legal responsibility on account of his participation in the atrocious crime. These overtures, it is further known, were made through Father Walters [*sic*], the Catholic priest who attends Surratt, and Miss Surratt, who daily visits her brother in his cell.[1030]

How could this newspaper reporter be privy to such inside information? Apparently he obtained it (at a price?) from one of the guards at the jail who claimed to be able to overhear most of Surratt's conversations, "although conducted in an undertone . . .." According to this jailkeeper, Surratt "is by no means confident of an acquittal, and is disposed to listen to any propositions, the acceptance whereof can save him from a felon's doom." The trial was postponed at the Government's request on May 28 to allow for the arrival of more witnesses. Soon thereafter, Surratt fell ill, perhaps from the strain of his situation. Anna argued that the continuance showed the weakness of the Government's case, but Surratt feared, to the contrary, that it proved they would leave no stone unturned to convict him, and that his attorneys were not as sanguine of his acquittal as they let on. To this, Anna supposedly responded that, "it was not too late for him to embrace the opportunity that had been offered him to save himself, and that she would, if he desired, go at once" to see the authorities in charge. Tentatively, Surratt said, "no – not now," then added a moment later, "I know not what to do . . .."[1031]

Surratt's concern was that even if his attorneys believed he would be convicted, they would nonetheless urge him to proceed to trial without taking the offer – in other words, that their real master was not their client, but Jefferson Davis. "Some of my pretended friends don't care a cent what becomes of me," Surratt added, "so [long as] they can chain my tongue."[1032] The idea, according to the *Herald*, was to get Surratt safely tried in order to protect the Confederate hierarchy, especially Davis. If Surratt was acquitted, then he would have no reason to tell what he knew of the involvement of Richmond in the assassination. If he was convicted, "any revelations he might [then] make, for the evident purpose of saving his life, would be discredited."[1033]

As Surratt awaited trial in the relative luxury of his jailhouse suite with his books and delectable treats, he had weighty matters to consider. But it was probably not as close of a call as the *Herald* – a Yankee paper – might have wished. Though doubtless Anna, having already lost a mother, implored her brother to save himself, it is unlikely that Surratt ever seriously considered playing Judas to Jeff Davis. Giving up his mother was one thing. Giving up the Commander in Chief of the Confederacy was quite another. What Surratt would have done if convicted to obtain commutation of a death sentence, no one can say. But rather than cast a permanent stain on the much-ballyhooed honor of the Confederacy, Surratt would stand trial for the murder of Abraham Lincoln.

* * *

In a letter to the editor of the *New York Tribune* dated May 22, 1867, Weichmann wrote, "I will soon be called to testify against Surratt."[1034] It could not have been a happy prospect. For his testimony against Mrs. Surratt, Weichmann had been publicly accused of confessing that he perjured himself to save his own skin, and denounced by a significant portion of the public as an "executioner."[1035] In an interview published in the *New York Tribune* on May 20, 1867, Weichmann acknowledged that Mrs. Surratt "died for that ride" to Surrattsville that she took with him in the carriage on the afternoon of the assassination. Nonetheless, Weichmann claimed to have no regrets: "I, who . . . had slept under her roof so long without unkindness given or received, do not shrink to say that I have never been sorry that I accompanied her." He added that, "when she died I felt saddened but not self-accusing; for if there is a doubt that she was a principal in the murder, there is no doubt . . . that she knew enough to prevent it, to save the President, the Secretary of State, Booth, and . . . perhaps, her own son."[1036]

Now it was that son who could hang based on Weichmann's testimony, and Weichmann could again expect to be showered in obloquy. But Surratt no longer held total sway over Weichmann's heart. After testifying at the military trial that he and Surratt had been "very intimate" and "shared the same bed,"[1037] he explained how he could justify appearing against him:

> I had been a companion of John H. Surratt's for seven years. *I did not consider that I forfeited my friendship to him* in mentioning my suspicions to Mr. Gleason; *he forfeited his friendship to me* by placing me in the position in which I now stand, testifying against him. I think I was more of a friend to him than he was to me.[1038]

In his May 22nd letter to the editor of the *New York Tribune*, Weichmann expressed reluctant determination. "I confess," he writes, "that I shall not do it readily as a child eats its bread and butter, for [Surratt] was once a dear schoolmate of mine." [1039]   Torn though he was, he had to go forward:

> [A]ll good people must remember that [Surratt] is alleged to have been engaged in a fearful crime, the mere report of which shook the world to its foundations . . ., and my heart bleeds that there is cause for me to testify, yet if [by] what I may have done, or may do, my actions shall help to render the future rulers of our country more secure in their positions, I shall be content.   I shall have performed a good work, which I am ready to sanctify with my now saddened though youthful life.[1040]

Weichmann's many detractors would read this as a sanctimonious cover for his own guilt. But whether guilty or innocent or somewhere in the gray area we call "not guilty," it is hard to deny that the position in which Surratt placed the loyal companion of his youth was a harsh one. Weichmann could not avoid the duty to testify, but for the first time he seems to be conscious that his testimony was as likely to destroy himself, as it was to destroy Surratt.

Weichmann was getting older and wiser – and sadder.

1001 David O. Stewart, *Impeached: The Trial of President Andrew Johnson and the Fight for Lincoln's Legacy* pp.81-83 (Simon & Schuster New York 2009) (hereafter *"Impeached"*).

1002 Henry Steele Commager, *Documents of American History*, vol.1 p.493 (Articles of Impeachment) (Meredith Corporation, New York 1968) (hereafter *"Commager"*).

1003 1 JHS Trial 469; Cable #237 from Potter to Seward (Oct. 27, 1865), *reprinted in President's Message re: Surratt*, p.6.

1004 *Impeached*, p.47.

1005 *Ibid.*, pp.18-20, 22-23; *Commager*, pp.458-60 (Presidential Reconstruction).

1006 *Impeached*, p.23.

1007 *Ibid.*, citing, *Report of the Joint Committee on Reconstruction*, 39th Cong., 1st sess. (1866).

1008 *Impeached*, pp.20, 36. The fact that Stevens suffered from a congenital birth defect known as "clubfoot", which is now treatable with early surgical intervention, doubtless shaped both his determination and some of the ire he raised in his opponents.

1009 *Ibid.*, pp.51-52 (speech given on Washington's Birthday, Feb. 22, 1866).

1010 *Ibid.*, p.22.

1011 *Ibid.*, pp.43-44, & 360 (note for p.51). The so-called "Black Codes" enacted in 1865 throughout the South contained a wide array of vexatious limitations on the liberties of "freedmen, free negroes and mulattoes," such as restricting where they could live, prohibiting interracial marriage, deeming them vagrants if unemployed or congregating together or intermixing with whites, and barring them from keeping or bearing arms. The Black Codes were a legal cover for imposing conditions akin to slavery. Contracts of employment (usually for one year) were deemed "entire," which meant that breach of the smallest part was breach of the whole, so that the employee could work for 364 days and then forfeit all wages by breaching the contract on the last day of the year. While the freedman had a formal liberty to choose his or her employment, once chosen he was forbidden to quit, and whites were empowered to arrest and forcibly return runaways. The right of "moderate chastisement" short of "cruel or inhuman punishment" was conferred upon the master. Any "negro" who committed "riots, routs, affrays, trespasses, malicious mischief, cruel treatment to animals, seditious speeches, insulting gestures, language or acts, . . . disturbances of the peace" or who did any of a number of other enumerated acts, was guilty of a misdemeanor and subject to a fine which, if not paid, permitted his sale for labor at public auction to any white person who would pay his fine. *Commager*, pp.452-57 (Black Codes of Mississippi and Louisiana). Thus, in the immediate aftermath of the Civil War, the so-called "freedman" was not free at all. If he didn't work he was a criminal, subject to fine and imprisonment. If he did work, he was a virtual prisoner at the mercy of his employer, subject to whippings, forfeiture of pay, and arrest and return if he tried to run. And, regardless of whether he worked or not, the slightest offense given to any mean-spirited white man or woman was a one-way ticket to the auction block, and involuntary servitude for "crime" - not technically a violation of the Thirteenth Amendment.

[1012] *Tennessee Encyclopedia of History and Culture, Memphis Race Riot of 1866*, http://tennesseeencyclopedia.net/entry.php?rec=900 (accessed March 3, 2014).

[1013] *Impeachment*, p.54; *The New Orleans Race Riot of 1866*, https://lcrm.lib.unc.edu/blog/index.php/2012/07/30/on-this-day-the-new-orleans-race-riot-of-1866/ (accessed March 3, 2014); *New Orleans Riot of 1866*, http://chnm.gmu.edu/courses/122/carr/riottext.html (accessed March 3, 2014).

[1014] *Impeachment*, pp.49-51, 53.

[1015] *Ibid.*, pp.359-60 (note to p.50), *citing, Letter from Philip Ripley to Manton Marble*, Feb. 8, 1868, Manton Marble Papers.

[1016] *Impeachment*, p.53.

[1017] *Impeachment*, p.57.

[1018] *Dred Scott v. Sandford*, 60 U.S. 393 (1857). The first holding of this hateful opinion was that "negroes" were not "citizens" within the meaning of the Article III §2 of the U.S. Constitution, conferring diversity jurisdiction over suits between citizens of different states. *Ibid.*, 60 U.S. at 404-07. The first line of the Fourteenth Amendment is, "All persons born or naturalized in the United States, and subject to the jurisdiction thereof, are citizens of the United States and of the State wherein they reside." *Commager*, p.501. This wording is obviously intended to abrogate the first holding of *Dred Scott*.

[1019] *Commager*, p.501 (Fourteenth Amendment §1).

[1020] *Ibid.*, §2.

[1021] U.S. Const., Amend. XV, http://www.law.cornell.edu/constitution/amendmentxv (accessed March 3, 2014).

[1022] Univ. of Missouri-Kansas City Law School, Douglas O. Linder, *The Impeachment Trial of Andrew Johnson*, http://law2.umkc.edu/faculty/projects/ftrials/impeach/imp_account2.html (accessed March 3, 2014); *Impeachment*, pp.75-77, 83-85, 94-96.

1023 Isacsson, *TAT*, p.30.

1024 *NY Times*, "A Visit to Surratt," p.5. The ensuing account is taken from this article.

1025 *Ibid.*

1026 *New York Herald*, "The Case of John H. Surratt," p.4, col. 5 (June 6, 1867) (hereafter "*NY Herald, Case of Surratt*").

1027 Encyclopedia Virginia, *Fort Monroe During the Civil War*, http://encyclopediavirginia.org/Fort_Monroe_During_the_Civil_War#start_entry (accessed March 3, 2014).

1028 *New York Times*, "Opening of the United States District Court in Norfolk - Jefferson Davis and John H. Surratt" (Dec. 19, 1866).

1029 *NY Herald*, "Case of Surratt," p.4, col. 5.

1030 *Ibid.*

1031 *Ibid.*

1032 *Ibid.*

1033 *Ibid.*, p.4, col. 6.

1034 *LA from Surratt Courier, vol.2, Card from Louis J. Weichmann, May 22, 1867*, p. IX-21, *reprinted in, Townsend Interviews Weichmann* (August 1991) (hereafter, "*Card from Weichmann*").

1035 *Brophy Affidavit*; Weichmann, p.285. The Brophy Affidavit is quoted in Chapter Eleven.

1036 *Townsend Interviews Weichmann*, p. IX-20.

1037 *Trial of the Conspirators*, p.116.

1038 *Ibid.*, p.120 (emphasis added).

1039 *Card from Weichmann*, p. IX-21.

1040 *Ibid.*, pp. IX-21 to 22.

CHAPTER NINETEEN

UNITED STATES VERSUS JOHN SURRATT: THE GOVERNMENT'S CASE

It was the hottest ticket all that stormy, hot summer of 1867. In the words of one juror, "[t]he people were . . . stirred up as never before since . . . the days of the Revolution."[1041] Everyone from Senators to commoners wanted to get inside the oft-neglected District of Columbia criminal court on D Street between Fourth and Fifth.[1042] Surratt's trial was so in demand that the Honorable George P. Fisher had to control the crowds by issuing tickets for admission, and then withdraw them and issue more restrictive passes to prevent the crowds from impinging on the attorneys and courtroom personnel, and to give the fetid air a chance to circulate a bit.[1043]

At the center of it all sat "the prisoner at the bar," twenty-three-year-old American celebrity John H. Surratt. About six feet tall and "rather slender in form – almost delicate," with "very light auburn [hair], nicely cut and trimmed, parted behind and combed forward," a "prominent forehead," "keen blue eyes" with lids "hidden under dark brows," reddish-brown mustache and goatee hung from a "haughty chin," pleasant, well-spoken, with an easy if somewhat disingenuous smile, he was the very picture of – if not quite innocence – at least the virile Anglo-Saxon rogue Americans love to forgive.[1044] Whether chastised for his abandonment of his mother or lionized for his Confederate service and daring leap over the prison parapet, celebrity then as now was a kind of currency. Like great wealth it took on a life of its own, divorced from whatever sordid means were used to acquire it. A recent Alexander Gardner photograph of Surratt in full Zouave regalia adorned nearly every saloon bar in Washington City, and his exploits were on everybody's tongue.[1045]

Surratt was adored by the Catholic hierarchy in Washington and Maryland. Weichmann tells us that priests "were almost constant in their attendance on court, and were continually hobnobbing with the lawyers for the defense, thus showing which way their feelings ran."[1046] The net effect of all this was carefully described by the correspondent George Alfred Townsend in the days before newspaper photographs, television or the internet:

> Dressed in neat new black cloth, with new boots shining black, a ring on his small hand, clean linen, a face well-shaven, good color in his lank cheeks – [Surratt] looked to be a good type of the middle-class young Maryland farmer, who had acquired self-reliance and the courage that comes from vanity as some of the ruinous compensations of slavery. Not a whit worse nor better than the average of what were considered the finest young soldiers of Rebel Virginia, sharing their common *animus*, as ignorant as a prejudiced education could make one, as well esteemed today in half the hearts of the South as the memory of Stonewall Jackson . . ., so valued in this national district that no jury will probably agree to find him guilty of any crime, the name of his mother a political beatitude to reject or nominate Presidents, himself a city favorite, petted in his church and among his schoolmates, John Surratt seemed to me to lose his special ignominy as an assassin . . ..[1047]

Three tall windows graced each side of the courtroom. Each was screened with red and blue linen in a nod towards the importance of the occasion, but their light fell upon a courtroom in disarray, empty brackets where whale-oil lamps had been removed, the hollow socket of a clock-well left gaping in the expanse of dreary buff wall, the room "like most city court rooms, full of smell and grime . . .." From the windows,

Surratt could see the forty-foot high statue of Lincoln cast by Lot Flannery, and further in the distance, the penitentiary where his mother had spent her final weeks.[1048] Lincoln was turned with his back to the courthouse, as if he could not bear to watch.

* * *

Surratt was tried from June 10 to August 10, 1867. The presiding Judge, George P. Fisher, was a tall, handsome abolitionist former Congressman from Delaware who'd been appointed to the bench by Abraham Lincoln.[1049] Fisher had been a Union Colonel who commanded the Third Delaware Regiment in which Henri Beaumont de Ste. Marie served.[1050] Although capable of ruling in favor of the defense from time to time, the general pattern of his rulings were biased in favor of the prosecution, and his jury instructions were patterned entirely on the Government's legal theories.[1051]

The Government called eighty-five witnesses in its case in chief, ranging from the lowest "negro" servant up to General Ulysses S. Grant. Not to be outdone, the defense responded with ninety-seven witnesses of its own, and so unnerved the Government that it called ninety-six witnesses in rebuttal. The defense then called twenty-three surrebuttal witnesses, and would have called more had they been able to arrive in Washington before Judge Fisher's patience ran out.[1052] The evidence closed on July 27, and then the lawyers began ruminating on the huge record like the great implacable bulls they were. The District Attorney argued for three full days. The first defense lawyer argued two days; the second argued another full day. The prosecution team's hired gun from New York City rebutted for two more days, making eight full days of nothing but lawyers rehashing the evidence and dressing it up or tearing it down to suit their client's needs.[1053]

The Government blundered right out of the starting gate in the opening statement of thirty-one-year-old Assistant District Attorney Nathaniel Wilson. After detailing the death wound inflicted on Lincoln by Booth on the night of April 14, Wilson promised the jury:

> We shall prove to your entire satisfaction . . . that at that
> time the prisoner at the bar was then present aiding and

abetting that murder, and that at twenty minutes past ten o'clock that night he was in front of that theatre in company with Booth. You shall hear what he then said and did. You shall know that his cool and calculating malice was the director of the bullet that pierced the brain of the President and the knife that fell upon the face of the venerable Secretary of State.[1054]

How Surratt's lawyers must have rejoiced to hear the Government overplay its hand in such a fashion. Hell hath no fury like a jury spurned; promises made in the first minutes of a trial must be kept. *What was the Government thinking?* It is not as if it had no inkling that Surratt was planning to set up an alibi defense. The *New York Herald* reported on June 6 that, "[t]he defence contend they can prove an alibi, whereas the prosecution are said to have witnesses to show that Surratt was in this city on the day in question."[1055] Under the law of conspiracy – as the Government would be forced to argue later, during its strategic retreat in the face of the Elmira evidence – it was not necessary for Surratt to be actually present at the scene of the crime in order to be found guilty.[1056] But by promising to prove that he was, the Government made Surratt's presence or absence the central question on which guilt or innocence would turn. Since the evidence on that question was so hotly contested and the Government needed a unanimous jury to get a conviction, that was a losing proposition.[1057]

* * *

The Government's case began with some lurid medical examiner details, followed by thrilling testimony of the actual assassination – something, of course, that nobody disputed.[1058] According to Lieutenant Henry Rathbone, who along with his fiancée Clara Harris was a guest of the Lincolns in the presidential box that fatal night:

> [W]hile I was intently observing the performance on the stage, I heard the report of a pistol from behind me, and on looking round saw dimly through the smoke the form of a man between the President and the door. I heard him

shriek out some such word as "Freedom." . . . I immediately sprung towards him and seized him. He wrested himself from my grasp, and at the same time made a violent thrust at me with a large knife. I parried the blow . . . on my left arm, between the elbow and shoulder, and received a deep wound. The man sprung towards the front of the box. I rushed after him, but only succeeded in catching his clothes as he was leaping over the railing of the box. . . . I instantly cried out, "Stop that man." I then looked towards the President. His position had not changed, except that his head was slightly bowed forward and his eyes were closed.[1059]

Attorney Joseph B. Stewart, seated in the orchestra seats below, took up the story of what happened when he heard the report of Booth's pistol:

I saw . . . a man coming over the balustrade, and noticed the curl of smoke right immediately above him, as he was in a crouching position, in the act of leaping out of the box. . . . As he cleared the box I heard him exclaim, "*Sic semper tyrannis.*" . . . This person came down to the stage with his back to the audience, crouched as he fell, and came down upon his knees with a considerable jar, but rose instantly with his face turned full upon the audience. I noticed at the same instant that he held a very large knife in his hand. . . . I stepped into the chair I occupied and jumped over on to the stage, keeping my eyes distinctly on the movement of this man, who I thought I recognized . . . . When I reached the stage this man crossed rapidly, not in a full run, but in a quick springing walk, over to the left-hand side of the stage. I saw him disappear in the passage . . .. I ran across the stage with all my might. I said to persons on the stage, "Stop that man; he has shot the President." When I turned around towards the back building, and had gone perhaps a second or third step, I heard the door slam at the end of the passage. As many as five persons . . . somewhat obstructed my movements . . ..

When I reached the door, which was in an instant, I first took hold of the hinge side, then changed to the other side, and opened it. . . . My attention was fixed on the movements of the man mounting his horse. He was imperfectly mounted; was in the saddle, but leaning over to the left. The horse was moving with a sort of jerking, agitated gait, as a horse would do if spurred or touched at the instant of mounting, describing a sort of semicircle from right to left . . .. I ran as fast as I possibly could, aiming to get at the reins . . .. I got up near the flank of the horse and nearly within reaching distance of the man – a stride further, and I might have got hold of the bridle. With an oath he brought his horse round so quick that his quarter came against my arm, so that I gave way towards the buildings. . . . I noticed that he leaned forwards, holding firm his knife. . . . When near the further side of the alley he brought the horse up and headed him off.

. . . I demanded of the person to stop. I had no doubt in my mind at all who I was speaking to. I believed I was speaking to John Wilkes Booth.[1060]

This was thrilling stuff, and it seemed as if the Government was off to a strong start. This impression was reinforced by the testimony of Sergeant Joseph Dye, quoted in Chapter One, which placed Surratt in front of Ford's Theatre on the night of the assassination, calling time.[1061] It was strengthened over the duration of the Government's case as witness after witness swore that they saw Surratt in Washington on the morning, afternoon or night of April 14, 1865.[1062] As we have already seen, the Government also found an honest Yankee railroad conductor from Vermont by the name of Carroll Hobart to establish Surratt's flight through Burlington and St. Albans towards Canada on the Tuesday after the Friday assassination.[1063]

But the Government's rambling case got bogged down by the sheer enormity of the leads that they attempted to follow from the witness stand. These leads would have been better explored in the privacy of District Attorney Carrington's office as part of diligent pretrial preparation, with only the strongest selected for presentation to the jury. For example, they brought in banking witnesses to tell the jury that Jacob Thompson, the Confederate Secret Service leader in Canada, withdrew $180,000 on April 6, 1865, but never tied any of the money to Surratt or the other conspirators.[1064] They blundered into retrying the case against Mary Surratt, apparently more for political than for sound legal reasons, thus reminding everyone of their sympathy for the executed woman. They used Sergeant Dye's companion, Sergeant Cooper, to testify that Mary Surratt was awake at midnight on the night of the assassination and asked about the commotion in town, but it turned out that in fact they had spoken with Frederika R. Lambert of 587 H Street, not Mary Surratt who lived in a similar-looking house at 541 H Street.[1065] They put Dr. J.T. May on the stand to testify that he identified the body of John Wilkes Booth onboard the *Monitor* from a scar left by an operation he'd performed, apparently to silence the "Booth escaped to South America" fringe, but the point seemed quite irrelevant, as did all the lengthy testimony about tracking down Booth and shooting him in Garrett's barn.[1066] They bored the jury to tears with pointless evidence about Atzerodt's comings and goings.[1067] Worse than boring the jury, the Government insulted them by putting scoundrels like convicted rapist Doc Cleaver on the stand, thus vouching for his essentially incredible testimony that Surratt told him back in January 1865 that he and Booth were going to kill Abe Lincoln.[1068] They offered vast quantities of evidence placing Surratt with Booth and the other conspirators, and very little evidence about what was actually said between them. A witness who testified to recognizing Surratt based on seeing him once for five minutes seated with Booth at a round table in a Pennsylvania Avenue music hall with a woman dancing on stage the afternoon of April 14th, allowed the wily defense attorneys to drag the prosecution into a contest over afternoon female dancing, and the shape of Washington music hall tables.[1069]

* * *

Weichmann probably attended all of John Surratt's trial, based on his reimbursement claim for sixty-six days of attendance.[1070] It proved to be as much a trial for Weichmann as for Surratt. According to Weichmann:

> On one occasion about twenty students from St. Charles College, the institution where Surratt and I had studied, with the Reverend John B. Menu, one of the professors, and my former father confessor, . . . came into court. All of them were permitted, by the marshal of the court, to approach the prisoner and to shake hands with him, and this in the presence of the jury.[1071]

"None of these men came to me," adds Weichmann, "and gave me his hand."[1072]

Weichmann probably had another issue weighing on his mind as he contemplated taking the witness stand: consciousness of his own guilt. Though it is doubtful that he knew much about the plot against Lincoln, it is likely that he committed treason by leaking dispatches from the War Department to Surratt, knowing that Surratt would carry them straight to Richmond. For this he was vulnerable not merely to cross-examination, but to self-incrimination. Weichmann must have known that Surratt blamed him for his mother's death and that Surratt's tough legal team would not hesitate to destroy him. As Surratt told his Rockville audience a few years later:

> I . . . pronounce [Weichmann] a base-born perjurer; a murderer of the meanest hue! Give me a man who can strike his victim dead, but save me from a man who, through perjury, will cause the death of an innocent person. Double murderer! Hell possesses no worse fiend than a character of that kind. . . . I leave him in the pit of infamy, which he has dug for himself, a prey to the lights of his guilty conscience.[1073]

Vulnerable and friendless, trapped between a Government with power over his life, an orphaned prisoner he once loved, and his own guilt, by the time he took the stand Weichmann was a nervous wreck.

* * *

That time came on June 27. Weichmann testified for a day and a half for the Government. He was then cross-examined for a day and a half by Joseph H. Bradley, Sr., long the bully of the District of Columbia criminal court, for whom Judge Fisher borrowed Horace's description of Achilles: "[i]mperious, irascible, unplacable, bitter."[1074] Weichmann's testimony takes up sixty-seven pages of the transcript, more than any other witness.[1075]

Weichmann started out sounding a bit loony. The simplest question in any witness examination is the first, but it is an important one because the jury immediately judges the witness's demeanor and first impressions are crucial. Here's what popped out of Weichmann's mouth:

Mr. Pierrepont: State your full name.
Weichmann: My name is Louis J. Weichman [*sic*]. Before the trial of the assassins I spelled my name Wie. I gave it distinctly to the reporters, as I thought, but they spelled it Wei, and since that I have spelled it that way.[1076]

With this answer, Weichmann made himself disagreeable to the average juror by demonstrating fussiness. Worse, he also demonstrated one of the principal public charges against him – that he had no spine. What kind of man would change the spelling his own last name simply because a court reporter had misspelled it? One is tempted to believe that the reporter at the Surratt trial deliberately left the second "n" off the end of Weichmann's name, just to test whether he would change it again!

Weichmann testified to a dramatic first-hand account of Surratt, Booth and Powell, immediately after the failed kidnapping attempt in mid-March, but he lacked any first-hand knowledge of what they had been up to that led to their momentary frenzy and despair.[1077] He placed Surratt in Richmond with Judah Benjamin and Jefferson Davis just prior to April 3, 1865, noted his return with plenty of gold coins in his pocket, but of course did not have any information about what precisely had been discussed.[1078] The rest of his testimony detailed many suspicious comings and goings of Booth, Surratt, Powell, Atzerodt, Herold, Mudd, Mrs. Surratt and Mrs. Slater, along with information about their aliases, weapons and disguises – all very fascinating – but it contained little concrete information sufficient to support a criminal indictment. Indeed, Weichmann even helped Surratt to establish his alibi by testifying that the last time he saw him in Washington was on April 3, 1865.[1079]

The rest of Weichmann's testimony, including the tenacious cross-examination, went as well as could be hoped from the perspective of the Government. Like the "twenty-four / seven" student of the assassination he had become, Weichmann knew the record, including his own prior testimony, as well if not better than defense counsel. The most significant challenge was over the date that Surratt first met Booth through Dr. Mudd. In the military trial of the conspirators, Weichmann had set the date as January 15, 1865, which later proved to be impossible, since Mudd had an alibi for that date. At Surratt's trial, Weichmann fixed the date as winter 1864-65, and then narrowed it down to late December about two weeks prior to Surratt's employment by Adam's Express Company.[1080] He was roughed up about this and a few other dates, but not significantly impeached in any respect. Oddly, while en route to imprisonment at the inhospitable Dry Tortugas, Dr. Mudd had confessed "that he was with Booth on the evening referred to by Weichmann in his testimony [at the military trial]; that he came to Washington on that occasion to meet Booth by appointment who wished to be introduced to John Surratt . . . ."[1081] Because the best evidence is that Surratt met Booth on December 23, not January 15, this is either the imprecise statement of a man trying to curry favor in order to obtain commutation of an awful exile, or a very calculated attempt to place Surratt in the conspiracy only *after* he had already bought the getaway boat.

Another point on which Bradley pressed Weichmann was his story that he could not hear the April 11 discussion between John Lloyd and Mary Surratt about having the "shooting irons" ready.[1082] It was Lloyd who filled in the gap about what was discussed with Weichmann seated next to Mrs. Surratt in the buggy as Lloyd stood by her side, and if Weichmann did actually hear the conversation that day, then he would be more deeply implicated in the conspiracy. Although Weichmann did not emerge totally unscathed by this line of attack, it did not undermine his testimony in any significant way.

Finally, Bradley attempted to show that Weichmann had only agreed to testify against the Surratts after being threatened with imminent hanging. This, of course, got to the crux of the cowardice and perjury issues foremost in the public mind. To the question whether "an officer of the government . . . [told] you that unless you testified to more than you had already stated they would hang you too," Weichmann gave what many in the legal trade would call a "non-denial denial": "I don't remember to have ever heard it. It is news to me. I never had any fear of hanging."[1083] Because there may have been truth to Bradley's line of inquiry, it seems that Bradley could have been on the verge of cracking Weichmann's veneer of calm truthfulness.

"Objection!" cried the prosecution's sharp New York lawyer, Mr. Pierrepont. Pierrepont led attention away from the damaging question, into a confusing argument about whether the alleged threat of hanging was made in relation to the present case or the military trial. Judge Fisher ruled that threats or inducements made in the present case were admissible, but threats or inducements made before the military tribunal were not.[1084] This seems a foolish ruling. A witness, once threatened, does not come out from the burden of that threat when the same subject-matter is brought before a subsequent tribunal. Perjury extorted under threat would compel additional perjury to cover up the first crime. This does not necessarily mean that Weichmann's testimony at the military tribunal was perjured, but it does mean that Bradley should have been allowed to explore this issue at Surratt's subsequent trial in the civilian court. He was not, and therefore Weichmann – with the help of Pierrepont – slipped off the hook relatively unscathed.

Though Weichmann's testimony generally went into the record without a hitch, the difficulty for the Government was that, with one notable exception, it was all smoke and little fire. The exception was Weichmann's testimony that Surratt obtained the Washington lodgings at Herndon House for Seward's would-be assassin, Powell/Paine.[1085]

While that alone might well have been, under other circumstances, enough to hang him, it seemed a slender reed in the face of the Government's bold start.

Aside from this, the most telling evidence Weichmann gave was against Mrs. Surratt, not her son. He was led again through the tale of Mrs. Surratt's fateful carriage ride on the afternoon of the assassination, and even permitted to dress it up a bit with her alleged statement on returning to the lights of the victory parade in Washington that, "I am afraid that all this rejoicing will be turned into mourning and all this gladness into sorrow."[1086]   This was a waste of everyone's time, and all it did was open the door to allow the defense to wrap the son in the protective cloak of his mother's allegedly unjust execution.

* * *

What of the testimony of Henri Beaumont de Ste. Marie tying Judah Benjamin – and therefore Jefferson Davis – to the assassination plot? Ste. Marie had attributed to Surratt the telling admission that the assassins had "acted under the orders" of persons acting under Davis, with enough detail to pinpoint Benjamin, the man "still . . . in London."[1087] Yet for reasons that are totally unexplained, Ste. Marie was the amazing disappearing witness. He was one of five witnesses on July 2, and his entire testimony covers barely a page and one-half of the transcript.[1088] The only significant revelation in his testimony was his claim that Surratt told him that he left Washington either the night of the assassination or the next morning, disguised as an Englishman with a scarf over his shoulder.[1089] Considering his previous statements, this is a long step back. Considering also that of all the witnesses Ste. Marie was paid the most and carried the furthest – $668.15 for 143 days' attendance and 4,894 miles traveled,[1090] plus $250 for expenses paid by Rufus King, and another $10,000 in reward money authorized by special act of Congress on July 27, 1867[1091] – this paltry testimony seems a very poor return on investment. What went wrong?

There is some evidence of witness intimidation. On June 26, Richard T. Merrick, the dashing thirty-nine year old member of Surratt's defense team,[1092] was reprimanded by the Court for making a joke that was picked up by the press about putting the prosecution witnesses in the penitentiary.[1093] On July 1, the day before Ste. Marie testified, Dr. McMillan revived the issue from the witness stand.[1094] The issue exploded on the very day of Ste. Marie's testimony, when defense counsel Bradley referred to the witness room as the penitentiary, and Merrick added that those witnesses would soon be in another kind of penitentiary. The District Attorney's demand that Bradley retract his remark only spurred him to repeat it with the guarantee that he could make good on it. The Court reprimanded both the witness and defense counsel, saying that, "I have never, in all my judicial experience, seen a case in which there has been so much trouble with regard to the examination of witnesses, and so much bitterness of feeling displayed."[1095] But this scolding did not cure any witness intimidation that may have occurred.

Still, for a witness as eager to talk as Ste. Marie had been in 1866 – even at the expense of his personal safety – it does not seem likely that this veiled threat would have been sufficient to dissuade him. It is not as simple, of course, as saying that so long as Ste. Marie was being truthful he had nothing to fear. A witness such as Ste. Marie could be truthful about what Surratt had told him in the hills of Italy, and still have much to fear from crusading lawyers and ex-Confederates. He might have been personally threatened, or he may have had family or some other interest that was threatened. We simply do not know.

On the other hand, it may be that his testimony was fraudulent, advanced solely for the reward money, and by the time of the trial he was having second thoughts. It does not seem likely that fear of perjury would have stopped him at this late stage, because he had already given the Government sworn affidavits containing the worst of the allegations against Surratt. He does not appear to have fallen out of the good graces of the Government, as a witness who suddenly recants or backs out would have, since he was the beneficiary of a special act of Congress awarding him $10,000 for information leading to the capture of Surratt, less than a month after the date of his testimony.[1096] When Ste. Marie renewed his claim for the full balance of the original $25,000 reward in December 1872, the Government did not raise any claim that Ste. Marie had recanted his testimony or acted under false pretenses, but merely defended based on revocation of the original reward, and Ste.

Marie's acceptance of the ten thousand dollar appropriation.[1097] If Ste. Marie had admitted to fraud, the Government would probably have said so at this time. Eleventh hour recanting of testimony is not the most likely explanation.

I believe that Ste. Marie's testimony was deliberately truncated by the Government in order to protect Weichmann. Indeed, the Government had no choice but to decide whether to stake its fortunes on Weichmann or Ste. Marie, and it had already chosen the former back at the time of the military trial. Remember that Ste. Marie had written a letter to Judge Advocate General Holt on May 20, 1865, attributing strong secessionist sentiments to Weichmann.[1098] Ste. Marie's letter went well beyond this, however, to argue for Weichmann's arrest:

> . . . Weichman [*sic*.] and Surratt were intimate friends, and I do not understand how blind the commission is not to arrest him at once.
>
> Weichman [*sic*.] is a base low minded and presumptuous man, he often acknowledge to me [*sic*.] that his opinions were for the South . . ..
>
> I have heard Wiechman [*sic*.] and Surratt say in my presence that they wished somebody would kill Lincoln, that he would die one of these day [*sic*.] by the hands of an assassin, that he was a tyrant, a base and vulgar man.[1099]

Though Ste. Marie offered to testify at the time, his letter indicated there was a personal grudge underlying his relations with Weichmann: "[h]ow I reached my native home and what suffering I endured by that vilain's [*sic*.] jealousy and false pride would be to [*sic*.] long to relate."[1100] The Government did not take Ste. Marie up on his offer to testify at that time, likely preferring to guard Weichmann's reputation. Those were the days long before the *Brady* rule required the prosecution to produce all evidence of possible innocence to the defense,[1101] so Mrs. Surratt's lawyers would not necessarily have been aware of Ste. Marie's letter to Judge Holt. But John Surratt was probably aware of Ste. Marie's opinion of Weichmann, either from their time together in Washington or in Italy. With very little inducement, Ste. Marie was ready to turn on Weichmann. If the Government had set Ste. Marie up as a principal witness subject to probing cross-examination, it risked playing directly into the defense claim that its star witness against both mother and son was himself a conspirator in the plot, turned to save his skin.

Politics probably added weight to the decision not to rely on Ste. Marie's more sensational revelations. The Johnson administration surely did not want anything to come out that would implicate the Confederate government, since its reconstruction policy was based on putting many former Confederates back in power. District Attorney Carrington was often asking the administration for advice.[1102] If told that the President wanted him to lay off Davis and concentrate on Surratt, he would likely have complied.

Ste. Marie, even if truthful, probably did not appear all that reliable. Recall that Captain Jeffers thought he was a braggart.[1103] The Government already had Dr. McMillan's testimony about Surratt's trips to Richmond, which might have seemed both more reliable, and enough on that subject. The question of whether direct charges against the Confederate high command would stick may have contributed to the Government's reticence. If Surratt wanted to serve up Davis on a golden platter, that was one thing. But in the Conover affair the Government had already been burned once when trying to land the biggest fish. For much the same reason that nobody really wanted Surratt captured in the first place, it may be that nobody wanted to stick their political neck out based on second-hand testimony about a conspiracy directed from Richmond. The public was war-weary and wanted to move on; there were state governments to be formed, freedmen to be enfranchised, and a bitter political fight to be fought between the President and Congress. Getting Surratt would be more than enough.

In the final analysis, we don't know for certain why Ste. Marie's testimony was truncated. Whatever the reason, powerful evidence against Surratt and the Confederate high command was suppressed.

* * *

The prosecution threw every scrap of documentary evidence it could find into the fray, without much regard to how it fit into the case against John Surratt. They put in the "Dear Al" letter about "all the pretty girls" and "Old Abe, the good old soul, may the devil take pity on him," – though the evidence showed that it had never been sent, and it didn't seem to mean much anyway.[1104] Mary Hudspeth was called to the stand to detail how she found the "Charles Selby" letter to "Dear Louis" dropped on the New York tram in November 1864 – most likely prior to the time that Surratt was even in the conspiracy.[1105]

Another tantalizing but most likely fraudulent document introduced at Surratt's trial is the "Friend Wilkes" letter. This time, the letter was not to the mysterious Louis, but was purportedly *from* "Lou." On May 24, 1865, while the military trial of the conspirators was going on, the desk clerk at the National Hotel where Booth had lodgings checked the mail rack and discovered a letter addressed to "J.W.B."[1106] The contents of the letter were surely provocative. As read into the record at Surratt's trial, it said:

> South Branch Bridge, April 6, 1865.
> FRIEND WILKES: . . . I saw French and Brady and others about the oil speculation. The subscription to the *stock* amounts to eight thousand dollars, and I add one thousand myself, which is about all I can stand; now when you *sink* your well go deep enough, don't fail, everything depends upon you and your *helpers*; if you can't get through on your *trip*, after you *strike* ile, strike through Thornton Gap and across Capon, Romney's, and down the branch, and I can keep you safe from all hardships for a year. I am clear of all surveillance now that infernal Purdy is beat. I hired that girl to charge him with an outrage, and reported him to old Kelly, which sent him in the *shade*, but he suspects too damn much now; had he better be *silenced for good?* I sent this up by Tom, and if he don't get drunk, you will get

it the ninth. At all events, it can't be understood if lost. I can't half write, I have been drunk for two days. Don't write so much highfalutin next time. No more; only Jake will be at Green's with the funds. Burn this. Truly yours, LOU.

Sue Guthrie sends much love.[1107]

Many researchers have put a lot of effort into deciphering this letter, but so far it has all been tilting at windmills. Taken at face value, the "oil speculation" is clearly code for the plot against Lincoln, and the command to "go deep enough" when "you sink your well" appears to be an order to kill. The part about "Thornton Gap and across by Capon" are directions for an escape route, followed by an offer to conceal the fleeing John Wilkes Booth for a year. All very exciting except for one crucial fact brought out by both the Government and the defense: *this letter was mailed on May 8, long after the assassination and even after Booth had been shot dead in Garrett's barn.*[1108]   No actual conspirator would mail a letter to Booth at that time, and the postmark is therefore not just a mark of the date of mailing, but also a mark of fraud. By placing such a transparent fraud in front of the jury, the Government could only harm its own credibility.

* * *

On July 5, the prosecution attempted to close its case on a high note by introducing what is known to assassination buffs as the "Dear John" letter. The envelope was addressed to "John W. Wise," a name that certainly brings to mind a sharp fellow like John H. Surratt. To add to the allure, the contents of the letter were all in cipher, albeit a simple letter-correspondence cipher of the kind that any reasonably bright ten year old could crack. But of all the dubious flotsam of Government evidence, the "Dear John" letter takes the prize: it was found on May 1 or 2, 1865, floating in the water in Morehead City, North Carolina, by Mr. Charles Duell and his crew of pile drivers.[1109]   Morehead City is located over three hundred fifty miles south of Washington, and there is no record of any of the principal conspirators being there the day after the assassination. As read to the jury at the Surratt trial by a Government witness, the "Dear John" letter states:

> WASHINGTON, April the 15, 1865.
> DEAR JOHN: I am happy to inform you that Pet has done his work well – He is safe and Old Abe is in hell. Now, sir, all eyes are on you. You must bring Sherman. Grant is in the hands of Gray ere this. Red Shoes showed a lack of nerve in Seward's case. But he fell back in good order. Johnson must come. Old Crook has him in charge. Mind well that brother's oath and you will have no difficulty. All well. Be safe and enjoy the fruits of our labor. We had a large meeting last night. All were bent on carrying out the program to the letter. The rails are laid our [*sic.*] safe exit. Old, always behind, lost the pass at City Point. Now I say again the lives of our brave officers and the life of the South depends upon the carrying this program into effect. No. two will give you this. Its [*sic.*] ordered. No more letters shall be sent by mail; when you write sign no real name, and send by some of our friends who are coming home. We want you to write us how the news was received there. We receive great encouragement from all quarters. I hope there will be no getting weak in the knees. I was in Baltimore yesterday. Pet had not got there yet. Your folks are well and have heard from you. Don't lose your nerve.
> O'B. NO. FIVE[1110]

The Government closed its case in chief on this absurd document, but subsequently had to agree to have it stricken from the record because it failed to produce a witness who could identify the handwriting. Perhaps not surprisingly, Mr. Duell, who authenticated the letter at the military trial, had disappeared.[1111]

* * *

Despite all these failings the Government did manage to assemble three very telling pieces of the puzzle before the jury: first, that John Surratt recruited Atzerodt and purchased a getaway boat with him; second, that Surratt arranged for Seward-assailant Powell's lodging and secret meals in Washington; and third, that John Surratt and David Herold arrived at Surrattsville with Booth's carbines, and Surratt caused John Lloyd to hide them between the joists.[1112] The law of conspiracy, as set down by Chief Justice Marshall in *Ex Parte Bollman & Swartwout*, a treason case arising out of Aaron Burr's exploits in Mexico, is broad:

> [A]ll those who perform any part, however minute, or however remote from the scene of action, and who are actually leagued in the general conspiracy, are to be considered as traitors.[1113]

However remote Elmira might be from the scene of the crime, it seemed to be beyond dispute that Surratt had played an important part in Lincoln's murder, and that he was actually in league with the general conspiracy. Thus, under Chief Justice Marshall's statement of the law, any one of these three proven contributions to the conspiracy should have been sufficient to convict Surratt of conspiracy to murder Lincoln. All three together constituted overwhelming evidence of guilt. What could the defense possibly say to that?

1041 JOH Papers - JHS, *Reminiscences of the Surratt Jury*, p.2, (undated manuscript reproduced from the Manuscript Division, Library of Congress) (hereafter *"Juror Reminiscence"*).

1042 *Townsend re: Trial of Surratt*, p. X-14.

1043 *New York Times, New Rules Regarding Spectators* (July 28, 1867); *Townsend re: Trial of Surratt*, p. X-14; *Washington Times*, John F. Doyle, "The Civil War," p.B3 (June 14, 1997) (hereafter, *"Washington Times*, Doyle").

1044 *Trial of the Conspirators*, p.116; *NY Times, A Visit to Surratt*, pp.1-2; *Townsend re: Trial of Surratt*, p. X-13.

1045 *Townsend re: Trial of Surratt*, p. X-15.

1046 Weichmann, p.376.

1047 *Townsend re: Trial of Surratt*, p. X-13.

1048 *Townsend re: Trial of Surratt*, pp. X-13 to 15.

1049 *Washington Times*, Doyle, p.B3; *Townsend re: Trial of Surratt*, p. X-14.

[1050] Weichmann, p.24.

[1051] *E.g.*, 1 JHS Trial 74, 285, 338, 702 (for defense); 1&2 JHS Trial 154, 168, 267-70, 420-21, 654-55, 768, 791, 793, 824, 837, 839-40, 869, 1047 (for prosecution); 2 JHS Trial 1072-73 (some both ways, but admission of evidence of shooting the starving Union soldiers with Mrs. Slater seems quite prejudicial and irrelevant to the charges); 2 JHS Trial 1368-78 (jury instructions).

[1052] 1 & 2 JHS Trial.

[1053] 2 JHS Trial 1073-1366.

[1054] 1 JHS Trial 118.

[1055] *NY Herald*, "Case of Surratt," p.4, col.5.

[1056] *Ex Parte Bollman & Swartwout*, 8 U.S. 75, 126 (1807) (Marshall, C.J.).

[1057] Modern lawyers will add that part of the problem was that the Government had the burden of proof beyond a reasonable doubt. However, in those pre-*Mullane* days the defendant had the burden of proving an alibi defense. 2 JHS Trial 1080, 1144 (arguments of counsel) & 1374-75 (charge to jury).

[1058] 1 JHS Trial 121-131.

[1059] 1 JHS Trial 124.

[1060] 1 JHS Trial 126-27 (paragraph break added).

[1061] 1 JHS Trial 131-57.

[1062] The evidence on this point has been detailed in Chapter Ten, and will not be repeated here.

[1063] 1 JHS Trial 169-73.

[1064] 1 JHS Trial 193-95.

[1065] 1 JHS Trial 186, 661-67.

[1066] 1 JHS Trial 270-71, 302-13, 315-22.

[1067] 1 JHS Trial 271-75.

[1068] 1 JHS Trial 204-13. See quoted testimony at the end of Chapter Five.

[1069] 1 JHS Trial 240-45, 632-35, 635-38, 638-39; 2 JHS Trial 783-85, 1121.

[1070] *New York Times*, "The Surratt Trial: Estimated Expense of Proceedings" (August 10, 1867) (hereafter "*NY Times, Estimated Expense*"). The trial itself was not that long, but some of those days are attributable to travel and witness preparation.

[1071] Weichmann, p.377.

[1072] *Ibid.*

[1073] *Rockville Lecture*, Weichmann, p.435.

[1074] *Townsend re: Trial of Surratt*, p. X-14 (bully); *Judge Fisher's Account*, p. X-18 (Horace).

[1075] 1 JHS Trial 369-436.

[1076] 1 JHS Trial 369.

[1077] 1 JHS Trial 399-400.

[1078] 1 JHS Trial 387.

[1079] 1 JHS Trial 388.

[1080] *Trial of the Conspirators*, p.114; 1 JHS Trial 371, 412-15.

[1081] Weichmann, p.258, *quoting, Sworn Letter from Captain George W. Dutton to General Joseph Holt* (August 22, 1865).

[1082] 1 JHS Trial 416-17.

[1083] 1 JHS Trial 420.

[1084] *Ibid.*

[1085] 1 JHS Trial 381-82.

[1086] 1 JHS Trial 393.

[1087] *Ste. Marie v. United States*, p.23 (Ste. Marie Statement, July 10, 1866).

[1088] 1 JHS Trial 492-93.

[1089] 1 JHS Trial 493.

[1090] *NY Times, Estimated Expense.*

[1091] Act of July 27, 1867, U.S. Stat. at Large, vol. 15, p.534; *Ste. Marie v. United States*, p.47 (Letter of Davis to Phillips (Sept. 29, 1873)).

[1092] *New York Times*, "Richard H. Merrick Obituary" (June 24, 1885).

[1093] 1 JHS Trial 326.

[1094] 1 JHS Trial 468.

[1095] 1 JHS Trial 469-70.

[1096] Somebody might suggest that this was hush money, but a *quid pro quo* seems unlikely. Why would the Republican Congress want to cover up evidence of Davis' involvement? On the face of the Acts, the money was awarded "for services and information in the arrest of John H. Surratt in the Kingdom of Italy," *Ste. Marie v. United States*, pp.49-50, and while of course that is not determinative, it makes sense in context. The Government has been accused in the military trial of paying for testimony, but it has never been accused of paying to prevent testimony, and such a bill could not have gotten through a politically charged Congress without someone calling it to public attention.

[1097] *Ste. Marie v. United States*, pp.12, 47, 49-53, 59-61.

[1098] *Ste. Marie Letter of May 20, 1865*, p.1. This letter is discussed in Chapter Three.

[1099] *Ibid.*

[1100] *Ibid.*

[1101] *Brady v. Maryland*, 373 U.S. 83 (1963).

[1102] *E.g.*, National Archives, *Letter from Edward C. Carrington to Acting Attorney General*, (June 5, 1868), National Archives Identifier 6783058 (hereafter "*Carrington June 5*"); National Archives, *Letter from Edward C. Carrington to Acting Attorney General*, (June 9, 1868), National Archives Identifier 6783059 (hereafter "*Carrington June 9*").

[1103] *Jeffers Testimony*, p.17.

1104 1 JHS Trial 403-05.

1105 1 JHS Trial 352-55. For details on the "Charles Selby" letter, see Chapter Three.

1106 1 JHS Trial 338-39.

1107 1 JHS Trial 339 (emphasis in original).

1108 1 JHS Trial 339.

1109 1 JHS Trial 527-29; *Trial of the Conspirators*, p.42.

1110 1 JHS Trial 528.

1111 1 JHS Trial 529; 2 JHS Trial 1065.

1112 Buying the boat is covered in Chapter Five; arranging Powell's lodging is covered in Chapter Eight; hiding the carbines is covered in Chapter Seven.

1113 *Ex Parte Bollman & Swartwout*, 8 U.S. 75, 126 (1807).

CHAPTER TWENTY

UNITED STATES VERSUS JOHN SURRATT: THE DEFENSE

From some unknown quarter influence and money were found to hire a stellar defense team for John H. Surratt, the pauper who arrived with only a few foreign coins in his pocket. At the head of the team stood sixty-four-year-old Joseph Habersham Bradley, Sr., dean of the Washington bar, who was as feared as he was respected.[1114] By his side sat his son, Joseph H. Bradley, Jr., who gave the defense's opening statement, traveled widely to perform background investigation, and handled the crucial task of care and grooming of the witnesses.[1115] Richard T. Merrick, a handsome Marylander at the height of his powers, wielded the sharpest tongue in the defense arsenal. Merrick parried prosecution arguments and skewered witnesses with honeyed diction in what newspaperman George Townsend called "his affected Virginia dialect, three-fourth negro and one-fourth boarding school."[1116] Mary Surratt had previously sought Merrick's help, knowing him to be a Catholic attorney of fine reputation and Southern sympathies. At the urging of his father-in-law he had refused, fearing in those dark days just after the assassination that taking her case would harm his political career.[1117] With the shift in the political winds towards former rebels and all things Surratt, Merrick was now willing and eager to serve.

The defense employed the shrewd tactic of reserving its opening statement to the start of its case. Bradley Jr. wasted no time in establishing the principal tenets of the defense. His very first sentence was most telling:

[G]entlemen of the jury, we have at last arrived at that stage of this case when an opportunity is afforded the prisoner for saying something by way of defence, not only of his own character, his own reputation, his life, and his honor, but also . . . something in the way of vindicating the pure fame of his departed mother.[1118]

Surratt intended to use his trial to expiate his guilt over the death of his mother by placing the blame for execution of an "innocent" woman squarely upon the Government. His lawyers' purposes dovetailed with his own. They knew that public sympathy for Mrs. Surratt and anger over the failure to commute her sentence was the Government's Achilles heel, and they exploited it from beginning to end. If sympathy for Mrs. Surratt would prevent just one juror from voting to convict John Surratt, then the case would be won and Mrs. Surratt's martyrdom would not be in vain.

But there was much more to the defense than sympathy for the prisoner's mother. First and foremost, there was Surratt's alibi defense.[1119] In addition to the upstanding Elmira merchants who testified to Surratt's haberdashery habits, and the mind-numbing deluge of railroad schedules, Surratt's team of detectives was able to unearth a mysterious man on crutches that Surratt recalled meeting in Elmira. The man was a New York City physician named Augustus Bissell, who testified that he was in Elmira on April 14 to track down a railroad employee to testify in his lawsuit against the railroad. According to Dr. Bissell, he happened to wander into Brainard House in order to lie down for a while in the lounge when a tall man came in and sat by him. The man, noting the doctor's injured leg, asked if he'd been to the war, but Dr. Bissell was suspicious that he was a hired railroad detective so he barely uttered a few words. Still, it was enough: Surratt was instructed to stand, and Dr. Bissell identified him as the man he saw at Brainard House in Elmira, on the morning of April 14.[1120] When asked how he could place the date firmly as April 14, he explained that he received a telegram from his wife that evening, saying that their child was very ill. He immediately boarded the train to return home, but his child died before he got there.[1121] While the world will long remember it as the night Lincoln died, the Bissell child slipped away quietly that same night and was forgotten by all but a few.

* * *

Beyond alibi and Mrs. Surratt's hanging, the defense had a third trump card in hand: *the indictment*. What was Surratt indicted for doing? The Government said it was conspiracy to commit murder. The defense said no, it was for simple murder.[1122] If the defense was right, the more restrictive law of accessory to murder might apply, but not the much broader law of conspiracy upon which the Government was relying.

In his opening statement, Mr. Bradley Jr. tried to cut the Government's case down to size:

> Heinous as this offence is, its moral qualities in the sight of the Almighty are no worse than when the commonest vagabond in the street is slain in cold blood. . . . [I]n the sight of the Judge of the quick and dead the life of the humblest man is as precious and sacred to Him as the life of the loftiest citizen.[1123]

This argument not only deflated the passions attending the enormous crime with which Surratt was charged, but supported the argument that the crime was murder, pure and simple, not treason or conspiracy. "[T]hey contend," said young Bradley to the jury, "there was a conspiracy to murder the president of the United States, and certain members of his cabinet; and our client . . . was one of the conspirators with John Wilkes Booth and others." But that was not how the defense read the indictment. "[W]e maintain that this is an indictment for murder simply . . .."[1124]

If Abraham Lincoln could not be known to the jury as President and Commander in Chief, how was the plot against Seward connected, and how were the broad doctrines of the *Bollman & Swartwout* case to be applied? Was the Government's case against John H. Surratt doomed by a fatal flaw in the indictment before the first juror was even sworn?

The defense argument seems to have moved even the Government itself, which re-indicted Surratt in very different language after his first trial.[1125] It has convinced a great many others as well. For example, an article in the *Philadelphia Press* dated August 11, 1867 states that, "had Surratt been indicted for conspiracy instead of murder, the jurors would have convicted him 'immediately on retiring to their room.'"[1126] This view was perpetuated by the *Baltimore News American* in a 1974 article about Surratt, which states, "because he was charged incorrectly with murder instead of conspiracy, the trial resulted in a hung jury."[1127] Even careful Lincoln assassination researchers such as James O. Hall have regularly referred to the first indictment as simply a "murder indictment."[1128] We must pause to parse the first Surratt indictment.

* * *

The original handwritten indictment that was filed February 4, 1867 against John Surratt in Criminal Case #4731, is housed in the National Archives building in downtown Washington, D.C., about halfway between the White House and Ford's Theatre.[1129] Those old handwritten Nineteeth Century indictments with their repetition and meter are a kind of poetry conjoined with the fire and brimstone of a sermon and the minute empiricism of a scientific dissertation. Here's the opening to the first count against Surratt:

> The Jurors of the United States of America for the County of Washington aforesaid upon their oath Present that John H. Surratt late of the County aforesaid, yeoman, not having the fear of God before his eyes but being moved and seduced by the instigation of the devil on the fourteenth day of April in the year of our Lord one thousand eight hundred and sixty five, with force and arms . . . in and upon one Abraham Lincoln, in the peace of God and of the said United States of America there being, feloniously, willfully, and of his malice aforethought, did make an assault, and that the said John H. Surratt a certain pistol of the value of ten dollars, then and there charged with gun powder and one leaden bullet, which said pistol he the said John H. Surratt in his right hand then and there had and held, then and there feloniously willfully and of his malice aforethought, did discharge and shoot off to against and upon the said Abraham Lincoln . . ..[1130]

It's hard to love an "aforesaid," and harder yet to love a whole gag-gle (flock? murder?) of them, especially when done "feloniously, will-fully and with malice aforethought," as is every aforesaid thing throughout this lengthy document.[1131] But as one trained in the law with over thirty years of practice, I can vouch that through three drea-ry pages, this first count of the indictment is for the crime of murder, pure and simple.[1132] Score one for the defense.

The second count has not Surratt but Booth holding the pistol that caused the "leaden bullet" to "strike, penetrate, and wound" Lincoln's "left and posterior side of the head," inflicting "one mortal wound of the depth of six inches and of the breadth of half an inch," of which Lincoln "did languish, and languishing did live," but then, alas, "died."[1133] By placing the pistol in Booth's hand, this count at least bears a credible resemblance to what actually happened. We might wonder why the first count was even in there, but it is probable that there is no good answer. The not-so-good answer is that lawyers would rather throw ten thousand words against a problem when ten would do than risk leaving out even one of those ten. The second count con-cludes that, "John H. Surratt then and there feloniously, willfully, and of his malice aforethought, was present, aiding, helping, assisting, and maintaining the said John Wilkes Booth in the felony and murder aforesaid,"[1134] and thus it constitutes a charge of accessory murder. Score two for the defense.

Likewise, the third count is for accessory murder, this time against Surratt in combination not merely with Booth, but also with Herold, "Atzeroth" [*sic.*], "Payne" [*sic.*], Mary E. Surratt, "and others to the Jurors aforesaid unknown . . .."[1135] Score three for the defense.

If there is to be a count of conspiracy to commit murder, it must be the fourth count of this four-count indictment. The fourth count (shorn of most of its "saids" and "aforesaids") charges "that . . . John Wilkes Booth . . . and . . . John H. Surratt . . . and . . . David E. Herold . . . and . . . George A. Atzerodt . . . and . . . Lewis Payne [*sic.*] . . . and . . . Mary E. Surratt . . ., together with divers other persons to the jurors . . . unknown, . . . unlawfully and wickedly did *combine confederate and conspire and agree together* feloniously to kill and murder one Abraham Lincoln; and that . . . in pursuance of said *wicked and unlawful conspiracy* in and upon the said Abraham Lincoln, . . . [they] did make an assault;

and that . . . John Wilkes Booth in pursuance of *said wicked and unlawful conspiracy* [shot Lincoln dead] . . .."[1136] It doesn't take a lawyer to recognize that this is a charge of conspiracy to commit murder, and not a charge of simple murder or even accessory murder. It is true that the Government, in its fear of leaving anything out, muddied this charge by adding that, "in pursuance of said wicked and unlawful conspiracy," all the conspirators "were present, aiding, helping, and abetting, comforting, assisting, and maintaining the said John Wilkes Booth" to commit the murder, which mixes in a bit of accessory-murder language.[1137] Still, in legal contemplation this is what lawyers are fond of calling "mere surplusage," and it does not detract from the charge of conspiracy to commit murder. Judge Fisher recognized this in his instructions to the jury: "The indictment in this case charges the prisoner with being engaged in a conspiracy with John Wilkes Booth and others to effect the murder of Abraham Lincoln, and with having succeeded in the accomplishment of that atrocious crime."[1138] Game, set and match for the prosecution!

Let's clear the historical record once and for all. John Surratt was charged in the original indictment with murder, accessory murder, and conspiracy to commit the murder of Abraham Lincoln. Surratt was tried for all these crimes, including conspiracy to commit murder. The only crime for which Surratt arguably should have been indicted that he was not, was conspiracy to *kidnap* the President. Any historical or contemporary source that says the prosecution failed because the Government did not indict Surratt for conspiracy to commit murder is simply not accurate.

Which brings us to the so-called "kidnap defense."

* * *

Surratt never lacked for *chutzpah*. Recall that his primary alibi defense was based on the premise that he was a Rebel spy, assigned at the time to surveil the prison in Elmira by General Robert E. Lee's cousin. In other words, his alibi defense was that at the time of the assassination he was busy violating *other* laws of war, for which he could have been summarily convicted and shot had he been caught. Addressing the charges directly, his lawyers added that Surratt knew nothing of Booth's "change of plan" to murder the President – at most, he was guilty of nothing more than *conspiring to kidnap the President of the United States.*[1139]

This is a pretty serious confession. Kidnapping was a felony then, as it is now.[1140] As even Surratt's counsel admitted in closing argument, the plan to abduct the President of the United States was "unjustifiable, . . . for which they might have been taken and executed . . .."[1141] Kidnapping the President of the United States strikes a blow at democratic government. Kidnapping the Commander in Chief in war time is an attack on the nation. A contemporary analogy to Surratt's bizarre defense is that an accused Nine-Eleven terrorist might argue that he did not conspire to fly a plane into the World Trade Center because he had only conspired to hijack the aircraft and hold it for ransom in exchange for release of other terrorists, and besides, at the time of the attack he was elsewhere, busily drawing up sketches of the White House for Osama bin Laden.

The law since at least the early seventeenth century, and certainly throughout the United States in the nineteenth century, has recognized something called the "Felony-Murder rule."[1142]   Under this rule, any person involved in a felony is guilty of any murder that occurs in the course of committing the felony – even if that person did not actually kill, and had no intention of killing anyone.[1143] As argued by the prosecution, if Surratt was part of a conspiracy to kidnap Lincoln, and Lincoln was killed by another conspirator without Surratt's knowledge or consent during the commission of that crime, Surratt would be guilty of felony-murder.[1144]

* * *

Surratt's kidnap defense, however, was more nuanced than this. By alluding to his role in the kidnapping conspiracy, Surratt contended that there were *two separate conspiracies* – one to kidnap, and one to kill – and that he was only part of the first abandoned conspiracy to kidnap, not a part of the second conspiracy, which was the one that culminated at Ford's Theatre the night of April 14.[1145]

There is a chance that Surratt was only aware of a plot to kidnap Lincoln, and not of a plot to kill Lincoln. Surratt admits that Booth mentioned killing Lincoln at Gautier's on March 15, but that was supposedly as a last resort after a failed kidnapping, and Surratt claims that it was opposed by all on hand.[1146] Surratt admitted to Dr. McMillan that he was informed of the change in plan by Booth's April letter to Montreal,[1147] but McMillan could be lying or simply confused. It may be that killing Lincoln was not discussed when Surratt met with Benjamin and Davis just before the fall of Richmond.

Booth claimed in his diary entry for April 14 that, "[u]ntil today nothing was even thought of sacrificing to our country's wrongs," and that, "[f]or six months we have worked to capture."[1148] This entry, probably written on April 15, is a transparent *post-hoc* whitewash. Booth had assassination on his mind no later than April 7, when he told Samuel Chester of the missed opportunity to shoot Lincoln at the second inaugural.[1149] On April 11, Booth urged Powell to shoot Lincoln as they listened to him speak from the White House portico, then said, "[t]hat is the last speech he will ever make."[1150] Clearly, Booth had killing Lincoln in mind for some time prior to the time that he actually carried out the deed – long enough for Surratt to have learned that his plot with Booth had become a plot to kill.

Regardless of Surratt's actual knowledge of the goal of assassination, the "two conspiracies" theory stumbles out of the gate for other reasons. Can it be said in good conscience that these were two separate conspiracies? The principal actors involved were the same ones Surratt recruited and conferred with regularly, the carbines hidden at Surrattsville were the same that Surratt secreted there, and the getaway boat stashed for transport back to rebel territory – though never used – still waited at Nanjemoy Creek. Considering the meeting at Gautier's Saloon at which both Ford's Theatre and killing were discussed, it does not even seem accurate to contend that the plan "changed" from kidnap to murder. Rather, the evidence suggests that the plan vacillated back and forth between kidnap and murder, depending on the opportunity that presented itself and the circumstances of the moment.

Remember that the idea of killing Lincoln actually grew in enormity after the fact, when the shock set in. Prior to April 14, plots against Lincoln's life were the coin of the realm in certain circles. To think that those circles would not have included John Surratt is to fail to understand both the man and the times.

* * *

From a legal point of view, Surratt's defense to the conspiracy charge in count four of the indictment is called "abandonment" or "withdrawal." While Surratt would have us believe that everybody abandoned the kidnapping conspiracy after the failed attempt at the play *Still Waters Run Deep* at Campbell Hospital, his many subsequent actions in furtherance of the conspiracy belie that claim. After the *Still Waters Run Deep* fiasco, Surratt hid Booth's carbines that were later used in Booth's escape, secured lodging for Powell, went to Richmond and returned with money and instructions, and likely even left Montreal on April 12 in response to Booth's letter about changed plans. The purpose of the conspiracy may have shifted, but under no reasonable view of the facts can it be said that the conspiracy was abandoned or that Surratt withdrew.

Under the common law, "if a person withdraws from a conspiracy, he may avoid liability for subsequent crimes committed in furtherance of the conspiracy by his former co-conspirators if he *communicated his withdrawal to each co-conspirator*."[1151] As stated in *State v. McCahill*, a nineteenth century Iowa prosecution for conspiracy murder in which withdrawal from the conspiracy was pleaded as a defense:

> His guilt, if he did not personally aid in the commission of the unlawful act, consisted in the encouragement he gave thereto. If he advised and directed the unlawful acts, he cannot escape responsibility by quietly withdrawing from the scene. His guilty act was the encouragement and advice he gave those who committed the crime. The influence and effect of this encouragement continued until he withdrew it by acts or words showing that he disapproved or opposed the contemplated crime. He cannot, by the coward's expedient of running away after he incited his associates to crime, escape punishment.[1152]

Surratt not only gave "encouragement and advice" to Booth and the other conspirators in Lincoln's murder, but he gave them his labor and specific material support. There is no evidence whatsoever that he communicated to his fellow conspirators any intent to withdraw from the conspiracy. Indeed, George Atzerodt was told by Booth that Surratt was present and participating on the night of the assassination.[1153] Even if that was not true, Surratt had no tenable legal argument for a withdrawal defense based on the facts as we know them, because he continued to participate and he did not tell his co-conspirators that he was withdrawing.

Hapless Mr. Atzerodt, who was assigned to kill Vice-President Johnson but got cold feet, was hanged for wandering off in the night without telling anybody about the plot against Lincoln. Why should Surratt have gotten off any easier?

* * *

Weichmann's worst fears were realized during Surratt's defense case. Actor and fellow Catholic Lewis J. Carland – the very man who claimed to have called time in front of Ford's Theatre on the night of the assassination[1154] – was recalled to the stand by Mr. Merrick to testify to a walk he took with Weichmann shortly after the conclusion of the military trial. According to Carland, Weichmann asked that they go together to St. Aloysius Church for confession, as "his mind was so burdened with what he had done, that he had no peace." Carland says that he told him, "That is not the right way, Mr. Weichmann, you had better go to a magistrate and make a statement under oath," to which Weichmann replied, "I would take that course if I were not afraid of being indicted for perjury." Weichmann elaborated that his statement had been written out for him, and he was forced to sign it to avoid being charged as one of the conspirators before the military commission. Had he been allowed to make his statement in his own way, he told Carland, "it would have been very different with Mrs. Surratt . . .."[1155]

Cross-examination did nothing to shake Mr. Carland's story. All it did was elicit the memorable image of their visit to Duaut's saloon after confession. It was there, said Carland, that Weichmann recited Hamlet's soliloquy on death.[1156]

To be, or not to be – that is the question:
Whether 'tis nobler in the mind to suffer

The slings and arrows of outrageous fortune
Or to take arms against a sea of troubles
And by opposing end them. To die, to sleep –
No more – and by a sleep to say we end
The heartache, and the thousand natural shocks
That flesh is heir to. 'Tis a consummation
Devoutly to be wished. To die, to sleep –
To sleep – perchance to dream: ay, there's the rub,
For in that sleep of death what dreams may come
When we have shuffled off this mortal coil,
Must give us pause. There's the respect
That makes calamity of so long life.
For who would bear the whips and scorns of time,
. . . But that the dread of something after death,
The undiscovered country, from whose bourn
No traveller returns, puzzles the will,
And makes us rather bear those ills we have
Than fly to others that we know not of?
Thus conscience does make cowards of us all . . ..[1157]

It was as if Shakespeare had written these words just for Louis J. Weichmann.

* * *

As the case wore on, Judge Fisher seems to have concluded that the Government needed his help. Three examples of evidentiary rulings against the defense stand out. The first concerns the hotel register for Webster House in Canandaigua, into which someone had entered the name "John Harrison of New York" on the page for April 15, 1865.[1158] The signature was identified as Surratt's by his cousin, Olivia Jenkins, a lodger at Mary Surratt's house who ought to have known his handwriting, and by other witnesses.[1159] The Government nonetheless objected to its admission because anyone – including Surratt himself while hidden in Canada – could have sneaked into Webster House over the following two years and entered the name "John Harrison" on the register. Judge Fisher agreed, and excluded it on that ground.[1160]

The Government's argument, while theoretically tenable, is quite unlikely. As a regularly kept business record, this register would normally have been admitted with the question of its genuineness left to the jury to decide. This is what lawyers mean when they argue – as Bradley Sr. did[1161] - that the objection goes to the weight, not the admissibility, of the evidence.

This ruling angered Surratt enough that he discussed it at length in his Rockville lecture:

> Now mark, ladies and gentlemen, if you please, my name was signed midway of the hotel register, with six other parties before and after. There was no doubt as to the genuineness of my signature, because the very experts brought by the United States to swear to my signatures in other instances, swore also that that was my handwriting. After all this the register was ruled out by Judge Fisher, because he was well aware if he admitted it my case was at an end. I could not be in two places at once, though they tried to make me so.[1162]

Surratt mocks Fisher's view that he might have slipped down from Canada to write his name in the register, saying that, "[i]t was a likely idea that the proprietor of a hotel would leave a blank line in the register for my especial benefit," and concludes that "the ruling . . . ought to damn the Judge who so ruled as a villain in the minds of every honest and upright man." The account of the lecture notes that this remark was greeted with "[l]oud and prolonged applause."[1163]

* * *

The second ruling that marked Judge Fisher as somewhat of a Government partisan was his decision to exclude the testimony of General Edwin G. Lee that Surratt was in Elmira to surveil the prison.[1164] This does not mean that General Lee was a truthful witness who should have been believed. To the contrary, he opened his testimony by failing to tell "the whole truth" when he explained his presence in Montreal with the cover story that he was on medical leave with a surgeon's certificate, leaving out the minor detail that he was assigned there by Judah Benjamin to command the Confederate Secret Service operations in Canada.[1165] The question for the trial judge, however, is not witness credibility, but admissibility.

The net result of excluding General Lee's testimony is that it deprived Surratt of the opportunity to prove his claimed purpose for being in Elmira. As the Government's theory of the case shifted in response to the strength of Surratt's alibi evidence from the bold assertion that Surratt was present at Ford's Theatre, to the fall-back argument that even if he was in Elmira, "modern" travel (railroad) and communication (telegraph) might have permitted him to participate in the conspiracy plot,[1166] it became more important for Surratt to show what he was actually doing in Elmira. The unfairness of excluding General Lee's testimony permitted Mr. Merrick to taunt the Government in closing argument:

> Does the gentleman mean to argue that [Surratt] was . . . [in Elmira] participating in the conspiracy? . . . [B]lush for shame, gentlemen, if that is your purpose, for when we offered to prove why he went to Elmira, and what he was doing there, you told the court that there had been no proof on your part as to what he was doing there, and therefore, we could not offer any; and so the court decided. If you mean to contend that he was in Elmira performing his part of the conspiracy, then I say you have tricked us . . ., for you remember, gentlemen of the jury, that we had General E.G. Lee on that stand, prepared to prove what Surratt went to Elmira for, and what he was doing in Elmira, and to show that it had nothing to do with this conspiracy . . ..[1167]

* * *

A third significant pro-Government ruling by Judge Fisher concerned proposed testimony by a Catholic priest, Reverend L. Roccofort, who claimed to have had delicate conversations with Weichmann outside of the confessional. Mr. Merrick's next question was, "[d]id he ever tell you that he was employed in an office in the War Department, and engaged to send information to the southern confederacy?"[1168] Mr. Carrington shot to his feet with an objection. Weichmann, who was in court that day seated immediately behind Judge Pierrepont, must have felt his stomach clench at Merrick's response:

> [The defense] charged that if there was any conspiracy at all, Weichmann was in that conspiracy. That his testimony was the testimony of an accomplice, seeking to save his own life by the betrayal of his associates.[1169]

According to Merrick's sound reasoning, Surratt was entitled to show that Weichmann was in the plot because the testimony of an accomplice is entitled to less weight than that of an innocent person due to the accomplice's motive to lie in order to protect himself.[1170] Playing not just to the Court, but also to the jury, Merrick laid out his evidence in no uncertain terms:

> Weichmann [told Father Roccofort] . . . that his business in the War Department was to hold the office . . . for the purpose of aiding the rebel government in Richmond; and that, in his office, he received information in an official capacity as an officer of the United States, which he did communicate to the confederate government at Richmond.

With a flourish he immediately came to regret, Merrick closed with the rhetorical question, "[w]as not that . . . a fact from which it might be inferred that [Weichmann] was an accomplice?"[1171]

"If it was," shot back Judge Fisher, "[you] should prove that the confederate government was the principal in the murder of Mr. Lincoln."[1172] This was territory that Merrick and the other defense counsel would avoid at all costs – perhaps, even, at the cost of sacrificing their immediate client. Merrick retreated, and Judge Fisher then excluded the proposed testimony on technical grounds: it was an effort to show a witness was less believable ("impeachment") that was based on questioning a different witness ("extrinsic impeachment") on a topic not directly relevant to the charges in the case ("collateral matter").[1173]

While the rule of evidence invoked by the Judge is sound, its application here is highly suspect. Whether one of the principal government witnesses was a co-conspirator and therefore less worthy of belief was central to the trial, and the defense ought to have been allowed to impeach him for that however they could manage it. But Judge Fisher's ruling probably made no difference. Merrick effectively smeared Weichmann before the jury, laying out his evidence and confirming the prejudices they carried into the jury box. The picture of a Catholic priest on the stand, silenced by Judge Fisher as he was about to damn Weichmann in Surratt's defense, likely made a deeper impression on the jury than any testimony Father Roccofort could have given.

If Fisher was pro-Government, as he appears to have been, it did not matter in the end. Though the Government was the beneficiary of most of the evidentiary rulings and of jury instructions that were based on its conspiracy theory of the case, this was not a military tribunal in which the judge decided the outcome. Instead, guilt or innocence rested in the hands of twelve jurors drawn from the District of Columbia, the majority of whom were born in the South.[1174] Some had been Union men, but it is likely that the sympathies of most of the jurors lay with ex-Confederates like Surratt.[1175] With the nation itself still quarreling over what it believed, how could the jury ever be expected to agree?

[1114] Birthdate from Find a Grave, http://www.findagrave.com/cgi-bin/fg.cgi?page=gr&GRid=46605697 (accessed March 8, 2014).

[1115] For example, he helped the notorious Rebel Stephen Cameron obtain his pardon in July 4, 1867, just in time to testify for the defense. 2 JHS Trial 814. He was also the fellow sent to Canandaigua to retrieve the hotel register. 2 JHS Trial 765-66.

[1116] *Townsend re: Trial of Surratt*, p. X-14.

[1117] *American Tragedy*, p.146.

[1118] 1 JHS Trial 530-31.

[1119] Most of the evidence for that has already been covered, and will not be repeated here. See Chapters One and Ten.

[1120] 2 JHS Trial 863-64.

[1121] 2 JHS Trial 864-65.

[1122] 2 JHS Trial 1060-61, 1065-66, 1066-67, 1068.

1123 1 JHS Trial 532-33.

1124 1 JHS Trial 533, 1060.

1125 *LA from Surratt Courier, vol. 2*, James E.T. Lange and Katherine DeWitt, Jr., *The Three Indictments of John Harrison Surratt, Jr.*, p. X-25 (Jan. 1992) (hereafter *"Three Indictments"*); see Chapter Twenty.

1126 LA from Surratt Courier, vol. 2, "Letter to the Editor from Joseph George," Jr., p. X-20 (Sept. 1987), *quoting, Philadelpia Press* (August 11, 1867) (hereafter *"Philadelphia Press* (August 11, 1867)").

1127 JOH Papers, J. William Joynes, "The Missing Link in Lincoln's Assassination," §B, *Baltimore News American* (Feb. 12, 1974) (hereafter *"Missing Link"*).

1128 *Three Indictments*, pp. X-25 (twice); JOH Papers - JHS, *Letter from James O. Hall to Joan Chaconas* (June 5, 1987); JOH Papers - JHS, *James O. Hall's Handwritten Notes re: The Indictments* (hereafter *"Hall Notes on Indictments"*).

1129 National Archives, RG 21, *United States v. John H. Surratt*, Criminal Case #4731, *Indictment* (Feb. 4, 1867) (hereafter *"Indictment*, Case #4731"). By letter dated March 2, 1867, Mr. Carrington asked Attorney General Henry Stanberry to review the indictment to "state whether in your opinion it is free from objection." National Archives, *Letter from Edward C. Carrington to Henry Stanberry* (March 2, 1867), National Archives Identifier 6783048.

1130 *Indictment*, Case #4731, p.1.

1131 The irony is that lawyers are so afraid of leaving something out that they sometimes cram their documents with so much redundant boilerplate that they end up unintelligible, which makes them nearly unreviewable, which frequently results in leaving out something important.

1132 *Ibid.*, pp.1, 1b, 2.

1133 *Indictment*, Case #4731, pp.2, 2b.

1134 *Ibid.*, p.3.

1135 *Ibid.*, pp.3b-4b.

1136 *Ibid.*, pp.5, 5b, 6 (emphasis added).

1137 *Ibid.*, pp.6-6b.

1138 2 JHS Trial 1372.

1139 2 JHS Trial 1201-02 (argument of Merrick).

1140 *U.S. Legal, District of Columbia Kidnapping/Abduction Laws*, http://kidnapping.uslegal.com/state-kidnapping-abduction-laws/district-of-columbia-kidnappingabduction-laws/ (accessed March 11, 2014).

1141 2 JHS Trial 1204.

1142 Peter J. McQuillan, *Felony Murder and the Misdemeanor of Attempted Escape: A Legislative Error in Search of a Correction*, 15 Fordham Urban Law Journal 821, 825-28 (1986).

1143 *Ibid.*, p.827 (*quoting*, Chase's *Blackstone's Commentaries*, p.940).

1144 2 JHS Trial 1091, 1151.

1145 2 JHS Trial 1202.

1146 *Rockville Lecture*, Weichmann, pp.431-32.

1147 *McMillan Judiciary Testimony*, p.13; 1 JHS Trial 471, 477.

1148 National Parks Service, Ford's Theatre Collection, *Pocket Diary of John Wilkes Booth* (emphasis in original).

1149 *Trial of the Conspirators*, p.45.

1150 *Come Retribution*, p.421.

1151 *Lexis-Nexis Capsule Summary of Criminal Law* §22.05[B][1] (2004) (emphasis in original). The contemporary Model Penal Code is even more strict, requiring that the withdrawing conspirator take affirmative steps to thwart the success of the conspiracy. *Ibid.*, §22.05[B][2].

1152 *State v. McCahill*, 72 Iowa 111, 33 N.W. 599, 601-02 (1887).

1153 *Atzerodt Baltimore American Statement*, p. III-28.

1154 See Chapter One.

1155 2 JHS Trial 814-15.

1156 2 JHS Trial 816.

1157 William Shakespeare, *Hamlet*, Act 3, scene 1.

1158 2 JHS Trial 761, 789-90, 792.

1159 *American Tragedy*, p.83; 2 JHS Trial 748.

1160 2 JHS Trial 764-68, 916.

1161 2 JHS Trial 767.

1162 *Rockville Lecture*, Weichmann, pp.436-37.

1163 *Ibid.*, p.437.

1164 2 JHS Trial 780-82; *E.G. Lee Offer of Proof*, ¶2. I have already expressed the view that the Elmira prison surveillance mission was a cover for something else, see Chapter Ten.

1165 2 JHS Trial 780; *E.G. Lee*, pp.121-25.

1166 2 JHS Trial 1064.

1167 2 JHS Trial 1166.

1168 2 JHS Trial 838.

1169 2 JHS Trial 837.

1170 *Ibid.*

1171 2 JHS Trial 839.

1172 *Ibid.*

1173 2 JHS Trial 839-40.

1174 1 JHS Trial 6-7; *Philadelphia Press* (August 11, 1867), p. X-20.

1175 Although an unidentified surviving member of the Surratt jury provided a "reminiscence" thirty years after the event, in which he asserted his belief that "all were . . . Union men," this seems unlikely. *Juror Reminiscence*, p.2.

CHAPTER TWENTY-ONE

CLOSING ARGUMENTS: CARRINGTON VERSUS MERRICK

O<small>N</small> J<small>ULY</small> 27, 1867, <small>FORTY-SEVEN DAYS AND OVER THREE HUNDRED</small> witnesses after the start of Surratt's trial, the lawyers began their final arguments. District Attorney Edward C. Carrington stood to face the jury. He carried plenty of baggage. On January 5, 1861, Mr. Carrington – though a native-born Virginian – issued a stirring letter calling out the District of Columbia militia in protection of the Federal Government, thus earning the enduring enmity of many secessionists.[1176] He did it, as he told the jury, "not because I loved Virginia less, but this Union more . . .."[1177] And so, as District Attorney Carrington stood to face the jury, he first addressed the elephant in the room – sectional bias.

> I cannot regard this cruel, miserable murderer and assassin as a representative man of the South; . . . and if an attempt should be made . . . by innuendoes . . . to present him to the imagination of this jury as an embodiment . . . of southern honor and southern chivalry, I call upon you to spurn it as an insult to every honest man, born and reared upon southern soil. Southern men do not justify assassination and cold-blooded, deliberate, cruel murder. I am aware that I address southern men with southern sympathies. . . . Loyal men, men true to the laws and the Constitution of our common country. What honorable man, north, south, east, or west, will proclaim to the civilized world that he justifies, palliates, sympathizes with a traitor, a spy, and an assassin . . . .?[1178]

Was this merely wishful thinking? It certainly seemed so, as Mr. Carrington pursued his rhetoric beyond the breaking point:

> Give me a jury of honorable confederate soldiers, give me a jury of young rebels, with arms in their hands, who entered into this fierce and cruel war, under the delusion that they were doing God's service, . . . misled by wicked, designing and ambitious politicians, and let me tell the sad story of this cruel, cruel murder, and they would hang this wretch as high as Old John Brown . . ..[1179]

More likely, like Booth himself who had participated in the deed, they would hang John Brown twice more and welcome Surratt into their fellowship.

Carrington then drew upon Milton's *Paradise Lost*:

> The Satan of this infernal conspiracy has gone to hell, there to atone in penal fires forever and forever for his horrid crime. But the Beelzebub still lives and moves upon the face of this green earth, as the dramatist says, "to mock the name of man." In John H. Surratt, the prisoner at the bar, you behold the Beelzebub of this infernal conspiracy.[1180]

Just as it was beginning to appear that Carrington had nothing to offer besides literate ways to call Surratt a bad fellow, he set forth five propositions by which Surratt should be found guilty, of which three are worth mentioning here:

First, that if Surratt was a member of a conspiracy to assassinate Lincoln, and he performed the role assigned to him, he was guilty no matter how far away from Ford's Theatre he may have been at the time of the fatal shot;

Second, even if the object of the conspiracy was to kidnap the President, and one of Surratt's co-conspirators killed Lincoln without the foreknowledge and contrary to the intent of the other conspirators, all conspirators including Surratt were nonetheless guilty of murder; and

Third, that Surratt, so long as he served his role in the conspiracy, or aided or abetted in the murder, was "constructively present" at Ford's Theatre – which simply means that the law would treat him as though he was present, even if he wasn't.[1181]

Because the evidence that Surratt was privy to a conspiracy to abduct was stronger than the evidence that he was privy to a conspiracy to kill, it was crucial to the success of the Government's case that the jury in effect adopt the 1862 reasoning of Jefferson Davis that an attempt to kidnap the President was tantamount to an attempt to kill him. As argued by Mr. Carrington:

> [W]here a number of men engage in an enterprise in the midst of war, when brother is armed against brother, . . . to . . . by force abduct [the President] and carry him to his enemies . . ., if human life is taken every man involved in that dangerous conspiracy . . ., though it was no part of the original plan, is guilty of murder. For although . . . I am not . . . a fighting man, yet while I had a heart to beat, while I had an arm to strike, . . . I would fight them to the death, and the inevitable consequences would be murder, bloodshed, and death.[1182]

With those as the ground rules, Carrington attempted to tie Surratt to the conspiracy, mixing good evidence indiscriminately with bad. He trotted out the Charles Selby letter that was possibly written by Booth, but most likely well before Surratt had any involvement.[1183] He referred to calling time in front of Ford's Theatre, quickly retreated to the position that whether Surratt was there or not was immaterial, then made it seem essential by spending much of an afternoon and part of the next morning reviewing the evidence that Surratt was in Washington on the fatal Good Friday.[1184] He reminded the jury of McMillan's testimony that Surratt came in response to a letter from Booth stating a change in plans.[1185] He painted the other conspirators with more quotations from Milton, bungling a few names ("Samuel Atzerodt"). He dredged up Surratt's association with Mrs. Slater – that "depraved and wicked woman"[1187] – and the killing of the Union soldiers, which had nothing to do with the great crime with which Surratt was charged.

Carrington indignantly defended Weichmann against the charge of complicity, but allowed that if Weichmann was in fact a co-conspirator, at least he had the sense to repent and turn state's evidence.[1188] He bored the jury by reading Greenleaf on "apparent accomplices" who turn government witness, and every scrap of paper put into evidence. He read from the Bible to demonstrate that God had delegated His power over life and death to the civil authorities in order to reassure the jurors that they could impose capital punishment consistent with God's will.[1189] He derided Mrs. Surratt, saying that she "unsexes herself" by plotting the murder of Lincoln, and got himself so worked up in a paternalistic rage that he again seemed to forget who was on trial:

> I believe in submission on the part of woman; submission to her God, to the laws of her country, and her husband.[1190] But when a woman opens her house to murderers and conspirators; infuses the poison of her own malice into their hearts, and urges them to the crime of murder and treason, I say boldly as an American officer, public safety, public duty, requires that an example be made of her conduct.[1191]

In short, Carrington by turns bored, confused and angered the jury, pandered to its worst prejudices, and baited it to revisit the controversy of the hanging of Mrs. Surratt even though that was a no-win proposition for the Government.

It was deep into this swerving and unstructured speech that Mr. Carrington finally struck upon the crucial facts that Surratt brought Lloyd "certain arms" and "show[ed] him where they could be safely concealed . . .," and that when Booth was captured and shot, "an arm [was] taken . . . from his dying grasp" that was "identified as the very arm which had been provided for him by the prisoner at the bar [Surratt] . . . ."[1192] Had he stuck to that point and hammered it home in light of his statement of the law, a conviction might have been won. But he could not control himself, and just a few minutes later he was back to beating the ghost of Mrs. Surratt:

> A woman's weapon is her tongue, . . . with which she sows the seeds of bloodshed, and violence, and discord. . . . I call

upon you as conservators of the public peace, as Christian Men, to say to woman, Keep your proper place; submit to the laws of your country; . . .. But if you dare to raise your arm, to unsex yourself and engage in a conspiracy against the nation's life and the nation's honor, . . . I call upon this honest jury . . . to spurn mawkish sentimentality.[1193]

Though a prisoner to the patriarchal and grandiloquent style of his day, Carrington goes on much longer than he should. Finally, two days after he began, Carrington finished this way:

[W]hat is this country worth if its highest officials are to be at the mercy of the assassin's dagger?

"Dagger?" Booth shot Lincoln!

. . . It has been said that this Nation was baptized in blood, the blood of our fathers; it has been preserved in blood, the blood of their children. But what is this country worth if your sons fight for its preservation and you fail by the execution of its laws to restrain and punish its enemies? I charge you by the solemn memories of the past, by the glorious hopes of the future, by the memories of the honored dead who have fallen in the service of the republic, to vindicate the majesty of the law, . . . and wipe this deep and damning stain from the escutcheon of your country. . . . I charge you, . . . gentlemen of the jury, assign to . . . the blood-stained prisoner at the bar, that punishment which he deserves by the law of God and man, for the great crime which he has committed in the face of heaven and earth. He is a murderer, and deserves a murderer's doom.[1194]

Carrington was plainly tone deaf, unable to hear his own words in the ears of a southern juror. In 1867 the wounds of the rebellion were fresh; any Confederate patriot smarted from the fact that the nation had been "preserved in blood," and did not consider it a point of honor. Their sons had not died to preserve the Government represented by

Mr. Carrington, and their "honored dead" did not fall in service of it; quite the contrary. If it was their country now, it was so not by choice, but at the point of a bayonet. Carrington's peroration was as if one of King George's be-wigged prosecutors had asked a Colonial jury to hang George Washington after an unsuccessful American Revolution, by appealing to the majesty of the Crown for which their Minutemen sons had died.

* * *

Merrick followed Carrington to argue for the next two days. To flip Charles Sumner's felicitous phrase, he was like "champagne after hog-wash."[1195] Arrayed against his client, Merrick told the jury, were high government officials, "a swarm of spies and detectives," and "the treasury of a government with hundreds of millions at its command," all "to pursue to the gibbet one penniless young man . . .." In their zeal to convict for a vague conspiracy even at the expense of suborning perjury, charged Merrick, "there have been other conspiracies in higher places to commit a murder through the forms of law . . .." Merrick ripped at the many irrelevancies relied on by the Government to "tear open the wounds of war and pour into your minds a torrent of invective calculat-ed to keep alive forever fraternal hatred . . . engendered in a war that is now at an end . . .." *"Shame on the United States!"* scolded Merrick, and one can already imagine the jurors looking down their noses at District Attorney Carrington.[1196]

Yet Merrick was not above poking at the wounds of the recent war when to do so served his cause. He characterized the prosecution of Surratt as "attempting now, after the war is over, to discredit a man because he followed . . . his honest conviction." Suddenly abducting – or even murdering – the President of the United States, was simply a difference between men as to their "honest convictions"!

Merrick played on the contemporaneous tensions between North and South:

> [W]ho has kept the faith the best between the two contend-
> ing foes, of the obligations that were entered into at
> Appomattox Court House, when Lee gave up his sword to

Grant? . . . Has the acquiescent and submissive southerner, keeping to the pledge he then gave of submission to the supreme law of the land? [O]r has the dominant spirit of incendiary fanaticism, seeking vengeance in the north, and now blotting out nine states of the south, and establishing military despotism where once in her glory rode and triumphed the goddess of constitutional liberty?[1198]

If the prosecution wanted to fight the Civil War again, Merrick was more than ready, and stood a much better chance on the ground of the D.C. Criminal Court than Lee had stood on Virginia soil.

Having framed the case in the context of sectional strife, Merrick got down to business. First, he knocked conspiracy right out of the indictment. Stressing the "did kill and murder" language of the fourth count, he asked, "Are you not trying John H. Surratt for the murder of Abraham Lincoln? Is there anything else in the case? Is there anything else in the indictment?" Then he added, "I am not surprised that my friends on the other side, having found their original theory of the case fail them, should be driven to the extreme principles of the law they have attempted to assert; but I should be surprised, I should be amazed, if they ever get this jury to adopt any such absurd notion."[1199] With a few dismissive comments, Merrick snatched out from under the Government the only realistic ground on which it could possibly muster twelve votes to hang Surratt.

Focusing more closely on the conspiracy count of the indictment, Merrick argued that the portion of the count stating that the conspirators "were present, aiding, helping, and abetting . . . the said John Wilkes Booth,"[1200] meant that Surratt had to be "present" to satisfy the charge of conspiracy. Merrick correctly noted that Chief Justice Marshall had distinguished his *Bollman & Swartwout* opinion in the main trial against Aaron Burr for conspiracy to commit treason. Even though the law does not necessarily require actual presence, Marshall held that where the indictment alleged a conspiracy in one place but the evidence did not support it having occurred in that place, the case had to be dismissed.[1201] It seemed that the Government had again made that error.

Was the allegation in count four that Surratt was "present" a fatal flaw in the conspiracy indictment? That was a question of law for the Court to resolve in its instructions to the jury. In this case, Judge Fisher told the jury that a member of a conspiracy is equally guilty if "he was present either constructively or actually, that is to say, either at the scene of the crime in person, or near enough to give . . . the slightest support or encouragement to the actual perpetration of it, or if he be remote from the scene for the purpose of aiding it, and in performance of the part of the plan assigned to him . . .."[1202] Clearly, the Judge treated the allegation of presence as satisfied by the legal fiction of "constructive presence." My Contracts professor[1203] taught us that whenever you see the word "constructive" in the law, it means that the next word means the opposite of what it says. So "constructive presence" means Surratt was absent, but the law for various reasons will pretend that he was present. Therefore, the indictment's allegation that Surratt was "present" should not have been a fatal flaw. Yet Bradley deftly convinced the jury that it should be.

* * *

Having cut the case down to the size he wanted, Merrick then rubbed the Government's face in its opening blunder. "You recollect, gentlemen of the jury, when Mr. Wilson opened this case . . . on the part of the government, he looked upon the indictment as a simple indictment for murder, and he said that they would prove the prisoner's complicity in the murder, and his presence in Washington, helping to do the deed of murder."[1204] Merrick detailed the Government's efforts to make this proof, and then how "[o]ne by one [the witnesses] . . . fell as they came" under scorching cross-examination, and the light of truth revealed by the witnesses for the defense. An honorable Government, said Merrick, "would have said we have been mistaken, . . . [our] witnesses . . . have told us falsehoods, . . . they are of infamous character, and have polluted and contaminated the court . . .." Instead, the Government pressed forward. "[I]nnocent blood must again be shed to wash out the damning record of innocent blood already shed," thundered Merrick, an obvious reference to Mrs. Surratt. And so, because it could not prove its indictment, the Government had changed its tactics to rely on conspiracy.[1205]

Merrick's argument on this point was all the more powerful because (with the exception of the dubious claim that mother or son were innocent) it was accurate. The Government had claimed it would prove Surratt guilty of simple murder by placing him on the scene, and it had backed off and changed its strategy to rely on conspiracy when it realized the strength of Surratt's alibi. Even if the fall-back argument was valid and Surratt should have been convicted for conspiracy to murder, once the Government changed horses in midstream it began to lose credibility. If the jury could not rely on the Government to know what it was doing, they were unlikely to vote unanimously on something so serious as a hanging offense. Merrick understood this, and exploited it with great skill. Thus, the Surratt trial is an example of a phenomenon succinctly parodied by Robert Frost nearly a century later: "A jury consists of twelve persons chosen to decide who has the better lawyer."[1206]

* * *

Astonishingly, Merrick as much as admitted that Surratt was a Rebel spy and part of a conspiracy to abduct Lincoln:

> Here were a number of young men, with their minds inflamed upon political topics, sympathizing earnestly with the South, . . . carrying despatches [*sic.*] between the United States and the Confederate States, and having arms for the purpose of their common protection; and further than that it is not improbable that there may have been some idea of abducting the President as a measure of war – a thing which was unjustifiable, and for which they might have been taken and executed; but it is not improbable, I say, for the reason that . . . the North refused to make those [prisoner] exchanges which were demanded by the rules of war and the laws of humanity.[1207]

This admission tied into the defense that the plan had changed from kidnapping to assassination without Surratt's knowledge, and that he was therefore part of a different conspiracy than the one carried into fruition.[1208] But it also shows the extent to which Merrick was confident that he knew the sympathies of his audience, and could rely upon them to share Surratt's view of the necessities of war.

* * *

Merrick argued that by elevating the murder of President Lincoln into something special, beyond an ordinary murder, the Government was tending towards monarchy:

> [T]here is a class of gentlemen in the United States who . . . seem to have . . . become dazzled with the prospective glory of . . . titles of nobility and rank, crowns and diadems . . .. Why, the very dead of the Revolution, of the last war with Britain, and of the late war for freedom and constitutional independence, rise to condemn the gentleman and to repudiate his doctrine. . . . The President is a simple American citizen, representative of the free people of America. The monarchy of this country . . . is the embodied will of the people in the Constitution of the United States; our only emperor, our only king, is the Constitution . . ..[1209]

Suddenly, the jurors had to acquit to avoid crowning the dead President King of America. One can only marvel at how far afield these arguments carried the jurors from the actual question of Surratt's tangible contributions to the conspiracy against Lincoln.

Notice also the different phrasing used by the prosecution and defense in referring to what we now call the Civil War. To Carrington and Pierrepont, it was a "rebellion." But on Merrick's silver tongue, it was "the late war for freedom and constitutional independence."[1210] That is what the southern jurors' sons fought and died for and, by implication, that is what Surratt was fighting for – and what the tyrant, Lincoln, denied the South.

Merrick told the jurors that in France it is treason to imagine the death of Emperor Louis Napoleon, then caused a sensation in the courtroom when he interjected into the proceedings the political firestorm over Andrew Johnson:

> Is it treason here to imagine the death of Andrew Johnson?
> Is it treason to wish his death? If it be, then when your
> grand jury meets, *charge them to indict Thaddeus Stevens and
> all his corps....* No, sir; it is not treason. We can wish what
> we please in this free land, and public men are open to the
> freest and severest criticism.[1211]

The United States Congress was working on impeaching President
Johnson even as Merrick spoke.[1212] How quickly the worm had turned.
Those who deified Lincoln and wanted special rules to apply to his
killing were now engaged in a form of "political assassination" against
his all-too-human successor. Those who had hated Lincoln now pros-
pered at the hand of Johnson. Merrick delighted in exploiting the
hypocrisy.

* * *

We will not revisit Merrick's arguments on the particulars of the
conflicting evidence of Surratt's whereabouts at the fatal moment. For
nearly the course of an entire day he effectively portrayed the witnesses for the prosecution as either confused or perjurers, and lionized the
probity of Surratt's witnesses.[1213] He also construed the train schedules to show that Surratt could not possibly have gotten to Elmira in
time to leave on the April 13th train that the Government needed him
to leave on, and to show that, even if he had, he could not have been
in Washington in time to be shaved on the morning of the assassination by the prosecution witness he derided as "the barber nigger,
Wood . . . ."[1214]

Casual racism of this sort pervaded the trial. Merrick attacked the
testimony of Susan Jackson, the house servant who claimed to have
served John Surratt tea the night of April 14, by relying on the contrary
testimony of Mrs. Surratt's former slave, Rachel Hawkins. Rachel testified that on the morning of the assassination Susan said she had served
tea to John Surratt "about two weeks before," and had not seen him
since.[1215] Merrick praised Rachel to the jury as "an excellent specimen

of that system [slavery] which is passing away, and which hereafter will be remembered in romance and in story."[1216] Mr. Pierrepont had shown in cross-examination that Rachel was biased in favor of the Surratts,[1217] but Merrick set him straight while simultaneously condemning the "ungrateful" Susan Jackson:

> [Mr. Pierrepont's] education in the north has not led him to be familiar with the institutions in our section of the country. The honest and earnest sympathy of these old family negroes is beyond expression. . . . Show me an old family negro who has dandled the children of her master in her arms, . . . and I will show you a specimen of honesty such as cultivated education or high civilization cannot exhibit. Show me a negro who cares not for the family in which he was reared, which has protected him, which has extended to him the kindly hand of charity, but whose heart has turned away from them, and I will show you as black-hearted and false a man as you can find in the wilds of Africa.[1218]

On Merrick's slick tongue, the forced labor of slavery mellows into "the kindly hand of charity."

Merrick even relied on "that accursed fiend, Weichmann," to discredit Susan Jackson. Weichmann testified that he was with Mrs. Surratt until ten o'clock on the night of the assassination and did not see Surratt there, and that he last saw Surratt in Washington on April 3. For purposes of Merrick's argument to the jury, that portion of Weichmann's testimony was gospel truth amidst a sea of lies.[1219]

1176 2 JHS Trial 1252.
1177 2 JHS Trial 1075.
1178 2 JHS Trial 1075.
1179 *Ibid.*
1180 2 JHS Trial 1079, 1131.
1181 2 JHS Trial 1080. For those eager to know, the fourth and fifth propositions were: *fourth*, that if Lincoln was killed pursuant to a conspiracy of which Surratt was a member, the jury should presume Surratt was present for the purpose of aiding that conspiracy unless Surratt could prove that assistance

was not his purpose; and *fifth*, that because alibi is an affirmative defense, the burden of proving it lies with Surratt. *Ibid.*

1182 2 JHS Trial 1091-92; *see also, ibid.*, 1085, 1090-91, 1097.

1183 2 JHS Trial 1098-99.

1184 2 JHS Trial 1101, 1117-28.

1185 2 JHS Trial 1116.

1186 2 JHS Trial 1100. Carrington seemed more offended by Mrs. Slater, whom the Government had been unable to track down, than by the man he was supposed to be prosecuting, saying that "when she casts aside her womanly nature and enters into a hell-inspired plot, she is, of all objects, the most offensive and disgusting, the depth of degradation being in proportion to the immense elevation from which she falls." *Ibid.*

1187 2 JHS Trial 1102.

1188 2 JHS Trial 1103-09.

1189 2 JHS Trial 1139-40.

1190 Who, by the way, was dead.

1191 2 JHS Trial 1112.

1192 2 JHS Trial 1113-14.

1193 2 JHS Trial 1115.

1194 2 JHS Trial 1148.

1195 Gerald T. Dunne, *Justice Joseph Story and the Rise of the Supreme Court*, p.365 (Simon & Schuster 1970), *quoted in*, Stephen B. Presser & Jamil S. Zainaldin, *Law and Jurisprudence in American History*, p.625 (Thomson-West 5th ed. 2003) (hereafter *"Presser & Zainaldin"*). Sumner said reading Chief Justice Roger Taney's majority opinion in the *Charles River Bridge* case after reading Joseph Story's dissent was "hog wash after champagne." *Ibid.*

1196 2 JHS Trial 1155-57 (some verb tenses changed).

1197 2 JHS Trial 1202.

1198 2 JHS Trial 1203.

1199 2 JHS Trial 1159.

1200 *Indictment*, Case #4731, pp.6-6b.

1201 2 JHS Trial 1176-77. The authority referred to by Mr. Merrick is *United States v. Burr*, 25 F.Cas. 187, 196-99 (C.C.Va. 1807).

1202 2 JHS Trial 1375.

1203 Professor Jon L. Jacobson, University of Oregon School of Law.

1204 2 JHS Trial 1159.

1205 2 JHS Trial 1160-61.

1206 Lawrance Thompson, *Fire and Ice: The Art and Thought of Robert Frost* (Russell & Russell, New York 1961). I don't know the page; I simply remembered the quote!

1207 2 JHS Trial 1204.

1208 2 JHS Trial 1202-03.

1209 2 JHS Trial 1165.

1210 *Compare*, 2 JHS Trial 1150 & 1165.

1211 2 JHS Trial 1173 (emphasis added).

1212 *Ibid.*

1213 2 JHS Trial 1179-1201.

1214 2 JHS Trial 1196-97.

1215 1 JHS Trial 693.

1216 2 JHS Trial 1191-92.

1217 1 JHS Trial 694.

1218 2 JHS Trial 1192.

1219 2 JHS Trial 1192-94.

CHAPTER TWENTY-TWO

MOTHER AND SON VERSUS THE UNITED STATES

MERRICK'S ARGUMENT TO THIS POINT WAS ENOUGH TO WIN JOHN Surratt's case, but the defense wanted even more. They wanted to clear the name of Surratt's mother. They wanted to bring down Judge Advocate General Joseph Holt, the man in charge of the prosecution of Mary Surratt, and the man the defense accused of suborning perjury in both trials.[1220] Through Holt, they may even have dreamed of bringing down Holt's boss, the irascible Republican Secretary of War, Edwin M. Stanton. Astonishingly, it seems that they succeeded beyond their wildest dreams, and that Merrick's side gambit in the Surratt trial pushed the President into taking actions that led directly to passage of the articles of impeachment.

In the days leading up to the Surratt trial the southern press accused the Government – and, specifically, Judge Holt – of various forms of duplicity, including the charge that he prevented President Andrew Johnson from receiving pleas for mercy on behalf of Mrs. Surratt on the day of the execution.[1221] Less sensitive to political nuance than a Washingtonian would have been, Mr. Pierrepont promised early on to show that all considerations of clemency were placed before the President and his cabinet prior to the execution.[1222] But no such proof was made, and Merrick pounced on this in his closing argument. "Where is your record?" he taunted. "Why didn't you bring it in? Did you find at the end of the record a recommendation to mercy in the case of Mrs. Surratt that the President never saw? You had the record here in court."

"And offered it once and withdrew it," added Mr. Bradley.

"Yes, sir, offered it once and withdrew it," confirmed Merrick.[1223]
Then he painted the pathos of execution day in his Virginia drawl:

> You remember that day, gentlemen. Twenty-four hours for
> preparation. The echoes of the announcement of impend-
> ing death scarcely dying away before the approaching guard
> was heard leading to the gallows. Priest, friend, philan-
> thropist, and clergymen went to the Executive Mansion to
> get access to the President, to implore for that poor woman
> three days' respite, to prepare her soul to meet her God,
> but got no access. The heart-broken child – the poor
> daughter went there crazed, and, stretched upon the steps
> that lead to the Executive Chamber, she raised her hands in
> agony and prayed to every one that came, "O, God! let me
> have access, that I may ask for but one day for my poor
> mother – just one day!" Did she get there? No. And yet,
> says the counsel, there was no one to prevent access being
> had. Why can't you prove it? O, God! If such a thing
> could have been proved, how would I not have rejoiced in
> the fact; for when reflecting upon that sad, unfortunate,
> wretched hour in the history of my country – an hour when
> I feel she was so much degraded, I could weep until the
> paper be worn away with the continual dropping of my
> tears. Who stood between her and the seat of mercy? Has
> conscience lashed the chief of the Bureau of Military Justice
> [Judge Holt]? Does memory haunt the Secretary of War
> [Stanton]?[1224]

Not yet satisfied, Merrick painted a scene of Mrs. Surratt haunting
Judge Advocate General Holt, worthy of any contemporary horror
film:

> [Mrs. Surratt's] spirit moves about, and the Judge Advocate
> General and all those men may understand that it is the
> eternal law of God . . . [that] the spirit will still walk beside

them. He may shudder before her, because she is with him by day and by night; and he may say,

> *Avant! and quit my sight! Let the earth hide thee!*
> *Thy bones are marrowless; thy blood is cold.*

But the cold blood and marrowless bones are still beside him, and her whisperings are presaging that great judgment day when all men shall stand before the throne of God, and when Mrs. Surratt is called to testify against Joseph Holt, what will he in vindication say?[1225]

As part of his strategy of shifting attention away from the very real charges against Surratt, Merrick was determined to put Judge Holt on trial.

This put the War Department in a tough spot. A written recommendation of mercy had been signed by five members of the military commission, asking the President to commute Mrs. Surratt's death sentence to life imprisonment. Yet it was never published in Pitman's Trial Report because it was not considered part of the official proceedings.[1226] The question is, *did Judge Holt show it to the President prior to Mrs. Surratt's execution?*

Merrick's taunt was made in open court on the afternoon of August 1, 1867. President Johnson learned of it that same day, and ordered his private secretary, Colonel W.G. Moore, to prepare the first version of a historic note, addressed to Secretary of War Stanton:

> August 1, 1867
> Sir: Public considerations of a high character constrain me to say that your resignation as Secretary of War will be accepted.
> Very respectfully yours,
> /s/ Andrew Johnson[1227]

Although surely mounting tensions over Stanton's interference with the President's attempts to frustrate Congressional Reconstruction were the long-term cause of this, the immediate cause – or "pretext," if you will – seems to have been the revelations at the Surratt trial.

* * *

On the morning of Saturday, August 3, as soon as the prosecution had another chance to speak, Mr. Pierrepont was on his feet responding to Merrick's charges of covering up the clemency recommendation. Every single member of the cabinet voted to confirm the death sentences, he told the jurors, "and when it was suggested by some of the members of the commission that in consequence of the age and the sex of Mrs. Surratt it might possibly be well to change her sentence to imprisonment for life, [the President] signed the warrant for her death with the paper right before his eyes – and there it is," at which point Pierrepont handed the mercy recommendation to Merrick, adding, "[m]y friend can read it for himself."[1228]

On Monday, August 5, President Johnson ordered Secretary of War Stanton to deliver to him all records that Judge Holt claimed to have shown him prior to the signing of the death warrants. The papers, delivered that same day, included the recommendation of five members of the Commission that "the President, in consideration of the age and sex of Mary E. Surratt, if he can . . . find it consistent with his sense of duty to the country, . . . [should] commute the sentence of death . . . to imprisonment . . . for life."[1229] Johnson declared that he'd never seen this recommendation before; that he had been reluctant to sign the death warrant for Mrs. Surratt and so he had questioned Judge Holt closely, but Holt had totally failed to bring the mercy recommendation to his attention.[1230] He ordered his secretary to re-date the resignation request August 5, and it was delivered that day to Secretary Stanton.[1231] Stanton, who had been primed to expect it, parroted the President's words back to him: "Public considerations of a high character, which alone have induced me to continue at the head of this department, constrain me not to resign."[1232]

The next morning, with rumors of the stand-off all over Washington, Mr. Pierrepont reassured the jury that he knew from Judge Advocate General Holt's own lips that the mercy recommendation had in fact been shown to the President.[1233] With characteristic good luck, Surratt had managed to trigger the political cause célèbre of the year, a standoff between the legislative and executive branches of government that would result in President Johnson's impeachment for violation of the Tenure of Office Act. And it was all thanks to his mother, who seemed to reach from the grave to put her protective arms around him.

Only much later would strong evidence emerge that Andrew Johnson either knew perfectly well that he had seen the clemency recommendation, or simply forgot about it. Judge Holt indignantly denied the charge that he had failed to show the President the clemency recommendation.[1234] His position was confirmed by a number of sources, including the Attorney General, Secretary of State, Secretary of War, and Secretary of the Interior.[1235] It was also confirmed by General R.D. Mussey, who was attending the President at the Executive Mansion that day, and remembers Johnson coming out of a long meeting with Judge Holt held to review the findings of the military commission. According to General Mussey:

> I am very confident, though not absolutely assured, that it was at this interview Mr. Johnson told me that the court had recommended Mrs. Surratt to mercy on the ground of her sex (and age, I believe). But I am certain he did so inform me about that time, and that he said he thought the grounds urged insufficient, and that he had refused to interfere; that if she was guilty at all, her sex did not make her any less guilty; that he, about the time of her execution, justified it; that he told me that there had not been "women enough hanged in this war."[1236]

That sounds exactly like Andrew Johnson.

* * *

The specter of Mary Surratt stalks every moment of the Surratt trial, and Merrick made her star witness and co-counsel for the defense:

> Gentlemen, this voice from the grave speaks in behalf of the child. . . . [T]here is one single voice rising from the tomb, and as it ascends to the heavens is re-echoed back, *protect that boy.* You [addressing counsel for the prosecution] have broken the cerements of that grave; you have

brought her before this jury; now close those cerements if you can. She sits beside him, and covers him with a wing you can never shut. . . . Her trailing garments from the tomb sweep through this room. We feel the damp chill air of death. You may bid the spirit down now, but it will not down. It is here, as it has been elsewhere. It speaks to this jury – a mother pleading for her son, testifying in his behalf. It lives upon earth; that spirit which speaks to living men hisses in the ears of those who did this damning murder.[1237]

Merrick berated the Government for trying Mrs. Surratt a second time:

[Then] comes Mr. Carrington, breaking the cerements of the tomb, and demanding your verdict against Mrs. Surratt. In God's name, isn't it enough to try the living? Will you play the gnome, and bring her from the cold, cold earth, and hang her corpse? Bring her in, but there is no occasion for doing so; she is here already. We have felt our blood run cold as the rustling of the garments from the grave swept by us.[1238]

Of course, had the Government not dragged "her in from the cold, cold earth," the defense would have done so itself. As the opening line of their opening statement shows,[1239] the defense needed a martyred mother to deflect attention from the deep involvement of the son in the plot against Lincoln.

The climax of Merrick's dramatic argument is an absurd, airbrushed scene of great pathos:

Think, gentlemen, of what disasters have fallen upon this young man. Three years ago, . . . [a]round the hearth was gathered a happy band. A mother blessed it with a mother's love. Her gentle daughter, budding into womanhood, gave to the scene the sweet hues of her devoted smile.

Beside her sat a brother, just bursting into the promise of the man. Think, gentlemen, what has transpired since that night. The bright fire is quenched and gone, the hearth is desolate, the mother sleeps in a nameless, felon's grave, the daughter drags out a weary life with a broken heart, and the son is before you pleading for his life.[1240]

It may have been morally reprehensible for John Surratt to remain in hiding while his mother was tried and hanged, but it was a brilliant legal stroke. Mrs. Surratt gave her life for her son not once, but twice.

[1220] 2 JHS Trial 1208-09.

[1221] 1 JHS Trial 27; *see generally, LA from Surratt Courier*, vol. 1, James O. Hall, *The Mercy Recommendation for Mrs. Surratt*, pp.VI-27 to VI-28 (August 1990) (hereafter *"The Mercy Recommendation"*). There were also allegations that he suppressed the Booth diary, and that he suborned perjury through "Sanford Conover" and his purchased witnesses.

[1222] 1 JHS Trial 27.

[1223] 2 JHS Trial 1207.

[1224] 2 JHS Trial 1207-08.

[1225] 2 JHS Trial 1209 (italics added). Counsel is quoting from Shakespeare's
[1226] Macbeth, Act III, scene 4.
      LA from Surratt Courier, vol. 1, *The Clemency Plea Debate*, p.VI-34 (May 1986), *quoting*, "Judge Holt and the Lincoln Conspirators," *Century Magazine* (April 1890) (hereafter *"Clemency Plea Debate"*).

[1227] *The Mercy Recommendation*, p. VI-27.

[1228] 2 JHS Trial 1249.

[1229] *The Mercy Recommendation*, p.VI-27; *LA from Surratt Courier*, vol. 1, *Andrew Johnson or Joseph Holt?* p.VI-30 (Nov. 1995), *quoting*, Will T. Hale, *Nashville American* (March 4, 1906).

[1230] *The Mercy Recommendation*, p.VI-28.

[1231] *Ibid.*, pp.VI-27 to 28.

[1232] *Impeached*, p.95.

[1233] 2 JHS Trial 1320-21.

[1234] Weichmann, pp.297-98.

[1235] *Clemency Plea Debate*, p.VI-35.

[1236] *Ibid.*

[1237] 2 JHS Trial 1194 (bracketed material in original).

[1238] 2 JHS Trial 1209.

[1239] 1 JHS Trial 530-31.

[1240] 2 JHS Trial 1212.

CHAPTER TWENTY-THREE

THE GREAT FIZZLE

TRIALS HAVE A WAY OF BECOMING INTERMINABLE AND BITTER. OLD Mr. Bradley filled up Friday, August 2, with what he announced would probably be his last speech to a Washington jury after forty years at the bar.[1241] As we shall see, he was closer to correct than he imagined.

Bradley, Sr.'s rather meager contribution to the arguments is mostly a plaintive wail against his age and lack of vigor to fight the Surratt case "to the death," claiming that if he were younger, he "would bring up [his] children . . . to continue the fight" for "the principle . . . that you shall not go outside the indictment to find weapons to kill other than those recognized by the law."[1242] Bradley also propagated the Confederate party line that Booth was "a fanatic and . . . a madman,"[1243] which effectively covered up possible Confederate involvement in the plot for over a century. He berated Weichmann mercilessly, reviewed all the evidence in favor of Mrs. Surratt, and asked in conclusion not only for a verdict in favor of John Surratt, but also for one in favor of Mrs. Surratt.[1244]

It then fell to Judge Pierrepont, the elegant New York City lawyer, to rise on behalf of the Government and try to reassemble the pieces of the shattered prosecution case. Pierrepont spoke all day Saturday, August 3, and Tuesday August 6. He lavished the jury with copious quotations from the Bible and admonishments about God's will, but he also assembled the key evidence against Surratt into a fairly coherent picture.[1245] It was the first time anyone from the Government side had done this with intellectual rigor and clarity, and it was probably too late. According to an enthusiastic letter dated August 9, 1867, from Secretary of War Stanton to Judge Pierrepont:

> Judge Wylie called last evening and was, as Lloyd said of Mrs. Surratt, "so smiling that you wouldn't have known" him. He said he didn't understand the evidence until he heard your argument.[1246]

The Government's momentary optimism was misplaced. The jury retired on Wednesday, August 7, at 11:32 a.m. Two times between then and the weekend it informed the Court that it was deadlocked, and two times the Court sent it back with instructions to keep trying to reach a verdict. Finally, on the afternoon of Saturday, August 10, at one o'clock, the jury was brought in before Judge Fisher, with Surratt and the various lawyers present. The Clerk intoned the age-old question, "Gentlemen of the jury, have you agreed on a verdict?" Mr. Todd, the foreman, responded "No."[1247]

Judge Fisher then disclosed that he had received a note from the jury that morning, stating that "they stand precisely now as when they first balloted upon entering the room, nearly equally divided, and they are firmly convinced that they cannot possibly make a verdict." Under the circumstances, Judge Fisher ordered them discharged, and ordered John Surratt remanded back to the custody of the marshal.[1248]

The only one hung that day was the jury. It was not an acquittal, but it was a major victory for John Surratt.

* * *

If the lawyers and this author have assumed that "southern jurors" would vote one way and "northern jurors" would vote another, the results in the jury room did not perfectly vindicate that thesis, but they were close. According to the *Philadelphia Press* the jurors, with their places of birth following, were not "nearly equally divided," but stood eight to four in favor of acquittal:

For conviction:

W.B. Todd	Newburyport, Mass.
J. Russell Burr [*sic.* – "Barr"]	Northumberland Co., Pa.
C.S. Schneider	Wurtemberg, Germany
Wm. McLean	Kilmarnock, Scotland

For acquittal:

James Y. Davis	Northumberland Co., Va.
Thomas Berry	New York City
Robert Ball	Alexandria Co., D.C.
George A. Bohrer	Georgetown, D.C.
C. Alexander	Alexandria, Va.
Benj. F. Morsell	Prince Geo. Co., Md.
Benj. Gittings	Mongomery Co., Md.
Wm. W. Birth	Washington, D.C.[1249]

The two foreign-born jurors immigrated to the United States at a young age, but we do not know where they settled. All the jurors had been residents of, and done business in, the District of Columbia for many years.[1250] If we assume that birthplace correlates roughly with inclinations, especially in the antebellum time when people were generally less mobile and there was no pervasive national media, and further assume that the foreign-born jurors were naturally "northern," then there is exact sectional correlation with the exception of Thomas Berry of New York City.

What do we know of Thomas Berry? Not much. We know from his *voir dire* (questioning of potential jurors by the lawyers) that he had both formed and expressed an opinion as to the guilt or innocence of John Surratt before the trial even started, though we do not know the substance of that pretrial opinion. In this respect, he was not so different from most of the other jurors sworn to the panel. Unlike many other potential jurors who were disqualified, however, Mr. Berry was willing to say that this preexisting opinion would not bias or prejudice his judgment after hearing all the evidence, and therefore he was accepted.[1251] But in this, too, he was like most of the other potential jurors who made it on to the jury. So Mr. Berry seems to be an average juror who just happened to have been born in New York City, and who had lived for many years in the District of Columbia. What his political allegiances may have been, we do not know.

Virginia native James Y. Davis was the only juror who claimed in *voir dire* to have no opinion on the case.[1252] How could somebody have no opinion in a cause célèbre over which, according to another juror, the "[e]xcitement was intense"?[1253] That should have been a red flag to disqualify him on the spot, but nobody challenged him. District of Columbia native George Bohrer not only had an opinion about John Surratt, but he added that he could not have voted to convict Mary Surratt. Judge Wylie, who was sitting in for a sick Judge Fisher on that day of jury selection, told him that Mary Surratt's guilt or innocence "has nothing to do with this case," and then he was put on the jury.[1254] Though legally correct, the Judge could not have been more wrong. In the final analysis, both Davis and Bohrer voted for acquittal.

Even if there had been complete sectional correlation, correlation is not causation. The Government had blundered out of the starting gate, and it was consistently out-lawyered. The Government was unable or unwilling to elicit the strongest evidence that Surratt had carried instructions from Judah Benjamin pertaining to the assassination plot. While it clearly had enough evidence to convict Surratt of conspiracy to kidnap the President, that was not the charge. Unbiased jurors could entertain reasonable doubt as to whether Surratt was guilty of conspiracy to murder the President.

* * *

An undated juror's reminiscence prepared thirty years after the event by one of the few surviving jurors provides a bit of insight into the jury deliberations.[1255] After noting that four jurors stood firm for conviction through all the ballots, the surviving juror says, "This result, in the face of the testimony of the proprietor and employees of a Clothing House in Elmira, New York, was cause of wonder!"[1256] This shows that the survivor who wrote this account was in favor of acquittal. He does remember that there was testimony on both sides of the question of where Surratt was on the night of the assassination, *but he makes it clear that Surratt's absence from Washington was the crucial deciding factor in the outcome:*

> The evidence of the Elmira people, proved conclusively that at the [illegible] time of the terrible deed, Surratt was hundreds of miles away from Washington. Therefore the acquitting Jurymen announced to their fellows that, from a conscientious construction of the testimony, they could not, without violating their oaths, render a verdict of condemnation.[1257]

The Government lawyers and Judge Fisher could talk about fancy notions of "constructive presence" till the cows came home, but these hard-headed businessmen knew the difference between being present at or absent from the scene of the crime, and apparently weren't interested in legal niceties.

This raises an interesting question: *did the jury deliberately ignore Judge Fisher's instructions on the law of conspiracy?* According to the same *Philadelphia Press* account that printed the alignment of jurors reproduced above, had Surratt been indicted for conspiracy instead of murder, they would have convicted him "immediately upon retiring to their room."[1258] This odd statement has sat unchallenged for nearly 150 years, because many people do not realize that Surratt *was indicted for conspiracy, and that Judge Fisher clearly instructed the jury on conspiracy.*[1259] What is really going on here?

Both Mr. Merrick and Mr. Bradley Sr. argued at length to the jury about their "right" to decide not only the facts of the case, but also the law applicable to the case.[1260] This is the ancient doctrine of jury nullification, which states that the jury is to follow its own conscience, deciding the law as well as the facts, even if their view of the law contradicts the instructions given by the Court.[1261] It was first introduced into American law by the colonial-era trial of John Peter Zenger, whom the jury acquitted of the crime of seditious libel even though he was probably guilty under the instructions given by the Royal Governor's hand-picked judge.[1262]

Defense counsel's jury nullification arguments were made in response to District Attorney Carrington. Early in his closing remarks, Carrington made such a clumsy argument about the jury's obligation to follow the law as given by the Court, that he managed to turn it into a threat:

> A juror who swears to decide according [to] the law, and departs but a hair's breadth from the instructions of the court, and decides according to his own abstract notions of right and wrong – pardon me for saying so, I do it in no offensive sense – commits the awful and Heaven daring crime of perjury.[1263]

If Carrington knew anything of English legal history, he should have been familiar with *Bushel's Case*, in which a juror was fined for refusing – against the Court's instructions – to convict the Quaker William Penn of breach of the peace. The higher court overturned the fine based on the principle "that the judges . . . have no right to fine, imprison, or punish a jury for not finding a verdict according to the direction of the Court."[1264]

Mr. Bradley took severe umbrage at Carrington's remarks:

> I heard with utter amazement another thing broached. That the jury in a capital offense, where they are to bear the burden of responsibility, . . . are perjured if they do not follow the dictates of the court. Is it possible, with all the information this day spread around us, . . . with all the learning coming to us from past ages, that a jury are to be considered perjured if they do not follow the dictates of the court?[1265]

Bradley then gave an excellent summary of the history of oppression under the English Star Chamber, and the rise of the jury in the *Case of the Seven Bishops* as a shield against that oppression. "[F]or the sake of the law of my country," he thundered, "I condemn, I repudiate, I trample under foot any such doctrine as this – that a juror commits perjury because, according to his conscience, he renders a general verdict of acquittal or guilty."[1266]

Judge Fisher instructed the jury that, while it may have the *power* to disregard a corrupt judge, it did not have the legal *right* to disregard the law he gave them.[1267] Eight jurors were not intimidated by Mr. Carrington's threats, and it seems that they either believed Judge Fisher was corrupt, or that jury nullification was otherwise necessary because of what they perceived as the injustice of convicting a man who was 280 miles away from the scene of the crime. Despite Judge Fisher's contrary legal instructions on conspiracy and constructive presence, the simple fact that Surratt was in Elmira was enough to convince those jurors that they should never vote to convict.[1268]

* * *

The surviving juror's reminiscence reveals one other matter that weighed on their collective minds: *a threat made by "a prominent New Yorker" engaged by the prosecution* – Judge Edwards Pierrepont.[1269] Capable though he was, we have already seen that, as an outsider, he sometimes failed to grasp the nuances of life in the District of Columbia. He should never have made this argument:

> A great many men from interested motives, some from political motives, and some possibly from patriotic motives, are very anxious to remove this capital from its present place. They say it does not belong here; that the people are not in sympathy . . . with this great government; that it is full of people who hate the government . . . . [E]very such man . . . wants to be able . . . to say in Congress, . . . "You see it is just as I told you. You cannot get justice in the city of Washington; a jury of the city of Washington refuses even to find guilty the assassin of the President, who is overwhelmingly proved to be guilty. We will remove the capital far hence. We will take it to a place where a public officer can be safe . . .."[1270]

Whether an accurate statement of a then-current political debate or not, such a consideration has nothing to do with Surratt's guilt or innocence. Pierrepont is essentially telling the jurors that their own property and business values will plummet – the obvious effect of moving the capital – if they vote to acquit. Stated bluntly, they should hang a man to protect their pocketbooks.

This threat may have had the opposite of its intended effect. After referring to this as Pierrepont's "attempt to obtain a verdict by intimidation," the surviving juror says that "[t]he jury were [*sic.*] very indignant as may be supposed, at this effort to drive them to a conclusion regardless of the convictions they might [illegible] after conscientiously, and deliberately weighing the evidence." He believed that "[t]his threat had an effect" after the verdict was handed down, upon an unspecified "man of wealth [who] was said to have been for a time seriously effected [*sic.*] in mind."[1271]

* * *

Immediately after the verdict was announced, the frustrations of a long and fruitless prosecution boiled over. A contemporary account by Secretary of the Navy Gideon Welles captures the scene:

> The judge was disgracefully partial and unjust, I thought, and his charge [to the jury] improper. The Senior Bradley was irascible, violent and indiscreet, some difficulty brought him and the judge in collision almost – and the judge, at the conclusion of the trial, ordered his name stricken from the roll of attorneys, an arbitrary act.[1272]

The "difficulty" alluded to occurred on July 2, the day that Judge Fisher, provoked by defense counsel's "penitentiary" remarks about the prosecution witnesses, admonished both sides for their lack of professional courtesy and overly adversarial tactics. According to Judge Fisher's order, as he was descending the bench on that day Mr. Bradley "accosted him in a rude and insulting manner charging the Judge with having offered him [Bradley] a series of insults from the Bench from the commencement of the trial."[1273] Fisher denied this charge, but Bradley was not satisfied, and he "threatened the Judge with personal chastisement."[1274]

Not surprisingly, Mr. Bradley's version of events is quite different. He says that when the Judge came back into the courtroom to get his umbrella, he (Bradley) asked him, "what do you mean by treating me as you have done today?"[1275]

> The judge replied, in great excitement, shaking his finger insultingly in Bradley's face, and, after some altercation, the judge said, "Step out with me, step out, if you dare." Whereupon Bradley stepped towards him, but was seized by some members of the bar and held, and the judge, holding his clinched [*sic.*] hand towards Bradley, said, "You know where to find me . . .," &c., with other abusive language.[1276]

Regardless of which version of the initial altercation you accept, it is undisputed that afterwards Mr. Bradley followed Judge Fisher onto a streetcar and handed him a note which – depending on whose version one believes – either accepts Judge Fisher's challenge ("You know where to find me"), or initiates a challenge to a duel.[1277]

Judge Fisher was incensed. He waited until the trial was over, then immediately ordered the name of Joseph H. Bradley, Sr., stricken from the roll of attorneys qualified to practice law in the District of Columbia Criminal Court.[1278]

On technical grounds too abstruse to be of interest, the Supreme Court of the United States held that the disbarment was improper. By order entered January 26, 1869, in conformance with the mandate of the United States Supreme Court, the lower court rescinded the order of disbarment.[1279] This tawdry footnote to the hung jury is but another example of what, in modern times, might be called Surratt's "teflon" coating. While his associates and defenders fell by the wayside, nothing ever stuck to Surratt.

Remanded to his comfortable suite of cells, Surratt waited. And waited. He spent his twenty-fourth birthday on April 13, 1868 still in jail awaiting trial. We don't know, but he was probably visited on that day by brother Isaac and sister Anna.

Meanwhile, the original Indictment #4731 sputtered forward. The case was set for retrial on May 12, 1868, but put off until June 22.[1280] On June 5, Mr. Carrington wrote to Acting Attorney General Oliver H. Browning, suggesting that they seek a further delay because Mr. Pierrepont would not be able to attend that term of court.[1281] This letter was replaced with a more detailed letter of June 9, which made clearer the Government's problems. First, the case would probably come before Judge Wylie, who could be expected to rule – unlike Judge Fisher – that Surratt had to be near enough to the scene of the crime to be able to provide assistance if called upon. Second, Carrington admitted that he had "no hope of securing [Sergeant Dye's] attendance at the next term [of court]."[1282] For whatever reason – whether inability to locate him, a change in his story, intimidation, or something else – the star witness who identified the "pale face" of Surratt as the man who called time in front of Ford's Theatre would not be available.

It was under these circumstances that Mr. Carrington recommended to the Acting Attorney General that they should *nolle prosequi* – in other words, drop the prosecution – on the original Indictment #4731 (which Carrington himself refers to as the indictment for "murder"), and instead bring a new indictment drawn to meet the objections raised by the defense. According to Carrington, this was necessary "to avoid a long tedious and expensive trial which would result either in an acquittal or another hung jury, and secure a conviction, which would, to some extent vindicate the cause of public justice."[1283] Acting Attorney General Browning replied with what some researchers have politely called "a gluteus-masking letter . . ., neither agreeing nor disagreeing with Carrington but saying, in essence, that it was worth a try."[1284]

To my knowledge, Mr. Carrington has borne the full brunt of history's condemnation for this move, but that's not quite fair. It was not Carrington, but Edwards Pierrepont, who first proposed a new indictment for Surratt. In a letter dated December 31, 1867 from Pierrepont to Assistant Attorney General Binckley, copied to Mr. Carrington, Pierrepont suggested a new indictment in response to intelligence from a juror:

> From intimation . . . which has been conveyed to me from one of the jurors . . . I wish to suggest whether an indictment can be framed so that, the jurors can find the prisoner guilty as an aidor [*sic.*] and abettor of the conspiracy merely – The juror says they did not doubt the guilt, but they wanted to find some verdict which relieved them of the necessity of a verdict of guilty of "Murder" . . ..[1285]

Of course, as District Attorney, it was Mr. Carrington who drafted and signed the new indictment, and who was ultimately responsible for its validity or invalidity. But he was neither the only nor the first member of the prosecution team to consider that a new indictment against Surratt might be necessary.

It proved to be a colossal blunder.

* * *

On Thursday, June 18, 1868, Carrington filed a new indictment in Criminal Case #5920 against John H. Surratt in the D.C. Criminal Court.[1286] The first count was for conspiracy to aid the rebellion by murdering Abraham Lincoln, "President of the . . . United States . . . and . . . Commander in Chief of the Army and Navy . . .." The second count was for conspiracy to aid the rebellion by kidnapping Abraham Lincoln, President and Commander in Chief. The third count was for conspiracy to aid the rebellion by providing specific material support to the plot to kidnap Lincoln.[1287] The fourth count was conspiracy to kidnap Lincoln. The fifth and final count was conspiracy to commit assault and battery upon Lincoln. A conviction on the second, third and fourth counts seemed probable.

Indictment #5920 became known in the press as "the rebellion indictment."[1288] It is significant that the new indictment repeatedly charged that Surratt intended "to give aid and comfort to the said rebellion and insurrection against the authority of the said United

States . . .."[1289] Under the Constitution, the crime of treason consists only in "levying war" against the United States, "or, in adhering to their Enemies, giving them Aid and Comfort."[1290] "Aid and comfort" was therefore a legal term of art, meaning that this indictment could be read as charging Surratt with treason.

Surratt was arraigned on the new charges on June 22, 1868, and pleaded not guilty.[1291] Trial was set for June 29 and bail set at twenty thousand dollars. Four men put up the bail money, thus betting that Surratt would appear for trial one week later rather than indulge in his now-legendary ability to vanish.[1292] With the posting of bail, Surratt was free for the first time since he was taken prisoner by Mr. Hale in Egypt on November 27, 1866.

Probably because of the new charges contained in Indictment #5920, trial was not held as scheduled. On September 21, Mr. Carrington formally entered a *nolle prosequi* on the first indictment.[1293] Surratt's lawyers were waiting to pounce. The very next day, September 22, Surratt raised as a special defense against Indictment #5920 that it was barred by the proclamation of amnesty dated July 4, 1868, which gave a general pardon to "every person who directly or indirectly participated in the late . . . rebellion, excepting such person . . . as may be under . . . indictment . . . upon a charge of treason or other felony . . .."[1294] This defense seems on its face to be quite weak. At the time of the proclamation, Surratt was of course under indictment (both ##4731 and 5920) for a number of felonies, up to and including providing "aid and comfort" to the rebellion, a form of treason. The Government "demurred," which is a fancy legal term meaning "so what?"[1295]

So plenty! On Thursday, September 24, 1868, Judge Wylie ruled against the Government and ordered that Surratt should go free "without delay."[1296] How did that happen? The Judge had been on the verge of ruling against Surratt's amnesty defense when his wily lawyers raised, for the first time, a new defense based on a 1790 statute of limitations.[1297] Judge Wylie was persuaded to find that the second indictment was barred by this statute because it had not been brought within two years of the crime.[1298] Since the first indictment, which had been brought within two years of the crime, was now officially withdrawn, this placed the Government in a terrible spot.

The Government took an appeal from this ruling. The merits of the appeal looked strong, because the statute of limitations relied on by Surratt said, *"[t]hat nothing herein contained shall extend to any person or persons fleeing from justice."*[1299] Surratt, of course, had spent nearly two years fleeing from justice.

But the appellate court would never reach the merits of this argument. Merrick and Bradley (Junior, we assume) filed a motion to dismiss the appeal. This motion argued that the Government was not allowed to appeal when it lost a criminal case. The appeals court agreed, and ordered the appeal dismissed.[1300] As a result, on December 7, 1868 the Clerk of the D.C. Criminal Court dismissed Indictment #5920.[1301] *There were no longer any indictments against Surratt!*

Frustrated by Surratt's absurdly technical victory, the Government attempted to press on with a third indictment, assigned as Criminal Case #6594.[1302] Some have concluded that this indictment was actually filed early in 1868, prior to Indictment #5920,[1303] but I am convinced that it was filed January 4, 1869.[1304] The third indictment was identical to the second. Most likely, the Government believed it could beat the statute of limitations argument based on the exception for "persons fleeing from justice," and that it could beat the amnesty proclamation defense based on the preexisting indictments for "treason or other felony." While the Government was probably correct on the law, it lacked Surratt's good luck. The Grand Jury Foreman ended all legal proceedings against Surratt by writing *"Ignoramus"* across the Indictment caption – Latin for "we ignore."[1305] Had he written ignominious he would have perfectly summed up the entirety of the legal proceedings against Surratt.

Surratt was set free by technicalities that, if read more carefully, should not have freed him. As stated by the newspaperman George Alfred Townsend in an October 4, 1868 article in the *Cleveland Leader*:

> This Surratt trial ranks like the trial of Aaron Burr at Richmond, a sensation without a climax. It seems strange, however, that Mudd, Spangler, and the minor conspirators against Mr. Lincoln, should be parboiling at the Dry Tortugas, while the glove-fellow and prime conspirator with Booth goes absolutely free.[1306]

There was an over-abundance of legality, but there was no justice to it. Surratt was at least Booth's second in command and yet he was now a free man. The law had no more claim on him. Whether his conscience did is an untold story.

1241 2 JHS Trial 1213.
1242 2 JHS Trial 1227.
1243 2 JHS Trial 1229.
1244 2 JHS Trial 1238-41, 1245-46.
1245 2 JHS Trial 1247-1366.
1246 JOH Papers - JHS, *Letter from Edwin L. Stanton to Judge Edwards Pierrepont* (August 9, 1867).
1247 2 JHS Trial 1379; *Judge Fisher's Account*, p. X-19.
1248 2 JHS Trial 1379.
1249 *Philadelphia Press* (August 11, 1867), p. X-20.
1250 *Juror Reminiscence*, p.2.
1251 1 JHS Trial 90.
1252 1 JHS Trial 98.
1253 *Juror Reminiscence*, p.2.
1254 1 JHS Trial 92.
1255 *Juror Reminiscence*, pp.1 & 2 (this would make it circa 1897).
1256 *Ibid.*, pp.4-5.
1257 *Ibid.*, p.6.
1258 *Philadelphia Press* (August 11, 1867), p. X-20.
1259 *Indictment*, Case #4731, Count Four; 2 JHS Trial 1372.
1260 2 JHS Trial 1161-62 (Merrick); 2 JHS Trial 1215-19 (Bradley).
1261 *Presser & Zainaldin*, pp.44-48.
1262 Frank B. Latham, *The Trial of John Peter Zenger*, August 1735 (Franklin Watts, Inc., New York 1970) (hereafter *"Latham"*); *Presser & Zainaldin*, pp.32-56.
1263 2 JHS Trial 1076.
1264 Latham, pp.52-53.
1265 2 JHS Trial 1215.
1266 2 JHS Trial 1215-19.
1267 2 JHS Trial 1375-76.
1268 *Juror Reminiscence*, pp.4-6.
1269 *Ibid.*, p.4.
1270 2 JHS Trial 1259.
1271 *Juror Reminiscence*, p.4 (one verb tense changed).
1272 *LA from Surratt Courier*, vol. 2, Joan L. Chaconas, *Legal Fireworks After the*

Surratt Trial, p.X-23 (July 1989).

1273 National Archives, RG 21, *United States v. John H. Surratt*, D.C. Criminal Case #4731, *Order of George P. Fisher, Jus. S.C. D.C.* (August 10, 1867).

1274 Ibid.

1275 J.T. Mitchell, *Professional Misconduct - The Case of Mr. Bradley and the Supreme Court of the District of Columbia*, American Law Register, vol. XVII, p.130 (March 1869).

1276 *Ibid.*

1277 *Ibid.*, pp.130-31. Referring to the "You know where to find me" remark, Mr. Bradley says, "There is but one interpretation of such an intimation among gentlemen. . . . I beg you will let me know, as soon as you conveniently can, when it will suit you to meet me out of this District, that we may arrange, to our mutual satisfaction, the points of difference between us without incurring the risk and odium which might accompany any controversy here, or in public." *Ibid.*, p.131.

1278 *Ibid.*, p.130.

1279 *Ibid.*, p.133, 134-35.

1280 National Archives, RG 21, *United States v. John H. Surratt*, D.C. Criminal Case #4731, *Orders of April 24, May 12 and June 15, 1868.*

1281 *Carrington June 5*, pp.1-2.

1282 *Carrington June 9*, pp.1-3.

1283 *Ibid.*, p.3 (emphasis in original).

1284 *Three Indictments*, p. X-25.

1285 National Archives, *Letter from Edwards Pierrepont to Assistant Attorney General* (Dec. 31, 1867), National Archives Identifier 6783055.

1286 National Archives, RG 21, *United States v. John H. Surratt*, D.C. Criminal Case #5920, *Indictment* (June 18, 1868) (hereafter "*Indictment*, Case #5920").

1287 *Ibid.*, pp. 1-10 (includes "b"-side pages).

1288 *New York Times*, "Trial of Surratt" (Sept. 20, 1868).

1289 *Indictment*, Case #5920, pp. 1b, 3, 3b-4, 4-7.

1290 U.S. Const., Article III, sec. 3, cl. 1.

1291 Isacsson, *TAT*, p.32.

1292 National Archives, RG 21, *United States v. John H. Surratt*, D.C. Criminal Case #5930, *Recognizance* (June 22, 1868).

1293 National Archives, RG 21, *United States v. John H. Surratt*, D.C. Criminal Case #5930, *Special Plea*, p.2 (Sept. 22, 1868) (hereafter "*Special Plea*").

1294 *Special Plea*, p.2; *ibid.*, *Proclamation of President Andrew Johnson* (July 4, 1868) (hereafter "*Amnesty Proclamation*"). It must have been painful for Secretary of State Seward to sign the certification of authenticity of this proclamation for Surratt's lawyers.

1295 National Archives, RG 21, United States v. John H. Surratt, D.C.

Criminal Case #5930, *Demurrer to Special Plea* (Sept. 22, 1868). I am indebted to my Oregon Practice and Procedure professor, Frank Lacy, emeritus of the University of Oregon School of Law, for this straightforward definition of a demurrer.

1296 *Hall Notes on Indictments, citing*, National Archives, RG 21, *United States v. John H. Surratt*, D.C. Criminal Case #5930 (proceedings of Sept. 22-24, 1868).

1297 National Archives, RG 21, *United States v. John H. Surratt*, D.C. Criminal Case #5930, *Brief of the United States*, p.1 (Oct. 23, 1868) (hereafter *"Brief of the United States"*). Specifically, the statute of limitations provided that no person should be tried for treason or other capital offense (other than willful murder or forgery) unless the charge was brought within three years; nor shall any person be tried for non-capital offenses unless the charge was brought within two years. *New York Times*, "The Surratt Trial - A New Plea Entered" (Sept. 25, 1868), *quoting*, Act of Congress of April 30, 1790.

1298 *Brief of the United States*, pp.1-2; *United States v. John H. Surratt*, 1 Mackay 306, 1868 WL 11041, p.1 (D.C. Sup., Nov. 6, 1868).

1299 *Brief of the United States*, pp.2, 3.

1300 *United States v. John H. Surratt*, 1 Mackay 306, 1868 WL 11041, pp.1-2 (D.C. Sup., Nov. 6, 1868).

1301 National Archives, RG 21, *United States v. John H. Surratt*, D.C. Criminal Case #5930, *Order of Dec. 7, 1868*.

1302 National Archives, RG 21, *United States vs. John H. Surratt*, Criminal Case #6594, *Indictment* (Jan. 4, 1868 [sic., 1869]) (hereafter *"Indictment*, Case #6594").

1303 Isacsson, *AFCT*, p. X-6; Isacsson, *TAT*, p.32. It has also been suggested without any citation to evidence that Indictment #6594 was stricken on November 5, 1868, before it was (in my view) even filed. *Three Indictments*, p. X-26. I could find no support for this.

1304 On its face it says "Jany 4, 1868," but all the surrounding evidence suggests this was due to the common mistake of jotting the just-expired year on the jacket of the indictment simply out of habit: (1) It has a higher case number than the preceding indictments; (2) neither Surratt's Special Plea to Indictment #5920 nor the appeals court decision of November 6, 1868 mention this indictment; (3) Surratt's Special Plea specifically says that Surratt is not under indictment except for the indictments it specifically mentions, *Special Plea*, p.2; and (4) Carrington stated at the hearing on September 24, 1868 that he "supposed a new indictment could be found at the next term of the Court," as soon as he heard Judge Wylie's ruling. *New York Times*, "The Surratt Trial - A New Plea Entered" (Sept. 25, 1868). A handwritten note in Mr. Hall's files confirms that he agrees with the

January 4, 1869 date for Indictment #6594. JOH Papers - JHS, *Hall Notes on Indictments*, p.4.

1305 *Indictment*, Case #6594, p.1.

1306 *Townsend re: Trial of Surratt*, p. X-13.

Chapter Twenty-Four

THE REVERSE OF TRUTH

AFTER THE TRIALS, LOUIS J. WEICHMANN SETTLED BACK IN HIS HOME town of Philadelphia, where he worked as a reporter and then at a plum government job for the custom house for seventeen years. In 1886 he followed his brother, a Catholic priest, to Anderson, Indiana, where he founded and ran a small business college until his death at the age of sixty, on June 5, 1902.[1307] He was known for "his culture and courtesy . . ., his gentility and amazing ability to speak eight languages . . . ."[1308] He spent nearly his whole life rebutting charges of perjury and cowardice.[1309] He was increasingly anxious during his years in Anderson. Monsignor Thomas Conroy wrote that, "in all the years of the [business] school's life Wechman [*sic.*] never stood with his back to a door . . . ." One of his students, Joseph Abel, said that Weichmann would go out only when necessary, "and then only on well-lighted streets . . . ."[1310]

While Weichmann's many detractors portray his nervousness as a sign of a guilty conscience, it may have been a reasonable reaction to actual threats and harassment. In an interview given to researcher Lloyd Lewis in 1926, Weichmann's sisters tell the following tales from Weichmann's Philadelphia years:

> One evening, as he was walking home from work, a neighbor woman screamed at him to run. A man was following him on the other side of the street and began to run as soon as Lou did. The woman held the door open and pulled

Lou in just as the man fired. The bullet stuck in the door. Another time, he was sitting in the second-story window at home reading when a revolver went off across the street and the bullet hit the window sill and fell down into a flower-bed where a little neighbor girl was playing.[1311]

Few people would stand with their back to a door after enduring such terrifying experiences.

Although a bachelor nearly his whole life, an obituary published by the *Muncie Morning Star* revealed that Weichmann was very briefly married in approximately 1872, to an unidentified woman in Philadelphia. "Domestic troubles soon came and they separated."[1312] Such a brief "show" marriage could be considered as much evidence of Weichmann's possible homosexuality as evidence against it. When he moved to Anderson, "[h]e didn't mix in a town where every one mixed."[1313] If Weichmann was gay in those closeted days it must have been especially painful, since he was already marked as an outcast in many circles.

According to the Muncie obituary, "although his evidence was true in detail, Professor Weichmann has always brooded over the matter, and frequently said that his testimony was the cause of the conviction and sentence to the gallows of Mrs. Surratt."[1314] His sisters confirm his state of mental turmoil, and even say that he would pace the floor at night, muttering about Mrs. Surratt.[1315] This brooding could be an indication of a guilty conscience, but not necessarily. Weichmann may have simply done his duty and then, as a sensitive man, been appalled at the rush to execution by the military commission and President Johnson – events over which he had no control. Mrs. Surratt cared for him like a son, and he had every reason to be fond of her regardless of any guilt she may or may not have borne. The sad fact, as stated by researcher Erich L. Ewald, is that "Mrs. Surratt's most ardent champions could not have devised a circle of hell more destructive of Louis Weichmann's mental health than the one he constructed for himself during his residence in this Indiana town."[1316]

* * *

On June 5, 1902, at the age of sixty, Louis J. Weichmann died peacefully of "cardiac asthma." He died at the home of his sister, Mrs. Charles O'Crawley, surrounded by his two sisters, his brother, and a few close friends.[1317] The Anderson obituary contains a fascinating account of an alleged deathbed statement made by Weichmann:

> During the afternoon, Mr. Weichman [*sic.*] realized that he must die. There seemed to be something on his mind which worried him. He called H.J. Creighton[1318] to his bedside and undertook to talk to him but was too weak. He wanted to talk about the assassination of Abraham Lincoln and the part he had taken as a witness in the trial of the conspirators. After a time he wrote on a piece of paper. He said that he realized that he was about to pass out of this world and was about to face his God in another world and he wished the people of this country to understand that in the great trial, and while on the witness stand, he told the truth and nothing but the truth.[1319]

This is a wonderfully dramatic, but probably embellished, version of what actually happened. It seems unlikely that a dying man so weak as to be unable to speak could manage to write such a long and cogent sentence as is attributed to Weichmann by the *Anderson Herald*.

There are at least two other versions of Weichmann's deathbed statement (which is sometimes called a "deathbed confession," but should not be since he did not confess to anything, instead merely confirming what he had always claimed). According to the *Muncie Morning Star*:

> [T]en minutes before his death came Mr. Weichmann called H.J. Creighton, a neighbor to his bedside. He was unable to talk and in a trembling hand he wrote the following:
>
> "Now, as I am so soon to meet my Almighty God I wish to state that my testimony in that great trial was the truth and nothing but the truth."
>
> It was the last thing he did.[1320]

Equally dramatic, and this time marvelously succinct. Still, could anyone write anything ten minutes before dying from cardiac failure, with the brain starved for oxygen? Again, unlikely.

The third version was told to researcher Lloyd Lewis by Weichmann's sisters in the 1926 interview. In this version, when their brother realized he was soon to die, he asked them to take down the following statement: "'June 2, 1902; This is to certify that every word I gave in evidence at the assassination trial was absolutely true; and now I am about to die and with love I recommend myself to all truth-loving people.'" "Then," reports Mr. Lewis, "he signed it 'Louis J. Weichmann' and died."[1321] Mr. Creighton is gone from this version, and Lloyd Lewis gets at least two things wrong on this same page – the date and cause of Weichmann's death. But there are enough versions of this story circulating to suggest that, although the actual document has never surfaced, some version of Weichmann's "deathbed statement" probably happened.

Weichmann was a very religious man. He feared God above all else. It is not likely he would have gone to his maker with a lie on his lips.

* * *

Except for one very serious problem with that theory. Mary E. Surratt was equally religious and God-fearing. On May 25, 1891, the Reverend J.A. Walter, confessor to Mrs. Surratt, read the following statement to the United States Catholic Historical Society of New York:

> On the . . . morning [of the execution] I went at 7 o'clock, carrying with me the Holy Communion, which I gave to Mrs. Surratt in her cell. I remained with her until the time of her execution, which was about 2:30 p.m. I can never forget the scene witnessed on that sad occasion. Poor Mrs. Surratt had been sick for several weeks and was quite feeble; she was lying on a mattress laid on the bare brick floor of her cell. Shortly before the hour of her execution, Mrs. Surratt was brought out of her cell and was sitting on a chair at the doorway. It was at this time that she made clearly and distinctly the solemn declaration of her inno-

cence. She said to me in the presence of several officers: "Father, I wish to say something." "Well, what is it, my child?" "That I am innocent" were her exact words. These words were uttered whilst she stood on the verge of eternity, and were the last confession of an innocent woman.[1322]

There is contemporaneous written proof of Mrs. Surratt's final declaration. On that fateful July 7, she wrote a note to a friend in a very shaky hand, asking her to "stay with Annie today," and then added, "God knows I [illegible] innocent but for [illegible] cause I must suffer today." "Good Bye" she added, then signed it: "God Bless You. Mary E. Surratt."[1323]

History is slippery like that. One might say that Weichmann could be truthful and Mrs. Surratt innocent if John Lloyd lied. But Weichmann tied Mrs. Surratt to acting as Booth's courier on the very day of the assassination, as well as to assisting with Powell's lodging. In the Surratt trial, he also testified to statements she had made that demonstrated foreknowledge of the awful events to come. It seems that, at best, if Weichmann was completely truthful then Mrs. Surratt could only have been "less guilty," not "innocent."

Perhaps the most credible explanation for these two dying declarations is that sometimes even pious people are more in the thrall of the earthly consequences they can still see and feel, than of the hellfire or heavenly reward that may or may not lie behind the veil of death. For Mrs. Surratt, one very palpable earthly consequence of whether she maintained her innocence or admitted guilt was the effect it would have on her son John if he were caught.

* * *

Within a month or two of the dismissal of the charges in September 1868, John Surratt left for a long sojourn in South America to recover his health. He did not return until April 1869.[1324] While he was away, Anna petitioned for and received permission from President Johnson to exhume the remains of their mother from the Old Arsenal, where she lay in unconsecrated ground. Father Walter, Anna Surratt and Dr. William Tonry were present for the exhumation. On February 9, 1869

Mrs. Surratt's body was placed in a "handsome walnut coffin" and rein-terred in a lot given to the Surratt family by the trustees of the Mount Olivet cemetery in Washington, D.C. Newspaper accounts said that Anna and Honora Fitzpatrick – who had shared a bedroom with Mrs. Surratt – were greatly affected by the reburial ceremony.[1325] John Surratt missed another opportunity to be present and pay respects to his mother.[1326]

He did not, however, miss his sister's wedding. On June 17, 1869, Anna was married to Dr. William P. Tonry, who was then employed as a chemist at the Office of the United States Surgeon General. The happy ceremony was performed by Father Walter at St. Patrick's Church in Washington. Isaac walked Anna down the aisle, while John looked on from a pew.[1327]

The groom "was fired by special order on June 21, only four days after their marriage, likely because his bride was the daughter of Mary Surratt."[1328] Dr. and Mrs. William Tonry moved to Baltimore, where they had a successful marriage and raised four children. Anna died in Baltimore at the age of sixty-one on October 24, 1904, and is buried at Mt. Olivet cemetery, next to her mother.[1329]

* * *

Upon his return from South America, John Surratt wrote to former Confederates under the heading "Produce and General Commission Merchant," seeking referrals for business.[1330] Possibly he had found some contacts for the importation for fruits and vegetables while he was on his trip. But the business did not work out, so Surratt secured a position as a public school teacher in Rockville, Maryland, where he worked from November 1870 to February 1873.[1331]

After Rockville, Surratt went on to become the principal at the Catholic Saint Joseph's Academy in Emmitsburg, located just south of Maryland's border with Pennsylvania. While there, Surratt mixed pub-licly more than he would later on. He enjoyed gathering with the men of the town at Gelwick's Drug Store to discuss politics, although he avoided direct discussion of the assassination. "Being a rather good shot, he also enjoyed target shooting with them."[1332]

St. Joseph's Academy at that time had an enrollment of about sixty students, and classes were held in the Fireman's Hall, directly across from St. Joseph's Catholic Church.[1333] According to an article in the *Maryland Historical Magazine*:

> [Surratt] rattled his classes and would resort to physical punishment to maintain discipline. On older boys, some of them twenty or twenty-one, he used his fists. The younger boys John would beat with a paddle after he had stretched them over a special punishment desk which he had designed. "The Old Bear," as the boys nicknamed him, swore at them in French when they overstepped the limits of his discipline.[1334]

Although corporal punishment was common at that time (and still is in most of the southern states), use of the teacher's fists was not common.[1335] It seems fair to conclude that John Surratt was a tough taskmaster who believed in strict martial discipline. We might also conclude that he was an angry man, not above taking his anger out on others weaker than himself.

* * *

Towards the end of 1870, Surratt apparently concluded that tempers had cooled enough to permit him to trade upon his fame and the public's insatiable appetite for information on the assassination, by giving a series of public lectures. A famous poster survives, advertising his lecture in Washington's Odd Fellows' Hall for the evening of Friday, December 30. The poster promised Surratt would tell of "THRILLING ADVENTURES DURING THE REBELLION, and introduction to J. WILKES BOOTH," "Kidnap, not Murder," "ARREST! TRIAL! ACQUITTAL!" "Life among the Papal Zouaves in Rome!" and "HONORABLE ACQUITTAL" – though of course he was never acquitted; there was a hung jury followed by a dismissal on technicalities. All this excitement could be vicariously enjoyed for the then-princely sum of "50 Cents."[1336]

The first lecture he gave was in Rockville, Maryland on the evening of Tuesday, December 6, 1870, and that is the one (in the form published the next day in the *Washington Evening Star*) that we have relied upon in this narrative. Surratt was among friends, and the lecture was warmly received with laughter and applause.[1337] At the conclusion of the lecture "the band played 'Dixie,' and a concert was improvised, the audience not separating till a late hour, during which time Surratt was quite a lion among the ladies present."[1338]

Surratt may have had a lot of fun reminiscing over old times with a gaggle of adoring ex-Confederates and southern belles, but he was not so well received in New York, where only a "small audience" of 150 heard him on December 9 at the Cooper Institute.[1339] A series of highly critical editorials marked the beginning of the backlash. Responding to "the furious outburst against [Surratt] of the [New York] *World*, the Cincinnati *Enquirer*, and some other papers," a December 16 editorial in the *Washington Star* set out to defend Surratt, but ended up joining the choir of condemnation:

> The good taste of portions of Surratt's lecture may be questioned, and especially . . . the flippancy with which he dwells upon his love adventures in Canada in the same breath with his reference to his mother's death upon the gallows . . . . Really the serious defect in the Surratt lecture was not what he said, but what he failed to say. He, if anyone was in a position to clear up his mother's memory and establish her innocence, if that were possible, and it would have seemed a filial and creditable act in him to have appeared before the public in her defence [*sic.*]. But it will be noticed that throughout his lecture he is silent in regard to the part she took or did not take in the plottings of the conspirators. He thus puts himself in the attitude of making an egotistical defence [*sic.*] of himself and of leaving her memory to take care of itself; and at the same time an impression is conveyed to the public adverse to her innocence.[1340]

While it is likely that both Surratts were guilty of some degree of complicity in the conspiracy against Lincoln, the *Star* is correct that so long as Surratt was going to the trouble of lying to the public in order to place his actions in the best possible light, the least he could have done was to lie a bit in favor of his mother's innocence as well. After all she sacrificed for him, he owed her at least that much. It was a cold and narcissistic heart indeed that failed to appreciate even that.

* * *

Surratt planned other lectures, but the experience was rocky, and soon he was forced to abandon the whole enterprise. On Thursday, December 29, he appeared at Concordia Opera House in Baltimore, an opulent hall designed to seat about 1,700 people, but drew an audience of only 250. Though the cold weather might explain it, the Concordia must have felt empty with the "slim audience present for so large a hall."[1341] Still, those who attended were ardent in their applause as Surratt lashed out at his critics in the press:

> I have been long enough an object of attack for the lying, envenomed tongue of calumny to have grown used to it. I can smile at its rage, its malice and its meanness, and so let it pass unheeded. And to you I beg leave to return thanks for the new proof, furnished by your presence here tonight, that the public mind has independence enough to hear and judge for itself, and will not allow itself to be dictated to by any newspaper autocrat, who, arrogating to himself the functions of both judge and jury, . . . passes such sentence as may best suit his own prejudices and his own gain.[1342]

Based on the size of the crowd even in a city so *seccesh* as Baltimore had been, one might better conclude that the public had made up its mind against Surratt.

Surratt gave the same lecture as in Rockville, but there was a surprise ending to the evening. As he left the stage he was arrested by a United States marshal on a charge of "being a retail dealer . . . in leaf tobacco . . . without having paid the special tax." This appears to have been a trumped-up form of harassment by officials who were warning

Surratt that he had better keep quiet. Surratt was compelled to post bail of $1,500 to get out in time to try to meet his other lecture commitments.[1343]

Although the famous poster for Surratt's Odd-Fellows lecture in Washington states, in bold letters, "J.H. SURRATT WILL MOST POSITIVELY DELIVER HIS LECTURE!" it does not appear that Surratt gave any more lectures after this arrest. According to an article titled "Surratt in Washington" dated December 31, 1870:

> John H. Surratt was advertised to repeat his lecture in this city ton-night [*sic.*], having with considerable difficulty, obtained a hall for that purpose, but to-day he was persuaded to abandon his intention in consequence of a letter from Mayor Emery stating that he had learned [of] . . . great opposition. Fearing it might cause trouble, he officially advised Surratt to withdraw his appointment to lecture. It is stated that a large number of persons had determined to prevent the lecture from being delivered.[1344]

Surratt was refused admission to both Odd Fellows' Hall and to Lincoln Hall, "but, still determined to meet his obligations, he finally secured Carnal's Hall . . . and was going ahead, when he got the mayor's note this evening, which finally settled the case." The paper added ominously, "[t]here were good reasons for apprehending trouble."[1345] Surratt's very short career as a public lecturer was at an end.

* * *

Surratt had experienced enough adventure for several lifetimes, and it was time to settle down. On May 21, 1872, at St. Mary's Catholic Church in Alexandria, Virginia, John Harrison Surratt married twenty-five year old Mary Victorine Hunter. Miss Hunter, the daughter of Thomas and Susanna Key (Scott) Hunter, who lived on the road from Rockville to Gaithersburg, was a second cousin of Francis Scott Key, composer of the *Star-Spangled Banner*. The wedding witnesses were "B. Hale & G. Buckley" – which suggests that Isaac may not have attended.[1346] Most likely Anna and Dr. Tonry were in attendance, but Anna would not have been asked to provide legal witness. After the kerfuffle over Surratt's public lectures, his wedding was probably a small private ceremony.

The marriage was to last a lifetime. An 1880 census of the house at 161 North Calvert Street in Baltimore lists thirty-six year old John H. Surratt with wife "Neary V." [*sic.*, should be "Mary V."], three sons and a daughter, brother Isaac, a sister-in-law (of Mary Victorine – Isaac never married), six boarders and a servant.[1347] In total, John and Mary Victorine Surratt would have three boys and four girls. Although it has frequently been reported that only one son and three daughters survived to adulthood,[1348] the Surratt Museum genealogy page reports that both John Harrison Surratt III and William Hunter Surratt survived into adulthood.[1349]

In a letter dated April 26, 1873 Surratt told Father Jolivet – the priest who had sheltered him in Liverpool – that his "greatest desire . . . is to leave this abominable country and go to Europe there to spend the balance of my days in peace and quiet."[1350] This was contingent on securing employment overseas, but it does not appear that Surratt's former benefactors in the Church were interested in sponsoring him. After he finished teaching in Rockville and Emmittsburg, he and his wife moved to Baltimore. One account says that Isaac was already there, employed by the Old Bay Line Steamship Company, and he was able to secure a minor clerking position there for his brother John.[1351] The family version, taken from an interview with Anna's son in 1931, is different:

> In 1869 [*sic.* – probably 1874] [John] and his brother Isaac came to Baltimore and going to the offices of the Merchants and Miners Transportation Company – the Bay Line – asked for work. "We do not employee [*sic.*] gentlemen," said the man they applied to. "We want work and will do anything," they replied. And so they were put to work weighing freight. In six weeks John was promoted to [illegible] and then became chief auditor of the company. Isaac became chief weigher and died in the employ of the company many years later. John Surratt remained with

them until he was 72 years of age [*sic.* – actually 71], when he was retired on a pension.[1352]

Thus, the elusive Rebel spy, feared and resourceful plotter against Lincoln, the man who escaped the best efforts of the United States government to put him to death, lived out most of his remaining years as a clerk with a steamship line in Baltimore. But Surratt could never quite fill the role of milquetoast clerk. A flattering account from 1881 described him as "straight, erect, lithe . . . [with] fierce, steady eagle eyes . . . [and] aquiline nose as pointed as the man's character," marking him as "a military man of martinet discipline."[1353] Mr. J. Friend Lodge of Philadelphia, who often encountered Surratt in his "Freight Auditor" office at the Old Bay Line, had this to say:

> What were my impressions of him? I met him many times, and he was always the same, pleasant and agreeable, but I usually had to make the conversation. He would always answer me very nicely and politely, but always there was that reserve . . . .. He impressed me as a man that always, under any and all circumstances, could be counted on to be in full control of himself.[1354]

In other words, Surratt was a man carrying secrets, who had no intention of tipping his hand.

Surratt was also carrying suppressed psychological trauma. After the Rockville lecture, when asked by a prospective life insurer, "[h]ow did your mother die," he responded, "[s]he was murdered by the United States government."[1355] Without going too far into the role of armchair psychiatrist, we might venture that Surratt's rigid control may have been a defense mechanism against suppressed anger at himself for playing a larger role than he was willing to admit in sending his mother to the gallows.

* * *

Surratt took his secrets with him to the grave. All his life he was engaged in writing a book about his experiences. When he retired, his son William, a Baltimore attorney, gave him space to work on the manuscript, which he did. The project got so far that his story was sold to a publisher. Then, shortly before his death, John Surratt gathered up his manuscript and all his notes and papers, and threw them into the furnace.[1356]

On April 21, 1916, one week after his seventy-second birthday, John Harrison Surratt succumbed to pneumonia. He lies interred at New Cathedral Cemetery in Baltimore. It seems a bit of a miracle that Surratt died at his home at 1004 West Lanville Street in Baltimore, in a bed surrounded by his wife and two daughters, an old man with a long droopy white mustache, rather than as a young man shot off a horse while crossing enemy lines, or with his hands tied behind his back and a noose around his neck.[1357]

But John Surratt was always lucky. He was the last survivor of the known Lincoln conspirators.[1358] He outlived Weichmann and also Ste. Marie, who had dropped dead on the street at the young age of forty-one.[1359] He outlived his sister and brother.[1360] He lived to see the motorcar, the light bulb, Woodrow Wilson, Ty Cobb, cubism, Charlie Chaplin, and the opening scenes of a horrific World War. He outlasted Ford's Theatre itself, which collapsed on an audience of government clerks in 1893, the same day that Edwin Booth was being buried in Boston.[1361] He lived through the fiftieth anniversary of the assassination, when the martyred Lincoln was again paraded before the Republic that he saved, and that Surratt had tried but failed to destroy. Though Surratt died in some circles as a respected member of the community for whom Bay Line Steamship Company officials acted as pallbearers, he lived long enough to see people cross the street to avoid him and his children.[1362]

No man could possibly live long enough to live down being John Harrison Surratt.

* * *

Though we have been hard on Mr. Carrington, he said something quite profound in closing argument: *"justice to the guilty is mercy to the innocent."*[1363] Tales of unjust conviction of the innocent are common, but careful consideration of the consequences of acquitting the guilty is less common. The high burden of proof in criminal cases is our society's embrace of the ideal that it is better to let ten guilty people go free, than to wrongfully convict one innocent person. But there are costs beyond the obvious.

Who were the victims in Surratt's case? Certainly Lincoln, who deserved to have this man who plotted against him punished. Lincoln's family, forced to entrust retribution to the law, but betrayed by its incompetence. Louis J. Weichmann, whose love for Surratt was manipulated and then cast off like so much rubbish, whose prospects in life were diminished, whose nerves were shattered, and who has been immortalized through Surratt's eyes as the consummate weasel. Add in public servants like Holt and Stanton, accused of hunting witches when they were hunting real assassins. The people of the North, who were deprived of their chosen leader by violence. The people of the South, deprived of a persuasive voice for fairness in reconstruction. The freedmen, who lost their great emancipator. Democratic government, usurped by a handful of hate-filled fanatics. And, of course, that elusive ideal, truth itself.

The sixteenth century philosopher of Bordeaux, Michel de Montaigne, wrote that "the reverse of truth has a hundred thousand shapes, and a field indefinite, without bound or limit."[1364] Surratt and his confederates were masters of the reverse of truth. They did not merely kill a man whose complexity and compassion they could never understand, but in covering their tracks they stole our history. To take the time as we have done to consider meticulously whether Surratt was unjustly set free for a monstrous crime, is to attempt to reclaim a small measure of that history from the hundred thousand fragments of untruth. It is of course too late by far to convict Surratt in a court of law. But he can still be convicted in another court – the court of history. History is a court of rigor that requires evidence, not unguided speculation. It requires general consensus among reasonable people. But it is not a court that requires unanimous agreement or proof beyond a reasonable doubt. It is not a court hobbled by meaningless technicalities. And it is not a court with a statute of limitations.

Ladies and gentlemen, on the charge of conspiracy to murder Abraham Lincoln, President of the United States, how do you find?

On the charge of conspiracy to abduct Abraham Lincoln, how do you find? On the charge of conspiring with Jefferson Davis and Judah P. Benjamin, how do you find? On the charge of abandoning his mother when she was on the cusp of hanging for the conspiracy he brought into her home, how do you find? Is the defendant, John Harrison Surratt, guilty or not guilty in the court of history?

1307 *Anderson Herald*, "Louis J. Weichmann Obituary" (June 6, 1902), reprinted in, Weichmann, pp.405-06 (hereafter *"Anderson Herald Obituary*, Weichmann"); Lloyd Lewis, *Myths After Lincoln*, p.226 (Reader's Club Press, 1942) (hereafter *"Myths After Lincoln"*).

1308 *Myths After Lincoln*, p.228.

1309 *LA from Surratt Courier*, vol.2, Erich L. Ewald, *The Witness and the Young Boy: New Information Regarding the Testimony of Louis J. Weichmann*, p.IX-4 (Oct. 1991); Weichmann, pp.284-85, 316-28, 398-400, 408-28, 435, 486-87 n.13; *Myths After Lincoln*, p.225.

1310 *LA from Surratt Courier*, vol.2, Erich L. Ewald, *The Witness and an Uncertain Sanctuary: New Information Regarding Louis J. Weichmann and the Surratts of Anderson, Indiana*, p.IX-23 (Nov. 1992).

1311 *Myths After Lincoln*, pp.225-26.

1312 *LA from Surratt Courier*, vol.2, Erich L. Ewald, *Louis J. Weichmann's Second "Deathbed Confession" and Other Tales from Behind the Curtain*, p.IX-28 (Sept. 1993), *quoting*, "Weichmann Obituary," *Muncie Morning Herald* (June 6, 1902) (hereafter *"Deathbed Confession"*).

1313 *Myths After Lincoln*, pp.227-28.

1314 *Deathbed Confession*, p.IX-28.

1315 *Myths After Lincoln*, p.227.

1316 *Deathbed Confession*, p.IX-29.

1317 *Anderson Herald Obituary*, Weichmann, p.405.

1318 Hugh J. Creighton was a local businessman, owner of the Perfecto Magneto Company. *Weichmann*, p.405.

1319 *Anderson Herald Obituary*, Weichmann, pp.405-06.

1320 *Deathbed Confession*, p. IX-29.

1321 *Myths After Lincoln*, p.232.

1322 Weichmann, pp.318-19.

1323 JOH Papers, *Last letter of Mary E. Surratt* (July 7, 1865), *copy from* Library of Congress, Ac 2670 (PDF courtesy of Joan Chaconas). This shaky and blotted copy is very difficult to read and subject to some interpretation. Mr. Hall and Ms. Chaconas read it, "God knows I am innocent but for some cause I must suffer today." *Email from Joan Chaconas to author*, April 1, 2014. Mr. Isacsson read it differently: "God knows I shed innocent blood for sinners course I must suffer today." *Mary's Offspring*, pp.VII-31 to 32. We all agree on the one word that really matters: *innocent*. But, quite frankly, even that word is blotted and difficult to distinguish.

1324 JOH Papers - JHS, *Letter from John H. Surratt to Major William Norris, former head of CSA Signal Bureau* (June 24, 1869) (hereafter *"JHS Letter to Norris"*).

1325 *American Tragedy*, pp.230-31; *Mary's Offspring*, pp.VII-31 to 32.

1326 The author of *American Tragedy* places John at the graveside, *ibid.*, p.231, but this is not possible. By his own admission, he was in South America from November 1868 to April 1869. *JHS Letter to Norris.*

1327 *Mary's Offspring*, p.VII-31.

1328 *American Tragedy*, p.231; *In Pursuit Of, The Children of Mary Surratt*, p.224.

1329 *American Tragedy*, p.231; *Mary's Offspring*, p.X-26. A fifth child died in infancy.

1330 *JHS Letter to Norris.*

1331 JOH Papers - *JHS, Letter from Montgomery County Historical Society to James O. Hall* (April 7, 1987), *quoting, Guy Jewell, From One Room to Open Spaces; Letter from John H. Surratt to Father Jolivet* (April 26, 1873), *reprinted in*, Isacsson, *TAT*, p.33 (hereafter "JHS Letter to Jolivet").

1332 JOH Papers - JHS, *Maryland Historical Magazine* (Dec. 1957).

1333 *Ibid.; JHS Letter to Jolivet.*

1334 JOH Papers - JHS, *Maryland Historical Magazine* (Dec. 1957).

1335 "Corporal Punishment in U.S. Schools," http://www.corpun.com/counuss.htm (accessed March 23, 2014).

1336 JOH Papers - JHS, *Surratt Odd Fellow's Hall Lecture Poster*, Courtesy Mark Neely's Lincoln Museum, #3458.

1337 Full text with applause and laughter interjected by the reporter, *Rockville Lecture*, Weichmann, pp.428-40.

1338 Weichmann, p.440.

1339 *In Pursuit Of*, Edward Steers, Jr., *John Surratt, Jr. Speaks at the Cooper Institute*, pp.283-84 (Nov. 1979).

1340 Weichmann, pp.440-41 (some italics deleted).

1341 JOH Papers - JHS, *Baltimore Sun*, p.1 (Dec. 30, 1870); W.H. Corwin, *A Guide to the City of Baltimore: Its Public Buildings, Places of Amusement, Commercial, Benevolent and Religious Institutions*, p.117 (1869).

1342 JOH Papers - JHS, *Baltimore Sun*, p.1 (Dec. 30, 1870).

1343 *Ibid.*

1344 *Baltimore Sun*, "Surratt in Washington," p.1 C 5 (Dec. 31, 1870).

1345 *Ibid.*

1346 JOH Papers - JHS, *Genealogical records from Montgomery County Historical Society, Hall's notes on witnesses, and Letter to James O. Hall* (March 22, 1987); JOH Papers - JHS, *1880 Baltimore Census* (June 8, 1880).

1347 JOH Papers - JHS, *1880 Baltimore Census* (June 8, 1880); *American Tragedy*, p.232.

1348 Isacsson, *AFCT*, p. X-6; *American Tragedy*, p.233; E.G.Lee p.222 n.3.

1349 *Children and Descendents of John Surratt, Jr.*, http://www.surrattmuseum.org/genealogy/su_genx.html#JOHN (accessed March 24, 2014). There seems to be some uncertainty about who survived and who did not. It seems likely that, at a minimum, the two sons mentioned in the text and three daughters survived: Mrs. J. Francis Hardy (born Susanna Scott Surratt), Mrs. Albert F. Dalton of Kensington, Maryland (born Mary Eugenia Surratt), and Mrs. Parker L. Weller, of Montgomery, Alabama (born Mary Victorine Surratt). *Baltimore Sun*, "John H. Surratt Dead," p.16 (April 22, 1916).

1350 *JHS Letter to Jolivet.*

1351 *Missing Link*, p. B1.

1352 *His Mother's Memories*, p. XI-26.

1353 JOH Papers - JHS, *Maryland Journal*, p.3 (Oct. 15, 1881).

1354 LA in Surratt Courier, vol. 2, *A Recollection of John H. Surratt Fifty Years Later*, p. X-46 (March 1988) (some italics omitted).

1355 JOH Papers - JHS, *Baltimore Sun* (August 10, 1889).

1356 *His Mother's Memories*, p. X-26; JOH Papers - JHS, *Letter from Henry B. Lee to "Rebecca"* (Nov. 30, 1937). The purported "Diary of John H. Surratt" that can be found on Amazon is the totally fraudulent creation of a nineteenth century "penny-dreadful" hack writer seeking to capitalize on Surratt's fame.

1357 *Baltimore Sun*, "John Surratt Dead," p.16 (April 22, 1916).

1358 *Ibid.*

1359 JOH Papers - HBSM, *Baltimore County Union*, "Obituary" (Sept. 19, 1874).

1360 *In Pursuit Of, The Children of Mary Surratt*, pp.222-23.

1361 Weichmann, pp.392-93. The Ford's Theatre you find today in Washington is a reconstruction by the United States Park Service.
Missing Link, p.B-1; Roger J. Norton, *Lincoln Discussion Symposium, Mary*

1362 *Victorine Hunter Surratt*, posts ##1 & 2, http://rogerjnorton.com/LincolnDiscussionSymposium/thread-116.html (accessed March 24, 2014).

1363 2 JHS Trial 1148.

1364 Michel de Montaigne, *Selected Essays - Of Liars*, p.13 (Thomas Y. Crowell & Co., New York, 1903).

BIBLIOGRAPHY & CITATION ABBREVIATIONS

Abolition in the District of Columbia,
http://memory.loc.gov/ammem/today/apr16.html (accessed Nov. 11, 2013).

Acton Institute, Religion & Liberty, *Onward Catholic Soldiers: The Catholic Church During the American Civil War,* http://www.acton.org/pub/religion-liberty/volume-21-number-4/onward-catholic-soldiers-catholic-church-during-am (accessed Jan. 15, 2014).

Anderson Herald, Louis J. Weichmann Obituary (June 6, 1902), *reprinted in,* Weichmann, pp.405-06 (*"Anderson Herald Obituary, Weichmann"*).

Andrew Jackson Narrowly Escapes Assassination, http://www.history.com/this-day-in-history/andrew-jackson-narrowly-escapes-assassination (accessed March 29, 2014).

The Atlantic, "But Were They Gay? The Mystery of Same-Sex Love in the 19th Century," (Sept. 7, 2012), http://www.theatlantic.com/national/archive/2012/09/but-were-they-gay-the-mystery-of-same-sex-love-in-the-19th-century/262117/ (accessed Nov. 11, 2013).

Baltimore Sun, John H. Surratt Dead (April 22, 1916).

Baltimore Sun, Surratt in Washington (Dec. 31, 1870).

Biographies in Naval History – Rear Admiral John A. Dahlgren, http://www.history.navy.mil/bios/dahlgren.htm (accessed Dec. 21, 2013).

Brigadier General Garbriel J. Rains, "Father of Modern Mine Warfare," http://gabrielrains.com/ (accessed Dec. 26, 2013).

Helen Jones Campbell, *The Case for Mrs. Surratt* (G.P. Putnam & Sons, New York 1943).

Canadian Catholic Historical Ass'n Report, vol.12 (1944-1945), Howard R. Marraro, Ph.D., *Canadian and American Zouaves in the Papal Army, 1868-1870* ("Marraro").

Charles Ciniquy, *Fifty Years in the Church of Rome* (Fleming H. Revel Co., NY, Chicago, Toronto 1886) ("Fifty Years").

Charlotte Corday,
http://www.britannica.com/EBchecked/topic/137301/Charlotte-Corday (accessed Nov. 9, 2013).

Children and Descendents of John Surratt, Jr.,
http://www.surrattmuseum.org/genealogy/su_genx.html#JOHN (accessed
March 24, 2014).

Civil War Maps, http://civilwardc.org/maps/ (accessed Nov. 8, 2013).

Civil War Statistics,
http://www.phil.muni.cz/~vndrzl/amstudies/civilwar_stats.htm (accessed Dec.
22, 2013).

Clinton Maryland Tourism, http://www.marylandtravelrecreation.com/mary-
land-cities/clinton-travel.html (accessed Nov. 26, 2013).

Henry Steele Commager, *Documents of American History*, vol.1 (Meredith
Corporation, New York 1968) ("Commager").

Thomas Nelson Conrad, *A Confederate Spy* (J.S. Ogilvie, New York 1892).

Thomas Nelson Conrad, *The Rebel Scout* (National Publishing Co.,
Washington DC 1904).

Correspondence Between His Holiness Pope Piux IX and President Jefferson Davis,
http://www.danvilleartillery.org/popeletter.htm (accessed Jan. 15, 2014).

W.H. Corwin, *A Guide to the City of Baltimore: Its Public Buildings, Places of
Amusement, Commercial, Benevolent and Religious Institutions* (1869).

Maria A. Dering, *The Twilight of Edwin Booth, in The New York Researcher*
(Fall 2005).

Otto Eisenschiml, *Why Was Lincoln Murdered?* (Little Brown and Co., Boston
1937).

Encyclopedia Virginia, *Fort Monroe During the Civil War*,
http://encyclopediavirginia.org/Fort_Monroe_During_the_Civil_War#start_
entry (accessed March 3, 2014).

Encyclopedia Virginia – Libby Prison,
http://www.encyclopediavirginia.org/Libby_Prison (accessed Dec. 21, 2013).

Ex Parte Merryman,
http://www.princeton.edu/~achaney/tmve/wiki100k/docs/Ex_parte_Merryma
n.html (accessed Nov. 7, 2013).

Exchange of Prisoners in the Civil War,
http://www.civilwarhome.com/prisonerexchange.htm (accessed Nov. 27,
2013).

Don E Fehrenbacher, *Journal of the Abraham Lincoln Ass'n*, "The Anti-
Lincoln Tradition," vol. 4, issue 1 (1982), Permalink:
http://hdl.handle.net/2027/spo.2629860.0004.103 (accessed Nov. 9, 2013).

Seymour J. Frank, *The Conspiracy to Implicate the Confederate Leaders in Lincoln's Assassination*, Mississippi Valley Historical Rev. 629 ("Conspiracy re: Confederate Leaders").

Alexander Gardner, http://www.civilwar.org/education/history/biographies/alexander-gardner.html (accessed Dec. 4, 2013).

James O. Hall, *The Veiled Lady, from North & South: The Official Magazine of the Civil War Society,* vol. 3, number 6 (2000) (*"The Veiled Lady"*).

James O. Hall Research Center, Mr. Hall's Papers on Lincoln Assassination, Surratt House Museum ("JOH Papers"). Whenever possible I note "JOH Papers – [initials]", which designates the group of files where the document appears, e.g., "JHS" for John H. Surratt files, "HBSM" for Henri B. de Ste. Marie files, or "SS" for Sarah Slater files.

JOH Papers, *A Biography of John Surratt by Alfred Isacsson, O.Carm. - A Dissertation to Faculty of Grad School of Arts & Sciences of Saint Bonaventure University for MA degree* (July 1957, Saint Bonaventure, NY) (*"Isacsson Dissertation"*).

JOH Papers, Boutwell Committee, *Report Of The Committee Of The Judiciary* (March 2, 1867) (*"Boutwell Committee Report"*).

JOH Papers, *Boutwell Committee Report, Testimony of William N. Jeffers* (Feb. 20, 1867) (hereafter *"Jeffers Testimony"*).

JOH Papers, J. William Joynes, *The Missing Link in Lincoln's Assassination, §B, Baltimore News American* (Feb. 12, 1974) (*"Missing Link"*).

JOH Papers – Clark Larsen, *Who Started It?* (Surratt Courier Vol. XXXVIII, No. 6, June 2013) (*"Who Started It?"*).

JOH Papers, *Diary of E.G. Lee* (April 6, 1865) ("Lee Diary").

JOH Papers, *Affidavit* [anonymous, but clearly of L.J. McMillan] (*"McMillan Affidavit of Dec. 8, 1866"*).

JOH Papers, 39th Congress, 2nd Session, House Of Representatives, *Message From The President Of The United States, Transmitting A Report Of The Secretary Of State Relating To The Discovery And Arrest Of John H. Surratt (Dec. 8, 1866) ("President's Message re: Surratt"*).

JOH Papers, *Report of the Committee of the Judiciary, Testimony of L.J. McMillan,* (March 2, 1867) (*"McMillan Judiciary Testimony"*).

JOH Papers, *A report of George H. Sharpe re: Assassination of President Lincoln* (Dec. 17, 1867) (*"Sharpe Report"*).

JOH Papers, *Microfilm of St. Lawrence Hall Register* (January 10, 1865).

JOH Papers, C.W. Taylor, *Report of Proceedings in Canada* ("Taylor Report").

JOH Papers, *Letter to Members of Madame Tussaud's Headhunters Society, from "Tyrone"* (a.k.a. Dexter) (April 3, 1990) (*"Tyrone letter"*).

JOH Papers – HBSM, *Baltimore County Union*, Obituary (Sept. 19, 1874).

JOH Papers – HBSM, *Hall's Handwritten JHS Timeline* (*"Hall JHS Timeline"*).

JOH Papers – HBSM, *Richmond Daily Examiner*, p.1 col.4 (Oct. 21, 1863).

JOH Papers – HBSM, *Typescript of Letter for Sale by Mr. Charles Appelbaum* (Oct. 23, 1866).

JOH Papers – JHS, *1880 Baltimore Census* (June 8, 1880).

JOH Papers – JHS, *Affidavit of John P. Brophy* (July 7, 1865) (*"Brophy Affidavit"*).

JOH Papers – JHS, *Baltimore Sun* (Dec. 30, 1870).

JOH Papers – JHS, *Baltimore Sun* (August 10, 1889).

JOH Papers – JHS, *Enclosure with May 23, 1865 letter from Consul-General Potter to Acting Secretary of State Hunter – Letter from Henri B. Ste. Marie, Laprairie Canada East* (May 20, 1865) (*"Ste. Marie Letter of May 20, 1865"*)

JOH Papers – JHS, *Letter from Edwin L. Stanton to Judge Edwards Pierrepont* (August 9, 1867).

JOH Papers – JHS, *Letter from Henry B. Lee to "Rebecca"* (Nov. 30, 1937).

JOH Papers – JHS, *Letter from J. Harrison Surratt to H. De Ste. Marie* (April 24, 1863).

JOH Papers – JHS, *Letter from John H. Surratt to Major William Norris, former head of CSA Signal Bureau* (June 24, 1869) (*"JHS Letter to Norris"*).

JOH Papers – JHS, *Genealogical records from Montgomery County Historical Society, Hall's notes on witnesses, and Letter to James O. Hall* (March 22, 1987).

JOH Papers – JHS, *Letter from Montgomery County Historical Society to James O. Hall* (April 7, 1987), *quoting, Guy Jewell, From One Room to Open Spaces.*

JOH Papers – JHS, *Maryland Historical Magazine* (Dec. 1957).

JOH Papers – JHS, *Maryland Journal* (Oct. 15, 1881).

JOH Papers – JHS, *James O. Hall's Handwritten Notes re: The Indictments* (hereafter *"Hall Notes on Indictments"*).

JOH Papers – JHS, *Notes of James O. Hall and Testimony of James H. Fowle, May 1866* (*"JOH Fowle Testimony"*).

JOH Papers – JHS, *Philadelphia Times* (Oct. 4, 1885), *reprinted in Pilgrim Magazine, reprinted in Surratt Courier, Pilgrim Interview* (July 1981) (*"Pilgrim"*).

JOH Papers – JHS, *Reminiscences of the Surratt Jury* (undated manuscript reproduced from the Manuscript Division, Library of Congress) (*"Juror Reminiscence"*).

JOH Papers – JHS, *Surratt Odd Fellow's Hall Lecture Poster*, Courtesy Mark Neely's Lincoln Museum, #3458.

JOH Papers – JHS, *Unfiled Papers & Slips Belonging in Compiled Confederate Service Records*, M-347, Reel 194, *Philadelphia Weekly Press, The Attempt To Capture President Lincoln* (March 13, 1880) (*"Attempt to Capture"*).

JOH Papers – SS, *Additional Fowle Testimony to Boutwell Committee 1866* (*"Additional Fowle Testimony"*).

JOH Papers – SS, John F. Stanton, *Attention Sarah Slater Seekers* (Surratt Courier, Vol. XXX, No.9, Sept. 2010) (*"Attention Slater Seekers"*).

JOH Papers – SS, John F. Stanton, Some Thoughts on Sarah Slater (Surratt Courier, vol. XXXII No.2 Feb. 2007) ("Thoughts on Slater")

Wade Hampton, http://www.history.com/topics/wade-hampton (accessed Dec. 23, 2013).

William Hanchett, *The Lincoln Murder Conspiracies* (Urbana, Univ. of Illinois Press 1983).

Alfred Isacsson, *The Travels, Arrest, and Trial of John H. Surratt* (Vestigium Press, Middleton, NY (2003) ("Isacsson, *TAT*").

Journal of the Southern Illinois Historical Society, vol.69, Joseph George, Jr., *The Lincoln Writings of Charles P.T. Chiniquy* (Feb. 1976).

Michael W. Kaufman, *American Brutus* (Random House 2004) (*"American Brutus"*).

Frank B. Latham, *The Trial of John Peter Zenger, August 1735* (Franklin

Watts, Inc., New York 1970) ("Latham").

Clara Laughlin, *Travelling Through Life* (Houghton Mifflin, NY 1934).

Letter from John H. Surratt to Father Jolivet (April 26, 1873), *reprinted in*, Isacsson, *TAT*, p.33 (*"JHS Letter to Jolivet"*).

Andrea Lee Levin, *This Awful Drama: General Edwin Gray Lee and his Family* (Vantage Press NY 1987) (*"E.G. Lee"*).

Lexis-Nexis Capsule Summary of Criminal Law (2004).

Library of Congress, *Letterbooks of Confederate State Papers, Canada, Feb. 15 1864-Jan. 8, 1865*, at Dec. 6, 1864.

Library of Congress, Manuscript Division, *George Nicholas Sanders Family Papers – Finding Aid Biographical Statement*, http://lcweb2.loc.gov/service/mss/eadxmlmss/eadpdfmss/2012/ms012053.pdf (accessed Feb. 9, 2014).

Douglas O. Linder, *The Impeachment Trial of Andrew Johnson*, http://law2.umkc.edu/faculty/projects/ftrials/impeach/imp_account2.html (accessed March 3, 2014).

Lloyd Lewis, *Myths After Lincoln* (Reader's Club Press, 1942) (*"Myths After Lincoln"*).

Manor House History, http://www.chapelpoint.org/historyManor.asp (accessed March 17, 2014).

Marauders of the Sea: Confederate Naval Vessels of the American Civil War – CSS Shenandoah, http://ahoy.tk-jk.net/MaraudersCivilWar/CSSShenandoah.html (accessed Jan. 31, 2014).

Burke McCarty, *The Suppressed Truth About the Assassination of Abraham Lincoln* (Self-published 1922).

Emmett McLoughlin, *An Inquiry into the Assassination of Abraham Lincoln* (Lyle Stuart, Inc., New York, 1963).

Peter J. McQuillan, *Felony Murder and the Misdemeanor of Attempted Escape: A Legislative Error in Search of a Correction*, 15 Fordham Urban Law Journal 821 (1986).

J.T. Mitchell, *Professional Misconduct – The Case of Mr. Bradley and the Supreme Court of the District of Columbia*, American Law Register, vol. XVII (March 1869).

Michel de Montaigne, *Selected Essays – Of Liars* (Thomas Y. Crowell & Co., New York, 1903).

Montreal History by Date, http://www.imtl.org/montreal/histoire.php?periode=1860 & http://www.imtl.org/montreal/histoire.php?periode=1870 (accessed Jan. 22, 2014).

Guy W. Moore, *The Case of Mrs. Surratt* (Norman: University of OK Press, 1954).

National Archives, RG 21, *United States v. John H. Surratt*, Criminal Case #4731, *E.G. Lee Offer of Proof* (July 15, 1867) (*"E.G. Lee Offer of Proof"*).

National Archives, RG 21, *United States v. John H. Surratt*, Criminal Case #4731, *Indictment* (Feb. 4, 1867) (*"Indictment, Case #4731"*).

National Archives, RG 21, *United States v. John H. Surratt*, D.C. Criminal Case #4731, *Order of George P. Fisher, Jus. S.C. D.C.* (August 10, 1867).

National Archives, RG 21, *United States v. John H. Surratt*, D.C. Criminal Case #5920, *Indictment* (June 18, 1868) (*"Indictment, Case #5920*).

National Archives, RG 21, *United States v. John H. Surratt*, D.C. Criminal Case #5930, *Recognizance* (June 22, 1868).

National Archives, RG 21, *United States v. John H. Surratt*, D.C. Criminal Case #5930, *Proclamation of President Andrew Johnson* (July 4, 1868) (*"Amnesty Proclamation"*).

National Archives, RG 21, *United States v. John H. Surratt*, D.C. Criminal Case #5930, *Special Plea* (Sept. 22, 1868) (*"Special Plea"*).

National Archives, RG 21, *United States v. John H. Surratt*, D.C. Criminal Case #5930, *Demurrer to Special Plea* (Sept. 22, 1868).

National Archives, RG 21, *United States v. John H. Surratt*, D.C. Criminal Case #5930, *Brief of the United States* (Oct. 23, 1868) (*"Brief of the United States"*).

National Archives, RG 21, *United States v. John H. Surratt*, D.C. Criminal Case #5930, *Order of Dec. 7, 1868.*

National Archives, RG 21, *United States vs. John H. Surratt*, Criminal Case #6594, *Indictment* (Jan. 4, 1868 [sic., 1869]) (*"Indictment, Case #6594"*).

National Archives, Letter from Edward C. Carrington to Henry Stanberry (March 2, 1867), National Archives Identifier 6783048.

National Archives, *Letter from Edwards Pierrepont to Assistant Attorney General* (Dec. 31, 1867), National Archives Identifier 6783055.

National Archives, *Letter from Edward C. Carrington to Acting Attorney General,* (June 5, 1868), National Archives Identifier 6783058 (*"Carrington June 5"*).

National Archives, *Letter from Edward C. Carrington to Acting Attorney General,* (June 9, 1868), National Archives Identifier 6783059 (*"Carrington June 9"*).

National Parks Service, Ford's Theatre Collection, *Pocket Diary of John Wilkes Booth.*

National Parks Service, Ford's Theatre Collection, *J. Wilkes Booth "To Whom it May Concern" Letter of 1864.*

National Parks Service, Ford's Theatre Collection, *Affidavit of John W. Westfall* (May 13, 1876) (*"Westfall Affidavit"*).

The New Orleans Race Riot of 1866, https://lcrm.lib.unc.edu/blog/index.php/2012/07/30/on-this-day-the-new-orleans-race-riot-of-1866/ (accessed March 3, 2014).

New Orleans Riot of 1866, http://chnm.gmu.edu/courses/122/carr/riottext.html (accessed March 3, 2014).

New York Herald, The Case of John H. Surratt (June 6, 1867) (*"NY Herald, Case of Surratt"*).

New York Times, "Census of 1865," http://query.nytimes.com/mem/archive-free/pdf?res=F10915FC3E59137A93CBA9178AD85F4 (accessed Nov. 9, 2013).

New York Times, Mr. [Edwin] Booth as Pescara, http://query.nytimes.com/mem/archive-free/pdf?res=F60C15FC3A5C15738DDDA80B94D9405B8584F0D3 (accessed Dec. 6, 2013).

New York Times, Opening of the United States District Court in Norfolk – Jefferson Davis and John H. Surratt (Dec. 19, 1866).

New York Times, A Visit to Surratt, Tuesday, April 2, (published April 8, 1867) (hereafter *"NY Times, A Visit to Surratt"*).

New York Times, New Rules Regarding Spectators (July 28, 1867).

New York Times, Trial of Surratt (Sept. 20, 1868).

New York Times, The Surratt Trial – A New Plea Entered (Sept. 25, 1868).

New York Times, Richard H. Merrick Obituary (June 24, 1885).

New York Times, The Surratt Trial: Estimated Expense of Proceedings (August 10, 1867) (*"NY Times, Estimated Expense"*).

Roger J. Norton, *Lincoln Discussion Symposium, Mary Victorine Hunter Surratt,*

posts ##1 & 2,
http://rogerjnorton.com/LincolnDiscussionSymposium/thread-116.html
(accessed March 24, 2014).

Papal Encyclicals Online, *The Syllabus of Errors Condemned by Piux IX*,
http://www.papalencyclicals.net/Pius09/p9syll.htm (accessed Feb. 15, 2014).

The Papal Zouaves, http://defidecatholica.blogspot.com/2011/02/papal-
zouaves_17.html (accessed Feb. 8, 2014).

Ben Pitman, *The Trial: The Assassination of President Lincoln and the Trial of
the Conspirators* (Edward Steers, Jr., ed., Univ. Press of Kentucky 2003) (*"Trial
of the Conspirators"*).

Photography and the Civil War, http://www.civilwar.org/photos/3d-photogra-
phy-special/photography-and-the-civil-war.html (accessed Dec. 4, 2013).

John Powell, *Two Years in the Pontifical Zouaves: a Narrative of Travel, Residence
and Experience in the Roman States* (R. Washbourne, London 1871) (*"Two
Years in the Zouaves"*).

Pratt Library, *Maryland in the Civil War*,
http://www.prattlibrary.org/uploadedFiles/www/locations/central/mary-
land/md_cw_complete.pdf (accessed Nov. 7, 2013).

Stephen B. Presser & Jamil S. Zainaldin, *Law and Jurisprudence in American
History*, (Thomson-West 5th ed. 2003) ("Presser & Zainaldin").

Hon. Sandy Prindle, Judah Benjamin: A Person of Interest (Surratt Courier,
April 2013) (*"Person of Interest"*).

Regiments of the Civil War, http://www.civilwar.org/education/history/warfare-
and-logistics/warfare/regiment.html (accessed Feb. 10, 2014).

Edward H. Ripley, *The Capture and Occupation of Richmond*, April 3, 1865
(G.P. Putnam & Sons, New York 1907).

Carl Sandburg, *Abraham Lincoln: The War Years*, vol. 1 (Harcourt Brace
1939).

Lynn Schooler, *The Last Shot of the Civil War: the Incredible Story of the CSS
Shenandoah* (Ecco 2005).

The Seige of Petersburg,
http://www.nps.gov/history/history/online_books/civil_war_series/20/sec8.ht
m (accessed Dec. 14, 2013).

Gene Smith, *American Gothic: the Story of America's Legendary Theatrical
Family, Junius, Edwin, and John Wilkes Booth* (Simon & Schuster, New York,
1992).

The Spencer Carbine,
http://amhistory.si.edu/militaryhistory/collection/object.asp?ID=117
(accessed Dec. 1, 2013).

State Archives of Rome, *Papal Zouaves Enlistment Records*, vol. 2, record
#1857.

State v. McCahill, 72 Iowa 111, 33 N.W. 599 (1887).

Henri B. Ste. Marie v. United States, United States Court of Claims, Docket
No. 6415 (1872) (Google digital book scanned from Harvard College
Library, Bequest of Evert Jansen Wendell, 1918) (*"Ste. Marie v. United
States"*).

Edward Steers, Jr., *Blood on the Moon: The Assassination of Abraham Lincoln*,
(Univ. Press of Kentucky 2001) (hereafter "Blood on the Moon").

Edward Steers, Jr., *His Name is Still Mudd*, (Thomas Publications, 2013),
Kindle edition (*"Still Mudd"*).

David O. Stewart, *Impeached: The Trial of President Andrew Johnson and the
Fight for Lincoln's Legacy* (Simon & Schuster New York 2009) ("Impeached").

Surratt Courier, vol. XXXVI No.8, John C. Stanton, *A Mystery No Longer –
The Lady in the Veil* (August 2011) (*"Mystery No Longer Pt. 1"*).

Surratt Courier, vol. XXXVI No.10, John C. Stanton, *A Mystery No Longer –
The Lady in the Veil (Conclusion)* (Oct. 2011) (*"Mystery No Longer Pt. 2"*).

Surratt Courier, Vol. XXXVIII No. 6, *President's Message, reprinting, Letter from
Anna Surratt, September 16, 1862* (August 2013) (*"Anna Letter Sept. 16"*).

The Surratt Family Tree,
http://www.surrattmuseum.org/genealogy/su_gen1.html (accessed March 17,
2014).

Surratt Society, *From War Department Files: Statements Made by the Alleged
Lincoln Conspirators Under Examination*, 1865 (Nov. 1980) (*"Statements"*).

> *Statement of Samuel Bland Arnold Made at Baltimore Maryland, April 18,
> 1865* (*"Arnold Statement"*).

> *Atzerodt Statement of April 25, 1865, Taken by Col. H.H. Wells Aboard the
> Monitor "Montauk,"* (*"Atzerodt Wells Statement"*).

> *Statement of David E. Herold, Made before Hon. John A. Bingham, Special
> Judge Advocate, on April 27, 1865, on Board the Monitor "Montauk,"*
> (*"Herold Statement"*).

> *Statement of Mrs. Mary E. Surratt to General Augur, April 17, 1865* (*"Mary
> Surratt 4/17"*).

Statement of Mrs. Mary E. Surratt, Carroll Prison, April 28, 1865 ("Mary Surratt 4/28").

Surratt Society, *In Pursuit Of . . . Continuing Research in the Field of the Lincoln Assassination* (Surratt Society, Clinton, MD 1990) (*"In Pursuit Of"*).

In Pursuit Of, The Children of Mary Surratt.

In Pursuit Of, Edward Steers, Jr., John Surratt, Jr. Speaks at the Cooper Institute (Nov. 1979).

Surratt Society, *The Lincoln Assassination: From the Pages of the Surratt Courier*, Vols. 1 & 2 (Surratt Society, Clinton, MD 2000) (*"LA from Surratt Courier"*, vol. #). Generally, this is followed by the citation to the reprinted article and date of the original article, and sometimes also with a citation to original source material quoted within the article, and the date of that source material. Specific articles cited with their abbreviations are:

Vol.1, at I-19, James O. *Hall, Hiding the Shooting Irons,* p. I-19 (March 1986) (*"Hiding the Shooting Irons"*)

Vol. 1, at III-19, *Unpublished Atzerodt Confession Revealed Here for the First Time,* p. III-21 (Oct. 1988), *reprinting, Statement of George A. Atzerodt to Prov. Mar. McPhail in Presence of John L. Smith* (May 1, 1865) (*"Lost Atzerodt Statement"*).

Vol 1, at III-23, *Atzerodt's Confession in the 7/9/1865 National Intelligencer* (*"Atzerodt National Intelligencer Statement"*).

Vol.1, at III-27, *George A. Atzerodt Confession in the Jun. 18, 1869 Baltimore American* (*"Atzerodt Baltimore American Statement"*).

Vol. 1, at VI-11, David Winfred Gaddy, *The Enigma of the Rebel Ciphers* (Sept. 1997).

Vol. 1, at VI-27, James O. Hall, *The Mercy Recommendation for Mrs. Surratt,* (August 1990) (*"The Mercy Recommendation"*).

Vol. 1, at VI-30, *Andrew Johnson or Joseph Holt?* (Nov. 1995), *quoting,* Will T. Hale, *Nashville American* (March 4, 1906).

Vol. 1, at VI-33, *The Clemency Plea Debate* (May 1986), *quoting, Judge Holt and the Lincoln Conspirators, Century Magazine* (April 1890) (*"Clemency Plea Debate"*).

Vol. 2, at VII-31, Alfred Isacsson, *Mary Surratt and Her Offspring, Anna and Isaac* (May 1986) (*"Mary's Offspring"*).

Vol.2, at IX-3, Erich L. Ewald, *The Witness and the Young Boy: New Information Regarding the Testimony of Louis J. Weichmann* (Oct. 1991).

Vol. 2, at IX-15, John C. Brennan, *Regarding George Alfred Townsend's 1867 Interview with Louis J. Weichmann* (July 1991) (*"Re: Townsend Interviews Weichmann"*).

Vol. 2, at IX-17, *Townsend Interviews Weichmann*, May 16, 1867 (August 1991) (*"Townsend Interviews Weichmann"*).

Vol. 2, at IX-21, *Card from Louis J. Weichmann, May 22, 1867, reprinted in, Townsend Interviews Weichmann* (August 1991) (*"Card from Weichmann"*).

Vol. 2, at IX-23, Erich L. Ewald, *The Witness and an Uncertain Sanctuary: New Information Regarding Louis J. Weichmann and the Surratts of Anderson, Indiana* (Nov. 1992).

Vol.2, Erich L. Ewald, *Louis J. Weichmann's Second "Deathbed Confession" and Other Tales from Behind the Curtain*, p.IX-28 (Sept. 1993), *quoting, Weichmann Obituary, Muncie Morning Herald* (June 6, 1902) (*"Deathbed Confession"*).

Vol. 2, at X-3, Alfred Isacsson, *John Surratt: the Assassination, Flight, Capture and Trial*, (July 1993) (*"Isacsson, AFCT"*).

Vol. 2, at X-9, Alfred Isacsson, *Some Points Concerning John Harrison Surratt, Jr.*, (August 1995) (*"Points Concerning"*).

Vol. 2, at X-13, George Alfred Townsend article, *Cleveland Leader,* Oct. 4, 1868, *reprinted in* President's Message, *The Trials of John Surratt* (Sept. 1988) (*"Townsend re: Trial of Surratt"*).

Vol. 2, at X-17, Alfred Isacsson, *Judge Fisher's Account of the John H. Surratt Trial*, (May 1987) (*"Judge Fisher's Account"*).

Vol. 2, at X-20, *Letter to the Editor from Joseph George, Jr.* (Sept. 1987), *quoting, Philadelpia Press* (August 11, 1867) (*"Philadelphia Press (August 11, 1867)"*).

Vol. 2, at X-23, Joan L. Chaconas, *Legal Fireworks After the Surratt Trial* (July 1989).

Vol. 2, at X-25, James E.T. Lange and Katherine DeWitt, Jr., *The Three Indictments of John Harrison Surratt, Jr.* (Jan. 1992) ("Three Indictments").

Vol. 2, at X-27, Robert Mills, *A Can of Worms* (Oct. 1990).

Vol.2, at X-29, William Hanchett, *We Told You So . . .* (Nov. 1990), *reprinting in part*, William Hanchett, *The Historian as Gamesman, Civil War History*, Vol. XXXVI, No. 1 (March 1990) (*"Historian as Gamesman"*).

Vol. 2, at X-35, Steven J. Wright, *More from the Can of Worms* (Dec. 1990).

Vol. 2, at X-45, *A Recollection of John H. Surratt Fifty Years Later* (March 1988).

Vol. 2, at XI-11, Rev. Dr. R.B. Garrett, *I Saw John Wilkes Booth Killed*, *reprinted from Alexandria Gazette* (June 8, 1903) (May 1999).

Vol.2, at XI-23, *His Mother's Memories*, (Interview of Dr. Reginald I. Tonry of Baltimore, grandson of Mary E. Surratt, son of Anna Surratt, by David Rankin Barbee, Nov. 13, 1931) (April 1987) (*"His Mother's Memories"*).

Vol. 2, at X-41, Steven G. Miller, *Ripples from the Hanson Hiss Article* (July 1996).

Vol. 2, at XI-5, Erich L. Ewald, *The Butcher's Tale: The Primary Documentation of "Chris Ritter's" Confrontation with Louis J. Weichmann* (April 1992).

James L. Swanson and, Daniel R. Weinberg, *Lincoln's Assassins: Their Trial and Execution* (William Morrow 2006) ("Swanson & Weinberg").

James L. Swanson, *Manhunt: the 12-Day Chase for Lincoln's Killer* (HarperCollins 2007) (*"Manhunt"*).

The Ten Costliest Battles of the Civil War, http://www.civilwarhome.com/Battles.htm (accessed Dec. 22, 2013).

Tennessee Encyclopedia of History and Culture, *Memphis Race Riot of 1866*, http://tennesseeencyclopedia.net/entry.php?rec=900 (accessed March 3, 2014).

William Tidwell, James O. Hall and David Winfred Gaddy, *Come Retribution: The Confederate Secret Service and the Assassination of Lincoln* (Univ. Press of Mississippi 1988) (*"Come Retribution"*).

Trial of John H. Surratt in the Criminal Court for the District of Columbia, (Washington: French & Richardson; Philadelphia: J.B. Lippincott & Co. 1867) ("[vol.#] JHS Trial [p.#]").

Elizabeth Steger Trindal, *Mary Surratt: An American Tragedy* (Pelican Publishing Co. Louisiana 1996) (*"American Tragedy"*).

Univ. of Maryland Library, *Slavery in Maryland*, http://lib.guides.umd.edu/marylandslavery (accessed Nov. 11, 2013).

Univ. of Missouri-Kansas City Law School, Douglas O. Linder, *The Impeachment Trial of Andrew Johnson*, http://law2.umkc.edu/faculty/projects/ftrials/impeach/imp_account2.html (accessed March 3, 2014).

U.S. Legal, District of Columbia Kidnapping/Abduction Laws, http://kidnapping.uslegal.com/state-kidnapping-abduction-laws/district-of-columbia-kidnappingabduction-laws/ (accessed March 11, 2014).

United States v. John H. Surratt, 1 Mackay 306, 1868 WL 11041 (D.C. Sup., Nov. 6, 1868).

Venice Preserved by Thomas Otway, http://www.gutenberg.org/files/21515/21515-h/21515-h.htm (accessed Dec. 28, 2013).

Washington Times, John F. Doyle, The Civil War, p.B3 (June 14, 1997) (*"Washington Times, Doyle"*).

Website of the English College, http://www.vecrome.org/ (accessed Feb. 8, 2014).

Louis J. Weichmann, *A True History of the Assassination of Abraham Lincoln and the Conspiracy of 1865* (Floyd Risvold, ed., Alfred A. Knopf, NY 1975) ("Weichmann"). This book includes:

> *The Hanson-Hiss Article, reprinted in* Weichmann, pp.441-52 (*"Hanson-Hiss,* Weichmann*"*).

> "The Rockville Lecture" (Dec. 6, 1870), *reprinted in,* Weichmann, pp.428-40 (*"Rockville Lecture,* Weichmann*"*).

> *Washington Evening Star* editorial (Dec. 16, 1870), *reprinted in,* Weichmann, pp.440-41 (*"Evening Star,* Dec. 16, Weichmann*"*).

William T. Sherman, http://www.civilwar.org/education/history/biographies/william-t-sherman.html (accessed Dec. 14, 2013).

When Liverpool Was Dixie, http://www.whenliverpoolwasdixie.org.uk/index.htm (accessed Jan. 31, 2014).

Jay Winik, *April 1865* (Perennial, Harper Collins 2002) (*"April 1865"*).

Yale Univ., Constitution of the Confederate States, March 11, 1861, http://avalon.law.yale.edu/19th_century/csa_csa.asp (accessed Nov. 8, 2013).

Yale Univ., Second Inaugural Address of Abraham Lincoln, http://avalon.law.yale.edu/19th_century/lincoln2.asp (accessed Dec. 4, 2013).

INDEX

ACKNOWLEDGEMENTS

Many PEOPLE HELPED ME WITH THIS BOOK; THE MISTAKES ARE THEIRS, the plaudits mine. Or did I get that backwards? Seriously, I am grateful to the entire staff of the Surratt House & Museum, especially Joan Chaconas, History Specialist; Sandra Walia, Librarian at the James O. Hall Research Center attached to the Museum; Laurie Verge, Museum Director; Lindsey Horn, Collections Manager; and Julia Cowderie, Education Assistant. I am grateful to the Surratt Society for the fine work it does preserving and exploring this history, and to all the members of that Society who support this important work. At the National Archives in Washington, D.C., my thanks go especially to librarians Robert Ellis and Nancy Wing. Thanks to the Library of Congress, to Allison Dixon of the National Parks Service, Ford's Theatre, and also to Park Ranger Roger Powell. In Veroli, Italy, I am especially grateful to Caterina Tartaglia & Antonio Zolfo of the hotel Tenuta del Massimo Feudo, residents Laura Fiorihi and Aurelio Campoli, and librarian Ivana Oddi, whose guidance enabled me to locate Surratt's prison cell. Thanks to Professor Giancarlo Onorati, author of *L'Ultimo dei Cospiratori*, for graciously sharing information with me, and to Joan Chaconas, Hon. Sandy Prindle, Bret Wirta, Ava Anderson, Garth Dennis, Carol Trenga, and Bob Jensen, for reading the draft manuscript and making helpful and perceptive comments. Much gratitude to my mother, Evelyn Schein, and to John Sessions and Garth Dennis, true patrons of the arts. Thanks also to all the folks at History Publishing Company, especially Don Bracken, publisher, to my publicist Marian Brown, to Robert Aulicino for his excellent book design and to web designer par excellence Scott M.X. Turner. A big thank-you to Celeste Bennett of Bennett & Hastings Publishing, who not only published my first two books, but was also kind enough to edit this one. Special thanks to my friend Christy McDanold of Secret Garden Books in Seattle for helping me with the title, and for running a beautiful independent bookstore in the Ballard neighborhood. Thanks to Ballard Writers Collective, and my friends at Tieton Arts, Mighty Tieton, LiTFUSE Poets' Workshop, Humanities Washington, and King County 4Culture, who have supported my writing as we have supported each other – it takes a village! Much love and thanks to my wife Carol Trenga, for interpreting with our English-Italian phrase book, and for her patience while navigating the narrow streets of Italy with a cursing author, chasing Surratt's ghost.

MICHAEL SCHEIN is an author, attorney, and former professor of American Legal History. He has previously published two historical novels: *Bones Beneath Our Feet* (2011), and *Just Deceits: a Historical Courtroom Mystery* (2008) (a #1-seller in the "legal thriller" category on KINDLE). Mr. Schein taught American Legal History at Seattle University Law School from 1988-2003, and since that time he has taught over one hundred continuing legal education classes, many focusing on legal history. He has served on the speakers' bureau of Humanities Washington, and he is Director of the annual LiTFUSE Poets' Workshop. His poetry has been supported by a grant from King County 4Culture, and has been nominated three times for the Pushcart Prize. Originally from Vermont, Mr. Schein and his wife raised two daughters in Seattle and then moved to the Snoqualmie Valley in the foothills of the Washington Cascades. Please follow @michael_schein on Twitter, and visit www.michaelschein.com

Selected praise for Mr. Schein's previous books:

***Bones Beneath Our Feet: A Historical Novel of Puget Sound* (2011)**
"*Bones Beneath Our Feet* is a complex, nuanced, revisionist epic with a massive cast of characters, pitched battles, reversals, small acts of human tenderness, and a climactic court scene. Characters seem both larger-than-life and humanely familiar. Schein excels at returning the Historical . . . to the human."   – Karl Wolff, *Driftless Area Review*

"One of the best historical novels I've read yet. The characters engaged me from the beginning. I learned so much about this area of the country. You must read this book. I still see the boy trying to keep his disturbed mother from jumping out her bedroom window. Excellent book."
– Ann Hite, Goodreads

"*Bones Beneath Our Feet* is a powerful and deeply moving historical novel . . . beautifully written with vivid descriptions of the landscape that we all love. The characters, both historical and created, come alive as they fight and love throughout this big book. . . . I highly recommend *Bones Beneath Our Feet* to all who love the land and its history as well as those who love a damn good story with fine writing. . . . *Bones Beneath Our Feet* has my highest recommendation!"
– J. Glenn Evans, author of Broker Jim and Zeke's Revenge

Just Deceits: A Historical Courtroom Mystery (2008)

"I love your book. In fact – it was one of those 'I can't wait to keep reading but I don't want it to end' books. I felt I was right there in Virginia with all the assorted characters - I felt the sweat on the horse, smelled the fields, as villains and heroes . . . made their way from one place to another, and I got scared and excited at all the right places. Bravo!"
– Note from a reader

"Michael Schein's excellent debut novel, *Just Deceits*, is the perfect book for lovers of courtroom thrillers, historical fiction, mysteries, or anyone looking for an exciting page-turner that also stimulates the mind. Schein's writing is crisp, the characters are vivid and engaging, and there are many unexpected twists on the way to a stunning ending. I couldn't put it down!"
– Robert Dugoni, New York Times bestselling author of
The Jury Master, My Sister's Grave, and many more